THE WIDENING WORLD OF CHILDHOOD

THE WIDENING

OF

LOIS BARCLAY MURPHY

and collaborators

WORLD

CHILDHOOD

Paths Toward Mastery

BASIC BOOKS INC. *Publishers* NEW YORK

The author gratefully acknowledges the kindness of the following publishers in allowing the quotation of copyrighted material.

The Journal Press, for permission to quote from "The Influence of Separation from the Mother on Children's Emotional Responses," by M. Shirley and L. Poyntz, published in the *Journal of Psychology*, Vol. XII, 1941.
Whiteside, Inc., for permission to quote from *The Lost and the Found*, by Robert Collis.
Tavistock Publications, Ltd., and Erik H. Erikson, for permission to quote from Erikson's remarks in *Discussions on Child Development*, Vol. 3, edited by J. M. Tanner and Bärbel Inhelder.

73 74 75 76   10 9 8 7 6 5 4 3 2 1

COLLABORATORS

To Gardner

ACKNOWLEDGMENTS

THIS BOOK IS ONE OF A GROUP of publications* based upon studies of normal children observed in infancy and periodically to adolescence. All of these studies have been supported by the Menninger Foundation and the United States Public Health Service. This work has been supported in addition by the Gustavus and Louise Pfeiffer Research Foundation. For the most part I have drawn upon data from the "Coping Project" supported by NIMH Grant M-680; but I have also made some use of data generously made available by Sibylle Escalona and Mary Leitch who directed the study of these children in infancy. Many chapters are based directly upon the records, case analyses, or discussions of specific aspects of behavior prepared by members of the research staff; thus in a real sense the book must be considered a product of group collaboration.

The idea for this study grew out of problems seen in earlier studies of personality development. However, our approach has been enriched by the suggestions and criticisms of many friends and supporters. Karl Menninger as Chief of Staff of the Menninger Foundation offered

* Publications on this research are listed in Appendix C.

guiding suggestions early in the research, and later for this book. Will Menninger supported the initiation of the research and has given its continued support his personal attention. Gardner Murphy in his role as Director of Research has been in close touch throughout our work, offering both technical assistance and warm support. Especially in the first year of planning and informally since then, Nelly Tibout shared the wisdom accumulated from years of psychoanalytic work with children. Ishak Ramzy contributed especially to my awareness of the potential meanings of the earliest beginnings, as well as to solutions of some of the problems we met.

In addition Robert Holt, George Klein, and David Rapaport, all formerly of the Menninger Foundation, contributed important suggestions, as did Margaret Mead, Peter Blos, Ruth Munroe, and L. K. Frank, who helped during the earliest spadework.

It will be obvious that our thinking has been stimulated especially by the work of Anna Freud and Dorothy Burlingame in the Hampstead reports; and by the approaches to experience in infancy and early childhood implicit in the work of Erik Erikson and of Ernest Schachtel.

Contributions of many staff members are mentioned at relevant points, but I wish here to add a special word of appreciation for the sensitive and eloquent reporting both of our staff observers and of two mothers, Gwen B. Zeichner and Jeanne Thompson; their records provided the warp and woof, the texture, and the fullness of the material with which we worked.

The manuscript was read in whole or in part by several of these friends and also Max Gitelson, and Eveoleen Rexford, who both contributed important suggestions regarding the presentation and use of the material. Wayne Holtzman, a consultant throughout, also participated in the planning of the book and read a late draft.

At different points in the development of the book Nelson A. Crawford, Annabel Learned, and Helen Friend contributed helpful suggestions regarding organization of the chapters; and Al G. Murphy's discriminating editorial criticism smoothed out many wrinkles in the verbal fabric.

I am grateful to Vesta Walker and her staff and to Dorothy Diehl for their expert help with references.

I owe a great deal to Katherine Stoner's meticulous work on the manuscript, and to Marie Smith's warm genius for keeping the subjects, their families, and the staff of the project in just the right mood for research.

We have thought of the "Coping Project" as an intensive pilot study whose purpose was to scrutinize children's ways of dealing with new demands and difficulties which they face in everyday life, and to offer tentative formulations and hypotheses regarding the processes involved in the solution of some typical problems. We hope that questions to which children have called our attention will stimulate others to work toward more understanding of children's ways of meeting challenges as they move into new experiences in their widening world.

Lois Barclay Murphy
Chief Investigator

CONTENTS

THE WIDENING WORLD OF CHILDHOOD

THE PROBLEM OF MASTERY

CHILDREN ARE THOUGHT OF as charming, resistant, or tragic, depending on the angle of our vision and the direction in which it leads us. Charming if they play a knowing part in a duet with an adult; resistant if they refuse to cooperate with a psychologist's irrelevant tasks; tragic when they withdraw in miserable bewilderment from a well-intentioned nurse in an evacuation center. Seldom do we think of the child as a small human being, carrying on his own struggle to make sense out of life, to meet his own needs, to master the challenges presented by life—but differing from adults especially in the proportion of newness to which he is exposed. If we think of children in this way, it is possible that by watching them, we may learn something about how all of us deal with new demands and stressful experiences, newness which cannot be met by well-established habits or ready-made answers. When responses are not automatic, when we do not know just what to do, we have to cope with the situation as best we can, trying to arrive at a solution that will enable us to get along. Much of what we call "getting experience" consists of just this, and out of these efforts to cope with new situations eventually develops a certain know-how, patterned ways of dealing with newness itself.

Newness of course does not present itself in pure form. It comes with aspects of challenge to new gratifications, difficulty or threat of failure, loss or the danger of it, pain or some threat to comfort and security. When newness brings fresh and interesting possibilities in its trail, there is motivation to master it for the sake of the obvious re-wards. When pain or loss or both are involved, the stressful aspects are multiplied, the rewards are uncertain, and the problem of mastery is intensified.

Backgrounds of our approach

It is something of a paradox that a nation which has exulted in its rapid expansion and its scientific-technological achievements, should have developed in its studies of childhood so vast a "problem" litera-ture: a literature often expressing adjustment difficulties, social fail-ures, blocked potentialities, and defeat. Since it came parallel with the muckraking and social criticism literature of the first half of the twentieth century, its emergence may, indeed, be considered partly due to different phases in our American history. Pioneer courage and the will to do were crystallized in the mottoes of the nineteenth cen-tury; in the twentieth century we became preoccupied with failures. In applying clinical ways of thinking formulated out of experience with broken adults, we were slow to see how the language of adequacy to meet life's challenges could become the subject matter of psycho-logical science. Thus there are thousands of studies of maladjustment for each one that deals directly with the ways of managing life's problems with personal strength and adequacy. The language of problems, difficulties, inadequacies, of antisocial or delinquent con-duct, or of ambivalence and anxiety is familiar. We know that there are devices for correcting, bypassing, or overcoming threats, but for the most part these have not been directly studied. Most impressive here is the work of Jean Macfarlane et al.,[1] who reviewed in detail the problem behavior and symptoms of more than two hundred children typical of a small city as these children were studied from twenty-one months to fourteen years; then they followed them into adulthood and found that, in general, clinical predictions were too pessimistic. As adults these individuals got along far better than had been antici-pated.

Too often in these studies we have been burdened by rigid biases and assumptions about the role of more or less statically conceived genetic factors or by standardized criteria of developmental norms. When the child does not "behave" as adults demand, he is said to have behavior problems or "symptoms." Temper tantrums, thumb-sucking, enuresis, etc., have been seen as problems even at the ages of three and four years because their occurrence deviated from the level of social conformity which it was assumed the child should be able to meet by the age of three or four or five.

Increasing flexibility in understanding children has gradually come from different sources. We are learning to look at both the organism and the milieu with which it is interacting more perceptively than was possible in earlier times, even though Freud,[2] Adolf Meyer,[3] Karl Menninger,[4] Gardner Murphy,[5] Erikson,[6] and others have long emphasized the necessity of giving weight to each. But from the time of Rousseau's[7] insight into the natural growth of a child it has taken nearly two hundred years for the psychological sciences to be able to identify with the young child enough to try to understand his efforts to deal with the world in terms of his childish experience of it. A wide variety of forces have biased our interpretations toward normative, moralistic, and clinical evaluations. None of these has much to do with the child's own need to make himself at home in the world, to find ways of coming to terms with it, and to manage his relation to the environment. To do this we have to observe what is going on, how the child seems to be experiencing a situation, and how he deals with it.

Possible implications of this approach

The revolutions in child-care patterns in recent years testify to the fluidity of our culture, its capacity for change, and the opportunity that both of these provide for influencing the culture if we can be sure of our ground in doing so. Difficulties in being sure come from disillusionments resulting from one-sided applications of insights into child development. The rigid routines of feeding, toileting, and sleeping advocated in the thirties grew out of an oversimplified concept of conditioning plus pediatric concepts that dealt with medical aspects of nutrition and physical hygiene, generally without regard to the emotional consequences. Later techniques went to the opposite extreme. Both excessive coercion and excessive indulgence brought problems for children.

There is no guarantee that we will not make just as many mistakes in the future. But the best insurance against that seems to lie in developing as balanced a picture as possible of the child's way of experiencing and responding, and of the child's ways of trying to satisfy demands of the culture. Dramatic and painful experiences of war have forced our attention to some of the most obvious interactions of events in the culture and child needs. For instance, the studies of Anna Freud and Burlingame,[8] Spitz,[9] Bowlby,[10] and others are significant in relation to problems of separation not only in wartime conditions of evacuation but also in our peacetime babysitting, and hospitalization of either the mother or the infant. Frequent moving, which uproots children from the home, neighborhood, and friends with whom they tried to establish firm relationships, sometimes involves more strain for children than for adults, because the task of familiarization in a new place is much greater for the child. We are beginning to learn how complex such demands are and how many factors both in the culture and in the child must be considered in our thinking about the development of the child's ways of handling the problems presented by these experiences in our culture. This can lead to new understanding of how adults can support the child's effort to manage these experiences.

Interest in positive ways of dealing with life's challenges has been developing in recent years. Murray's[11] approach to needs (leading to action) led to studies by McClelland et al.[12] of the achievement drive, and White's[13] studies of competence. Piaget[14] has contributed a new vocabulary of the cognitive process of adaptation in the infant and child. In psychoanalysis, Hartmann,[15] Rapaport,[16] and others following them have been explicitly concerned with adaptive functions and the process of coming to terms with the culture. Karl Menninger[17] has discussed the healing contribution of hope. Erikson[18] has most comprehensively outlined the positive residues from successive phases of psychosexual development available for active response to the environment. Anna Freud[19] has outlined positive lines of development in the young child, and long before had given many illustrations of children's active ways of dealing with stress.

From this background our own point of view has evolved: the ways in which triumph can be achieved both in the large and in the small, the ways in which human beings handle new demands, everyday problems and difficulties, need to be studied in their own right.

Problems of the child in our culture

American children have been observed in longitudinal studies for some thirty years.[20] To be sure, the number of children is relatively small; most of those studied were in cities or university centers, and all too many of them came from faculty families who had placed them in university nursery schools or experimental schools. Such centers had the facilities for carrying out careful studies and the children in them were easily accessible. Thus the samples are not by any means representative of even the major subcultural groups in the United States.

Even so, these samples of middle-class normal children have produced data to support some important conclusions. It is clear that whether children grow up in the San Francisco Bay area, in New Haven, or in suburbs of New York City, they have many problems to face. Some of these problems grow out of the normal expectable stresses of childhood: childhood diseases and infections or accidents that may require hospitalization, separation from the parents when the child starts to nursery school or school, sometimes before he is ready to leave the nest. Others are less predictable and are often the outgrowth of the times in which we live: tensions between parents, which are widespread and which increase in times of ill health or stress in the larger family of in-laws; the uprooting from friends and a familiar neighborhood as the father gets a better job in another town or the family moves into a better house in a very different neighborhood; tensions bouncing onto the child from international relations; war anxieties, or actual absence of the father for military service. We can think of an expected average of stresses, everyday demands, and difficulties typically confronted by children today.

Our research opportunity

Coming to the Menninger Foundation in 1952, we found unique opportunities to become acquainted with the various ways in which children meet these difficulties.

Escalona and Leitch[21] had already made exquisitely detailed records on over a hundred normal infants selected to exclude defects and deviations beyond the normal range. A number of these still lived in Topeka. As growing children they could be studied further (and we have now followed them to the edge of adolescence). This group provides a unique sample of initially normal children observed intensively in infancy and at successive levels of development. the availability of both Menninger Foundation support and support from the National Institute of Mental Health of the United States Public Health Service, stimulated us to plan to study through their childhood years the resources which these normal children mobilized and the methods they developed in their efforts to cope with life. This was the beginning of our "Coping Project," focused on the behavior of thirty-two preschool children, at our first level of research.

The concept of coping

When we speak of "coping efforts" we are not dealing with a concept with an established theoretical lineage. Anna Freud [22] and many others have used the term in the context of the individual's failure to cope with certain external difficulties or with his problems. "Mastery" has been discussed by Karl Menninger,[23] Ives Hendricks,[24] Bernfeld,[25] and others. Since it seems unsound to prejudge the ultimate outcome of the processes we are studying, we refer in the subtitle to *"paths toward* mastery." Although the term "coping" has long been used, it has merely crept in without being noticed and has not been dignified by systematic discussion; nevertheless, it seems most natural as a way of talking about and thinking about what we see when children confront new situations and challenges calling for responses not previously crystallized.

We do not include in our conception of coping devices or mechanisms such inborn and universal patterns as sucking reflexes and "riddance" reflexes; these are precursors of more complex forms of activity to deal with stimulation. Nor are other general capacities of the human organism such as the capacity for vocalization or locomotion to be regarded as coping devices, even though they may be used in very specific ways in the process of coping.

Coping devices involve choices in ways of using these resources, and also new structures and integrations developed by the individual organism to master its individual problems with the environment.

Nor are we concerned here with crystallized or automatized habits or other more or less institutionalized action patterns. Coping patterns are most easily seen when a child or an adult is confronting a new situation which cannot be handled by reflex, habitual, or other routine or automatic action. In this sense, the study of coping puts the emphasis on the process of developing ways of dealing with new and difficult situations. Once such methods are consolidated, competence or mastery may result.

The reader may ask, what is the relation between coping efforts and adaptation? "Coping" points to the process—the steps or sequences through which the child comes to terms with a challenge or makes use of an opportunity. "Adaptation" is the result. Adaptation is sometimes achieved by automatic or reflex responses which we do not include in "coping efforts." Similarly, "competence" refers to a skill achieved, not to the processes by which a level of competence in a functional area is reached. The "drive toward mastery" underlies coping efforts, and is expressed in them—indeed, in new situations it can hardly be gratified without them except when necessary skills have been perfected in similar situations previously.

Defense mechanisms may be, and often are, part of the over-all coping effort; they sometimes assist in dividing a complex situation into manageable parts, through repressing the excessive threat and focusing on the one that can be mastered.

More important at this stage than theoretical clarification is the way of thinking invited by the term "coping"—a way of thinking which pays attention to the child's own manner of dealing with pressures and threats, potential or actual. This way of thinking involves awareness of the individuality, spontaneity, even creativity characterizing the new patternings of response we see, as well as the gallant persistence and repetitive efforts which are often necessary in the struggle toward mastery.

Our methods of studying coping behavior

As in any other scientific research which has to explore new territory and build hypotheses out of fresh observations, it has been necessary for us to begin literally at the beginning: by using simple "natural history" observations as they might be made by an anthropologist or botanist or any other scientist who starts by careful observation of the phenomenon before he gets to the point of making formal hypotheses regarding determinants or causes.

A variety of scientists from different disciplines—such as Darwin,[26] Freud[27] and Hebb,[28] in addition to the anthropologists and students of personality like Allport,[29] and Wolff[30]—have fully appreciated the potential productivity inherent in full records of detailed observations. From these can come new hypotheses not always deducible from a tight theoretical system. The rewards of experiments focused on the task of proof of hypotheses developed from systematized theory has in many groups dimmed the awareness of the values inherent in this other method. Beyond this, methods for the use and analysis of natural history data have not been adequately developed. Consequently many people are not familiar with the kind of records used here.

L. B. Murphy and E. Lerner[31] presented suggestive outlines for observation of child behavior in 1941; and in 1956 presented a first study of a normal young child's struggles in growing up. Revisions of the outlines developed in this early study were studied by the members of this project. These approaches were enriched by the contributions of staff members. Grace Heider had already given much thought to the problems and coping efforts of deaf children. Alice Moriarty had worked with children handicapped by emotional problems and retardation. Such experiences aroused special interest in watching the efforts of normal children to deal with the everyday problems they confronted.

The permanent members of the staff were not only professionally experienced psychologists but also had children of their own. This meant that they were familiar with the day-to-day richness of childhood behavior and its way of bursting out of the conceptual tracks and fences of psychology. Part-time staff members included highly trained professional workers who carried out technical examinations such as psychiatric examinations and psychological tests. In addition, we used detailed records on "salient episodes" not otherwise accessible to us, made by mothers of a few children. These contributed invaluable sequences in the children's successive ways of handling problems at home. No one method is able to deal with all of the questions which we need to ask; consequently we found that at this stage it was most practical to use formal methods in order to obtain data relevant to certain kinds of questions for which these methods are appropriate, while other methods are used to obtain data not available from the formal procedures. The variety of training and of people making observations results in a variety of styles in the records we shall utilize; we have not tried to force either the recorders or their reports into a common mold. A full discussion of our methods appears in a separate volume.

The necessity to evolve ways of studying steps and processes of mastery and integration means that we have had first to look differently, to observe differently. Instead of studying "themes" or symptoms or conflicts or following any of the "objective" approaches by counting items of overt behavior, we observed extended segments and sequences of behavior in response to such opportunities, difficulties, and challenges as were presented to the children by a party or an intelligence test. Then we had to find ways of formulating what we found without burdening ourselves with unnecessary new or clumsy terms. A third step was to state the generalizations and hypotheses which our data could document. In order to alert ourselves to the steps, sequences, changes, and patterns visible through time, and the goals and methods of the child moving through these sequences, we had to set aside at first some of the usual labels of behavior. We had to reexamine what the child was doing and what were the specific sequelae and meaning of behavior often prejudged as "resistance," for example.

In order, then, to study the child's resources and their use in patterns of coping, we decided to make two kinds of records of the total behavior seen as the child responded to each situation. In addition to the usual technical methods employed in standard procedures which we used in order to compare these children with others, we added "parallel" descriptive records of the children's ways of dealing with the examiners and the demands they made—i.e., the "natural history" records.

Methods of the research included pediatric examinations, psychiatric interviews, psychometric and projective tests* such as Rorschach, Children's Apperception Test, and Miniature Life Toys, primarily, and standard body photographs.† Interviews with mothers provided data both on the home setting and on the child's ways of dealing with dilemmas at home. Observations of children going to and from testing sessions, at parties, at the zoo, and at home were included, in addition to the "parallel observer's" records of the child's ways of dealing with every new situation and every examination. So we saw the children in relatively standardized situations, both "structured" and "unstructured," as well as in situations similar to those of their everyday experience. The parallel observer could watch both the examiner and the child, and was responsible for a running record of the child's spontaneous behavior, over and above the technical record by pediatrician, psychologist, or psychiatrist.

Throughout our studies from the preschool level on, electrical recording has been used where feasible. Thus the record of a Rorschach session at the preschool level included (1) the recording of all of the conversation between the examiner and the child by a Time Master Dictaphone with the aid of a desk microphone, (2) the usual technical records by the examiner, (3) a running descriptive record of the total event including the child's behavior, by the parallel recorder. The examiner carefully synthesized (1) and (2) to obtain maximal accuracy and fullness of his own record. The behavior record was used along with similar records of other sessions by parallel recorders, for analysis of coping devices and processes. At later age levels all examinations were tape-recorded; these records were transcribed, checked, and integrated with notes of observers.

* Projective tests provide an opportunity for the child to interpret blots or pictures or to select, arrange, and act out fantasy themes with toys. Ordinarily psychologists pay attention to the organization or structural aspects of the child's response and to the feelings, conflicts, wishes expressed or implied. In this project we also noted carefully the child's ways of dealing with the experimenter and the real or fantasied demands he made.

† The Witkin tests of field independence and the Engel Insight Test were added at the early latency phase of the study, but are not reported here.

The children

All but one of the thirty-two children included in the Coping Study had been studied in detail as infants at some time between the ages of four and thirty-two weeks in the Infancy Study,* directed by Dr. Sibylle Escalona and Dr. Mary Leitch.[32] This one was an older sibling of one of the Infancy Study subjects.

These children may be seen as a sample of the middle-class white majority in a middle-sized town of the Midwest. They were chiefly of old American background. Many of their grandparents had been Kansas pioneers. For the most part they were tied rather closely to Catholic or Protestant churches of conservative leaning with an emphasis on strict control of behavior in tabooed areas, repression of sex, and consistent discipline of children to block early destructive impulses.

The environment of Topeka offers large open areas for movement and exploring. All but one family lived in its own separate home with a yard, and of these all but two lived in sections where even the youngest child had the freedom of the neighborhood and was free during most of the year to push open the screen door and "run." Neither fences nor hedges bar the free movement of children in this community; they are often seen in little neighborhood groups playing out fantasies of family life, traffic management, or other adult activities.

Our observations, begun in 1953, carry these children from two or three years of age up to the age of eleven or twelve, but in this book we have used chiefly the data from the preschool years. For that phase we saw each child in a dozen or more different sessions. We began simply by watching their ways of managing new or strange situations, separations from mother, difficulties, threats. From the home interviews and our own observations when we entered the homes to collect and return the children we obtained records of the family atmosphere, interaction, and events which created difficulties for the child. Conversations with the children going to and from test sessions often gave the child's point of view about events which the mother had described.

At the time of the infancy study and again at the preschool study most of these rather isolated mothers welcomed the research experience as an opportunity for a novel experience, an interruption of confining routine, a chance to share their experiences with their children

* In Topeka in 1948-1952, also with the joint support of the U.S. Public Health Services and the Menninger Foundation.

with people who were interested. On the surface there was little or no evidence of hesitation or resistance, with the exception of a few mothers who wished to come along in order to be satisfied that we were doing what we described. Some of them, whose children had not been away from home alone before, assumed the children would need support.

At no time in the twelve years of this study have parents been offered help. A few mothers have requested help for a child at one time or another and in each instance they have been referred to local resources. We felt that it would confuse the purposes of the research if we provided therapy.

We did not have the clinician's privilege to probe into intimate family relations and never initiated discussion about marital relations of the parents, for instance. Since we were not making demands of this sort, our work had both certain advantages and certain limits. We focused on the child, and the mothers volunteered out of sheer interest; consequently, there was little in the experience to arouse anxiety about what might be revealed—mothers were free to reveal what they chose. This doubtless has something to do with the fact that over these years we have lost contact with only two families. On the other side of the ledger, of course, is the fact that data regarding certain factors important in the deeper dynamics of family life are unavailable to us. We not only do not have psychoanalytic data, we do not have data in sensitive areas which might have been explored in a child guidance clinic. However the clinic has to give priority to depth of understanding within a limited time. The children in our group are now in their teens, and we feel that maintaining the active cooperation of 93 per cent of the families in the intensive group over these years has justified itself in terms of our research goals.

The plan and scope of the book

Books are written or constructed in many different ways: some books are elaborations of an a priori outline which moves step by step through close sequences developing a concept or pattern. Others are developed by arranging in a series a group of originally separate essays which are subsequently set in relation to each other and integrated into one whole. This book proceeds in a different way, and it can hardly be described without referring to both the children who were observed, and the observers—who were in some cases also analyzers of the observations on the children—as *dramatis personae*.

First we shall describe a number of children confronting one or another new experience in the project as seen by different members of the staff; these provide the materials from which the discussion of the children's responses to new situations is developed.

Next we move, just as we often do in going from one room to another in a museum, to the presentation of the children's responses to difficulties in the intelligence test as Dr. Moriarty observed and studied these. Quite a different area is seen when we move outdoors to observe the children confronting a variety of opportunites and challenges at "parties." Mrs. Pitsa Hartocollis reviewed the records of these experiences and analyzed them to provide the basic materials for this chapter.

In the next section we see a small boy and his mother coping with an accident, and a gallant girl struggling with serious motor difficulties following polio. We watched the way in which she mobilized her physical and intellectual resources in a play session where she was not able to move around the room freely as other children did. In the following chapter, "Some Processes of Mastery," we use records which illustrate some of the steps in different ways of conquering obstacles.

Following these descriptions of children's ways of meeting different challenges, we shall review in Part III some of the major coping devices and patterns which were particularly important in the situations just described. This section concludes with a formulation of the strategy of coping. Part IV deals with contributions of coping efforts to development. Some of our results are relevant to psychoanalytic ego psychology; here we are discussing a few topics such as coping styles and the contributions of mastery to the sense of identity.

The Widening World of Childhood is intended for a varied audience and omits technical details of method and findings, which are treated separately elsewhere (L. B. Murphy and W. Raine: *Methods in the Longitudinal Study of Children*). Analysis of what contributed to coping capacity, both in terms of ability to deal with the demands of the environment and in terms of the capacity to maintain internal integration, is presented in that report. A study of vulnerability in infants and preschool children by Grace Heider presents a first analysis of the data from the point of view of maintenance of integration. A more intensive study of some of the processes of outgrowing vulnerability is presented in *Vulnerability, Stress, and Resilience,* by Murphy and Gupta. Another monograph, by Alice Moriarty, deals with coping patterns of preschool children in response to intelligence test demands. A list of some current and forthcoming publications based on the data of this research is given in Appendix C.

In this book, then, we present many records of episodes of dealing with the environment and some extensive sequences of the behavior of the children. This is in line with the practice in some of the classical literature in the field of child development—the work of Scupin,[33] Shinn,[34] Buhler,[35] Piaget,[36] and from the psychoanalytic field, Susan Isaacs,[37] Anna Freud and Burlingame,[38] and others. This procedure has the advantage of giving the reader an opportunity to do his own reflecting, dissecting, and interpreting of the data in addition to acquainting himself with our concepts and hypotheses.

While the first focus of our interest was always the children's many ways of handling problems whether in the environment or within themselves, we were also looking for relations between style of response and evidence of constitutional tendencies in the infancy pattern as well as at later ages. For instance, are the active babies now active preschool children? What is the relation between other persistent aspects of equipment or temperament and the techniques used by each child as he confronts the demands made upon him? What unpredictable patterns of responding to the world and dealing with problems did the years after infancy produce?

Even though we give a few conspicuous examples of precursors of the child's own ways of dealing with the environment, we are not in any instance presenting a full and deeply interpreted case study here. This is being done in more technical monographs. Since we are not dealing with etiology, we do not discuss here the contribution of the mother or other members of the family to the child's coping attitudes or style.

Although we have provided some first interpretations, we do not wish to present final integrated interpretations of the children's behavior at this time but rather to make available a range of data in its natural richness. The strategy and the meaning of behavior are often lost when we destroy its natural complexity by premature dissection. Furthermore, the over-rigid formulation of explanatory concepts can result in a freezing of thought about child behavior at a time when our thinking should be kept as mobile and evolving as possible.

There are other reasons for remaining cautious about broad conclusions. With such a small sample in a relatively homogeneous subculture the proportions of children using one or another coping method may not be representative of patterns found in children of different national or subcultural groups. Moreover, our numbers are not large enough to be unequivocally typical for "native American white middle-class groups" in other sections of the country. Our contribution is not in any way "normative." Instead, we are interested in describing coping methods both at the level of specific devices and also in terms of hierarchies of devices and methods, their sequences, and the steps by which children find a coping style of their own in the subculture in which they are growing up.

There is much more to learn; this is just a beginning. We are trying to blaze a trail; as others join us, veering off in different directions to explore this aspect of development with quite different groups, we can gradually develop a more comprehensive picture of the ways in which children in different environments handle their challenges and difficulties, and manage to grow up to be competent adults.

In brief, the aim of this study is best expressed by the statement made in the first "grant application" to the National Institute of Mental Health: To initiate the study of children's own efforts to cope with their own day-to-day problems. This is not a one-variable experiment, but a broad effort to advance thinking toward (1) more awareness of the positive resources which both children and adults use in handling their limitations and problems; (2) more awareness of how to help young children deal with their difficulties.

We do not expect prescriptions to result from a study of this sort. But we hope to find insights and hypotheses regarding children's ways of handling some of the demands which life presents to them. Through these insights we may be led into new understanding of the relation of adults and children in various settings, as well as greater clarity as to the nature of the demands placed on children as they are experienced by the children themselves, and better ways of supporting children's efforts to help themselves.

THE CHILDREN

Nine of our 32 children studied at the preschool phase in the "Coping Project" were from devout Catholic families, and these children later attended parochial schools. Even at this time they were living in an unusually homogeneous group of relatives and acquaintances. Another nine children were from equally devoted Protestant families; five of these attended evangelical churches in which revivals or early commitment to Christ played an important part in the children's lives. Only one family reported no church affiliation and one was "mixed" Catholic and Protestant, but the attendance and involvement of the rest of the children was less intense and deep.

Fathers of about half of the children were skilled or semiskilled workers (carpenter, linoleum-layer, etc.) and fathers of the other half were businessmen or professional men with the exception of one who was in the Army. When we began the study two families were living in upper middle-class neighborhoods, while the others were in comfortable plain middle-class settings with the exception of the three or four families who were "poor" in earthly goods though not in spirit.

After the first interviews with mothers and some preliminary testing in the spring and summer of 1953, our formal research observations and examinations began in September. Using September 1, 1953, as a baseline against which to compare the ages of the children, they can be grouped as follows:

The youngest boys were from two years, eight months to four years, one month old on that date. These included the boys referred to by the following pseudonyms:

Raymond	2:8
Lennie	2:10
Brennie	2:10
Donald	2:10
Vernon	3:2
Ronald	3:5

There were nine two- and three-year-old girls on September 1, 1953:

Vivian	2:6
Molly	2:7
Sheila	2:8
Darlene	2:10
Diane	3:5
Sally	3:5
Rachel	3:8
JoAnne	3:7
Daryl	3:10

I have introduced these youngest children first because they include those who had had the most limited experience away from home; for them the project with its new places and people presented the most difficulty and challenge. In the first chapters of this book, we shall therefore find ourselves paying most attention to them.

The ten older boys ranged from almost four years to five years and three months; the older girls ranged from three years, three months to five years, seven months. In general these older children responded to the new experiences in terms of the interesting opportunities they saw in them; these children were independent and had many spontaneous ways of dealing with us. Except for one or two instances, the four-year-olds were quite able to leave their mothers at home. These older children included:

Boys		Girls	
Ralph	4:0	Barbie	4:3
Tommy	4:1	Karen	4:8
Chester	4:5	Susan	4:9
Gordon	4:7	Patsy	4:9
Greg	4:11	Janice	4:10
Martin	4:11	Trudy	5:2
Roddy	4:11	Cynthia	5:7
Teddy	4:11		
Steve	5:0		
Terry	5:3		

We have noted above that we do not here present intensive histories of the children's early development, the deeper relationships in the families, or a thorough study of the etiology of their behavior.* Our first step is the description of what the children themselves did, and their ways of meeting the situations they confronted.

NOTES AND REFERENCES

1. Macfarlane, J.W., Allen, L., and Honzik, M. *A Developmental Study of the Behavior Problems of Normal Children between Twenty-one Months and Fourteen Years.* Berkeley: University of California Press, 1954.

2. Freud, S. Three essays on sexuality. *Standard Edition of the Complete Psychological Works of Sigmund Freud,* Vol. 7. London: Hogarth Press, 1953. (Many other references to possible constitutional factors in the development of neurosis, choice of symptom, etc., are made throughout Freud's writings.)

3. Meyer, A. *Collected Papers of Adolf Meyer.* Baltimore: Johns Hopkins Press, 1950-1952.

4. Menninger, K. Psychological aspects of the organism under stress. *J. Amer. Psychoanal. Assoc. 2,* 1954.

5. Murphy, G. *Personality.* New York: Harper, 1947.

6. Erikson, E. H. *Childhood and Society.* New York: Norton, 1950.

7. Rousseau, J.J. *Emile.* New York: Dutton, 1911.

8. Freud, A., and Burlingame, D. *Infants Without Families.* New York: Medical War Books, International Universities Press, 1944.

9. Spitz, R. Anaclitic depression. *Psychoanalytic Study of the Child,* Vol. 2. New York: International Universities Press, 1946.

10. Bowlby, J. Separation anxiety. *Intern. J. Psychoanal. 41,* 1960. See also

* These will appear in forthcoming publications; see Appendix C.

Grief and mourning in infancy and early childhood. *Psychoanalytic Study of the Child*, Vol. 15. New York: International Universities Press, 1960.

11. Murray, H.A. *Explorations in Personality*. London: Oxford University Press, 1938.

12. McClelland, D., *et al*. *The Achievement Motive*. New York: Appleton-Century, 1953.

13. White, R. Motivation reconsidered: the concept of competence. *Psychol. Rev.*, 66, 1959.

14. Piaget, J. *Origins of Intelligence in Children*. New York: International Universities Press, 1952.

15. Hartmann, H. *Ego Psychology and the Problem of Adaptation*. New York: International Universities Press, 1958. See also Hartmann's writings in Vols. 2, 5, and 7, *Psychoanalytic Study of the Child*.

16. Rapaport, D. *Organization and Pathology of Thought*. New York: Columbia University Press, 1951.

17. Menninger, K. Hope. *Amer. J. Psychiat. 116*, 1959.

18. Erikson, E. H. *Childhood and Society*. New York: Norton, 1950.

19. Freud, A. Four contributions to the psychoanalytic study of the child, summarized in the *Bull. Phil. Psychoanal. Assoc. 2*, 1961.

20. Longitudinal Studies at the University of California, under the direction of J. Macfarlane, Nancy Bayley, Harold and Mary Jones, are outstanding examples.

21. Escalona, S., and Leitch, M. *Early Phases of Personality Development: a Non-Normative Study of Infant Behavior*. Evanston: Child Development Publications, 1953.

22. Freud, A. See *Ego and the Mechanisms of Defense*. London: Hogarth Press, 1937, and *War and Children*. New York: War Medical Books, International Universities Press, 1953.

23. Menninger, K. Psychological aspects of the organism under stress. *J. Amer. Psychoanal. Assoc. 2*, 1954.

24. Hendricks, I. Instinct and ego during infancy. *Psychoanal. Quart. 2*, 1942.

25. Bernfeld, S. *Psychology of the Infant*. New York: Brentano, 1929.

26. Darwin, C. *The Expression of the Emotions in Man and Animals*. New York: Appleton, 1873.

27. Freud, A., and Burlingame, D. See *Infants Without Families*. New York: Medical War Books, International Universities Press, 1944. Also note Anna Freud's discussions of the contributions of observation in psychoanalytic understanding of children; her article on infant observation, in *Psychoanalytic Study of the Child*, Vol. 8, is one example. Sigmund Freud expressed interest in the need for observations in *Three Essays on Sexuality*, 1920 edition, and used observations of children in *Little Hans* and *Beyond the Pleasure Principle*.

28. Hebb, D.O. *The Organization of Behavior*. New York: Wiley, 1949.

29. Allport, G., and Vernon, R.E. *Studies in Expressive Movement*. New York: Macmillan, 1933.

30. Wolff, W. *The Expression of Personality*. New York: Harper, 1943.

31. Lerner, E., and Murphy, L.B. (eds.). Methods for the Study of Personality in Young Children. *Monographs of the Society for Research in Child Development,* Vol. 6, No. 4. Washington, D.C.: Society for Research in Child Development, National Research Council, 1941. Revised by L. B. Murphy and published as *Personality in Young Children,* 2 vols. New York: Basic Books, 1956.

32. Escalona, S., and Leitch, M. The Infancy Study at the Menninger Foundation was supported by grants from the National Institutes of Health.

33. Scupin, E., and Scupin, G. *Bubi's Erste Kindheit.* Leipzig: Greeben, 1907.

34. Shinn, M.W. *Biography of a Baby.* Boston: Houghton-Mifflin, 1900.

35. Bühler, C. *The First Year of Life.* New York: John Day, 1930.

36. Barker, R. W., and Wright, H. *One Boy's Day.* New York: Harper, 1951.

37. Isaacs, S. *Social Development in Young Children.* London: G. Routledge and Sons, 1933.

38. Freud, A., and Burlingame, D. *Infants Without Families.* New York: Medical War Books, International Universities Press, 1944.

PART I ❀❀❀

THE NEW AND THE STRANGE

2

CHILDREN
ENCOUNTER NEWNESS

PROFESSIONAL WORKERS, RELATIVES and many other people who are encountered by a young child are apt to expect him to take for granted their friendly interest and benign intentions, and to respond acceptingly. From the child's-eye view, new people, places, experiences can seldom be experienced so casually. We can see this in one of the vivid children we met in the first weeks of our study as he moved into the play session with a young male psychiatrist, a situation free of the threats met in a doctor's office or hospital or the demands for conformity found in a school setting—a situation which was simply new:

Chester, an alert, active child (age four years, eleven months) came up the stairs somewhat expectantly, as though not certain as to what was in store for him. He walked into the room cautiously and in a rather methodical deliberate way went around the room exploring an unknown and uncertain situation. He was a handsome child, wide-eyed with the mysteries of a new person, at a loss to know what to expect, and apparently wondering what was permissible for him to do and how this person would respond to him. When permission for playing with the toys was granted, in the form of the question, "What toys do you like to play with?" he immediately went over to the brightly colored plastic engine and in a rather excited way began to handle the toy.*

Chester's response, once he realized that this was a place where he was expected to play freely, was much quicker and more sustained than that of some other children who could not accept the new situation quickly in a wholehearted way, but had to go through many steps in getting acquainted with it. By contrast with Chester, Donald, a tall, stocky, blond, wide-eyed boy not yet four, seemed to re-experience newness repeatedly at several points during the same sort of session with a psychiatrist:

In unfamiliar situations, such as the beginning of the hour, Donald thrust his hands deeply into his pockets and leaned back on his chair as far as he could, assuming an attitude of "move me if you can." He obviously wanted to appraise the situation before he could enter into it. Such withdrawal into a "closed position" occurred several times during the session, once because Donald had worn himself out and needed a rest. Not at any time did his watchful position appear "frozen" as in some children. Even while immobile, he would be fairly relaxed and merely seemed to have pulled himself out of the situation for a while. Tension was only apparent when in the beginning of the hour he attempted to pick up a peg from the floor, while keeping his seat glued to the chair. Noticeable also was his inability to get up a little later to inspect other toys though his face beamed with interest and anticipation. Even then his body was fairly relaxed. Later in the hour Donald manifested a great variety of comfortable postures, relaxing and seeming very much at ease despite the erectness of his body. He then moved very freely around, sometimes in almost an erratic fashion.†

From such observations we realized that the new qualities of much of his experience in the first years of life provide a considerable proportion of the challenges met by a young child under the age of four. The children's very first encounters with the people and the new situations with which we confronted them, both in the experience of a new visitor at home and their own excursions to the testing offices and parties, thus provided an important area to study. As we accompanied them one by one into their new experiences, we simply described them as a botanist would describe the behavior of the growing things he was observing. Only with this kind of naturalistic description was it possible to approach something of the unique quality of each child's

---

* From a record by H. Plotsky, M.D., substituting for Dr. Toussieng on this examination.

† From a record by Povl Toussieng, M.D.

encounter with newness. When later we came to the processes of dissecting and abstracting, analyzing and generalizing, we had to remember constantly that all such abstractions are made at a price—that each child's individual style of response represents his own unique integration of many different processes, only some of which are shared by any of the other children.

For our children, most of whom were growing up in small, modest homes, almost every part of the Project brought newness. The tests were at first conducted in a generous house of ten large rooms, colorfully decorated and furnished in a comfortable, traditional upper middle-class style. No child in the study lived in such a large house, and only a few came from homes so well-furnished. The first testing room itself was a large, bright bedroom lit by the sunshine which streamed in through a huge bay window, a pleasant room quite different in size and equipment from any room in the house of any of the children at that time.

For these children, most of whom had not been to nursery school and had not been around widely outside of the family home and the homes of a few relatives or neighbors, each testing experience contributed an additional surprise: the multitude of toys in a Miniature Life Toy Session, with its Sensory Toys and Bonhop Play House sequel, the toys in the psychiatric play session, the strange pictures in a Rorschach session, and the Children's Apperception Test session. All of these things offered a situation with a degree of newness beyond what would be experienced by a nursery school child or a city child whose room had been equipped with a large number of varied toys.

Added to this newness was the challenge of separation from the mother when this occurred. Actually, many of the mothers took it for granted that young children need their mothers when meeting a situation for the first time, and accompanied the child to the testing place. We shall deal with separation problems later and confine ourselves now to the child's ways of dealing with newness, and the mother's ways of helping when she felt help was needed.

These first experiences of mother and child in a new situation gave us a chance to see how the mothers handled the child in circumstances they thought the child might find mildly strange or disturbing. There were few instances of mothers scolding for shyness or fear or resistance; no instances of taunting with "don't be a baby," such as one often sees in large cities when a child is taken to a store to try on shoes, or introduced to some other strange, inhibiting, and fearful situation. On the contrary, most of the mothers assumed that it was natural for the child to feel shy, and offered support of one kind or another; a mother held her child's hand, put him on her lap, let him snuggle up against her in the car; or she soothed, explained, coaxed, as the case might be, physically and verbally comforting and supporting and encouraging the child. In other words, in the "new situations" in which we saw many of the children they were not expected by mothers to handle newness stoically.

Some children not only see the world of newness as innocent until it has been proven guilty but also seem to regard it as a potential reservoir of new delights, whereas other children seem to suspect the worst until the new situation has proved itself to be safe. Children who marched into new experiences with assurance included Sheila, not yet three, and three-year-old Brennie as well as four-year-old Teddy and Chester, Diane and Susan. More dramatic and swashbuckling or provocative in a counterchallenge to newness was Karen. At the other extreme were Daryl and others who were at first distrustful or very anxious. We shall look at more examples from each group, starting with a three-year-old boy who was eagerly interested in the new prospects:

Brennie's coping devices *

Brennie may have experienced less sense of newness in this situation than did most of the group; he alone lived in the same neighborhood and was accustomed to see such houses. He did not have to make the long trip to the testing center that most of the children did who lived in far-removed neighborhoods. For him it was the test experience primarily which was new.

An active, round-faced, brown-haired, alert three-year-old, he was riding his tricycle out in front of his house when Mrs. Heider and Mrs. Smith arrived to pick him up. He came along to the car without any delay or anxiety. It was his two-year-old brother who got upset and began to cry when he saw Brennie getting into the car and leaving. Brennie smiled and explained that Danny wanted to come along. Their mother was completely absorbed in trying to comfort Danny and promising him that Brennie would soon be back.

During the ride, Brennie was absorbed in the environment; he alertly observed and pointed out different children and objects along the way, different trucks and automobiles, enjoying his ability to name them, sharing his observations with the testers. He was quite at ease with the two new adults and used a little physical support when he needed it, resting his hand casually on Mrs. Smith's shoulder as the car rounded curves, slowed up, or stopped for signals. His beaming

* This summary parallels but is less detailed than that found in Dr. Moriarty's monograph.

smile seemed to express an immense enjoyment in new experiences and gave the adults the feeling that he was extremely happy just to be alive.

When the car stopped in front of the testing house, he paused for a moment, waiting for a cue, and got out as soon as he realized that he was expected to do so. He continued to chat about people he saw going by, enjoying himself and charming everyone with his smile. He accepted Mrs. Smith's hand, holding it all the way up to the house, then waited willingly downstairs until Dr. Moriarty was ready for them to come up.

Going upstairs to the testing room, he seemed to "take it all in with one look" as he entered the room and immediately walked over to the table and chair where Dr. Moriarty suggested he might sit. With continued responsiveness he asked, "Should I draw a picture on this?" when he was asked whether he would like to. Smiling softly at Dr. Moriarty he asked, "Are you the teacher?" and contentedly proceeded to draw, occasionally asking additional questions to orient himself, such as "Is this the school?" He appeared to include the adults and to trust them completely. He seemed to have little or no anxiety about his lack of clarity regarding the new situation.

When asked what he was going to draw, he said, "A horsey!" Then after drawing something like a small circle, he himself asked, "What's dat?" and as if answering his own question said, "Might be a heart." As he heard a car outside he asked, "What was that?" and when Dr. Moriarty suggested it was probably a car, he exclaimed, "Yes, sir! Think it was," again smiling happily . . .

During a rather long period of coloring, Brennie carried on a conversation with the tester, asking her the names of colors, asking her about a light which he saw on the ceiling and about the chimes he heard outside, finally asking, "What shall we do now?" although when she tried to find out whether he was all through coloring, he said, "No." Most of his initial questions appeared to serve the purpose of orienting himself to the roles of new people and objects, and the procedures to be followed.

He drew "a stop line" and then another line "that spells me." "That's my name right there." When Dr. Moriarty responded to his smile with a question, "Would you like to look at some other things?" he agreed eagerly, "Yes, I sure would."

When she offered him the string on which to string beads, he thanked her amiably. As she suggested, "Let's see how many you can put on," he remarked thoughtfully, "I think I will take a round one and see if a round one will go on," as if he were accustomed to do his own reality-testing. When he started with the end of the string that had a knot in it so that he could not put the bead on, he thanked the experimenter for explaining that it would work better if he started with the other end. Then he wanted to know what the knot was for. As Dr. Moriarty showed him how the beads did not fall off the end where the knot held them, he was delighted and tested her statement, commenting, "They *don't* fall off, do they?" and held up the string with the satisfaction of a great discoverer. When asked whether he could make a block structure like hers, he said rather doubtfully at first, "I guess I could," and then on a second questioning decided, "I couldn't do it like that." Evaluating how things work, what they could and could not do was evidently a typical part of his coping procedures.

He was thoroughly cooperative in naming the objects in a series of pictures and again said, "Thank you" when the task was done, continuing through other tests until he was shown the snowman with the missing leg. After drawing the missing leg immediately, he refused to complete the snowman, saying, "I couldn't do it now. I'm too tired to do it," and went back to his bead string. The "incomplete" (damaged) body evidently aroused some anxiety which he handled by retreating to a familiar area of achievement.

When shown the next series of small objects from which to choose "what we buy candy with," his attention wandered. He began to play that he was drinking out of the little cup, but when asked, "Are you having a drink?" he laughed and realistically remarked, "Just pretending." And again realistically, when asked if he rode in the car he said, "No, I don't ride in that car." Here he was discriminating between pretending and reality, although there is a childish lack of insight regarding the fact that an adult could not possibly expect him to take a ride in such a tiny car. After cooperating a little longer, naming parts of the body of the boy doll, he spied a train in the test material and asked rather sweetly, "Let's take a look at the train, do you want to?" He seemed to adopt the tester's manner, using it in his own dealings with her. When the train was brought out and he was asked whether he liked trains, he enthusiastically agreed, "Sure do," and then urged, "Let's look at the rest," pointing to another box of material. As Dr. Moriarty brought out the small formboard, he did the tasks immediately. He kept moving the test along with his questions, "Can I see more of those?" indicating another box, and readily responded to the series of requests which were now made of him.

Through the rest of the period of the test he continued in a cooperative mood, stopping only to be sure that he understood the requests of the tester, and at any free moment moving around to explore the room, change the position of his chair, and in some other way follow his own impulses. When Dr. Moriarty suggested that it was time to go and perhaps he would like an ice cream cone, he responded with a beaming smile. Going downstairs, he asked Mrs. Smith to hold his hand so that he would not fall; he managed the steps quite carefully, bringing his second foot down to have two feet squarely on each step before going to the next one, a procedure which seemed to contrast with his very grown-up "thank you" and "yes, sir."

In the car he again kept his right hand on Mrs. Smith's shoulder for support with increasing pressure when the car went around curves or slowed up. In the drugstore he chose to sit on a stool instead of in a booth and asked for a small cone with pink ice cream which he ate slowly and carefully.

This consistent, careful control of his body in order to avoid falling, bumps, or spilling involved greater impulse control, however, than he could sustain indefinitely. Having finished his cone, while passing some open shelves of candy on his way out of the store, he grabbed a candy kiss and as many balls of bubble gum as his hand would hold, then reached for a candy black hat which he tasted and put back on the shelf—all this without any indication of guilt or concern about whether it was permitted or not. When the group reached home, smiling and nodding, Brennie agreed that he would be happy to come back again for another session with the research group.

Here is a little boy who moved into the new situation warmly and spontaneously, quickly orienting himself by his own alert, widely ranging observation, and supplementing his own grasp by asking questions to clarify things further. He seemed to perceive the situation as one in which he was being given to, and responded for some time with polite thanks. Only at the end did his impulsive taking suggest that he may have expected to be given more, or felt that he had not been given to after all, but had done most of the giving himself. He was well able to manage for himself and to use the available adult for help and support, and to fit into the situation as far as he understood it, including an ability to postpone certain gratifications to a later time. Discovery of the phenomenon of a knot at the end of a string which would hold the beads on was a source of intense delight and he had the usual small-boy enthusiasm at a tiny gun. He preferred to continue activities which he could handle well rather than to attempt tasks he felt were beyond his ability, or which aroused anxious conflicts, and when pressed set limits to the examiner and stated his own limits. He was quite free to ask for further opportunities to explore objects in which he was interested and to hold onto an activity which he wished to continue. A hint of conscience was reflected in his "I'd better pick that up" when he dropped a small object on the floor, and anxiety was noted only when he was drawing the incomplete snow-

man. At the end his enjoyment seemed unalloyed and he was quite
ready to commit himself to a repetition of the experience.

Donald's steps in accepting the new situation

Very different in Dr. Moriarty's intelligence test situation was the
behavior of three-year-old Donald whom we saw briefly with Dr. Toussieng earlier. Donald came from a tiny crowded home in a remote neighborhood, and a family which probably never had visited a home like
that of the Observation Center. Donald's warm, ample mother held
his hand as they came out to the car on the first trip. He silently accepted a place on the front seat between his mother and Mrs. Heider.
While the grownups chatted he continued silent through the entire
trip, even when his mother told how his father accompanied Donald's songs on the guitar, and how Donald would not sing with other
children even though he would sing with his father at church. As he
quietly sat very close to his mother, she now and then stroked his hair
or wiped his nose. Even with this close physical support which continued as they came up to the house and on up to the second floor, he
was silent and increasingly reluctant. When they paused outside the
door, Donald's mother urged him to come in but he watchfully clung
to her, sober and unsmiling, though without any evidence of panic or
resentment.

Finally, Dr. Moriarty suggested that his mother could stay in the
room if Donald wished. And so she did, trying to help by urging Donald to go and sit in the little red chair provided for him. He continued
to stay close to her, standing with his hand against the wall, almost as if
needing it for support since his mother had now let go of his hand.
Although his mother several times added her weight to Dr. Moriarty's suggestion that he sit in the chair and see what she had to show
him, he stood his ground quite firmly and resolutely, with his feet
spread just slightly, showing no intention at all of leaving his mother's
side or sitting in the chair next to Dr. Moriarty.

The tester now took the tests to him, starting with beads to string;
but when they were offered, he stepped slightly behind his mother's
chair, looking first at the beads and then at Dr. Moriarty. She showed
him how the beads went on the string but he continued merely looking at them and at her, unsmiling, as he continued to stand close to
his mother. Dr. Moriarty then suggested that perhaps his mother
could string a few and show him how.

His mother took the bead string, asking him to tell her how many
beads she had put on it. Still he would not answer, although she
asked him many times. But now he watched his mother quite intently

and shook his head yes or no, as she asked him numbers. For example, if she held up two and asked him if it was three, he would shake his head no; he nodded his head yes when she asked the correct number, doing this up to five. Finally his mother coaxed him to take the string into his own hands and to sit down on the floor, which he did at first in a sort of squatting fashion.

Once started on the bead project, he showed very definite preferences: he had a little difficulty getting the round beads he wanted and with no seeming hesitation dumped all the beads out onto the floor, then picked out the round ones which were easier to find when separated on the larger area of the floor than piled in the small box.

But when Dr. Moriarty seated herself on the floor a few feet away from him and offered him a small blue car, suggesting that perhaps he would like to run it on the wooden floor close to the edge of the rug where he was sitting, he ignored her offer and persisted with his bead stringing, and he continued to do this subsequently when she scooted a yellow car toward him. He worked very slowly and deliberately with his bead stringing. Dr. Moriarty suggested that he come over to the red table when he was through with the beads. He had almost filled the string and looked up at his mother saying very softly but audibly, "Look at all those," as if impressed with his achievement. Although the string now was completely full he tried to get one more bead on; and only when he found it was impossible, after two further efforts, did he finally drop them and then take them off the string.

At the next stage of the test when Dr. Moriarty brought out the picture of the doll and asked him to show his mother where the different parts of the doll were (since it was obvious that he was not yet sufficiently related to the tester to tell her), his mother supported the effort. For her he pointed to all the different parts of the body quite readily, though slowly and deliberately. Tactfully, his mother asked him to take the picture over and put it on the table so she wouldn't have to hold it, but Donald could not yet accept her effort to make a bridge to Dr. Moriarty's area; as a compromise he put the doll on the floor about one step away.

Inch by inch he made a little progress. Dr. Moriarty offered him the box with the kitten, thimble, spoon, cup, and block and he now took them from her, going directly to his mother with them and naming the different objects in the box for her. When Dr. Moriarty gave him directions to put the spoon in the cup, the thimble on the block, and hand his mother the kitty, he accepted the directions and did so.

Now he made an important new step. He piled cup, thimble, and spoon all on top of an orange block, an accomplishment of his own devising not requested by the tester. She acknowledged it with an appreciative remark that he might grow up to be a juggler or do a balancing act in the circus.

This led to a definite step forward: since she had accepted him on his terms, evidently Donald was now able to cooperate with her on her own terms. Still sitting down on the floor a few feet away from Donald (recognizing his need to maintain some distance), Dr. Moriarty offered him the formboard and he put the forms in directly at her request without any encouragement or support of any kind from his mother.

Another step came when he got up very slowly at both Dr. Moriarty's and his mother's urging to get the crayons, taking them from Dr. Moriarty's table while keeping a sharp eye on her "as if she might be about to bite him." He took the crayons back to his mother, sitting down in front of her, turning his back to Dr. Moriarty who had moved back to the table. When she offered him some drawing paper, he reached out to accept it from her, and then chose a red crayon and drew something quickly. He followed his mother's instruction to draw a man, drawing with black at her suggestion of a dark color. His mother asked questions, "What is his name?" "Is that a cowboy?" and so on, but Donald firmly resisted her questions and said, "No, 'Popeye'!"

He still used a soft voice in answering his mother, although he had relaxed enough to respond more freely. Evidently attempting to help him to loosen up, his mother asked him to name colors one by one as he picked them out of the box and then asked him to count the crayons, which he did several times. After a few tries he counted up to eight without a mistake.

After this much expansion and demonstration of his ability to respond verbally, Dr. Moriarty attempted to get him to name pictures of objects on cards for her. He was able to go to her table and tried to take them, but she said she wanted to hold them while he named them. This manuever failed; he refused to do it this way, and she suggested then that he take them over to his mother and name them for her. The mother again followed the tester's style and routine, and Donald named them for his mother still speaking very softly, so softly that once in a while his mother would say that she couldn't hear, stimulating him in this way to speak a little louder. When he couldn't name the knife, he separated it from the rest, and his mother commented that that was the way he did in music if he couldn't name a note. At this point his embarrassment regarding ignorance and limitations appeared in a special kind of motor tension, hunching his shoulders.

Moving back and forth now between his mother and the tester's table, he took the cards back to the table and chose the green blocks to take back to the area where his mother was. Seeing the stopwatch on the table he decided to take it, but he did not protest when Dr. Moriarty suggested that he had better not, since it was delicate and could easily be damaged. He did take the blocks out and built a pyramid of nine of them, sitting now so that both Dr. Moriarty and the observer could see him. Though he was again in front of his mother, he did not shut out others to the extent he had done up to this point.

His slowly increasing expansiveness was next expressed in spontaneous activity with a blue and yellow car which he ran into his pyramid knocking it down. When his mother suggested that he build a garage, he immediately began to make a square structure putting both cars in it.

Dr. Moriarty now came to him again with more objects to name, and pink blocks with which to build a tower. He did the former but was not willing to bother with the tower. Instead, he wanted to make his own structure using the pink blocks along with his green ones. Only after his mother warned him to pay attention to Dr. Moriarty's requests and repeated instructions did he focus on the pink blocks and the tower required by the test. When the tester showed him a nest of cubes, he took them apart but did not want to put them together, again preferring to include them with the blocks; he did finally cooperate after repeated suggestions.

The tester did not attempt to work with him further at this time but suggested that he could stop and have an ice cream cone if he liked. Still he made no answer to her, but his eyes lit up a bit and the observer felt that he was responsive to the suggestion. He accepted her help in putting the objects back into the proper boxes and appeared to enjoy this restoration of order.

It is interesting to see that after all of this extreme caution, closeness to his mother, and limited responsiveness to demands and requests from a stranger, once Donald was out of the door of the testing room, instead of going downstairs he started up the steps to the strange third floor. He came back when his mother told him he should not go up there—that everybody was going home now. Out on the porch he wanted to climb up on the step railings but his mother again discouraged this, holding him by the hand and guiding him off the railing.

On the way home, while Donald sat in the front seat between his mother and Dr. Moriarty; instead of clinging so closely to his mother, he knelt on the front seat and faced the back, looking pleasantly at Mrs. Smith, and accepting a package of gum from her. His mother told the others how much Donald enjoyed taking pictures but still Donald did not venture any comments. When ice cream cones were brought out, Donald accepted his and approached the job of consuming it in the same slow and deliberate fashion as he had strung the beads.

Here we see a record of a very cautious little boy who manages to keep a new situation under control during the entire period; while his behavior would be frustrating to many examiners because of his firm determination to keep things on his own terms, and to do only what he wished to do where he wished to do it and with whom he wished to do it, there was actually no disintegrative response at any point. Donald handled the situation by very slow, selective, and controlled giving of himself combined with a differentiated use of support from his mother, which included both leaning on her to an extreme degree at points and at other points venturing off with surprising autonomy.

If we consider this record of a small boy's attempt to keep things within manageable limits, it is easy to see how disturbing it could be to such a child to be taken into a situation where he was expected to conform at every point to adult requests which not only did not make sense to him but were physically threatening, as a hospital situation might be.

Over the years we have seen Donald this pattern has continued: cautious, deliberate, watchful entrance into a new situation, keeping his distance at first, quietly, firmly maintaining his right to move at his own pace, to make his own choices, to set his own terms, to cooperate when he got ready. These tendencies persisted long after he became able to separate from his mother. We shall see more of this sturdy boy and his autonomous coping methods later.

Rachel, a child bewildered by newness

Still more cautious, though she had been quite willing to come along in all situations, was four-year-old Rachel, from the only family which felt acutely conscious of being "poor," and the only family which did not own a car and was therefore confined to its own meager home and neighborhood. Here Dr. Moriarty summarizes her first approach to the intelligence test situation.

Rachel on her first meeting was the epitome of the wide-eyed sober street gamin. Her broad face with its wide nose and large brown eyes expressed wonder and bewilderment. Her skin was pale, with a blue transparency except for a rough red spot on one cheek, the result of an allergy. As she spoke in hoarse whispers, stiffly controlling her bodily movements, there was a desperateness about Rachel that had a pathetic appeal. As the session proceeded, Rachel was able to progress from whispering to speech of normal intensity, from awkward, stiff movements to rather easy, functional movements in compliance with the examiner's instructions, from bewilderment to quite enthusiastic delight with some of the small toys and the ability to ask the examiner for more of them. My impression was that the initial aloof reserve was not as deep or uncomfortable as the tension one felt in her cousin, Vernon, but might at least in part be a result of inexperience with strangers or with the variety of stimulating play equipment which the various project sessions offer. . . .

Rachel seemed to want to explore and examine, to find out for herself before she was willing to give any indication of her own feelings. This seemed to be particularly true of the trip to and from her home, when she sat on the very edge of the car seat, looking from side to side intently. Her language was never profuse but spontaneous comments were made from time to time which indicated that her wide eyes were observing quite minutely. . . .

Although it is not easy to be sure of what is going on in such a quiet child, it appeared that she needed and used much time for looking, for visual orientation to and cognitive mastery of a new situation, and that her real investment was in this rather than in action.

Since Rachel showed such an extreme response to new situations —despite her willingness to separate from her mother—a closer examination of her behavior is worthwhile in an effort to understand what strangeness meant to her. The following is a review of behavior obtained in three play sessions with miniature toys with me:

Everything Rachel did the three times we saw her in the Miniature Life Toys play situation must be thought about in relation to the impression of four observers, that a new situation is overwhelming to her, almost paralyzing, certainly fraught with potentially threatening unknowns. At these times she looks like a lost child, a war-orphan or a child in some similar circumstances who is haunted by a fear of some dreadful destiny, or as WM commented, with a "fatiguing, paralyzing sense of apartness," expressed in her "far-away, vaguely drooping attitude." It should also be remembered throughout that on the way home from each situation she relaxed quickly, seemed to be a different child, able to talk with the adults with considerable freedom, responsive to her environment, radiantly expressive when a special treat appeared, and bubbling with eagerness as she rejoined her family. Details of her behavior can be seen then as expressions of an impressionable, reactive, resilient little personality with extremely wide swings from paralyzing anxiety to glowing delight. Verbal, motor, affective, cognitive responses to these situations were all deeply affected by this persistent apprehensivness about the unknown situation, the unknown person, from which she recovered as soon as she left the strangeness behind her, and returned to safe familiarity, or even the prospect of it.

All MLT records also express the bewilderment of the observers who are strained to interpret the behavior of this silent, masked, little girl as she very slowly expands into very personal, unusual, and sometimes unintelligible play. Her lack of language and also of facial expression during the MLT play,

combined with the idiosyncratic nature of some of it, invited the speculation
and fantasy of the observers who emphasized widely different possibilities in
line with their respective frames of reference, or avoided making any commitment beyond a summary of what went on, sometimes translated into abstract
terms. Not having seen her on the to and fro trips where her gazing and her
occasional remarks seemed natural, and being therefore unaware of the special
demands which the strange MLT situation and my strange self put on her, I
was even more puzzled than other observers.

My notes on the beginning of the first session will illustrate this:

She came up the steps silently with a slow cautious pace, big wide eyes,
cheeks gradually flushing, and stood near the toys and near me, immobile
and frozen. She tried to move her knees but the movement was hardly per-
ceptible; she stood and looked at the toys, face drooping, twisting her handkerchief. Since it seemed so difficult for her to relate to me or to the toys (although I had not had to do this for any other child in this group), I took
out some dollies, asking if "this could be" mother, father, etc., and she nodded
ever so slightly each time, her face still expressionless, movement still frozen.

After some five minutes I suggested that she sit on my lap. She did not
resist, but let me draw her down, where she continued to sit stiffly, head to
one side, not melting. Finally I suggested that I would go out to get a drink
and she could play with Dr. Moriarty, with whom she was familiar from the
previous testing sessions. After five minutes, I returned to the room. When I
came back she did not look up, as she sat in front of a group of Housekeeping Toys arranged in a unique way.

While she expanded into the situation very slowly, she was ultimately,
like other Kansas children,* able to use almost all parts of the room, including
the suitcase and space off the rug, suggesting freedom from deeply internalized
constrictions; this emphasized the situational and reactive nature of her inhibition. Her marked increase in tempo during the hour, also pointed to the
close relation between a sense of security and freedom to respond naturally.

Along with that of her sister, her surprise and pleasure in the windshield
wiper on WM's car revealed their lack of experiences common to the other
children; things which are everyday matters to most children can seem new,
magical or awesome to Rachel and her sister.

Her "shy, dumbfounded . . . gradually more open and radiant delight,"
her "lips parted in happy wonder" at the blonde doll which I gave her following the visit to our house, suggested further that she felt remote from what
must have seemed like an almost unearthly fairyland of toys. WM noted that
the word "curlers" seemed new to her, even this she repeated with a "rapt
musing expression."

Rachel's need for an unusually long orientation time, and her slow
tempo during her initial play with the toys was compared by LW with the
problem of a delayed first experience in a new sensory modality as of Senden's

---

* Children in Westchester and New York rarely used the whole room but
confined their arrangements of toys to assumed limits.

subjects after removal of congenital cataracts. However, I felt that her stiffness and emotional resistance and masking pointed to more anxiety than sheer newness of the cognitive situation to a rather deprived child would account for. The fact that she began play rather quickly in MLT after I, the new adult, left her alone with the tested and familiar Dr. Moriarty supports this hypothesis.

Rachel's occasional glances at the observer as if for reassurance seemed to imply insecurity about the right way to do things, or fear of reproof or disapproval. This may also be related to her undoing and shifting, and interfered with a free flow of play.

In all records there are repeated comments on her deep sighs and heavy breathing; and occasional remarks about paling and flushing which point to deep physical responsiveness to experience, at an autonomic level. Feelings pervade her whole self while all motor-expression through locomotor, facial, or overtly emotional outlets was blocked, so that we would expect gastro-intestinal or other physiological expressions of her reactions. (I did not know that she had a history of severe eczema, currently controlled by diet.)

Speculations about her inability to express the flood of feelings in a new situation which everyone sensed behind her silent gaze included the following: that she did not feel free to fully exist in an unfamiliar setting, or to call attention to herself in any way. Or perhaps she was full of awe of an outside unknown, perhaps higher-class world. Perhaps she had been overly conditioned to a brand of manners epitomized by unquestioning obedience, conformity or inconspicuousness; or perhaps she had an underlying sense of weakness and helplessness which kept her from meeting a conflict situation with any overt effort.

But she also showed a remarkable flexibility and resilience which enabled her to respond freely once she was out of the awesome or frightening new experience, and a capacity for deep sensuous delight and gratification and for sensitive non-verbal interpersonal communication through smiles and eyes, along with her capacity for representation and symbolization of experiences in fantasies which seemed to contradict the view of her as a deeply inhibited child.

It seemed clear that she was able to use tender and loving care as a reinforcement to her own coping efforts and resilience, despite her resistance when first confronting a new situation, and that she was much more free in her home setting.

Sheila's method of dominating a new situation

Lest the reader conclude that Rachel is typical of the girls, we shall present immediately a brief excerpt from Dr. Toussieng's report on Sheila, not yet three, whose approach to her first examination was an assertion of control.

"No," said Sheila with a finality which did not leave room for doubt. Her broad figure with rounded contours leaned forward, her arms and her legs flexed somewhat as if she wanted to roll herself up into a ball of firm, tense, immovable flesh. Even her square face, made more square by her straightly cut bangs and complete absence of curls in her blonde hair, seemed to draw itself together around the little mouth. Her pale face seemed to become even paler. Certainly here was the impression of a solid rock deeply imbedded in the ground, impermeable and hard cut.

The "no" was accepted, not challenged, and suddenly the stony features disappeared, melted away, and with unexpected, stunning grace Sheila smiled broadly and seductively and did what she had just refused to do. One realized that once more one had been allowed to witness the age-old tricks of femininity in our culture. Thus having assured herself of her complete control of this situation, Sheila was willing to relax, to enjoy herself, to explore the world around her, even the dangerous aspects of it. Few children turn to the instruments as quickly and experiment with them as freely as Sheila did. Assured of complete control Sheila was even willing to yield graciously to masculine requests, though she made sure in between that this miserable specimen of the male sex was still her slave whenever she wanted it. Then, very suddenly, she would become a little, whiny child who complained, "I can't," though she had just done it or proceeded to do it directly afterwards.

A lack of social anxiety in all these maneuvers was revealed most glaringly during the physical examination when her kicking made an examination of the abdomen futile. Mrs. H. was asked to hold her legs. A scared child would have cried out, but for Sheila it was merely a clear defeat which she accepted with grace and equanimity, waiting only for a moment when she could resume control of the situation. And she did! . . .

I have introduced here only the child's responses to new external situations; if we had ways of knowing about them, we could and should also study the infant and young child's discovery of newness in himself. Occasionally we do catch his surprise, puzzlement, or even anxiety as the child reacts to the sensation of a new tooth, his first haircut, the first time he accidentally bites a finger when putting something into his mouth, the first sensations of walking or of running or of being able to swing himself. This universe of feelings, tactile, painful, soothing, kinaesthetic, rhythmic, etc., to be discovered in new experiences of oneself would take another research endeavor, focused on experiences and behavior observable chiefly at home.

Coping with the new situation

We began our exploration of children's ways of dealing with new situations by following a few children whose approaches were widely different. We can now look at the group as a whole, and review the major steps in coping observed in a majority of the group. About half the group needed "time to see, look, take in" a new situation.

Sometimes, as we saw, this took the form of a cautious survey before the child committed himself to anyone or anything:

> With a steady, unblinking gaze Diane surveyed the situation and me; standing with the poise of a Flagstad, she continued to look steadily, unfalteringly, keeping her motionless quiet stance.

> Wide-eyed, hands in pockets and glued to the spot, Donald looked at all the toys, and me, and back to the toys, with a slowly shifting gaze blandly absorbing, appraising, ungiving. Unsmiling, he chewed his gum very hard, making no response to my suggestion that he could do anything he wanted to with the soldiers as he looked steadily at them.

I commented that he did not have the quick, immediate, sharp form perception characteristic of some of the other boys but he might achieve it at an older age as a result of practice. Donald had to make repeated efforts with the Bonhop Play House roof forms before he inserted the blocks correctly; but he could and did differentiate clearly as a result of persistent careful effort to do so. His interest in details, in differentiating form, was expressed in his characteristic wide-eyed staring gaze. He looked and looked and looked, not just at the beginning of any new experience, but especially then. The fact that it took a long time for him to master a situation perceptually may account to considerable degree for the long period of immobilization typical of him in any new situation.

Roger also went through a slow orientation period; but he moved around with an even tempo, easy fluid movements and a wide range of postures. Even the forthright Sandra had to have an initial period for appraisal and Karen, though often ebullient, was sometimes hesitant to commit herself. Vivian was also cautious and required a very long, slow warming-up time though without the extreme paralysis we saw in Rachel. In some cases the child seemed vague, hesitant, or puzzled; the slowness in orientation appeared to reflect a feeling of bewilderment with the strangeness of the situation and a need to withhold any emotional involvement while going through the initial period of survey. Ronnie was "reluctant to enter into and deal with a situation without familiar landmarks." Ray "required a long warming-up period."

While many of the children thus needed time to see, look, take in, this was by no means always a focused or systematic process. For some, the effort to get oriented had the quality of feeling one's way, at times concentrating with a focused gaze and at other times glancing about in a more haphazard way. We are not justified in saying that a systematic and active exploration was any more effective in terms of later behavior—or as effective—as the process engaged in by the child who slowly felt his way into the situation.

Each child brings his own good or bad expectancies or assumptions into new situations, and his own basic ways of dealing with these anticipated pleasures or threats; the extra energy mobilized to deal with newness seems to intensify these central coping patterns so that the small child is most uniquely himself in the spotlight of newness.

Jean Macfarlane[1] has commented that wide differences in sensitivity to overstimulation from different sensory areas may accentuate or in part account for differences in reaction to new situations. Nancy Bayley[2] observed that sensitive children may also have a wider range of variability, being shy and inhibited at first in new situations, later very talkative; they may seem to change more while the rest of the group remains more consistent. Children may also differ in variability, some being more labile earlier while others become more labile later.

As fast as the children discovered what to do, they became more alike; after the newness had worn off and all were engaged in a common activity, such as pinning the tail on the donkey at the party, their differences became muted by comparison with the vividness of differences at first. Still later, after four or five years of school, it was hard to believe they had appeared so very different at first.

Without further attention, for the moment, to individual children, and we can review the initial sequences in one of the experiences which appeared most unusual to them. While the Miniature Life Toy play situation came after a first test (usually the structured test with Dr. Moriarty), for most of the children it presented a surprising opportunity. Confronting a couple of hundred small toys in five heaps on the floor was a decidedly novel experience to these children, all but three of whom had never been to nursery school with its rich array of play materials, and many of whom had few indoor toys at all.

At first the response of the majority was simply to stand and stare. Some children went from staring to autonomous exploration of the room, acquainting themselves with all its resources, even looking into chests and drawers or under the bed and out of the window. This may have involved some stalling or a way of supporting the delay needed before deciding what to do, but several of the children actually used the room as part of their play, putting toys on or under the bed, on a window sill, on the suitcase, or in some other way integrating the space and large objects into their handling of the small toys. Thus the initial exploration seemed clearly a process of collecting data for appraisal of the scope of the opportunity. The time required for this initial appraisal and the tempo of active approach to new situations varied greatly from child to child. In some instances a child kept a bystander-watcher-observer attitude throughout an entire session, although in other situations this same child could be an active participant.

The orientation pattern differed for different children. Ralph, Chester, and Tommy seemed to attempt a comprehensive grasp of all the major resources of the situation, in contrast to Donald who limited what he took in at one time, sizing things up with a slow appraising regard which took in small details and selectively avoided what might be threatening.

This procedure of looking, observing, exploring, taking their own time to orient themselves to and appraise the situation, was very different from the typical behavior of hundreds of nursery school children in New York and its suburbs with whom Miniature Life Toy sessions had been carried on in previous years. Those children who typically had many toys at home usually dropped to the floor immediately, in some instances picking up some of the toys in an exploratory way, but more often making an almost immediate choice and beginning to play, with some incidental exploring interspersed through their play as they went along.

Other children used delay as a way of reducing the initial impact of a situation. Temporary postponement or taking time out to become clear about what was involved, to give oneself a feeling of control and security or moving into a situation slowly step by step, restricting the amount of stimulation to which one would expose oneself at any given moment, interposing delay in the form of "I'll do it when I feel like it," allowing time for mobilizing energy, characterized a number of them.

More daring children explored their own capacities and limits by trying things out; when they found themselves involved in something they could not manage, shifted to something which was within their ability. This capacity to shift also appeared when a child found himself engaged with some material or activity which stimulated impulses that tended to get out of hand. Such a child would stop himself when he felt he could no longer control his impulses, while another would turn away from and exclude from awareness things which threaten to be overwhelming.

Although the Miniature Life Toys session as well as the intelligence test and pediatric examination were all conducted by women who were themselves mothers as well as professional women (and whose attitude was permissive and tempo unhurried), and perhaps for this reason relatively easy for the children to feel at home with, the psychiatric examination and the projective tests such as the Rorschach and the CAT were conducted by men, whose approach was more rapidly paced, more demanding, partly because their research time was narrowly sliced from a crowded clinical schedule. Thus the atmosphere in these situations was different and presented another variation, another sort of new situation even to children who had had a couple of the previous tests with women members of the research team.

From the intensity of the reactions of some of the children, especially to the examinations conducted by men, we assume that new situations can readily mobilize anxieties and conflicts, perhaps because the lack of familiar content in the unknown itself removes the natural healthy supports to reality-testing which provide a normal challenge to threats from the child's inner world. The paralysis in new situations shown by some children suggested that the stress involved in "not knowing what to do" or how to manage, is part of the problem for children in new situations. Being overwhelmed by a multitude of new stimuli so that one cannot choose, select, or start directly to master the situation, contributes to this.

We may contrast this with the stress of sensory or perceptual deprivation, and call the present threat that of perceptual flooding in new situations, involving the feeling of inability to master stimuli: we may infer that such perceptual flooding is more likely to occur in children who (1) respond to a wide range of sensory and perceptual stimuli, (2) have rich associations to every stimulus, (3) are slow to select, to impose their own structure or to find structure in complex stimuli, and (4) are inhibited in the assertiveness required to detach part of the stimulus situation from the rest. These are possible factors in the stressfulness of new situations where neither pain nor loss is implied.

If we consider that the children's ability to survey a situation for themselves and achieve some degree of cognitive mastery in relation to it, on the one hand, and their ability to express their feelings clearly, on the other hand, indicated a foundation of independence, we should not be surprised to find those who could be assertive and able to make clear choices for themselves when opportunity offered. Tommy, Ronnie, and Chester all showed this capacity for assertion or frontal attack or action independent of public opinion, and even Vivian could choose her own path at times even though she was often plastic to others' initiative and control.

While much of this sounds mature, these were still very little children and we have seen that they could also use very childish ways of coping with situations which were beyond their own direct efforts. Vivian, Ray, Lennie, Karen, and others would seek support through bodily contact, physical help, encouraging words or manner, or by inviting affection. Sometimes these demands for physical support took a form which might ordinarily be considered quite infantile—clinging to mother, fingering her dress, or parts of her body, head, ears, hair, and so forth, depending on the physical situation in which the child found himself. Along with this, Tommy and others could get the adult to protect him from an external threat or from something he himself might do.

In our previous discussion of the children's way of surveying a situation in order to orient themselves clearly to it, we emphasized the active mastery in this procedure. While this aspect of mastery—the attempt to understand, to make a cognitive map, to clarify as many aspects of the situation as possible—seems to be involved with practically all of the children who took a watchful, observing attitude in new situations, it was also true that some children were not able to act upon their observations as other children did. We saw that Rachel seemed to be position-bound in a new situation; Martin, a fragile and sensitive boy, showed very closed, restricted postures for long periods, although he was capable of being very much more relaxed when a situation had become familiar to him. Vernon appeared equally mute, inhibited, and constricted when confronted with new children and new adults.

The autonomy of some children took a wider variety of forms than that of others. For instance, Jo Anne could reverse roles with the adult or accept limits as she could also set limits for the adult. She could structure the environment for her own comfort, arranging a room, opening a window, and in general behaved like an autonomous grownup. It was she who felt stronger than adults in some ways, not being afraid of mice as her mother was, and she exercised her right to decide whether or not she would play the offered "game," and if she did decide to cooperate would still retain areas of free choice. Other expressions of a clear sense of self appeared in Jo Anne's emphatic insistence that her name be understood in its full detail and used accurately.

Along with making his wants known and accepting or refusing suggestions from the adult, Chester could give instructions to the adult with a sense of equality expressing his feeling of self-respect and ability to hold his own.

A child with the independence of Teddy could show a proud self-control during a period of uncertainty or pressure which gave way to increased activity when he felt clearer about the way ahead.

With all of this strength to appraise, explore, accept or refuse, select, utilize, structure and restructure, which many of these children showed, they appeared to assume areas of freedom and areas of control and were able to use both when they felt safe in the former and when the latter made sense. Their strong drive to understand for themselves and clarify their own perceptions and grasp of situations, objects, and people was not defensive or rebellious.

Separation from known, and from mother

In our group, the child who felt anxiety at separation usually succeeded in holding the mother's support until he had secured sufficient footing and sufficient security in the new situation and with the new people to let his mother go, confident that he would soon rejoin her; the mothers often facilitated this confidence by asking the child to tell her all about it afterward. So long as it was his choice, the separation has no element of rebuff, rejection, or abandonment; and separation anxiety was momentary.

Nearly all of the four-year-olds were able to leave their mothers. This was also true of some three-year-olds and one child, Sheila, who was two years and ten months old. Here we find that the understanding of time, of going away for a short while, of coming back later—concepts which are not generally available to the two-year-old—appear to play a major part for children four years old, and older, in making separation possible without anxiety. From this point of view we can look in a new way at such data as the record of separation anxiety in Robertson's *A Two-Year-Old Goes to the Hospital*,[3] Spitz's observations[4] on infants separated from mothers in the first year of life, Anna Freud's[5] observations on evacuated children in wartime, and Bowlby's[6] discussions of separation anxiety. We can suggest that the feelings which overwhelm the child are not due simply to loss of the love-object, and to the feelings of abandonment as such. They involve feelings of uncertainty about many aspects of ability to handle a new situation, feelings which are greater where the child cannot grasp time and the validity of promises regarding mother's return "later."

It is interesting to note that the two-year-old Sheila who was able to separate at an early age had grown up in a family who lived with grandparents, and had had already deeply satisfying ties with other persons than mother. This leads us to infer that when a child has been early accustomed to tolerate routine separations from mother with the help of satisfying experiences with supplementary love-objects, new experiences involving separation can be accepted more easily. Leon Yarrow's[7] recent work on separation of infants cared for in foster families is congruent with this; infants developing in families where older sisters supplemented the care by the mother were better able to separate than babies who were cared for solely by the foster mother. A very young child who is cared for in his familiar setting by moderately familiar grandmother during mother's absence suffers far less, if at all, than he does when cared for by a strange person or, more drastically, when he is removed from home to be hospitalized and is cared for by a series of people no one of whom can be counted on to understand his still uncertain language, and his other ways of expressing needs and of gaining comfort.

Thus we need to sort out the various elements which may be involved in separation from mother: loss of mother's presence, love, and familiar ways is intensified by anxiety regarding the unfamiliarity with the new person who is substituting and perhaps frustration in his effort to make a new relationship, a frustration increased by the shortness of time each of a series of new persons is with him. New gross surroundings and the absence of familiar orientation, mastery, and comfort points in his environment make him feel unsure of his ability to deal with the new situation; the crib, bed clothes, night clothes, and even toys, in a hospital look, feel, and smell differently and may be less comfortable. In addition, there may be new demands for action. All of this is overwhelming for some children. In order to see more clearly what is involved for different children and what they do about it, let us turn again to the records.

Lennie copes with newness and separation

We might think that in view of the child's great need to understand what is going on, his ability to cooperate with the short-time separation involved in our study would have been greatly facilitated simply by taking sufficient care to explain to him what would happen and what he could expect from the new experience. Lennie's mother did just this but, as we shall see, a verbal explanation at this age did not help sufficiently to make it possible for him to handle the experience by himself, and to leave his mother at home.

As Dr. Moriarty and Mrs. Smith drove up to his home, and Mrs. Smith went to the door to pick up three-year-old Lennie, he was standing at the window. He waved at her but she noticed a slightly worried look on his face. Inside she was greeted warmly by his mother who was ironing and who introduced Lennie casually saying, "This is the lady that you're going with." He had met Mrs. Smith the day before at the time of Dr. Heider's visit to his mother. Holding his jacket in his hand, he said he wanted his mother to go with him, but she immediately explained that she had too much to do, that he would not be gone very long, that he would come back afterward and tell her all the things that he had done.

Lennie now began a series of delaying maneuvers. First, he

wanted a drink and his mother got him one, glancing at Mrs. Smith meaningfully, apparently well on to his purpose. Again he asked his mother to come with him and again she said she had too much to do. Then he asked for his hat and mother accompanied him to get it. He came back with the typical red cowboy hat which was the fad at the time and Mrs. Smith commented on it with appreciation. His mother said he was "Cowboy Joe in that hat." Lennie was quite proud of it but still asked his mother to go along. Then he asked her if she would cry while he was gone. She laughed and replied that she wouldn't and Lennie finally started out the door.

At this point she asked him to kiss her goodbye and when he did this and then interrupted his leaving to cling to her, asking her to come out with him, she agreed and came out on the porch. Seeing his scooter in the yard he stopped for another delaying action, starting virtuously to put it away. His mother told him to go ahead, that she would take care of it for him. He was now holding onto her as she came across the yard out to the car with him. As they approached the car he clung closer to his mother, his face flushed, his lip was beginning to pucker and tremble and he looked quite unhappy.

Mrs. Smith opened the back door and his mother attempted to coax him in, then tried to lift him in. Everyone attempted to give him a good picture of what lay ahead, explaining to him about the toys that he would play with, the ice cream cone he would have afterward but all to no avail. By this time he was pleading with tears in his eyes for his mother to come with him, pulling at her dress. She laughingly told him that he was "undressing her." He then pulled away and ran crying back into the sanctuary of his house. His mother followed and reminded him how much he had wanted to go and how he had been planning on it all morning.

At this point the testers had a quick conference and decided to invite the mother to come along. She agreed saying that she "could" but was not dressed very well. She was reassured when told that no one else would be around and she looked perfectly all right.

As soon as his mother promised to come Lennie's face was wreathed in smiles and his expression was one of definite relief. Everyone now went to the car and Lennie got in with no hesitation except a backward glance to be sure that his mother was actually coming.

He had been told he could have an ice cream cone even before the session with Dr. Moriarty if he wished and the testers felt ethically bound to carry out this promise. When asked whether he wanted a little one or big one his mother suggested a little one but Lennie said with a rather worried look "a big one" and it was brought to him. When he received it his mother helped him to keep it from dripping, indicating where to eat while he licked at it in a rather gingerly way. He had a very bad cold and runny nose; his mother alternated between wiping his nose and wiping the drippy ice cream from his mouth.

Arriving at the testing house, Lennie got out of the car readily and walked up to the house but still looked back to make sure that his mother was coming along. When they got in Dr. Moriarty asked Lennie, his mother and Mrs. Smith to wait downstairs while she got things ready upstairs and Lennie kept asking "why?" over and over again, not understanding at all what a getting ready process might mean. Aware of the fact that he was expected to go upstairs and leave his mother downstairs, he started assuring her that he would not be upstairs long. Then his interest shifted and he wanted to go back outdoors again and although his mother protested and told him to stay inside he responded emphatically that he wanted to "get some air!", with a slight stamp of his foot, his hands on his hips. He then went outside waving at his mother and Mrs. Smith through the window of the door, leaving it partly open, letting the screen bang, both of which his mother reminded him about. After a couple of other instances of exploratory ventures outside and returning inside, Dr. Moriarty called down that she was ready for him. At this time he again insisted that he wanted his mother to come along and despite her effort to resist and explain to him that this was like school and they didn't go to his older sister's school room with her, he still insisted that she come along and stopped ascending the steps to be sure that she was coming. Everyone went into the testing room together; Lennie sat down, looked things over quickly, still licking the ice cream cone in his hand and again asked his mother to stay. When she said she would go out in the hall and look around he permitted her to do this and the door was left open during the entire session. The situation now rigged to his own satisfaction, he jumped into the experience with Dr. Moriarty with energy.

Molly's postponement of separation

A more subtle mixture of protest and control was characteristic of two-year-old Molly's management of the testing situation with Dr. Kass as she refused to be separated from her mother. (Molly's four-year-old sister had previously accepted separation without resistance.) Dr. Heider described the experience with Molly:

> When Trudy, Molly's sister, and I reached the house, Molly was still asleep. Mrs. Thornton had Jimmie, the baby, in her arms, and after a few minutes she decided to waken Molly. I took Jimmie and played with him

while she went upstairs for Molly. She carried Molly down, who was clinging to her mother, and clearly in a mood in which it did not seem likely that she would be willing to be separated from her. However, Mrs. Thornton urged her, as did Trudy. I asked about Molly's new jacket, and little by little she was gotten into it; her mother, who often employs a stepwise procedure with her with a good deal of success, got her interested in going out to the car to see my dog Tony, who was whining in it.

We got out as far as the car, and Molly was quite willing to pat the dog and even feed him some sugared corn crispies which her sister Trudy had been given when she came home from her own testing session. I believe that Mrs. Thornton even persuaded Molly to sit in the front seat; Molly made it clear that any attempt by her mother to leave her there would result in tears. We suggested that Trudy go along to keep Molly company, but this was not sufficient, so it ended up by the whole family going, that is, Mrs. Thornton and the baby, and Trudy and Molly.

I had suggested to Trudy that she bring along a book or something, so that she could wait in the living room, a hint which worked out quite well when we once got there. Molly was now quite cheerful, and she and Trudy together were feeding the dog and enjoying the ride. When we came into the house, however, Trudy went into the living room instead of into the study, and once more Molly was crying her unwillingness to be separated from her mother. It ended with all of us going into the study, where the mother, holding the baby, sat in the wicker chair, GH in a chair further to one side near the fireplace, and Trudy stood near as Molly settled herself in the little chair at the table.

Dr. Kass got out a little picture book, and Molly, who was holding a handful of the sugared crispies in her right hand and feeding herself from it with her left, was describing the pictures to him with delight in her tone. She was sitting in a sidewise position, swaying on the chair, and distinctly flirtatious.

By this time, Trudy had tactfully left the room and Mrs. Thornton had followed with the baby a few moments afterward. Molly did not appear to notice, although she probably knew that they had gone.

Mrs. Thornton said that this is characteristic of her, that once a thing happens and she is established in a new situation, it is perfectly all right. She protests only in advance, before she had experienced the new situation. When she finds she can manage all right she lets her mother go.*

Molly was a child of high intelligence, who already as a young baby of eight weeks was reported by her mother to be sensitive to change. The arrival of a new baby and mother's absence in the hospital a few months before this test session probably intensified her resistance to separation from mother. Lennie, at the time we saw him, had a tested intelligence score at the average level although he had

* In this instance, the fact that Molly was wakened from a nap may have been an important factor in her resistance at this time. But she was hesitant about many new situations where this was not involved.

been considered very superior as a young infant. His mother had gone back to work when he was nine months old, after which he failed to develop well; the family pediatrician had later urged her to give up her work and stay with him, which she did. In other words, both of these children had had infantile difficulties with newness and separation, which continued into their preschool years.

Competition for mother

Even the visit of Dr. Heider to the home for an interview with the mother was experienced as something threatening for many of the children. A glimpse of some of the ways in which these experiences were handled will give us a picture both of the meanings to the child and to the mother, and the coping methods of both.

Tommy was playing outside when Dr. Heider arrived and stayed outside for quite a while. When he finally came in, he ran over to his mother and threw his arms around her skirts, peeking at Dr. Heider rather shyly. Then he climbed on the arm of his mother's chair and from there got down to the floor to play with the baby. Climbing back again on his mother's chair, he patted her tenderly and combed her hair for a moment. When his mother urged that Tommy tell Dr. Heider something, he became a little rough with his mother in his combing and hit at her arm. When she protested, he playfully ran away saying that he would play with his older brother's toys.

A little later he called to his mother as he banged on the bathroom door that he needed help because he had locked himself in. When his mother let him out, he brought her a scrap of paper saying that he wanted to show it to her, but was soon willing to go off to the bedroom. Shortly he came back again to show his mother something else and she went along with him accepting his request. Soon they returned together and Tommy showed Dr. Heider a new plaid shirt in a friendly and matter-of-fact manner. Dr. Heider then went on with the interview. Tommy was not inclined to leave his mother alone with the interviewer but asked her where something was and, although she urged him to find it himself, he insisted that she go with him, kept holding her hand and pulling on it until she did go.

After this the mother made coffee for Dr. Heider, and Tommy joined them in the kitchen, finally making contact with Dr. Heider by showing her some pictures his older brother had made at school and pointing out details. He now made himself part of the group, sitting down at the table with his mother and Dr. Heider; he picked out two of the largest cookies on the plate, putting them at his own place. He dunked the cookies in his mother's coffee ignoring her mild reprimand.

He seemed to be enjoying himself and said, "good" as he ate his dunked cookies. Dr. Heider went on with the interview as Tommy seemed to pay no attention to the conversation. After he was finished with his cookies, he leaped from his chair, said goodbye and ran out.

This spontaneous separation did not last long, however. He was in and out of the room, locked himself in the bathroom again and called to his mother, "Take care of me again." When he came out, he said he wanted to whisper a secret to his mother, cupped his hand to do so. Apparently this made little sense to his mother and she told him playfully that he was being silly. He began talking in a bragging way about going out and beating up the kids in the neighborhood. His mother advised against this, but did not command. Tommy went outside again and stayed out for the rest of the interview.

This type of behavior is more characteristic of the two- and three-year-olds in our group and does not appear in the records of the children over four and a half. As we noted briefly earlier, it was not at all unusual for the child to resort to close body contact and playful handling of the mother, either at home or when the mother brought the child for the first testing situation. This was tolerated by the mothers who generally yielded rather easily to demands for help or other manipulations of the child.

The easy recourse to body contact with mother at moments of insecurity in new or strange or threatening situations is reflected in many other instances when children would sit very close to mother riding in the car for the first visit to the testing house, would hold her hand, pull her along, cling to her skirts, pat her, hide behind or at one side, or in some other way use mother's body for protection; absorb her sole attention by telling her secrets, distracting her, monopolizing her with questions or mischievous acts, or by asking for help or by offering help.

Separation from mother in Shirley's research

The value of such close physical support can be seen more sharply when we contrast these records of maternal support and tolerance with Shirley's[8] records of the behavior of children who were separated from their mothers to be taken for mental examinations.

Timothy: 2 years. Timmy was brought to the Center by his father, who remarked, "I expect he'll have a hard day, for he never has been away from home before. Now goodbye, Timmy. Be a good boy." Timmy at once began crying in a complaining voice, uttering, "Mamma, Mamma" at every breath. He could not be quieted for a mental examination and continued to cry throughout the entire period in the playroom.

2½ years. Timmy's mother brought him and reported that he was interested in coming until he reached the door of the Center, whereupon he burst into violent crying and offered physical resistance. Mother said, "Now, Timmy, mother is going to the dentist to have her teeth fixed, and you will stay here and have your dinner and your nap; then mother will come and take you to grandma's." She added to a staff member, "If Timmy cries, tell him he is making mother unhappy. I find that is the best way to handle him." Timmy cried violently for several minutes but finally quieted enough to be given a mental test. Upon coming to the playroom, he cried, "Mamma! I want Mamma," for five minutes, then stood disconsolately looking down at the sidewalk. When asked what he saw there, he chokingly said, "Mamma, Mamma, dad gone."

3 years. Timmy was brought by his mother. He began sobbing, "I want Mamma!" the moment his mother left and kept this up for nine minutes in the playroom. He then gradually subsided but kept worriedly questioning the observer, "Mamma come back soon? Atter num-num (dinner) Mamma come back?" or attempting to bolster up his courage by saying, "No Timmy c'y" (apparently meaning to convey the thought "Timmy will not cry"). But his voice continued to tremble, and his brow never lost its pucker.

Merta: 2 years. Merta's mother brought her to the Center and had to go home at once to care for another one of her children who was sick. Merta herself had a nose cold. Merta cried continuously, "Mamma! Mamma!" in a half-ill voice, coughing at intervals. She repeatedly went to the playroom door and clung to the knob. After ten minutes she was taken to an examination.

2½ years. Merta, who was brought by her mother, entered crying but was taken at once to the mental examination. Her mother remained throughout the test and then carried the child up to the playroom. Merta began crying as soon as her mother put her down, unconvinced by her mother's kiss bestowed with the well-intentioned deception, "Mother won't leave you, Merta dear; she'll stay right downstairs." As the mother disappeared through the door, Merta ran after her with her arms outstretched and had to be caught and held to prevent her escape. She then stood facing the door, crying and sulking for thirty minutes.

Shirley reported that fewer of the older children were upset by parting from their mothers, but those who were upset had quite as great difficulty in overcoming it.

Simon: 3½ years. Simon's mother brought him and did not leave until after he had been given one examination. Although he had cried at being separated he had quieted by the time he came to the playroom. There he witnessed Anne's tearful leave-taking from her mother and he at once began to cry, "Where my mother? Where my mother?" He continued until his mother, who had not left the Center, overheard him and came to see what was up. Upon sight of her his cries became louder, but when she took her leave the author was able to quiet him. At intervals, however, he again cried and invented several excuses for going downstairs, his real object being to go in search of his mother.

4 years. Simon was called for by the technician, who reported that he cried all the way. He came at once to the playroom where he continued to sob in a grating voice that sounded very much forced. After five minutes he ceased crying and stood idly gazing out the window. He responded to questions, but his only spontaneous speech concerned his mother's coming.

4½ years. Simon shrieked at leaving home and cried or sulked all the way to the Center and could not be drawn into speech. He was not crying when he entered the door but began as soon as he was inside.

5 years. Simon came without objection but was entirely silent and now and then trembled. He was sent up to the playroom before the attendant arrived and she found him standing in the upstairs corridor silently crying, though the playroom door was open and toys were available.

Even children who had been stable during their early visits were disturbed when home conditions changed:

Although Joan previously had enjoyed three periods of nursery school experience at the Center, she was somewhat upset on her first all-day visit at three-and-a-half years. She was then eager at the next two visits but at five years was very upset. Possibly, the fact that a man called for her might have been a little upsetting, since she was a little upset the first time, when the X-ray technician had called for her. It is far more likely, however, that this serious upset at five years was due largely to the recent hospitalization of the mother, the birth of the new baby, and the breaking of home routine occasioned by the family's temporary move into the grandparents' home for the period of the mother's confinement.

In these records and other records by Shirley there are hints of the roles of numerous factors in the child's distress beyond those already discussed, and even the separation from mother as such: suggestion from the parent that the child will be upset expressed in the hearing of the child; separation feelings intensified by the emotional stimulation induced by mother's requests for extra kisses, etc.; (after the first experience), memories of previous distress in examination situations.

We are not told anything about the previous experience or early development of the children who were "upset" by the clinic visits, nor do we have any information about relevant characteristics of the child at the current period.

When we see the sturdy independence with which most of our group of children later surveyed the test situation once they had been separated from the mother, this child-mother behavior seems quite babyish; but, as a matter of fact, it is not by any means uniquely characteristic of Kansas children. All across the country it is a familiar matter to have nursery school teachers, doctors, nurses and others complain that the child is much fussier and more infantile with his mother than he is after the mother has left the situation. This is often handled in hospitals, nursery schools and other places by urging the mother to leave the situation as rapidly as possible in order that the more "mature" and controlled behavior of the child may be mobilized. Such practices leave out of account the effect on the child's later attitudes to professional workers of the anxiety repressed but unrelieved in their early encounters.

From observations of our children in this setting, it would seem that the opportunity to have the security-giving contact with the mother in strange or new situations or at times of anticipated separation may be very important in the child's ability to handle the demands of the separation subsequently. Here it seemed normal for our children in this group at the age of three to expect physical comfort and reassurance from mother at times of even mild, every-day kinds of stress, and normal for mothers to offer support in physical ways.

With our practice of permitting the child to retain the support of his mother in his first encounters with us, all but one child became able to tolerate and for the most part to enjoy subsequent sessions in the preschool phase. Lennie, Ronnie and Ray, who were fearful at first, surprised us with their responsiveness and active enjoyment of sessions a few weeks later. Daryl, Vivian, and Rachel were slower, but here there were backgrounds of a special kind which we shall discuss later.

Group patterns of coping with new experiences
and separation from mother

We can now look briefly at the group as a whole in terms of their handling of separation from mother, and their response to the new examiners. About one third of the children had some problem of separating from their mothers in the earliest experiences of the project— either difficulties in leaving mother at home or in leaving her downstairs when they went upstairs to the testing room. In two or three instances the separation problem seemed equally great for the mother —as illustrated by the mother who would interrupt the small boy on his way out to ask, "Aren't you going to give me another kiss?" The girls who found separation difficult had younger siblings, while fifty per cent of the girls who separated easily were themselves youngest children. The boys with severe separation problems had erotically excited relations with their mothers in contrast to the fact that only two out of nine boys who separated comfortably from their mothers had relationships with this quality.

Of the children whose mothers accompanied them, ten were able to cooperate with the intelligence test without special help while ingenious efforts of the tester were required for ten. Nine out of twelve children whose mothers stayed at home were able to handle the test without unusual help by the tester. These last children were not completely free from anxiety, as we shall see at a later point when we describe their ways of expressing anxiety and the part it played in their testing experience—all of them showed some tinge of anxiety at one time or another.

By contrast with the intelligence test, the pediatric examination was a relatively familiar experience, and was conducted after the child had already been through two or more sessions with our staff. Moreover, our doctor expected the mother to stay with the child in order to give her the history of the child's medical experience and to answer any questions that came up about his present physical condition. The examination was given in the examining room of the large city hospital where Well Baby Conferences were held, to which some of the mothers had brought these children as babies; to these mothers the place itself was a familiar one. Under these circumstances, it is not surprising that most mothers seemed thoroughly at ease and most of the children of these mothers cooperated easily and with little tension. However, three children cried or were extremely tense at one point or another during the physical examination, even though their mothers were present. Where a child had marked fears of body intrusion or pain, even the presence of the mother did not prevent anxiety in a situation where these fears were aroused. In view of this it is easy to see the probable role of fears about possible body damage in separation-anxiety. In the face of unknown physical danger the small child feels the need of his mother as protector. The projective element here is suggested when we note that all three of these boys were impulsive or "high drive" children who may have feared the consequences of their own impulsiveness if mother's control were not present.[9]

Lennie had actually had a bad experience as a result of impulsiveness: he had fallen into a lake at the age of two following which he had a severe infection, some loss of hearing, and speech difficulties. Ray's feeling of a need for protection seemed to be confirmed later when he fell from a tree and broke his leg. Ronnie had vigorous aggressive impulses which he worked hard to direct. Comparing these children with others like Barbie and Teddy, who always separated easily, we note the balanced development, relatively slow tempo, and smooth control of the latter children. These evidently contributed to experiences of mastery both of environment and of impulses, and this strength made it easier for the child to separate.

Backgrounds of responses to the new and the strange in these children

How can we understand widely different responses to new situations which actually involved no real danger? There were no similarities between the pleasant homelike setting of the first tests and a hospital setting where some of the children might have experienced pain. There were no white coats, no special bewildering apparatus, nothing in the immediate situation to be actually frightening insofar as we could possibly eliminate anything potentially frightening to a child. The child's feeling about newness, whether eager and expectant or anxious and suspicious, came from inside. Is three-year-old Donald less brave than three-year-old Brennie? Why is Rachel's behavior in the new situation so different from that of Sheila?

And even before the children came into the new situation, the threat of separation was disturbing to a few of them. Are we to think of Molly and Lennie as neurotic? We shall have to give attention separately to responses to newness and to the problem of separation.

Our data from the Escalona-Leitch records of the children's early experiences as infants are limited to one period of their infancy and this was at different ages for the different children, but limited as this material is in this respect, it gives us some very important clues. Other clues come from the interviews with the mothers, by the pediatrician and Dr. Heider.

When Donald was seen at the age of sixteen weeks, his mother reported that at about the age of eight weeks he had been frightened by an elderly woman who was deaf, who talked with a loud voice, and who handled him too roughly. After that, he continued to be afraid of her and cautious of other elderly people. He tended to be more cautious with the gray-haired "Mrs. Murphy" than with younger members of the staff. All this we can understand in terms of conditioning, but when conditioning takes place at such an early age when differentiation is so incomplete, it can send ripples much farther than would be true at later ages. Perhaps it is fair to say then, that the experience of startle or even a discomfort bordering on pain, which Donald received at the hands of a strange person at that early age, provided a massive or generalized conditioning which underlay his negative attitude toward new situations generally. As he grew into a small boy, his parents' critical attitude toward neighbors and their tendencies to judge people by strict moral standards probably contributed to his tendencies to look people over and appraise them. The fact that there was very much in his life that was good, including a warm and understanding relationship with his need to "size up" new people and new situations, doubtless contributed to his ability to struggle with his anxiety about newness and bring himself to venture forth in active testing out of its possibilities after his preliminary detached appraisal.

Molly, as early as the age of eight weeks, had been observed by her mother to be sensitive to new places, and it may well be that this early tendency simply persisted unabated. In addition to this, however, we saw that a new baby, a younger brother at that, had recently provided a threat to Molly's security with her mother; Molly's determination to keep a close hold on her mother might be seen as in part a way of dealing with anxiety created by the arrival of the baby, in part an understandable effort to keep the warmth and closeness provided by her mother, in part a realistic need for support in a two-year-old still immature in language, locomotion, and orientation outside the home.

As we saw Molly later fighting against the plan to move to another town, to leave home and, as she thought, everything that was familiar to her, we must assume something more than insecurity about her relation to her mother since the move in itself did not involve any separation between Molly and her mother at any time. Each confronting of newness may imply a relinquishing of old satisfactions and old loves to a child like this, even after she was able to understand that the whole family would go, including pets and furniture. Even after the move itself, Molly's difficulty in shifting her attachment continued for a long time; it was a year and a half before she completely accepted the new home. It does not seem unreasonable to offer the hypothesis that Molly's sensitive reaction to strangeness, especially strange places, at the time when perceptual functions were in the process of emerging, was patterned into a generalized perceptual orientation to new worlds which continued more or less unabated through the time of the move we just described, and even later. At the age of ten she still did not like to leave home to visit other places. Since several siblings showed no such dislike of newness and adventure, we have to assume that factors in Molly and in her earliest experience were responsible. It would take much more than an experimental study or an observational study of a baby's responses at certain given times, to have an adequate picture of the development of the reaction to strangeness such as we see in her. We would need a careful diary record which included a full account of the baby's response to new objects, new places, new people, including the sequences through which the baby came to terms with each of these new experiences, and the patterns of gratification, frustration, difficulty, or pain that were associated with different ones. Her distrust of strangeness is particularly interesting because she had an exceptionally good relationship with her mother as judged not only by members of our staff at the time of the pre-school study, but by Dr. Sylvia Brody[10] in her study of patterns of mothering based on the data of the infancy study. There is thus no basis that we could find in the relation between the infant and her mother to expect a lack of trust if we assume that a satisfying relationship with the mother is the best foundation for trust.

If, however, we remember Spitz's observation[11] that the babies who had the best mothering suffered from the most severe anaclitic depressions when separated from the mother, we can explore a hint from this; it seems possible that the sensitive babies with excellent relationships with their mother found the contrast between the comfort of mother's presence and the discomfort of places or people who were new and strange too great to absorb. They could assimilate the new only in terms of being where mother is, where the familiar is of which mother is a part, in terms of safety and comfort.

This hypothesis gains some weight when we look at Brennie, whose mother was not very strong or well and was full of anxiety, much of which had a very realistic foundation in her own life before Brennie arrived. When Brennie was five months old his mother became pregnant again, giving birth to a baby brother when Brennie was thirteen months old. Mother substitutes came to him early. To Brennie, new people and new experiences may often have provided satisfactions he did not have in the relation with his mother. We had some hints of this in his pattern of exploring the neighborhood to play upon the motherly interests of other women down the block. When things were not too satisfying at home, he was lucky enough to find another mother. This could have provided some of the motivation for his eager response to certain members of the staff of our study. Seen in this light, the new experiences offered new possibilities for satisfaction for Brennie, where with Molly and Donald, who had very early experienced newness as painful or threatening or disappointing, any new situation could by definition hardly be anything but inferior to the satisfactions and securities of home, the familiar and mother.

When we come to Rachel, we have to recognize that we are discussing a child from one of the two poorest, most deprived families in the study, a child whose mother felt poor, more poor than did any other mother, in addition to the reality of limited economic resources. In other words, we have to take account of the fact that newness which was comparatively mild for the other children was startling to Rachel.

Beyond this, her enforced passivity in the hospital with severe eczema in the second year of life came at a critical phase in the development of motility and of the autonomy that comes with trying one's wings when motor coordination becomes available to the young child. Just at this important time when most children are getting the full exhilaration of exploring for themselves, discovering where locomotion can take them, Rachel was totally confined to a crib and immobilized almost completely for three months. It was impossible for her to pursue any curiosities, or follow any impulse; she had to wait until something was done for her, or to her, or with her. If this hospitalization had occurred at another time, either before the critical phase of development in motility or after motility had been well established, it is possible that we would not have seen such a profoundly rooted pattern of "wait and see."

Now, if we go back still further to the Rachel whom we saw in the infancy records, we do not find the kind of precursors for the preschool pattern of sensitivity to newness which we saw with Donald and Molly. Rachel was a baby of somewhat less than average activity and not unusually sensitive. There was no evidence at the age of twenty weeks of any special concern with the strange. In other words, here we have quite a different factor operating from the factors which we noted earlier with the children who were particularly shy in new situations. Since her communication afterward did not reflect that she went through feelings of anxiety (rather her reports to her mother were eager and spontaneous) nor did her play show disintegrative tendencies, we cannot assume intense fear of the new and the strange. She was not actually paralyzed by anxiety; she was trying to understand what she was expected to do. This interpretation was dramatically confirmed at a later period when a member of Dr. Witkin's staff joined us to carry through a series of perception tests.

In these situations, the child is put through a training series before the test proper, and in the training series is told exactly what to do. Rachel was at her best under these conditions. She walked with a lightly swaggering pride and handled the three-dimensional embedded figures test with high efficiency and confidence. She was not inhibited at all. To be sure, the embedded figures test focuses on a *perceptual* problem; the motor demands are very simple—to walk twelve or fifteen feet to the test board and pull out the appropriate block. Still this was a much greater demand than sitting on the floor to play with toys—a "free" situation in which she was totally unfree, until the examiner gave her a start. Through the succeeding years Rachel remained a child who had to be told, or had to be shown, what to do. She could not initiate spontaneous organization of a new situation.

External evidences suggest that a combination of several factors are involved in Rachel's severe reaction to strange situations: (1) deprivation, which means that our situations are actually more strange to her than to other children and expose her to more new objects in addition to including an aspect of feeling apart from a world of a different socio-economic class; (2) her world allowed little room for choices required here, in contrast to the body-photograph situation where she willingly, even eagerly accepted the role of "going first," following directions easily; (3) possibly rigid parental demands or strongly emotional reactions of parents to nonconformity; (4) some actual experiences with chaotic disturbing events.

Through such records we can see how different the meanings of new and strange situations can be for different children, and how different attitudes toward newness shape the challenge presented by the specific pattern of objects and people confronted by the child.

All together, we can see that responses to newness often have foundations in the earliest infantile experiences of newness—the satisfactions, comfort, pain, or frustration associated with these experiences and the residues or expectancies resulting from them. The role of mothering persons in helping the smallest baby to get used to newness and to find it satisfying, interesting, and manageable is obvious.

NOTES AND REFERENCES

1. Macfarlane, J.M. Personal communication.
2. Bayley, N. Personal communication.
3. Robertson, J. *A Two-Year-Old Goes to the Hospital*. Film. London: Tavistock Clinic, 1953. See also Robertson, J. *Young Children in Hospitals*. New York: Basic Books, 1959.
4. Spitz, R. Anaclitic depression. *Psychoanalytic Study of the Child*, Vol. 2. New York: International Universities Press, 1946.
5. Freud, A., and Burlingame, D. *War and Children*. New York: Medical War Books, International Universities Press, 1943.
6. Bowlby, J. Separation anxiety. *Intern. J. Psychoanal., 41*, 1960.
7. Yarrow, L.J. Maternal deprivation: toward an empirical and conceptual reevaluation. *Psych. Bull., 58*, 1961.
8. Shirley, M., and Poyntz, L. The influence of separation from the mother on children's emotional responses. *J. Psychol., 12*, 1941.
9. Heinicke, C. Some effects of separating two-year-old children from their parents: a comparative study. *Human Relations, 9*, 105-177, 1956.
10. Brody, S. *Patterns of Mothering*. New York: International Universities Press, 1956.
11. Spitz, R. Anaclitic depression. *Psychoanalytic Study of the Child*, Vol. 2. New York: International Universities Press, 1946.

3

A WIDER WORLD

Up to this point we have been discussing responses of the children to relatively brief situations, sessions of about an hour, where the child knows that he will return home and where there is no demand from his parents or from us to accept any long-time commitment beyond returning for some later visits.

The child is faced with a more difficult demand when at the age of two or three years he is expected to leave home for a part of every week day, and to make himself at home in nursery school. And even though the entire family goes along when the family moves from one location to another children are often anxious about the move. In this section we shall discuss examples of these experiences.

Getting used to nursery school: a home away from home

Few of the children from our original infancy group had been to nursery school and in no instance was it possible to secure a detailed

record of the process of entering and getting used to this new world
with observations made in the nursery school itself. However, the
mother of Sam* kept detailed records over a period of time of his steps
in getting oriented to the idea of going and then getting used to nursery school. Because of the period of time covered, we have had to reduce the narrative to manageable dimensions; consequently it has a
different flavor from the moment-by-moment records we have seen
up to now. I shall first tell the story as his mother told it, then review
the dilemmas Sam expresses and his steps in dealing with them. Sam
was three years old in May; play space was limited inside and outside
of the apartment where he lived with his family.

During the spring there was occasional conversation about going to
nursery school next year. On two different occasions we had stopped by at a
little school where several of Sam's friends go, but he flatly refused to even go
in for a visit. It is in a half-basement, and he just said it was "too little."
Every once in a while we stopped by at the Country Day School to pick up
his friend Mikey on the way to an excursion to the park, or to help a friend
in collecting and delivering donations for the hospital. Sam would freely and
happily help carry things into the building, and he gradually came to feel
quite at home and at ease in going in and out there, but he had not actually
visited the children's group. After I had visited, I had described something of
the setting and the equipment, including the fact that they had blocks that
fitted together to make long trains.
        As we began to talk about a planned visit to the school his interest in
the resources and the limits of the nursery school became more specific: "Do
they have a place to get a drink of water?" "Can I make a train, or not?"
"Will we have juice and crackers?" "I want to wear my engineer's suit 'cause
I want to make a train out of the blocks."
        The day came and he seemed at ease as we entered the building and
proceeded through the long passageway. He was aware of many aspects of
the environment, including the "three sets of stairs" as we climbed them.
Once in the nursery school room, he moved about freely, spending most of
the time putting together a "Santa Fe" train, using up practically all the
blocks in the process. The teacher, Miss Lund, proposed to him that she un-
couple the train so that she could divide up the blocks for another child
to have some, and Sam acquiesced to this fairly easily. There were a few
minor skirmishes with other children, but for the most part he pretty much
went about his own business. His second favorite activity was the easel painting, which he did with a great flourish, even though this was his first experience with this kind of paint. He also observed and reported his observations
—tracing the way the pipes went into the radiators, and noting that there
was a train book like one he has at home. He was curiously attentive to the
tantrum of another child, and also, on the way out, to a little girl who was
crying in the hall.

        * A child observed by the writer from infancy.

During the next day or two he shared many impressions, feelings, wonderings: "They have wonderful blocks there." "They have lots of sweet teachers at school." "When can I go again?" "Why was the girl crying?"

A few weeks later, when we stopped by to pick up Mike, Sam saw Miss Lund in the hall. He was shy and speechless, and later commented, "I felt so confused." It was as if he had an image of the nursery school room with her in it and he was disoriented when he confronted her out of that context.

At various times during the summer, there were questions or conversation about going to school and what it would be like: "Do you think Miss Moor would show me how to build a painter's truck?" "When I go to school I want you to pick me up the way you do Mikey sometimes." And in talking to his father: "When the leaves turn pretty colors, then I'll go to school—and mommy will take me there—and you know, daddy, the mommies can stay a little while!" As the time approached, he became worried: "But when I go to school I'll be lonesome—would Mikey's teacher let Mikey come up and see me?"

During one of his conversations with his mother about what he might do at school, she explained to him about "rhythms" and he said, "But I don't know *how* to dance." His mother suggested that this was probably in part a reflection of an experience during the summer, when the father of a five-year-old girl was urging Sam to learn to do the Cha-Cha-Cha, that it was important to know how to dance, and later he had asked, "*Why* is it important to learn to do what Susie 'doose'—the Cha-Cha-Cha?"

Ten days before he was to enter, his teacher visited him at home; after a brief initial period of shyness he was bouncy and exuberant— at ease with her alone, and spontaneously proposing various activities —playing "service truck" and baseball, and finding it hard to relinquish her. Later he asked emphatically, "*When* am I going to start school?" His mother told him that she wasn't sure, since in his group, different children started at different times. (For the first ten days, the total group was divided in half, each half going on alternate days.) It finally worked out that he was to go on September 24, then there would be an interruption and he would start going regularly on September 30.

On September 24 he asked whether this was the day he was to start school, and wanted to know whether his mother would stay with him a little while. She explained to him about the "cubby room" (coatroom) next door, where mommies stayed while the children were playing in their room. As they started out the door to school, he turned back to pick a flower to take to his teacher. He seemed relaxed and happily anticipating the experience. But at the nurse's office, where children passed inspection before entering nursery school, he was unwilling to open his mouth; the nurse did not insist, giving his O.K. slip anyway. He was a little puzzled about this, apparently feeling that he really wasn't entitled to it. His mother explained that the nurse understood that it often took children a little while to get used to opening their mouths for her.

On the roof, after standing around close to his mother for a little while and surveying the scene, he became intrigued with the hand trucks and soon was pushing one around vigorously, running with it and swinging it around in big swoops, then loading it with blocks, carting them over near his mother to unload them, and building a house. He called the teacher over to help him, whispering to her, "It's the Empire State Building." Several times he came to his mother for help, but she explained to him that at school the teachers were the ones who did the helping. At one point he started over to the slide, then came back, saying, "I changed my mind."

In the room, he repeated the activities of his first day, and again painted. He was especially responsive to being asked to help put the blocks away, contriving a special system of carrying them tucked under his chin. He spontaneously ran up and gave Miss Moor a kiss just before leaving. During the next week, he often made eager and appreciative comments about school, "Miss Moor is a nice teacher."

On September 30 the whole group was together for the first time. On the roof he stayed close to the mother but was quite active—playing telephone repair man, painting with water, sliding down the board once. But in the room he was so subdued and wary that both the teacher and mother wondered whether perhaps he was not feeling well; he looked pale and had none of his usual bounce and vigor. He finally got busy painting again and continued at this while his teacher was reading a story about animals to a small group. With one ear cocked for the story, but still painting, he began to sing, first softly, then finally almost shouting the song *What Do Animals Talk About?* straight through several verses and the chorus. After leaving the school, he gradually seemed more himself, so that it seemed quite likely that his appearance and behavior had reflected a feeling of being overwhelmed by the larger group of children, and especially by the fact that Miss Moor was now more busy with other children, and could not always respond when he called her.

The next day his mother suggested that he could have a Life Saver to pop into his mouth just before they got to school so the nurse would be surprised when he opened his mouth—and it would be a crystal mint, so she could see through it. This strategy worked well, but had to be continued for several weeks before he felt able to do without the Life Saver.

He soon became freer and more active, still very watchful of everything going on, and still very much aware of what his favorite teacher was doing. He called her for help several times, and once when she was busy and couldn't come right away, he told her when she did come, "You know, Miss Moor, the other teachers can take care of the other children," trying to organize the situation so that his needs would be met. He moved out into the play space on the roof fairly freely but often came back to visit or just to lean up against his mother. He left his "wagon" parked near her for safekeeping even when he wasn't using it, and once said, "If somebody comes to take my wagon, you say, 'No, no, my little friend'." He made some tentative efforts to get Carl (who was not yet three) to play with him, but without success. (Several of the other children had already made rather definite relationships: one boy and girl who live next door to each other were constant companions, and two little girls just "found" each other the first day and were always together.)

Apparently transitions from one place to another were hard for Sam. This continued as a pattern with only one or two exceptions as long as his mother stayed around. It was one of the indications that suggested to her that as long as she was available he was going to make use of her, rather than moving out with the group. As the children were gathering together to go down to their room, he came over and tugged at her, and wanted her to go down the stairs with him. Once downstairs, however, he went off quite cheerfully into the room, after reminding his mother to stay in the cubby (coatroom) so she would be there "in case I need you." About an hour later he came prancing into the cubby room and wanted her to come back into the room with him so she could see his picture. He was not able then to let her go back into the cubby again. Along with his own activities, he was interested in other things going on and once said, surveying the various block constructions in the middle of the room, "It looks like a city!"

Along with his feeling more at home, there began to be various kinds of provocative aggressive actions—snatching things away from other children, knocking down buildings, walking through paintings they were making on the floor, pushing, tugging at clothes, etc. It was hard to tell what was behind this—perhaps some of the time it was showing off, sometimes an effort to get the attention of the teachers, sometimes an effort to get a reaction from the other children, sometimes just an expression of boredom and not knowing what to do with himself.

There was no question about the fact that he was enjoying the school experience in many ways. On October 2 during the roof time, at a moment when his mother thought he was looking very alone and perhaps forlorn and wistful, just standing around rather aimlessly, he came over to her and said, "I just love it on the roof." He seemed very much aware of the differentness of the roof situation, often studying and commenting about the number and variety of chimneys, and the other things visible, and enjoying the feeling of openness, and the wide sky.

He was quite clear at every point about his own readiness for things; when his mother talked with him in advance about rhythms, he said, "I'll have to get used to it first." During the first period of rhythms he was fascinated, and very much attracted by it, but clung close to his mother and would not take off his shoes and socks. During the second rhythms period, Sylvia, an assistant teacher, came over and playfully tugged at his shoes, and he let her remove them; then, after his mother literally gave him a little push, he was off at full speed—galloping around and around the room with grace and utter pleasure. For several weeks afterward, however, it always took him a few minutes to warm up, and when anything new was introduced he was a little hesitant to take part at first, and tended to come back to hanging around mother.

The transition from the rhythms period to returning to the room was especially difficult; the first time his reaction was one of bitter disappointment—bursting into deep sobs, inconsolable for quite a few minutes, "I didn't want to leave." On subsequent occasions, it was more a feeling that there just wasn't any point in staying around any longer; once rhythms was over he would sit at the top of the stairs, tugging at his mother, trying to convince her that they might as well go home. It was as if rhythms was the high point of the day and everything afterward was an anticlimax. Gradually he learned that there were still interesting things to do back in the room.

The same day, after noticing that some of the children stayed to lunch, he decided he wanted to stay also, and he was allowed to. The next day, however, he decided, "I'll stay to lunch when I get to be a bigger boy." (He had not liked the scrambled eggs they had had for lunch, protesting, "I always like peek-a-boo eggs.")

Miss Moor agreed with him that it would be better to wait for a while. Later on, when he again began to show interest in staying for lunch, he was told that the way it usually worked is that children might stay for lunch once they were able to let their mothers go away for the whole morning, and this was mentioned again occasionally to help motivate the separation.

For some reason, he seemed to need to have his mother stay with him more on the roof than in the room—perhaps because this was the first activity of the day, but more likely because of his sensitivity to the

feeling of openness, and the fact that the whole roof setting was different from anything he had experienced before coming to nursery
school. Even though he engaged in many different activities, he still
tended to try to use his mother in his play—bringing over a load of
barrels—"fresh pears for you" or "ice cream," or sometimes just coming over to whisper, "I love you."

Occasionally he would make an overture to another child; when
he was rebuffed he would retaliate in a very direct way, like throwing
a bucket of water into the child's box. For a while the most obvious
progress was in his readiness to form a relationship with the other
adults—first Gloria, an assistant teacher; on October 7 he told his
mother glowingly, "I gave Gloria a kiss." The next day, "Charlotte is
my favorite assistant teacher." When asked about Gloria he said,
"She's my favorite too—and Sylvia—I just love the whole group." He
was quite ready to engage the help of any of the teachers in various
projects, and would often report such things as "Gloria helped me
build a subway."

In fact he was very much aware of adults throughout the building.
From the beginning he had done a lot of snooping, poking his head
into every open doorway, becoming well acquainted with the resources
of the shop and the clay and the science rooms, curious about the stair-
way down into the basement, and invariably stopping to watch whatever was going on in any of the play yards. He got into the habit of
stopping to say, "Hello" to Ethel in the office, and the nutritionist and
cooks in the kitchen, and hardly ever let a morning go by without
these greetings, which were his way of making himself at home.

Once in a while his imaginary elf-friend, "Woody," showed up;
on October 3, "Woody was at school today—nurse said he didn't
have to open his mouth—he's still a little shy," but he didn't seem to
be needed much of the time.

By mid-October his provocation of other children had taken the
form of saying very emphatically (with or without any basis for it),
"You're a bad boy." When he said this once to Gina she responded,
"I'm not a boy—I'm a girl—see my hair—you like my hair?"

When this became quite a persistent pattern for dealing with the
other children's interferences, his mother told him that it made children very unhappy when he said this, and it would work out much better if he would just say, "Please don't do that." She asked him if he understood, and he said, "No"; when she wondered why not, he said, "I
don't want to." Two days later, however, he proudly announced to his
mother, "I started to say to Chris—'You're a bad'—and I changed it and
said, 'Please don't do that Chris'."

It began to be evident that his relationship with other children was gradually taking a more positive direction, even though there were ups and downs. On the same day as the incident just described, there was the retort, "No, you can't—I already have some," when Chip asked if he could be his best friend, and then a little later, a request to Chip to watch his wagon for him while he went to the bathroom. That same day Steffie asked if she could come into his boat and he said expansively, "Sure—see what we're building here?" He also carried on quite a professional sounding conversation one day with Chip: "You have a runny nose?" "No." "You have a regular runny nose?" "No." "You have a runny nose from crying?" "No." "You shouldn't go outdoors with a runny nose."

By the third week of school it seemed as if there would have to be a decisive step forward or he would bog down into a habit of expecting his mother to be around all the time. He had been taking it more and more for granted that she would be available whenever he wanted her —would come into the coatroom to get her when he wanted to go to the toilet, and on at least two occasions laboriously pulled a chair over next to the easel for her to sit and watch while he painted. A few tentative efforts to absent herself had not been successful—once on the roof she told him she was going in to the adjoining, glass-walled room and after a few minutes he had run in to get her, crying and pulling at her, and distracting several children in the process. But there also had been occasions when he had willingly let her go out for a while on an errand or to get some coffee.

Since he was now "at home" with both teachers, and children, and materials, and also wanted to stay for lunch, his teacher and mother agreed that he would be able to tolerate the separation. When his mother talked this over with Sam he agreed on the surface but suggested that she stay downstairs on the bench near the front door. The next day, after being bitten by another child he cried and begged her not to go downstairs, but a few days later spontaneously suggested in the middle of the morning that she go home and do her work and come back later. He stayed to lunch alone.

A couple of days after this he let her stay away all day and seemed to get along all right at school, but cried at bedtime. He wanted her to read the book, *A Tree Is Nice* and commented, "But it isn't nice when the leaves change color and leave the tree!" That weekend he woke up from a Saturday afternoon nap crying, "Why do you always go away from me?" But the following Monday he announced, "Cecily (his music teacher at school) loves me too—doesn't she just love my beautiful galloping? And she helps me put my socks on!"

He was much interested in the piano: "The piano can say, 'Come over here.' It can say 'run run run, run run run.' It can say 'gallopy, gallopy, gallopy.' It's fun to learn what the piano says. It almost has a mouth."

From that time on, he was able to stay at school alone; he continued to share his observations, thoughts, and feelings. "My teacher scolded me for knocking down a building. I thought just guards scolded, not teachers—assistant teachers scold too! . . . Today I ate spaghetti with sauce and meat underneath. . . . We had something new today in rhythms—balloons! The other children threw them up in the air but I didn't throw mine . . . I just sat with it next to me." He complained once that "Hester doesn't wipe my nose for me." After Thanksgiving vacation he exclaimed, "I'm so happy to go back to school—that's why I'm so bouncy. . . . Teacher didn't have to scold me today—she just *told* me not to pull Mark's hair."

One day in April he said, "I wish teacher was my mommy, then when she gets very old and ready to be died she'd call you up and say, 'Come back and be Sam's mommy again'!" He was very unhappy about the school year ending late in May.

Sam was helped to enter school by his anticipation of new achievement, by expressing his doubts to his mother and getting her support. His teacher's visit before he entered school helped him to get acquainted and to feel at home with her, to develop the beginning of a warm feeling toward her. He resisted the body intrusion involved in morning mouth inspection, and his mother helped him with this by transforming the situation into a game. Often for long periods he was cautious, and at times seemed overwhelmed by the number of children, and perhaps by the differentness of some parts of the situation such as the roof.

On the roof play area the first day he kept close to his mother until his interest was drawn to an attractive toy. The second day he appreciated the feeling of being included or having a role in school, when asked to help put blocks away, and his feeling for his teacher blossomed into love and a desire to have her all to himself. Gradually he came to love the assistant teachers too.

He reserved the right to stand aside and watch new activities at first, but responded to a well-timed push. As he became freer to try out activities, express aggressive and retaliative impulses, perhaps aroused by his feelings of being inhibited in the new situation, as he became acquainted with and got used to all the newness, his enjoyment increased.

He used his mother an an anchor to familiarity, for help, as a playmate, and as a love-object during the early period of getting acquainted in the new situation. His imaginary companion "Woody," an elf, also helped him.

Sam expressed directly at different times his concerns about the new experience—that he might be lonely, that he might not get the protection he needed for his injured hand, that he did not know how to do things that would be expected of him and by implication felt inadequate, that he might not get help when he needed it. Indirectly also we see that he was concerned about love, and self-defense, and punishment.

Step by step and very thoroughly he familiarized himself with the place and the new activities, elicited help when he needed it, offered love, actively defended himself, accepted new social techniques, learned to accept limits and the scoldings, felt as punishment for infractions of rules against hurting children. His ability to share his feelings, discoveries, needs, and wishes contributed to the process, along with the ability of mother and teachers to help him understand, to make limits intelligible, to tolerate his pace of relating to the new situation.

Leave-taking continued to be difficult from time to time, not only from mother at first but from his favorite activity, rhythms, and finally from his teacher and from school itself.

Here we see the interesting combination of capacity for strong attachments, deep involvement in activities and experiences, combined with slow development of new relationships and slow relinquishing of attachments. The slow pace of making new commitments can be seen in relation both to his awareness of the many implications of change and his sensitivity to the nuances and qualities of many different aspects of experience—which he communicated directly and indirectly more fully than would have been possible for some three-year-olds.

Sam as a baby of three months had expressed his awareness of change and new places by restless, alert looking around. He also had difficulties in sleeping when he went on a visit to relatives with his mother; back at home, he relaxed into his familiar crib and sleeping problems vanished. He shared with some of the other children we have just seen a persistent sensitivity to newness and change from infancy on, despite the fact that he had never experienced prolonged separation from his mother.

But much of what he shows us is probably felt by other two- and three-year-olds who enter new situations and have to be separated from mother. We can sum up his uncertainties with these questions: Who will take care of me? Who will help me? Will I be able to do what is expected? Will I be able to control my feelings and actions or will I get scolded or punished? Whom can I love and who will love me?

We saw Sam's clear differentiation of situations and his relation to them, his capacity to identify qualities of people, places, and also his feelings. This evidently gave new experiences richer and more personal meanings than less perceptive children would find in them.

Moving to a new home

Moving from one house to another, from one neighborhood to another, from one town or state or even country to another, is a common part of contemporary life. Some occupational groups, such as the armed services, corporation junior executives, faculties of universities, ministers of churches and others, accept moving from one location to another at intervals of a year, or two or three, as part of life. In some communities there is thus a real estate turnover of forty per cent or more each year. Part of this, of course, represents moving to a different home in the same community. Even in our unusually stable group one third of the families moved out of town and a total of half of the families moved at least once during the child's first ten years.

The stress for some people—parallel with the challenge for others —of leaving home for new territory is expressed in Rølvaag's *Giants in the Earth*[1] and in stories of pioneer life in our country. In general, moving is a different experience for parents as compared with children. Adults living in a wider world have images of the place they are going to—they may have had gratifying fantasies about it. For adults, moving is often going to something expected to be more gratifying—for the husband, a promotion, a better opportunity, or better salary, or better living situation, better neighborhood, better house.

The child lives in a narrower world of time and space; present satisfactions are real; in general, the future is vague and hard to imagine. Hopes, plans, and ideas of progress for the family may not have developed. What means most to him are his friends, familiar surroundings, his present home. It is often impossible for him to imagine feeling at home anywhere else. Unlike his father, his entire feeling may be one of going away from, of loss, separation from the beloved realities of the present with no capacity to conjure up a potentially satisfying new at-homeness. This is reinforced by the feelings of loss felt by the child's companions.

We can illustrate some of these feelings by excerpts from a mother's account of two of our children:

At the time of the family's first move to a new house, Molly was an intelligent, sensitive, active three-year-old child with two older sisters and a baby brother a year old. Sequences over a period of almost two years show to some extent how Molly felt about and coped with the move of her family from Kansas to Iowa.

When the family was discussing the impending move, Molly insisted that she would not leave Topeka. Finally her mother said, "Don't you want to go live with us in a new house? You could take your cat and dog and play with them." Molly said, "Well, if you'll take Snooks and Scotty [pets] I'll come, too." Mother stated that Molly's present reaction was mostly that she didn't seem to care where they went so long as they all went—which in this instance included the pets.

At this early stage, the vagueness of the talk about moving around seemed to be the disturbing factor. Molly did not know what would go and what would be left behind. Vague anxieties about what would be left behind seemed to be uppermost.

Two months later, Molly began to cry when prospective buyers began to look through their house, saying, "I don't want those people to live in my room." Mother held her and reassured her for quite a while that their new home would be a nice big place, that there would be lots of new things to see, and that they were taking everything and everybody with them, including the pets. Finally Molly said, "Well, it's all right, I guess, only I don't really want to move."

Molly's self-feeling seemed to be intense at this point and seemed to be connected with everything she had been part of or felt close to—she seemed to think of losing her room almost as if it were part of her body; she did not want to give it up to anyone else. In her mother's report of her efforts to comfort Molly, there is no mention of any attempt to convey to Molly that she would have her own room in the new house, but only that the belongings would go along. This may have had some part in the fact that Molly's feeling did not change but was simply more controlled.

She grudgingly said, "It's all right, I guess, only I don't really want to leave." Later she told her father that "We are going to take *all* our family when we leave, and we are even going to take our pets."

About three months later her mother became cross with Molly, who was extremely fussy and had been crying off and on all afternoon as her mother was busy packing. Molly left and soon her mother heard anguished howls from the cat. Mother found Molly had stuffed the cat in the clothes hamper. When her mother asked what was wrong, Molly began to cry, saying, "Well, I'm just not happy." When her mother attempted to comfort her, Molly began to wail, saying, "I don't want to move, I want to live here with my own bed!" Mother suggested a popsicle and a swing on the front porch. Molly quit crying and as they sat on the porch, mother talked about the kind of pony they would get in Iowa. After a while Molly hopped out of the swing and said, "If I could find a box, I would put my stove and doll in it

and then we could move it too." Mother gave her the box and Molly began
to pack her valuables.

Again Molly's wail has to do with loss of possessions very close to
her. Again her mother's report does not include any indication of reassurance that she can take the bed with her but seems to focus on all
the other precious things she can take, to which Molly responded
actively.

The next month, at age three-and-a-half, her mother reported the following scene which happened several times. Molly wept for quite a while when
Trudy was invited out to lunch, saying, "I'm not happy. I want daddy, I'm
not happy." Mother held her for a while and then Molly said, "A bottle
would make me feel happier." Mother produced it and Molly took the bottle
to her bedroom, drank the contents, and went to sleep. She seemed much
happier when she awakened. Mother noted that it was not Trudy's absence
that was bothering her as much as the prospective move.

Here, as the threat of loss came inescapably closer Molly regressed
and sought a dependable infantile comforter which succeeded in as-
suaging her still intense distress. Her mother reported later that as the
moving date drew nearer Molly became more uncertain about moving and asked for her bottle oftener and seemed to want her family
around her more. The mother stated that sometimes Molly didn't
drink the milk but seemed to want the bottle to hold on to—she would
sometimes lay the bottle beside her or carry it around with her—
it seemed to be a real comforter at these times.

Four days later, the move was accomplished. Mother was showing Molly
the outside of the house first. Molly spied an outhouse and quickly said, "I
don't like this house—it has an outdoor john." Mother assured her that
there was also one inside. "Well, let me see the one inside," she said doubtfully. Mother showed her and she was reassured. Later she asked, "Can I go
to the outside john when I'm outside?" Mother agreed. "Well, just think,
two toilets at this house!" Molly exclaimed, a bit smugly.

Molly first rejected the outstanding feature of the new home that
was different from the old home, the "outside john," but as soon as she
found that the new house included the familiar inside toilet, the new
one was accepted positively as an asset. That is, if the threat of loss of
the familiar is removed, new items can be enjoyed.

About two weeks later her father had lit a fire in the fireplace. Molly
beamed, then said, "Mommy, is the fireplace ours too? Can we have a fire
in it any time?" Mother agreed. Molly ran to get the others to come see.
"We never did have a fireplace before. I like this fireplace a lot." Molly
then began to plan where she would hang her stocking at Christmas; she
kept peeking at the fire to be sure that it was still burning.

The vivid sensuous value of the fire in the fireplace aroused new strong positive feelings of delight and liking the new home, even in this child whose feeling of loss had been so intense.

Other new positive responses gradually emerged. About a week later Molly was heard to say, "There are so many instering (interesting) things here!" Mother stated that Molly found some new kind of insect or bird almost every day. One morning there was a mantis on the living room wall and Molly was intrigued with her father's name of "devil's walking-stick." Also, there was a barn owl in a nearby tree and Molly listened for him each night.

But at the end of the first month in the new home, Molly had difficulty getting to sleep. When mother asked what was wrong she said, "Mommy, this room just isn't like my room in Kansas—the bed's wrong." When mother asked what they should do, Molly said, "Could we move the bed so my pillow looks out the door into the hall?" (This would enable her to see her family as they went by.) Mother complied and Molly said, "That's better—that's like it used to be." Molly went to sleep immediately.

The loss or separation from family involved in going to bed and going to sleep was handled by reinstituting an old familiar coping pattern—diminishing the feeling of separation by maintaining visual contact.

Her mother stated, however, that she felt Molly was becoming happier in her new home and that she sang and played quite happily all day long. She seemed to feel that if the rest of her family was happy, everything was all right. Still, separations were threatening and she needed some familiar support to deal with them.

One evening, as mother and daddy were preparing to go out (first time away from home since the move), Molly began to whimper saying, "I don't know the sitter. Is she nice? I want you to stay home. How long will you be gone? Is Anne [oldest sister] going to be home?" Mother assured her that Anne and Trudy would be there. "Could Anne put me to bed?" Molly asked. Mother agreed. "Well, if Anne will put me to bed, I'll stay." Mother had planned on putting Molly to bed before she left, and this worked out so that Molly was almost asleep before the sitter arrived. There was no further trouble.

Three months later, at five years less six weeks, mother reported Molly as saying quite frequently, "I'm glad we have a big house and not a little hot apartment like we did at Sunnyside." Molly loves the fireplace and likes nothing better than to put the shades down at night and sit in front of the fire, discussing Christmas, where the tree will go and what she and the others will receive. About six months later, they were discussing a visit from one of the project members. Molly said, "I'm so glad Grace is coming to see our nice big house." Mother stated that Molly had been looking forward to this visit for some time and they have had many discussions as to where she will sleep, etc. Molly is beginning to like having company and enjoys planning for them.

About five months later, the children had been out Hallowe'ening quite successfully, and Molly said, "We have so many friends here. It's just like it was in Kansas." (This complete acceptance of the new home occurred a year and three months after the move was made.)

The story of Molly illustrates the need for constancy in the mother-child relationship in younger children during the moving process, and the need for a period of time to work through feelings about moving before the move, a chance to participate with the parents in the moving plans, opportunities to get information and answers to questions about the move and the new home in order that understanding and awareness can be increased and the possibility for distortions and misconceptions minimized. In addition, Molly illustrates how a child needs to make the new home conform in certain physical aspects to the old home as a method of keeping anxiety within limits while moving forward in the new adjustment.*

It is also worth observing how Molly's sister Trudy coped with the move. She was two years older than Molly, with more concern about her parents and more ties outside the family. Her approach to the problem differed, although many of her feelings were similar. The steps in her process of handling the move are as follows:

At five-and-a-half Trudy asked her mother, "Why do we have to move, anyway?" Mother explained the "new job for daddy." Trudy asked, "Where will his new job be? Will it be a nice place?" Reassured by mother Trudy said, "I guess if daddy likes the place, it will be okay with me." Mother stated that Trudy ruminated over these discussions for days and weeks, then finally she would begin to talk about them. (Note the importance of love for her father in motivating her acceptance of the move.)

About three months later, Trudy smeared mud all over her mother's freshly scrubbed porch. When mother questioned Trudy, she said, "Well, you said nobody would buy our house if it wasn't pretty, so I put mud on it so it wouldn't look pretty, then no one would buy it, and we wouldn't have to move." Mother again explained that they would have to go where "daddy's job" was and explained further that in order to buy a new house they would have to sell the present one. Trudy agreed but mother felt that she wasn't

* It is interesting to note that in the military services where family mobility is an expected routine, this latter method of coping with the concerns associated with moving may long ago have been unknowingly included in official protocol for officers. Not longer than four days after reporting aboard to a new station (family move), an officer and his wife are expected to make a visit to the home of the commanding officer and his wife. Implied in this action is an indication that the officer and his wife are prepared to receive a return visit. Such a custom makes it absolutely necessary that the new home be put in order immediately.

convinced. Trudy helped mother scrub the porch again and apologized for getting it dirty.

It was extremely rare at this age for Trudy to be aggressive or to use sabotage. It is not unusual at this age for a child to resolve a problem temporarily, then feel a resurgence of it perhaps at even greater strength because of the repression previously used.

About two weeks later, Trudy asked her mother if her teacher couldn't move to Iowa with them. Mother explained that her teacher had her own family who would want her to stay in Kansas. Mother suggested that Trudy would probably have a nice teacher in their new home. Trudy said, "Well, I don't think she will be as nice as Mrs. M. Mother, if I learn to write next year, I could send Mrs. M. a letter."

It is important to note that the need to cope with loss of her beloved teacher motivates her purpose to learn a new skill which will help to ameliorate the loss by keeping in touch with her.

About five weeks later, the last day of school, Trudy came home crying, saying she would never see her teacher again. Mother held her as she cried for about five minutes. Then she asked if mother could get her teacher's address so that when she learned to write she could write to her. Mother agreed. Trudy then got her picture of her class at school and asked her mother to put it away so she could have it wherever they moved. Mother felt the outburst was a protest against the whole idea of moving, not just the idea of leaving her teacher.

Trudy's foresight in realizing that a picture would help to keep her memory of her class at school and her teacher alive was in marked contrast to three-year-old Molly's inability to foresee the new situation.

About two months later (age six years, one month) Trudy came in from playing, asking if their new home in Iowa was "to be for one family or a lot of families?" Trudy listened to her mother's explanation, then remarked, "Well, I like the Hermans [neighbors] real well, but I don't like them so close. With a yard by us and then the H.'s on the other side I would like them better. And when we move to Iowa, I'm going to invite people to my house and then maybe they won't come unless I invite them." This seemed to be Trudy's first recognition that something good might come out of the move.

After six months of discussion of the move Trudy was able to develop increasingly realistic images of what the new situation would be like, to think in problem-solving terms which included some new advantages in the new situation.

Four days later, Trudy awakened in the night crying but wouldn't tell her mother what the trouble was—she cried hard for about ten minutes.

Finally, after her mother's repeated urgings she sobbed, "I just don't want to move." Mother again explained the need and generally tried to comfort her. Trudy said she didn't want to go to a new place and that she wouldn't "have any friends I know to play with." Mother suggested that she would make new ones, etc. Trudy asked, "Will Anne [older sister] go to the same school as me?" and "Can I really have a kitten?" When mother agreed Trudy stopped crying, and said, "Well, I guess it won't be so bad." Mother stated that they had tried very hard to point out all the advantages to Trudy but it still seemed pretty vague to her despite her efforts to develop a picture of how it would be; her home town was very near and dear.

Trudy's separation problem was still intense and she dealt with it by asking for reassurance that some aspects of the new situation will be like the old—she will still have her sister and she will have a cat as she has now.

About two weeks later, after the move had been completed, Trudy said she was afraid to go to bed and wanted to sleep with Anne, her older sister. Mother discouraged her and Trudy cried, saying, "Well, could you leave the door open to Anne's room and let me have Snooks [dog] on my bed?" Mother agreed and Trudy seemed happy. Mother states that Trudy loves the new house in the daytime but at night there are bad things in it and she needs a lot of reassurance that her family is close. They have told her that they are always available and that she can come to them anytime in the night that she becomes frightened. This seemed to help.

It is not unusual for phobic ideas to emerge when a child has lost the familiar supports. In this situation it is important that she was able to communicate her fear to her mother and to suggest specific, reassuring comforts that would help her to cope with her fear.

The next day Trudy asked Mr. McN., their landlord, who was doing some repair work on their garage, to come to the house for coffee. Mr. McN. declined. Trudy came to the house saying, "Daddy, Mr. McN. is kind of bashful—I think if you invited him he'd come up to the house for coffee." Daddy agreed, and Mr. McN. came. Trudy brought the cream and cookies and was delighted to play hostess to her guest. Mother felt this illustrated very plainly Trudy's need to put her roots down—having someone who would sit at the table and talk with her parents while they had their coffee, just as her older friends did in her former home.

Here and in numerous subsequent episodes Trudy took the initiative in helping the family to experience old satisfactions in the new setting, initiating relationships and making friendships at both the adult and childhood level.

About ten days later, after her mother had put Trudy to bed that night, she came downstairs looking very sad saying, "Mother it just isn't like Kansas at night here. It's big upstairs and I can't sleep. Could I leave the door open, and would you sing while you wash the dishes? Then it would sound like home and I could go to sleep." Mother went back upstairs with Trudy and sat talking to her about things they would do the next day. This seemed to cheer Trudy and after a while she said, "I could go to sleep now if you'd sing downstairs—sing loud so I can hear you." When mother started to sing *Swing Low Sweet Chariot* Trudy called, "Mother, don't sing any sad ones —just sing fast happy ones." Mother agreed and Trudy went to sleep shortly afterward.

Here and in more clear-cut phobic moments Trudy was always able to communicate her worries and to suggest specific ways of dealing with them. Her mother always used these suggestions of Trudy's or gave her support in other ways which helped to build positive feelings about the new house.

About five months (plus) later, Trudy was heard to say as mother put her to bed, "Mother this is the happiest place—there's all my family and a big house for us to play in, and I have Cuddles [her cat] and I never want it to change." Mother states that Trudy is very happy these days, loves everything and everybody, frequently says how happy she is, sings to herself as she paints or colors, or grabs someone for a kiss. Mother says they should have moved to Iowa long ago!

In summary, we see Trudy's self-insight, her capacity to express her feelings in words, to trust in the help of adults and to communicate stress to them, to prescribe remedies which would help and enlist assurance which would supplement and support her own counterphobic devices, in addition to her capacity to mobilize positive forces in the new environment. Important in all this is her capacity to link the new with old satisfactions, to get familiar comfort, and in general to initiate positive efforts to deal with situations.

With both of these children there was a high degree of spontaneous expressiveness and freedom to communicate their feelings to their mother. The mother in her turn had a high degree of patience and resourcefulness in making the reason for the move intelligible, making the new home a real image, reassuring the children about continuity of family and possessions, and supporting the children's ways of trying to make themselves at home in the new locality. While with both girls the idea of the move was threatening before it took place, the new satisfactions and the opportunity to sink in new roots produced in the end a perspective which could be expected to contribute toward greater flexibility and response to the challenge of newness and change in the future.

The capacity to respond to the new after loss or stress

In times of great stress, as in war or other disasters such as auto accidents, when a child has lost his family and everyone he has been close to, his capacity to respond to new interests, relationships, and sources of security may make the difference between his capacity to survive or not to survive. We do not know as much as we need to know about what is involved in this capacity to make a new life, but we have some varied reports on it. One from Anna Freud's account[2] of a group of concentration camp children who made a life for themselves together when transplanted to a group living situation in England; another, the patently autobiographical record of *Child of our Time*[3] where step by step we see the crucial role of an affectionate hand, a sacrificial and loving bit of food, in sustaining a child's fading morale.

Most fully in the story of two children of the war who were rescued by Dr. Robert Collis[4] do we have a record of the struggles with mourning, with anger, despair, and longing, which very slowly yielded to a re-emergence of the capacity to love new people and new places. Margaret Mead's introduction to this book comments that it is "not a book about horror, but a book about strength and trust." As she says, Dr. Collis traces the story of these children from the Carpathian Mountains, the warm, understanding, family life from which they emerged, and how after the horrors of war, the memories (conscious and unconscious) of these early years stood the children in such good stead that they were able to accept love offered by a new family.

We cannot review here in detail the long series of steps by which the children, especially Eva, emerged from desolation and misery into contentment. I shall quote an important climax in this story; it comes after a period of time when, at Christmas, Eva had become very withdrawn and desolate, not crying or complaining but silent and unreachable. Then "toward the end of the holidays a change occurred while the family was on a visit to their vacation cabin at Bo-Island.

The snow came, first appearing on the high mountains and then on the plateau around. From the first Eva revelled in it. Perhaps it stirred something in her memory—those wintry days in Presov when the High Tatra pine-trees were weighted down by masses of white snow, and even the hill torrents froze in long, beautiful icicles.

During the day she pursued Rusty through the drifts, was chased by Robbie and chased him, screaming and laughing as he hurled snowballs at her with far greater accuracy than she could match. Each night she slept in her corner by the big fire. There, snugly warm, she could hear the wind in the Scotch firs. Lying in bed, she could see out through the little window and watch the snow-covered trees in the wood shining like silver in the moonlight. Thus contentedly she would doze first into a light sleep and then sink downward into deep sleep.

Now Rusty on one of these cold, snowy nights climbed upon her couch when she was still dozing. She stretched out a small hand and patted his head. Thus encouraged, he not only decided that he would sleep upon her bed, but insinuated his silky person upwards until his golden head rested on the pillow beside hers. The child turned, and, nestling her face in the ruffles of his breast, slipped her arms around his neck, and thus fell asleep. The two presented a picture of great beauty. Eva's face was completely peaceful. Her whole attitude was one of relaxation. What deep association this strange slumber reunited in her mind while she lay asleep, again under the presence of high, snow-covered mountains in a small, warm house, what unconscious memory it stirred, I do not know; but from now on she appeared different, freer, less shut up inside herself, and the next day she called Bo-Island "home."

We can see here the reverse of the process of traumatization and the development of disturbance as we retrace the steps of these in our case studies and therapy with disturbed children. We uncover the chronic or the climactic wounds, angers, conflicts, which the child was not able to resolve and which lead to neurotic disturbance. Here in this book we are still interested in beginnings, but in the beginnings which poets are more apt to talk about than clinicians, the beginnings of the feeling of home, of closeness, security, love, and trust.

Poets share with psychoanalysis a deep respect for the integrity of the felt moment, the specific quality of experience as it was known, selected, polished, and embroidered by the individual child's imagination, then fitted into one or another area of the multidimensional inner world. Inexplicably, specific experiences form themselves into foci of early feelings of contentment, satisfaction, and hope.

Just as the shape and weight and terror of each new threat has been molded by, and reflects the shape and weight of, early threats and pains and disappointments, so the shape of the opposite—what Margaret Mead calls "blessing"—is similarly patterned. In fact the shape, color, and meaning of every piece of newness, whether new threat or new hope, emerges from the echoed meanings of former newness which it evokes. Just as each new threat summoned shadows of old pain, each new love glows with warmth from the earliest loves of all.

In the story of Eva, we see how elements of a new situation which overlapped with satisfying elements of old familiar situations finally helped her to feel "at home," in the new situation. Familiarization is reaching this feeling of "at homeness," or "getting used to things," and this is a process that has to go on all through life.

NOTES AND REFERENCES

1. Rølvaag, O. E. *Giants in the Earth*. New York: Harper, 1927.
2. Freud, A., and Dann, S. An experiment in group upbringing. *Psychoanalytic Study of the Child,* Vol. 6. New York: International Universities Press, 1951.
3. Del Castillo, M. *Child of Our Time*. New York: Knopf, 1958.
4. Collis, R. *The Lost and the Found*. New York: Woman's Press, 1952.

4

MEETING
NEW DIFFICULTIES*

So FAR, OUR DISCUSSION of the children's behavior in new situations has focused attention on the role of orientation and familiarization and the various processes of looking and appraising that go on before a child selects a portion of the stimuli in the environment to explore or manipulate. These processes were involved, of course, over and over again as different experiences presented themselves, but we shall not discuss problems of orientation as such again; we shall move ahead to other aspects of situations that were challenging or difficult as we followed the children through their responses to the many demands of the intelligence tests and later to the challenges at "parties."

Since an intelligence test consists of an extended series of quite

* Based on Dr. Moriarty's analysis of behavior in tests; see Coping patterns of preschool children in response to intelligence test demands, *Genetic Psychol. Monographs, 64:3-127, 1961.*

specific delimited tasks and demands, it permits as it were a microscopic scrutiny of the child's response to such demands and especially to the difficulties and threatened or actual failures involved. This will occupy the present chapter.

During the first four or five years of life most children are confronted with demands to accept and come to terms with numerous new situations. Some of these involve challenges to engage in new activities which may require the integration of new coordinations and skills, however well established some of the elements of these may be. Some of the skills demanded are not merely new, but difficult for the child's level of maturity and capacity. When this is so, he faces possible failure. New challenges may accordingly arouse some apprehension. The effort to deal with both internal tensions and external pressures optimally evokes spontaneous, constructive efforts which are however realistically limited by the child's total resources at that point. These coping efforts are enhanced in certain children, and in other children constrained or decreased by the tension aroused by the possibility of failure.

In our study, the tests have provided experiences which were by turns challenging, demanding, difficult, or frustrating. The test not only gives a general measure (of I.Q.) permitting comparisons of our subjects with other children; it also provides a pointed and detailed record of how the child uses his resources under such conditions. This includes the range of coping devices used in managing difficulty, the systems and functions heightened or diminished in response to successes and failures; his way of relating to the examiner, and to the situation as a whole including the parallel recorder. The observations thus reveal how the child selectively balances his need to comply or cooperate with the tester's demands with his own needs for spontaneous self-expression, protest, choice, and autonomy in solution of problems and the preservation of his own identity.

Coping styles of two young children in test situations involving pressure from the adult *

Dr. Kass' session at which an attempt was made to administer both perceptual and projective tests within one test period was more demanding than Dr. Moriarty's sessions; he made much less allowance for the child's own impulses and expected consistent cooperation on a long series of tasks. Some children fell in with the procedures in a free and spontaneous fashion; for others it was a situation where if test results were to be obtained at all the examiner had to use pres-

* Based on summaries by Grace Heider for Progress Report, 1954.

sures which, however skillfully applied, were coercive in their effect. Following are brief summaries of the ways in which two different three-year-old girls responded to adult control and pressure in test situations handled this way:

SHEILA

In the test room Sheila (age two years and ten months) at once made herself at home with toys that were available. She had objected firmly to taking her snow suit off when the observer offered help on arrival but soon chose to allow the examiner, Dr. Kass, to help her with it. She was amenable to being seated at the work table and cooperated with the first two CAT cards but soon announced, "We don't want to watch these" and then, "I don't want to watch these." Her posture now reflected marked distaste for the situation and she did not allow herself to be even temporarily caught by any of the usually successful approaches that the examiner then made. She announced, "I want to play with toys," then leaving her seat, "I play with toys."

Soon she was gay and playful with a game of her own devising involving the examiner but which she conducted from a distance and which left her master of her own movements. There was some aggression against the clown Bobo during this intermission and she continued to resist the examiner's leading questions like, "Want to sit down?" with a firm, "Want to play with toys." This was spoken with special energy when she momentarily allowed herself to sit in one of the chairs, only afterward, perhaps, realizing that in doing so she had really moved in the direction in which the adult pressures were being applied. Having made this pronouncement she was quickly out of her chair. After another excursion she played a two-way game with the examiner using toy telephones. The examiner, in the meantime, had set out a performance task which finally aroused Sheila's curiosity and she seated herself to begin the game, her face showing excited interest. Her manner was playful but gradually as she was urged to follow his rules instead of her own in the game she slipped away, announcing gaily, "I want to do *this*. We don't like the game. We don't like the game we had."

Dr. Kass lured her back to partial compliance with a more active phase of the task where at each step she announced, "I can't put this in" and soon left the scene. He then tried to utilize her decision to use crayons by introducing the Bender Gestalt drawings, a situation which Sheila again structured in terms of her own mood.

By this time there were indications that a definite relationship had been established; the examiner left the room for a moment and Sheila showed real concern as to whether he would return. She welcomed him with pleasure on his return, but did not allow this admission of a relationship to lead her to conform. The game continued on her own terms.

Another attempt to obtain responses from Sheila to the CAT cards was made with a toy telephone and her responses showed perhaps partial conformity for a brief period. This was quickly followed by another retreat with aggressive vocalizations that led up to a mild tantrum and a demand to leave the room. Her independence now established, Sheila again played with toys and the examiner began to put his material away. Sheila at this point approached him but was told "next time." The examiner suggested that she should go home. The immediate answer was, "Don't want to go home," but having affirmed her independence of the adult suggestions she said, "I want my mommy." There was another alternation of direction in regard to the process of putting on the snow suit—and then mild social interchange with a gentle blow at Bobo, reminiscent of, but no longer carrying the meaning of her previous attack on him.

Here we see a child who in the face of continuing and skillfully applied adult pressures maintained her own autonomy. And it was not merely a matter of refusing and rejecting; it was a matter of doing this without allowing the pressures to depress her mood or to restrict her freedom of movement. Instead, during most of the time, the pressures served to stimulate her to her own best efforts in structuring the situation and obtaining enjoyment from it and from the relationship with the adult. And during the brief intervals when it seemed possible that the pressures might win out to the extent of directing her behavior she quickly regained her independence, either by direct refusal, or, when she more nearly gave in, by a mild outbreak of anger. She made a frontal attack on the situation before there was any question of a paralyzing panic.

This high degree of autonomy was typical of Sheila, breaking down only when she was scratched and then abandoned by a cat she had been loving perhaps too vigorously. Sheila at two years and ten months was a child whose mother found it difficult to answer the various questions by which the interviewer tried to obtain descriptions of her behavior in frustration situations at home. The picture given was of a child who rarely, in this relatively permissive home, experienced anything akin to frustration. The reason for this was that what Sheila wanted she straightaway found devices to obtain, whether the temporary obstacle was impersonal or human.

VIVIAN

Vivian, at the age of three years and two months, was described by her mother as easy going in comparison with a sensitive older sister. But the mother also reported that although she was less prone to fears and anxieties than her sister she could be frightened by external threats, like attacks by neighboring children or the appearance of a strange dog. How she dealt with threats or pressures at home was not made clear.

On the trip to the Observation Center Vivian was chiefly engaged in comforting her somewhat tearful sister, Daryl, who was older by fifteen months. But once in the room with the examiner she herself wilted down, with gentle, quiet tears. She allowed herself to be led from one occupation to another, making minimal responses, and sucking a finger most of the time. From time to time she held up her head to have her eyes wiped by the examiner and showed touching dependence on him especially when, in hopes of changing the mood of the situation, he proposed that they take a little walk.

On her return she worked again at the tasks that were set her, still with no indication of enjoyment. In placing forms in the board she would lay one on the hole but seemed to lack the additional energy that it would have taken to turn it so that it would fall into place. Her decision not to repeat the task was indicated again by a minimal push that was applied to the board. And the slightest possible negative shaking of her head indicated her unwillingness to comply with other requests. Her CAT responses were meager and barely whispered. Finally she indicated by the direction of her glance and a slight push of the material that she was ending her contact with it.

Once the session was at an end and she was again with her sister, she gradually became an apparently secure and quietly happy child; on the trip home she proudly displayed her own gaily decorated handkerchief that had been in her pocket all the time that she was holding out her head to have her eyes wiped with the examiner's handkerchief.

Here we have an entirely different way of dealing with the examiner. The negative situation, instead of serving as it did for Sheila as a challenge and a stimulant, seemed to drain her energy, acting as a depressant. Whether one should think of this lowering of the level of energy available for action as a direct effect of the pressure felt in the situation or as a means of coping with it is a question that is not easy to answer. Certainly it did not affect the possibility of action to the extent of producing a state of panic where positive action would be possible. Instead, on this reduced level of activity, the child was easily able to lean on the adult figure and to utilize the support that he offered. And whether she perceived him at the same time as the source of the pressures that were being exerted on her or whether it was rather, as it seemed from the outside, a sorrowful situation in which he, a stronger figure and she, a weaker one, were involved together, one cannot say. But in any case her method of dealing with it had certain positive aspects, despite her inability to make constructive use of the material resources of the situation, to mobilize any aggressive protest, or to derive real enjoyment apart from the gratification of evoking the tender solicitude of the male examiner.

DIANE

Dr. Moriarty summarized Diane's approach as follows:

This attractive, well-groomed, composed, gentle little girl handled the newness of the situation by quietly surveying the room, by speaking softly, by drawing with minimal pressure, as though holding in abeyance deep participation until a comfortable oneness with the two observers was established. Diane worked with unhurried efficiency, calmly and evenly, so that one felt in her an almost regal acceptance of her rightful security. She welcomed intimate closeness and personal help, yet maintained always a sense of comfortable autonomy in an integrated self-percept. Quite early in the sessions, she seemed to experience the tests as something special, like school, and therefore pleasant since school represented growing up and doing things her older siblings did. She adapted herself to the situation, speaking softly in the quiet house and arising to praise with self-assured realistic acceptance, "Oh yes, I do very, very well." (Bead stringing.) She was delighted with small and pretty things and seemed to anticipate pleasure, basking in her successful performances (i.e., repeating three-hole formboard six times), partly because her unruffled calm protected her from anxiety in potential failure.

The parallel record of Diane's response to the intelligence test conveys the attitudes of a happy three-year-old who assumes that she has the right to define her own terms. Parts of the second and third session are quoted here.

Now AM said, "Shall we string some beads?" "Yup," she said and went after them quite eagerly. "Come on," she said a little impatiently to the first bead as she attempted to get it on the wrong end of the cord where there was a knot which would not let it go on. AM directed her to the other end. She seemed to enjoy the bead stringing immensely but did not follow AM's pattern at all. "I'm gonna do it clear clear to the bottom," she said as she worked. . . .

When AM got out the green blocks and said, "Could you give me three of these?" she said, "OK, wait 'till I get done," but in a very sweet voice.

Now she engaged AM in conversation that went something like this. (She is still stringing beads.) "Do you know what a bear is?" "Yes, do you?" AM said. "Uh-uh (meaning no) I don't know either," still preoccupied with bead stringing.

Again AM tried, "I'd like to show you these pictures before we go home, Diane. Do you think you could stop stringing beads now?" "Oh, no, I couldn't do that," she said, still in the same sweet voice but very matter-of-fact. Now AM said a little firmly, "I think we *really* do have to stop now." "OK," said Diane not seeming to mind at all.

When AM asked her to draw with the pencil "the shortest way to school" she took the pencil but was evidently not marking hard enough for AM to see. "Can you make it a little darker?" AM asked. "Uh-uh" (meaning no), she said. From what I could see she didn't seem to get the idea of what AM wanted her to do, but seemed to be playing with it going all over the paper.

Now AM asked her, "What would you do if you had broken something that belongs to somebody else?" "Throw it in the trash," she answered promptly.

Now she picks up the blocks that were still in front of her, giving them to AM as if a gift saying, "You can have this many," giving her a few, and then tells her she can have all of them and gives them to her. (I thought perhaps she might have realized she had failed on some of the tests and was giving these to AM to make up for her inadequacy.)

"I want to play with some of them," pointing to piles of boxes AM had on a bench. "OK," AM said, "would you like to look at this one?" Nods. "These are like this," AM explained, taking out the little boxes that are inside of each other (different colors). She took them from AM and said, "I know how to do them." She lined them up in front of her, looked at them a little, then said, "I want to see some of those others," pointing to some more boxes on the bench. She started to put them back together, made one mistake and then righted it, getting them all in correctly.

AM now gave her the buttons to do. She wasn't very interested in these and said she wanted some of the other boxes. AM said, "OK," but asked her if she could do this first. "But I don't know how to work it," in a very sweet voice. AM encouraged her and she did it even though she wanted to look in the other boxes. Now she said that she got one button, and AM said, "You *did* do it!" AM encouraged her and she got the other one. Now AM gave her the 4 button one; she did not want to do this either, saying, "I don't know how!" "Just try," AM said. "OK, just twy," she said. Now she sat down saying to AM, "You do two of these and I do two of these." AM said, "Let's see if you can do them all." She finished one, making "too too too" noises as she worked, then said, "twy and twy and twy." She was now standing with one knee on the chair, one foot on the floor. She finished two of them and handed them to AM telling AM to do two of them. AM said, "You do it. If I do it I won't know if you can do it." She finally finished them for AM. "Fine! You did them," AM said. "Now, which box would you like to look at?" She smiled as if accepting the reward and picked one out.

This is the matching cards. "This is a coffee pot," she said, "and this is an apple" as AM explained what she wanted her to do. Now she began and as she matched the cards her voice and manner were most delightful to see and hear as she said, "Dat one wight dere, I can take this, put it wight heah, and take this and put it wight up heah, and I can take this and put it wight heah." "Where does this go?" she said as she worked, and then again, "and this goes wight heah." After she completed the task she said, "Like me to put these away too?" putting the small ones on a pile on the table. "I don't like to put the little ones away," she said. "You don't?" AM asked. "No," she said stacking the big ones in the box. "Now you can put the little ones away," she said to AM. AM said "OK" and put the little ones in. Diane made little "dit dit dit" noises, hitting her feet together under the table. Now she got off her chair, then sat down with one foot under her very gracefully. . . .

"You do well," AM said. "I do very very well don't I?" but somehow there was no bragging in her voice, just a sort of sweet rapport with AM. And then again, "I do *very very* well!" as she worked putting them away and over on the bed.

Next was the Manikin. "I want to put the mans together," she said when she saw it. Now she sang as she worked, and then said, "There," as she finished, very quickly. "He looks like a mule," she said.

In the preceding examples we can see how differently the test situation was experienced by three young children; at the early age of three years each one had her own assumptions about ways of handling adults.

Group responses to difficulty

Since the intelligence tests are always continued through that test level at which every test task is failed, the design of the tests provides a fairly standardized experimental situation which forces every child to undergo the stress of handling difficulty and failure in the area of cognitive efforts. Thus we can compare individual reactions in regard to how the child "takes it," when fronted with difficulty or failure. Since a parallel observer was always present we had a full record of behavior and conversation as well as the examiner's technical record of test successes, failures, efficiency with different tasks, and reactions to her. The parallel record especially contained a detailed account of the choice and organization of behavior which might or might not lead to solutions to standard test tasks as these are expected from the adult point of view, but which often did express the child's way of solving the problem as he saw it in his own way. The record also noted attempts to seek refuge, support or escape. The examiner observed especially ways of releasing tension and of maintaining integrity in the ongoing situation.

More than half of the children participated eagerly, agreeably and willingly following directions during the test as a whole. These children appeared to be comfortable in the testing situation. While almost half of the children indicated distaste for the specific task at one time or another, only one sixth of them actively resisted test items per se. Some children typically responded by withdrawal, and others occasionally withdrew with the clear purpose of taking time out for survey, appraisal, and mobilization of resources, as we have illustrated these processes in earlier chapters. Withdrawal of this sort was at times a positive coping procedure, leading to a subsequent active effort.

Most children felt free to express their own needs independently, and actively did something to change the situation when they wished. All but four of the children (all boys) at times also expressed autonomy passively by evading tests they did not wish to try.

A majority of the children could casually ask for help when it was objectively needed. The group of one third who sometimes refused help included both some typically withdrawing children, and some highly autonomous children who seemed to feel that the offer of help implied that they were not competent.

Twenty-seven of the thirty-two children (eighty-four per cent) realistically accepted or recognized limitations in their skills or capacities. As a group the children were overtly proud of their own achievement and realistic in evaluating good performances. Only occasionally were they self-critical in a derogatory sense; sometimes they were embarrassed but feelings of humiliation were conspicuously lacking. Along with observers in other situations Dr. Moriarty felt in most of these children a strong sense of personal worth and competence.

Evidence of mild anxiety which appeared to be realistic or protective was observed at times in the majority of the children. This was clearly not overwhelming since the children were usually resilient and did not show pervasive or persistent effects beyond the response to the item in question. In other words, anxiety usually was mild, limited, and transitory rather than overwhelming, diffuse, or persistent.

All children at one time or another used defense mechanisms, particularly when uncertainty, difficulty, or failure was involved; usually these were employed flexibly without evidence of rigidity or pathology. Three fourths of the children used realistic defense mechanisms (substitution and compensation), avoiding direct and final failure and protecting their autonomous position. Defense mechanisms involving some distortion of reality (denial, projection, displacement) were also used at one time or another by nearly half of the children. Over a fifth of the group used fantasy in this testing situation, sometimes as a diversion, sometimes in the context of converting the situation into a pleasant social interchange; almost the same proportion enjoyed such regressive behavior as mouth or lip play when they were successful, while nearly half of the children regressed under tension.

Defense mechanisms were used in flexible ways, more frequently by the more competent, more affectively comfortable children. Children who cooperated eagerly more frequently used the kinds of defense mechanisms mentioned above than did those children who simply resisted the tests actively or passively. The cooperative children more often expressed fantasy and more often regressed when comfortable or gratified, less frequently needing to do so for tension release. Children who expressed autonomy needs actively were more apt to use a variety of defense mechanisms than did those who expressed autonomy needs passively. Similarly, children who realistically and openly recognized and accepted their own limitations used such defense mechanisms more frequently than did those who tried to conceal their limits by overtly ignoring, hiding, or minimizing them. That is, defense mechanisms at an intrapsychic level seemed to be the price of maintaining a cooperative, competent coping orientation rather than overtly refusing demands or hiding their limitations.

Demands of performance tests were less difficult than verbal tests, perhaps because they more closely resembled home demands or play experiences (such as buttoning, cutting, coloring, putting puzzles together) and because they eliminated potential difficulties in communication through speech at this stage when speech is not yet well consolidated. Sixty-seven per cent of the children oriented themselves quickly when performance tests were given, as compared to quick orientation on the part of just half of the group to verbal tests. Pride in accomplishment was more often expressed with performance tests than with verbal tests. In general the children appeared to be happier and more confident to be doing something than merely to be explaining or describing something. Thus it was to be expected that evasions of test demands were less frequent in performance tests than in verbal tests, and that there was less evidence of tension and anxiety on performance tests than on verbal tests. Although the absence of anxiety on the part of the boys in performance tests largely accounted for this difference, there was also slightly less anxiety on the part of the girls during performance tests. The children's bodily coordination was best with many children on performance items, perhaps because these tests directly demanded motor integrations and focused the child's attention on it. In line with this, meticulousness increased in the performance tests, and was thus an expression of increased focus in preferred motor situations rather than a need for defensive compulsive effort. At the same time certain children were more strained, awkward, or jerky in movements during the performance tests. While "realistic" defense mechanisms occurred more frequently on verbal items, unrealistic defenses were more frequently used on performance items.

Dr. Moriarty made an intensive analysis of the children's reactions to especially difficult tasks in the intelligence test. Their coping devices included cognitive efforts which implied recognition of the difficulty and an attempt to clarify the nature of it: taking time to explore, survey, feel out tactually, visually, motorically, or verbally; looking ahead to avoid errors; verbal clarification and self-orientation. Asking questions seemed to clarify the task. Staying with known success in the test, often continuing beyond satiation was used in the attempt to maintain the level of competence. ("We ought to do that some more." Repeating Seguin formboard four times and offering to do it again.)

In other instances the child provided evidence from his personal experience of what he could and could not do: buttons: "I can't. I'm sure I can't. I can button my coat. I have to put my finger in there." Thinking out solutions in a logical way, a child sometimes used past experience to meet the intellectual challenges.

Other devices included using environmental cues, as in word naming. The children also proceeded through various steps of categorizing: classifying, comparing, differentiating, qualifying, comparing size, color; naming, counting; insisting that the examiner explain in these terms.

Efforts directed toward staying in control of the situation while not rejecting the intention to cooperate, included delay or stalling as "I couldn't do that right now." "I'm not ready yet. I gotta tie it. Pretty soon I'll be ready."

Similarly, or more positively, some children asserted wishes, refusing to be bound by prearranged plans, or made their wishes known: "I want to make it zissaway." "Do you have something else? Don't want to play with these." Setting self-imposed time limits, for example, suggesting that the examiner count to ten and that the task would then be done, appeared to be another way of making the task manageable or tolerable.

Assuming the examiner's role modified the situation in the direction of reducing the examiner's dominance and increasing one's own: asking questions for the examiner to answer, sitting in her chair, "explaining"; shifting responsibility: "You tell me." Sharing responsibility: "You do two of these and I do two of these," was a more modulated form of the same effort. Modifying instructions: turning around or looking at the ceiling instead of closing eyes as asked, had the effect of maintaining some autonomy while still cooperating.

Facing the difficulty, some children invited the examiner to understand their plight: "I can't do it best . . . It's a little hard for me." "I said it was too hard." Some of them directly asked for legitimate help or reassurance: seeking more information, clarification or assistance; obtaining physical contact by rubbing or patting the examiner, placing his head in her lap, pressing close. One child made the examiner a virtual mother-substitute.

Efforts to exert greater care included becoming overmeticulous; extreme deliberation in making choices: unusual care in handling test equipment; pedantic verbal expression; wish for correctness, completeness. About one half of the children increased their precision with difficult tests, whereas half passively gave up. Boys seemed to be somewhat more persistent than girls.

Efforts to compensate by substitution were varied. Occasionally a child attempted to make failure less obnoxious by pointing out where success occurs: "I can't build this, but I got that." Other substitutions included shifting to an easier or more familiar but related task: as cutting out a smaller piece of paper than the one requested, building a tower instead of a bridge, making a circle instead of a square, counting instead of repeating digits. Or a child shifted to an easier, different task: (Asked to copy a star, one child said, "I'm making a garage. I'm making a garage. I can't make that one. It's too hard. I ca-a-ant"). A more positive form of this pattern involved shifting attention to a less ambitious project: "Do you want me to do something I *can* do?" "I can do something else."

More resourcefully a child shifted to a new approach after discarding a first unworkable method. Another realistic effort involved the attempt to rest and try later: certain children would put aside the difficulty and then attempt it at a later time. When such possibilities were not available some children sought to leave the task by changing the subject, reporting fantasies, or announcing entirely unrelated achievements: "I can dance; I can skip" (when unable to handle scissors).

Efforts to avoid the task also included more direct attempts to terminate the test or to suggest that items be omitted altogether. "That's all I want to say." Sometimes an acceptable reason for termination was offered: "I'm getting tired—that's all I want to do. I need a drink." "Oh, I've got a headache." In other instances a frank overt protest was expressed: "I can't . . . 'cause I don't want to. I don't care. I just don't want to."

These devices appeared to be useful to the child in his efforts to handle test difficulty. Other devices served to maximize gratification or to control or decrease his tension level; a child would support his self-esteem by asserting his own prowess or that of someone with whom he identified. He would cite superiority over a sibling: "I can stay inside the lines. That little kid goes outside the lines." Or he would maintain a front of superficial self-assurance, or of bravado.

Strong familial identification provided a kind of reassurance for some children; when they felt doubtful about what they could accomplish they talked in some detail of mother's skill in sewing, or father's athletic prowess. Regarding the examiner as an ally seemed to have a similar flavor of maintaining self-esteem through a sense of joint achievement. *"We* got nine points."

Self-esteem was also supported by anticipation of a better capacity in the future: a child who could not tell time said, "No, but I will some day." Minimizing, or excusing failure, was accomplished by pointing out lack of previous experience. "Well, I'll tell you. I never made a kite" (copying a diamond); "I forgot." Projective overtones could be seen in such protests as "There ain't any." "Mother didn't tell me." "I bet no one can make one like that." Projection also took the form of criticism of the examiner: "You didn't give me enough blocks." "I can put it away more neatly." "Hook, what's the mattah? Am you teasing?" Or criticism of tests or materials: "I can't believe this. There's no horsey. This was never a cut-up horse." "They can't cut, can they? . . . I don't like your scissors." Referring to test items as "silly," "nutty," "crazy," "dumb." Jabbing the pencil into the paper, pushing, squeezing, crumpling, biting, mutilating test material or handling them roughly and handing materials to the examiner with sharp thrusting movements expressed anger, hostile, perhaps primitive feelings arising in reaction to frustrations in the test. Less realistically a child dismissed a task by saying it was already done: "I told you! That's what I said!"

Keeping "face" was a more resistant device, and seemed to be involved when a child suggested that success depended on a wish to try, or that it was a matter of choice: "I don't know if I want to." "I can do it as fast as I want to," showed a superficial self-assurance, studied carelessness.

Occasionally a child blamed himself for failure in a self-critical way with such comments as, "I gotta think first . . . That's crazy that I don't know." "What's the matter with me?"

Difficulty was avoided in various ways by: shoving away, scattering, dumping, hiding unpleasant or unsatisfying objects; accidentally dropping objects; concealing work; physically leaving the field or turning away, seeming not to hear, looking at the ceiling, lowering eyes, going to sleep, or absolute denial.

Nearly all children, even those most active, were sometimes quiet

and uncommunicative. This appeared to serve the purpose of keeping affective relationship at a low level by remaining aloof, indifferent, uncommunicative, or not getting involved.

Preventive coping or forestalling stress occurred when a child refused to push beyond the point where he felt involved in an impossible task, and when a child made failure less striking by anticipating the difficulty, protecting himself from failure by not expecting success nor permitting the examiner to expect it: "I don't know if I know."

Indirect outlets of tension or compensatory soothing were provided by primitive gratification such as enjoyment of sound effects which often seemed to have release value. Imitating animal or mechanical sounds, nonsense sounds, exciting squealing, singing, humming, remarking on the clatter of blocks or other noises from manipulating of equipment by examiner or child also released tension. Varying the intensity of speed of speech with soft, slow sounds occurred more often when the child was failing. Baby talk was occasionally consciously used, almost as though the child were saying, "I'm little yet. Why do you expect so much of me?"

Abortive nods, whispering, tightness of voice, seemed to serve as a defense against possible spillovers of tension. Hoarseness or huskiness may have occurred as a compromise expression in the effort to avoid crying, as did chattering in agitated, "whistling in the dark" fashion. Crying occasionally appeared to control adult behavior.

Movement often seemed to facilitate release of tension. At times it was definitely purposive, as pantomime or tapping in rhythm to the examiner's speech. At other times it was automatic or close to reflexive, as ritualistic repetition, hunching shoulders; scratching, rubbing (sometimes masturbatory), fisting or pressing hands tightly against sides, compressing lips or tightening facial musculature, staring vacantly, remaining immobile. Some other bodily adjustments seemed to postpone test interaction: tripping, falling, balancing precariously, or moving with postural awkwardness, stiffness, or lack of tonus.

Soothing activities used various sensory modalities: rubbing, patting, tracing, fingering materials or own body; delight in visual detail: expressing pleasure in many rarely noticed details of room, test, objects seen on trips to session.

Coping efforts such as these need to be seen in the context of the child's over-all approach to the test which was summarized for each child in detail; we shall quote here only a portion of the summary as background for a review of Chester's ways of handling difficulty. We saw Chester earlier, but here we find some differences from the approach he made to the situation with the psychiatrist (Chapter 2, pp. 21-22).

Chester in the intelligence test situation

Chester is a sturdy, tall youngster, very neat and clean in appearance, as though freshly scrubbed for a special occasion. His sparkling brown eyes seemed always to emanate social warmth and personal security. Within this framework of comfortable interchange, one experienced in Chester subtle differentiation in moods in different situations. For example, he initially seemed subdued and shy in structured test situations with less of the ready confidence which was so apparent during the MLT. At the same time, ideas bubbled over in varied and original use of materials, in imaginative, semirealistic tall tales, and in his humorous, exaggerated similes, especially in his interpretation of auditory stimuli. Radiant delight, fleeting facial expressions of wistful longing, and inordinate pride in personal possessions added to the impression of a full, rich personality.

SPEED OF ORIENTATION

Though somewhat shy and subdued, Chester rapidly adjusted to the test demands and was quick to understand directions. Especially with motor tasks, he was likely to survey the total situation so that few errors occurred. He often looked ahead on the test blank to inquire what was coming next and how the illustrated or covered material (mazes, M-P boxes) would be used. He clarified his progress verbally as he worked.

PLEASURE, DELIGHT AND SATISFACTIONS

Chester was readily stimulated by all the test materials, utilizing them in personal ways for his own satisfaction. Blocks, beads and scissors seemed to offer special pleasure, which he expressed in happy smiles and enthusiastic participation in the tasks presented. Motor tasks were performed in a uniformly superior manner with considerable satisfaction in doing well and in working rapidly. He was delighted with the sound of clattering blocks. He often sang as he worked on the tests, offering for the examiner's approval various little songs he had learned. Chester drew satisfaction from neatness, care and orderliness in his performances, and post-test straightening up. This seemed to be not so much compulsive in quality as an awareness of the value of things and a need to prolong their usefulness. Several times, for example, he commented on the "nice little chairs and table" as he gently and carefully moved them into convenient positions.

REACTION TO DIFFICULTY, FAILURE

With difficulty or failure, Chester was not easily discouraged, and often made repeated efforts even after he had said he did not know an answer (Mutilated Pictures, erasing and correcting reproduction of a square). After stating that he did not know, he sometimes asked for further clarification of directions (Paper-folding). When he was uncertain, he sometimes offered approximations, of the inadequate nature of which he was fully aware. (He suggested that the folded paper, IX-1, would have a circular hole in the center; unable to make change, he offered the response, "lots of money.") He sometimes avoided difficulty by attending to something else (playing with the stopwatch when he could not answer the similarities and differences items) or by temporarily removing himself from the situation (going to the window to see a passing truck when he did not know the rhymes). Early in the test, when he was somewhat shy, or perhaps cautious; in a new situation, he discharged tension by restlessly moving his feet under the table. Late in the test sessions, when test items were realistically difficult, his over-all bodily restlessness increased. Embarrassed giggling, accompanied by slouching in his chair, appeared when failures accumulated toward the end of the test.

ANXIETY

Always comfortable, though mildly shy at first, Chester seemed imbued with the seriousness of living and of the implications of the test. As he encountered difficulty, he breathed rather heavily and we saw that as he met failure, he giggled in an embarrassed, self-conscious manner (copying the diamond, and comprehension at year VII, verbal absurdities and reversing four digits at year IX). Once he flushed as the examiner repeated instructions which he seemed to have failed to understand (covering his eyes while formboards were laid out). Just once, in copying a diamond, did he place his finger in his mouth, as though thoughtfully considering how best to proceed. Toward the end of the test, with difficult items, he slid down in his chair, partially removing himself from embarrassing failure. One always had the feeling that he was aware of and in control of his own behavior and that any temporary setbacks cast only momentary shadows on his self-assurance.

In conclusion we can note that these children had not yet entered school with its rigid limits upon spontaneous solutions to such dilemmas as those in which the intelligence test placed them. Nor had they been taught many of these solutions at home. In fact, their naive surprise, and sometimes reproach to the examiner, that they would be asked to carry out tasks beyond their capacities implies that home demands were usually well within their scope, and that they had been permitted to protest, or to deal actively with the situation in other ways when excessive demands were placed upon them.

5

RESPONDING TO
NEW CHALLENGES
AT A "PARTY"*

The nature of the opportunity and the challenge

THE "PARTY" of the Coping Project was utterly different from any party the children had ever attended before; at the preschool age few of the children had been to any sort of party at all. The situation was also very different from their previous experiences with the research staff. Their tests and examinations had all been conducted individually in the now thoroughly familiar upstairs room of a private home in a typical residential area. But for the party they came to the rustic, and to them strange, Murphy home in a terraced, wooded area at the edge of town, on a bluff above a wide cascading creek. Half a dozen other children were there whom they had never met before. In addition to the hostesses there was one observer for every child, and a

* This chapter is based upon analysis of the party records by Mrs. Pitsa Harto-collis.

camera man who photographed selected segments of the children's activity.

There were four parties at different hours of the same weekend. Each of the "parties" followed the same plan with the successive groups of children: a "hello" period with juice; invitation to try the climb-run-jump board; races; blindfold games; going-down-steps pictures; table activities with clay, beads, and favors; ice cream and cake; balloon play. There were tricycles, large blocks, dolls, and large toys in the open double-garage area. There were some periods for free play and other periods of guided activity which involved specific demands or challenges.

The presence of adults who made specific suggestions at certain times evoked from each child one or another of many kinds of behavior partly dominated by the question of how to deal with one's own autonomy: to defend it, modify it, or surrender it. The children's responses to such invitations seemed to be influenced more by the objective aspects of the equipment or social situation involved in the demand, while behavior in the free play periods took its direction from inner wishes, fears, or individual needs. The periods of freedom at the party, and the variety of opportunities provided by the space, the peer group, the various adults, the range of material things, the sensory, motor and emotional experiences, made it possible for us to watch rather complex coping efforts. These we shall outline later in a discussion of the process of mastery.

There were, then, certain situations which every child had to face: he was introduced into a group of peers and secondarily adults, within a new social and physical setting, with certain opportunities for exploration and certain demands for participation.

There were also situations which seemed to arise only with certain children and to be created by the child's private subjective world. These include occasions which for an individual child contain a threat of making mistakes, of isolation from the group, and the challenge of raising or maintaining self-esteem by exhibiting achievements to the others, by competing vigorously whenever competition was possible.

Although the nature of a situation like the party is partly determined by the available opportunities or difficulties, the child's orientation helps to determine how the situation is going to be experienced—whether as an opportunity for gratification, a challenge (promise of growth), or as a stress, burdened with apprehension.

Our discussion of the party behavior will have a different character from the previous discussion, which was based solely on adult-directed tests and examinations. In an intelligence test situation, each small task is followed by another demand, and this new demand may be easier or harder for the child than the preceding one. This constant change in the character of the stimulus situation together with the unremitting directing presence of the adult prevents the occurrence of spontaneous sequences of behavior which we can now see in the party records.

Children who were "ready to go" typically gulped down their initial large paper cups of juice in a few swallows and made off without asking permission from the adults, taking it for granted that this new world was theirs to enjoy and explore. The more hesitant children by contrast used the initial juice-drinking period as an island of safety; they drank in small, prolonged sips which enormously extended the time during which they could peer over the edges of their paper cups at the surroundings, and at the new children—observing carefully, gradually taking things in. They sorted out the opportunities in terms of what they might like to do, or used up the time while the more active or less hesitant children were energetically trying out the resources of the place. Behind the screens offered by their large juice cups, children like Tommy did not seem uneasy, but rather appeared to take their own time to decide for themselves what they wanted to do. But Darlene appeared awkward and tense even with this protection, as if the lack of direction left her totally at sea and uneasy about what might or might not be the proper thing to do.

After juice some of the hesitant children like Rachel, and Martin whom we shall describe at greater length before long, found other safety spots. From the haven offered by the garage and the toys which it held, they could further postpone commitments to the territory or to the new group of children—they could fend off overtures and demands from adults or children. Donald, however, did not use this protection but merely stood his ground, wide-eyed, looking and looking and looking, longer than did any of the other children, before he finally blossomed into very active participation in the party. It was in the free situations, such as the party, and the Miniature Life Toys play session, that the role of initial orientation, observation, achievement of cognitive mastery before action, and preparation for selectivity, struck us forcibly as basic coping steps when children are not initially clear about the nature, demands, scope, and limits of a situation.

Of this group of children approximately two thirds of the boys and one third of the girls responded to the party setup as an opportunity for spontaneous fun, flexibly moving into the situation and following their own impulses when the coast was clear, cooperating with the request from the adults during the organized phases of the party. One third of the boys were extremely hesitant, slow to warm up, suspicious or anxious, and in one way or another showed difficulty in responding freely to the undirected opportunities. Even these boys found something to do, and either made a safe place for themselves or gradually moved into activities with the others as we shall see from some of the records shortly. About two thirds of the girls were slow to warm up, or even quite inhibited during the free periods of the party and seemed much more at ease during the planned and directed activities except for those which involved some motor risks. Girls like Karen, Jo Anne, Janice, and Cynthia were the exceptions, jumping into the party opportunities almost as freely as the boys.

It is probable that sex differences in getting started at the party reflected differences in home handling. The boys took for granted freedom to roam and explore, whereas the girls did not venture far from the adults as if they were usually expected to stay with mother, to "help" about the house, etc. We also found differences in level of activity, as well as cultural standards of "being a lady"; Sheila's mother offered this advice on several occasions as we started out.

Boys like Ralph, Roddy, Gary, all of whom were active, extremely well-coordinated, and energetic, hardly waited for permission before racing and jumping down the terraces to get to the creek. Teddy was somewhat limited by his greater weight in contrast with the lithe, agile skill of the boys we just mentioned, but after they had all succeeded in climbing a stone wall about a foot higher than their own height they cooperated in giving Teddy a boost so that he could make it too. (Neither he nor they seemed particularly self-conscious about this. He was too heavy to lift his weight up with the help of precarious toe holds on the stone wall. The boost the boys gave him was as matter of fact as that of a parent who recognizes the limitations of a small child who is attempting to do something physically beyond him.) None of the girls leaped and scampered over the territory as did the boys we have just described, but some active girls explored the area freely if less dramatically and made contact with other children and grownups spontaneously. Cynthia and Janice came together with hilarious giggles which seemed to involve some release of tension as well as the delight of discovering a congenial companion.

In contrast to the spontaneity of these children for whom the party was so much fun that they referred to it in the following years as a very happy memory, Martin could not be enthusiastic. Another boy suggested to him an exchange of guns. This approach could be taken as a challenge, an opportunity to make a friend or to develop interpersonal relationships; but for Martin, this was a situation of stress, and was reacted to as such. After this, Martin did not seem very happy, nor did he become more relaxed during the whole party. He was not participating in the activities on his own. Here we see how a given coping response may be instrumental in determining the subsequent reaction. A child unsuccessful in trying to cope with a certain situation might be more eager to seize upon opportunity present in a subsequent situation than a child who found satisfaction. On the other hand after failure he may be more deterred by the fear of another disappointment.

Let us follow a few children into this situation before reviewing further the coping patterns of the group as a whole; here we shall begin with Donald and Martin as they come to the "party."

Sequences in Donald's response to the party*

. . . As I approached Donald's house, he emerged and met me . . . scrubbed-looking (as usual), smiling diffidently and with a quiet, bashful air that nonetheless suggested he was pleased to be coming to the party. He had on a red seersucker shirt imprinted with blue and white circles, and blue jeans. These gave him a more natural look than he'd had in the stiff and formal Sunday school attire he wore to a recent MLT session. But whether his outfit helped to create, or was merely consistent with, an easier and less constrained appearance, one became more aware of the quality of "resonance" in him, i.e., the quality of being tuned to, and in contact with, the environment, rather than walled away behind some isolating barrier. WM asked him some questions on the way to Sheila's house, and he answered readily, although, because of immature speech, his pronunciation at that time was unintelligible to her. BW asked him how old he was, and he promptly held up three fingers, and after a moment, stuck out his thumb also. He turned to inspect her with a bright, bold glance that was at the same time a fixed, unwavering stare. His manner appeared comfortable and amicably curious.

Sheila was called for soon after, and Donald turned his glance on her— the same clear-eyed, open expression that, in its own way, showed a certain readiness for interpersonal exchange. At one point during the trip, when BW admired Sheila's shoes, Donald immediately called attention to his own by a mixture of eager though incomprehensible vocalization, and gestures urging us to look at his feet. He managed to make us understand that the shoes he was wearing were new.

Throughout the remainder of the auto ride, Donald stood on the front seat, with chest propped against the back, and inspecting the two who were sitting in the rear (BW and Sheila). This actively watching, relatively unguarded, and accessible mood lasted until the moment of disembarking from the car. (He had been with one adult he knew, and the two strangers had both been introduced to him one at a time, i.e., in small and manageable doses.)

As soon as he arrived, however, he seemed to contract, pull back into

* From Wilma Miller's record of Donald at the first preschool age party.

himself—not in a sudden or dramatic way, but more as if he had undergone a transformation from "person" into "thing." Still animated, indeed, by the impulse to escape, still "coping" (though apparently feeling utterly helpless to keep at bay a potentially menacing outer-world), he turns himself into a nonresponding, nonreacting object . . . thus perhaps rendering the unmanageable, unpredictable environment powerless to affect or harm him.

What you can't alter or control, you can at least deprive of its power to sting. Automatically, he clung to the low stone wall as he entered the Murphy grounds and made his way to the garage. There he accepted the lemonade that was offered to him, and, gripping it in his right hand, stood so rigidly that he seemed to be locked within a skin-tight prison. Only his eyes roved, first to one side, then back to the other, where they clung for a split-second, to WM's. He swallowed once, fastened his eyes to a point just beyond her, and he may have ground his teeth together very hard, because a muscle at the side of his temple bulged momentarily. Then he stared ahead in a grave, quiet, solemn manner.

A couple of adults had also gathered round, and he was successively (but not insensitively or overwhelmingly) invited to use the climb-run-jump apparatus, asked if he would like to play with some of the toys in the garage, and shown the other children romping on the lawn outside. To each and all of these he remained absolutely, uncompromisingly silent. The group of people eventually dispersed, leaving only Donald and me in the garage. He soon set the lemonade down, almost entirely untouched. Then he turned his head slowly from left to right, eyes stationary and unblinking. So gradually and smoothly did his head turn, that it seemed to pivot with his neck in faultless, mechanical slow motion. His eyes, however, while absolutely quiet, still seemed alive to and registering external impressions.

I now invited him either to play with the toys or to join the other children on the lawn, and Donald, looking over in the direction of the doll house, remarked, "Bobby [his older brother] has a ha-hie house." I made him repeat this at least half a dozen times, but could not fathom what he meant until someone [MS] came by and translated! it as "army" house. Having divulged this bit of information, Donald turned and stared out toward the lawn, his expression that of someone able to receive but not to engage or react to external stimuli, much like a traveler passively watching the scenery slip by his window. In this instance, however, underlying tension was manifest in the infinitesimal curling of the fingers of his right hand (only the third finger hung straight and independent of the others). Then his whole hand fisted slightly, while the fingers of his left hand underwent discrete, tentative little curling movements.

Now I stretched out my own hand to Donald suggesting that he might take me wherever he wished to go, and to whatever he wished to see. He solemnly accepted the offer, and led me, somewhat uncertainly, out of the garage. At this point Brennie came running over, face wreathed in smiles, bearing a rifle which he extended to Donald with both arms. Donald simply took no notice, and walked on, stopping for a while halfway between the garage and the lawn. Now LBM hurried over, and (having previously found

Donald able to use direct physical support at a testing session) smiled and addressing Donald in a warm and merry fashion, scooped him up under one arm and carried him off to the activity area.

Donald, finding himself hitched over LBM's hip, and being borne swiftly toward the area of the party, into closer proximity with the other children and into the center of considerable hurly-hurly, allowed himself to dangle stiffly and expressionlessly, marionette-wise, from the circle of her arm. Once he was set down, he resumed his wooden pose, and again met all invitations to join the other children with the same dumb stare. Seeing that he resisted additional coaxing in this mute and strained fashion, I told him he could look at the toys in the garage if he wanted, or explore any other place he chose.

He moved back into the safety of the garage, and once there, went over to where blocks were stored. For the first time since his arrival, he began to develop a moderately animated expression. He placed a cardboard block in a horizontal position, stood another one on top of that vertically, then added a few smaller blocks, and, as though proceeding in logically successive steps, immediately knocked them over. The second time he stood up three of the cardboard blocks and placed them side by side. Then he stood a small rectangular block in the center of the left most block, and to this he added a triangular block. He knocked this over, saying very clearly, and with a suggestion of a smile, "I push."

Now he erected another structure, using the large blocks only, and alternately putting a vertical block on a horizontal one. This edifice, in some manner un-noted by the observer, toppled over, while Donald said, "Let this fall." Then he set to work rearing an even more elaborate one—three stories tall with a double foundation—saying, "This will work." As he stretched to put the last block in place, he exclaimed delightedly, and with clearly intelligible pronunciation, "Bigger than me," and turned a radiant smile on me. Then, with equal pleasure, he knocked and pushed the whole thing down. Without a pause, he built two more structures and knocked each of these down also.

Almost totally immobilized less than fifteen minutes before, Donald was now full of zestful energy, worked rapidly, effectively, and did not show even the slightest trace of being slowed up in his play by indecisiveness, dreaminess, or other activity-hampering states.

He then kicked and knocked over an endless variety of things at hand. He put a block on top of a toy car, a leaf on top of that, then knocked the leaf off. Then he turned a truck over on its side, put a block on top of it, moved over to the car, stacked three blocks on top of it, and knocked the whole structure over. He took the car again, spanked it as if it were a doll, knocked it upside down, placed a leaf on top of it, then swept the leaf off. He played a little longer in this way, then ran out of the garage.

He veered over into the direction of the stairs (WM had suggested he might like to have the photographer take his picture along with the other children) but then ran past them, turned and ran back into the garage. For five or ten minutes he raced the length of the driveway bordering the steps down to the lower terrace, back and forth, back and forth.

He finally walked with WM to the head of the steps where he grasped the bannister and clung to it. WM was now at the foot trying to entice him down. He told her he was going to walk down backwards and did so, clinging to the railing as he went, then back up again—he did this several times. The last time he descended he added a variation: with left foot planted on one step, he crossed his right foot over till it hit the step beneath, then crossed his left foot over till it reached the step beneath that, and so on till he reached the bottom (always he clung to the railing).

The children were all seated at the table stringing beads and Donald now joined them (probably by invitation). Before beginning the bead-stringing Donald spied a grasshopper which he captured and played with for a while before Sheila, sympathetic to the grasshopper, took it away from him. With the bead-stringing he made appropriate playful sounds and movements. He refused the ice cream saying simply "Me don't want none." When asked if he didn't like ice cream, again a simple reply, "Me do, but me don't want none." He continued to string beads quite happily. When he saw LBM taking pictures he said, "Don't take a picture of me." A few minutes later he called out, "Look at mine!" and displayed his string proudly. Once he glanced at LBM, a bit imperiously, a bit challengingly, as though daring her to take a picture of him.

With the favors Donald quickly said, "Me want," and bent over to inspect them. He watched the others spellbound as they blew their horns and whistles, then chose a serpentine. After his first rather gentle blow he then blew repeatedly, tirelessly. He next joined Brennie (after Brennie had first blown at him) in a play of blowing their favors at each other and at the same time racing up and down the steps. From the moment Donald first blew, the serpentine barely left his mouth—he blew it continuously, excitedly, assertively. They chased each other up and down the steps—then they chased up one stairs over the road and down the other stairs, around the walk (where the party tables were set up) and generally all over. When Donald's whistle became soggy he showed it to WM and was given another. As Donald continued to chase he seemed to have lost all his cautiousness of mounting and descending the steps—his left hand was even swinging free.

He accepted the invitation to try the climb-run-jump apparatus. He climbed up quickly but crept across on all fours. When someone else jumped up and down on the board Donald clung rigidly with some signs of distress showing on his face. When the jumping child stopped he continued creeping gingerly across; only toward the end did he pick up enough courage to stand up, walk, and jump off. Once the ice was broken, he again entered into the activity with zest and taste for repetition. As he approached the middle he would deliberately let himself drop off the side and roll along the ground. The last time he did this the plank came down with him. He was not hurt, nor did he look scared. He said, "Now no one can walk." He helped put the plank up and then turned his attention to the balloons.

He dipped eagerly into the basket and ran with his selection. It slipped away from him, and as he chased after it, it burst with a "bang." At first he seemed a bit startled, then became seized by an all-absorbing purpose—to break balloons. He squeezed, pinched, puckered and prodded their surfaces until he achieved his purpose. "There," he said looking up happily, "Me pop a balloon." With a large and particularly "tough" one he had some difficulty and finally tried sitting on it, but it kept bulging out in different places. With untiring persistence he attacked it with his hands and finally achieved his purpose with this one also. Often he raced another child to a balloon, but when he came out second best he was able to change his goal quickly and search for another one he could explode.

From initial paralysis during the first twenty minutes after his arrival at the party, Donald had emerged as a vigorous energetic participator, tireless until the party broke up.

This pattern of initial immobilization followed by vivid release was also typical of Donald in each exposure to another new situation and another examiner. For the present we can content ourselves with the observation that here Donald shows the tension aroused in a new situation which he handled by: his initial deerlike immobility permitting maximal observation with his wide roving eyes; his resistance to being forced to participate at a more rapid pace than he can manage during his orienting phase; his freedom within a safe area when he finds one after initial orientation and selection of an activity; his fantasies and impulses: I (want to) push (someone?) ; (I might) fall; (if I were bigger, I could manage) "work"; (I can defend myself against the ones) "bigger than me." These fantasies evidently had to do with the question, what might these big boys and grownups do to me? Can I manage these activities?

Martin's way of maintaining safety

Let us now watch Martin,* whose problems of coping with the party were deeper and more complex than Donald's:

Martin, cautious and perhaps more suspicious, made for himself an "island in the garage"; but he was not able to succeed in working through the anxious feelings and aggressive impulses as well as Donald had done. After he focused on his safety spot in the garage he played with the blocks for nearly forty minutes without interruption. He paid no attention to anyone, didn't even once look up at the rush of people coming in—but, standing very stiff and straight, oblivious to the environment, carried on his work. He wore a half bored, half contemptuous expression, although his eyes seemed quite alert.

He repulsed another boy—who uninvited started to help him rebuild his

* Based on record of Martin at the party by Baljeet Malhotra.

structure which had just fallen—by throwing the multicolored plastic ball at the structure in a very aggressive, challenging, showy manner, until the other boy turned away. He then started building again. He waited for LBM to take a picture of it before he knocked it down again—almost falling over it in order to do this.

He stopped building long enough to watch, rather longingly, another boy on a pair of stilts. Then he turned back to the safety of his blocks. He built some more and sat by his tower for a while. He knocked it down and then continued building again. This was repeated several times.

Finally when specifically invited by LBM to the climb-run-jump board with the rest of the children, he joined them reluctantly. He repulsed all overtures of friendliness on the part of the other children.

When asked after the party whether he enjoyed it, Martin replied "Not really." For him, more than any of the other children, the group of new peers evoked feelings of threat and hostile self-protection maneuvers to avoid getting genuinely involved.

Sequences in dealing with challenge

But even though a situation may have elements of actual rejec-tion, it is not always experienced as overwhelmingly stressful; with an optimistic child like Brennie* it may very well constitute an additional challenge:

Brennie ran and picked up his gun lying on the grass. He offered it to Donald who completely ignored him. Brennie then tried offering it to Sheila. Brennie held his gun in both hands and extended it in front of Sheila but she turned her face and walked away. He hurriedly walked up to the side lane of the garage and started shooting like an inspired soldier. After a few shots he joined Sheila in the garage and demonstrated his gun to her. Having thus captured some bit of her attention, Brennie ventured again on his former invitation "You like to play with the guns?" But feminine Sheila walked away without even a reply.

Brennie did not look a bit disconcerted at being refused twice. Instead he knelt before the wooden bench in the garage and used it as a shooting range.

We see that in the case of this child, when his attempt to challenge his peers brought no response at all, when his persistent attempts were ignored, he simply took this as a further challenge to cope with it as such, to try to win a peer's attention, instead of being deterred by the stress.

A new social situation also often involves specific or vaguely an-ticipated "difficulty." But there are children for whom a situation of

* Based on party record on Brennie by Baljeet Malhotra.

difficulty constitutes more of a not unwelcome challenge than a threat. In some cases, a situation can be both threatening and challenging. When two situations overlap in their possible meaning for the individual involved (or for the observer?), the coping devices corresponding to such situations could be described under different categories. Thus a device described as "defining a safe area" used in a "strange new situation" could sometimes be described as "restructuring the situation." The nature of a situation may be defined either in terms of the external reality or on the basis of the inferred subjective experience. Which approach is better to use is an open though not necessarily difficult question to answer. The problem would arise when there is no clear-cut approach possible, as in a situation which involves failure, gratification, criticism, and the like simultaneously. Any one of these conditions can be described objectively, but no one of them needs to correspond to equivalent experience, and vice versa.

Let us return to a detail of the record of Martin:

> When I arrived at the Murphy house for the party Martin was busy building high, narrow structures with big sized cardboard bricks. He paid no attention to anybody, didn't even once look up at the rush of people coming in, but standing very stiff and straight, oblivious to the environment, he carried on his work conscientiously.

Martin's defensive self-isolating stance suggested anxiety in the new situation and the coping device he used is referred to as "restructuring the situation." The child here was actually having difficulty integrating or sharing the experience of coming to a party with the others; he then occupied himself with an activity of his own (building an ambitious structure), and worked on it very conscientiously, oblivious to the environment and the activities of the other children. He restructured the situation to make it appear that this was the important thing for him (building), not the party.

Sometimes a situation involving anxiety-arousing stress at first may, without external interference, develop a more positive quality of challenge just because the child tries effectively to cope with the given stress. Thus we see that any situation (particularly the more complex or ambivalent ones) calls for a sequence or hierarchy of devices. Take, for example, the device of "surveying the situation" which occurred frequently in situations of challenge like the party and the free play with Miniature Life Toys. This surveying often implies "defining a safe area," since in order to be able to survey a given situation, one must have secured first a safe observation point. The ability to survey a situation, that is, to pay attention to the outer environment, presupposes a certain amount of protection of individual serenity, of safe autonomy. Tommy with his hands in his pockets, looking around when he arrived at the party, expressed the sense of such a safe area, making possible his survey of the situation. Darlene sat on a low wall, peering over the edge of her juice cup, while she sipped as slowly as possible, as if to prolong the safe activity.

Kicking or pushing a stone, arranging clothes, etc., would be other examples of "primitive" coping devices serving the purpose of releasing tension while delaying entrance into the party itself. These are more vigorous forms of behavior than we just saw but they are also part of a more self-absorbing search for a safe area before actively surveying the situation so that selection and participation can become possible.

The initial survey of the situation may be followed by an attempt to expand the safe area. In doing that, the child's chances to meet an opportunity for new gratification becomes greater. Thus we see that a situation of potential stress, as at the time of entering the strange new place, may resolve itself into a situation of opportunity or challenge, after the child has tried to cope with the initial stress, in contrast to the sequence we saw with Martin, whose initial restructuring isolated him from the situation instead of giving him an opportunity to survey and move into it.

A situation may also change for the child without any visible change in external reality. This is demonstrated in the record of Tommy.

Greg took Tommy's bead string saying, "You didn't want it, did you?" So Tommy gave it up.

Tommy had responded to apparently the same threat of "deprivation" in a different fashion earlier. The first time he defended his property, but the second time he gave it up without comment. But is the second situation the same for the child concerned? The subjective element of boredom in the second instance may be more crucial than the objective deprivation, present in both instances.

Ways of reacting to the strangeness of the party

Some children seem to have the capacity to react to a situation as a whole, while others react to it piecemeal. Thus for some children the situation as a whole seems to remain strange even when it is no longer new; they may continue to react to the many aspects of a situation with the same original restriction. It seems difficult for them to get over the stress of the strangeness which remains for a long time as various novel aspects arise one after the other.

Brennie was working the trigger of the gun, which made some clicking noises. Vivian blinked slightly, but her facial expressions were neither annoyed nor frightened. Daryl put her hand around Vivian's. Vivian, although she had been at the party for a while, was still reacting to the challenge of her peer with great reservation, no response, as if the situation were still new, not letting herself familiarize herself with it.

As the entire group walked over to the garage the feeling of constraint was still very much present. Inside the garage, Barbie leaned back against AM's bag. Sally stood quietly, sucking in her lower lip and sighed gently.

Children who appear to have the capacity to become familiar with or to catch onto the situation as a whole rather than to master specific parts of it in a piecemeal way familiarize themselves with the situation rather easily. Whether a situation ceases to be strange or not may depend on the capacity of the child initially to grasp the situation as a whole, and also to the readiness of the child to abandon his lonely position as an outsider. It is the children who cannot wholly do this who may attempt to define a stable safe area by staying close to a familiar person or object or activity, or by occupying themselves with some comfort activity. They may expect the environment to come to terms with them; that is, expect the others to approach them rather than seeing the situation as a challenge to their own effort, or trying actively to get into the new situation, to modify it, or to understand it.

Active and passive coping in relation to subjective experiences of challenge or stress

On the basis of what was just described, we can distinguish passive versus active coping devices; the coping device that is shaped by the environment versus the coping device that shapes the environment. In both cases the sense of challenge is present. In some instances of passive methods the challenge is evidently felt like a stress; where active methods are used, the challenge remains exciting. Coping with the challenge then generates energy to meet other challenges.

Sometimes a challenge newly introduced by others may be stressful if it creates a conflict with (and thus threatens) an existing goal in the child such as the one implied in the case of Gordon:

On the bottom of the hill was a small stream. Ronnie suggested "Let's go down the hill." Gordon said, "No." Ronnie, "Yes, let's go down." Ronnie started to lead down but Gordon again said, "No."

When a challenging situation is met by the child with such a "resistance" or a coping device of refusal, the child's autonomy may seem to be threatened. This is especially true of suggestions offered by adults.

Since the photographer was waiting in the yard to take additional pictures, AM now suggested that she and Ronnie go back to the yard where the others were engaged in various activities. To this he responded, "OK, I'm gonna build a house first. I want to build little houses." He had picked up several small geometrical shapes in various colors and laid them on one of the large cardboard blocks which resembled bricks. He set this up to look like a roof on the top of the large blocks. He stayed with this activity only very briefly however and then moved over to examine an additional box of toys. After thus expressing his autonomy he acted on AM's suggestion, saying, "I'll beat you out" [to the yard where the others were playing].

He had to delay long enough to make the cooperative response seem to be an autonomous decision.

Whether a social situation is going to involve a positive challenge or tension-laden stress seems to depend largely on the child, or the child's relation to the situation.

Constructiveness of coping devices

Coping devices oriented to meet a challenge, insofar as they aim at a new balance may be seen as constructive. Coping devices in response to stress, inasmuch as they aim at maintaining an old balance, may be seen as defensive devices.

In general it is easier to see the fact that the child is using coping devices than to be sure about the subjective nature of the situation that elicits the device. Devices are neither specific to situations nor uniformly successful; the same device used in one situation successfully may be quite unsuccessful in another or even the same situation at another time.

A coping device may be defined chiefly in terms of the situation that calls for it. Thus, a child like Martin who, confronted with the stress of a "strange new situation" such as a social gathering, occupied himself with the lonely building of a tower with blocks, was not likely to enjoy his activity or to feel sorry for errors, because the purpose of this activity was simply to shut off the stressful reality. He was not freely using his resources for achievement in its own right; achievement served a defensive role.

The situation was similar with the child who ran to escape danger. The child was not concerned with the competence of his performance; and if he fell down, he was likely to get up and run again, oblivious of any injuries—just as, when Martin chose to occupy himself with the building of a house rather than to participate in the group activity, he mechanically started the reconstruction when his structure fell down.

Complexity of coping

Coping devices may represent behavior of various levels of complexity. The simplest level of behavior would be equivalent to a simple response hardly more complicated than a reflex; for example, "surveying the situation" might begin with a simple startle reaction. Another child confronted with a strange new situation may stand staring at the situation with wide open eyes. As the situation becomes more familiar and less stressful, the process involved in simple orientation is followed in time by real cognitive skill which the child can use more effectively in order to cope with the situation. To illustrate the idea of a hierarchy of coping devices: a superior development from the same cognitive skill of "surveying the situation" is "planning."

Sticking to a safe area in a situation felt as stressful has an aspect of "constriction"; the child does not apparently feel free to move around and simply continues to protect his narrowed definition of the situation. And "negativism" or resistance could be considered to be the counterpart of "constriction" when the situation is primarily one of challenge, rather than threat.

She picked up the musical dog in one hand, the dolly in the other, went and stood in the sun, watching the other children. LBM came over and talked to Patsy for a little while and showed her how the dolly walked. Patsy stood with a frozen face, absolutely no expression registered.

Coping devices may be used in combination, in response to the same situation; for example, surveying while also keeping close to familiar persons; a child may use protection while taking steps toward a more active way of using the opportunity.

Barbie entered the gate with Kathy. She remained silent while Kathy talked on in a friendly way. . . . During these six minutes as far as I could tell from the corner of my eye, Barbie had been standing close to Kathy quietly. Barbie continued to remain silent, standing still, simply waiting for instructions, even though Kathy before and now Sally provided an opposite example. Sally spontaneously and eagerly offered to help LBM take the lemonade cups apart. Sally talked freely, but until now Barbie needed to hold back until she got a more secure feel of the situation. During this time Barbie was silent but not anxious or withdrawn. She was merely holding her own until she found out what was expected of her. She accepted the lemonade when it was offered her and sipped it in a ladylike fashion. She fingered the cup somewhat self-consciously, but on the whole simply did not do very much because she hadn't found out what the permitted possibilities were.

She became absorbed with the cup handle which was pressed into the side and kept working at it until she succeeded in pulling it out. Her cup was half full of lemonade and she was very careful not to spill it in her maneuverings. She continued to sip the lemonade, occasionally looking around at the children and remained rooted to the spot. Her tiny sips of lemonade seemed also to be an expression of an effort to make her behavior as inconspicuous as possible.*
[Subsequently she participated fully in all the activities of the party.]

Sometimes one coping device may be necessary in order to make possible another needed device. For example, a challenge may be coped with by "surveying the situation"; as we have seen, such a coping device requires a certain preparation, courage, or security, which may be made possible by "defining a safe area." In other situations, a child may need to prepare in any of various ways for a coping device in order to be able to make use of the latter.

Sometimes a coping device may be challenged by the environment; for example, a child who is resisting the unknown may be challenged and supported by an adult to give up this attitude and participate, as when an adult reassures the child and points to the good aspects of a party. This may change the situation which now takes on a new aspect, as the child becomes aware that the difficulty to which he had just reacted with resistance was a strange adult whom he is not sure of. All this involves a new kind of stress, and calls for a new coping device.

He simply stood, looking close to tears, and after some delay said, "I don't want to go to the party." Both the mother and AM tried to reassure him, the mother pointing out that he had previously enjoyed the visits, that he had also first been reluctant to go to the pet parade, but later found it most agreeable. . . . For several minutes, his own only response was a sad shaking of the head. Finally, he said with some air of reassuring AM, "I like Mrs. M., but I don't know that other girl," defending his aloofness.

A child may meet a recurring situation with various devices; and vice versa a child may use the same devices in different situations. The choice of the particular device depends sometimes on the results of an earlier use of it; sometimes it is determined by accompanying secondary situations which may orient the child's activity while the primary situation may remain the motivating factor. For example, in a situation involving the threat of "social isolation," a child may decide to turn toward "gratification" or "a curious new situation" (new toy), away from people; or try to impose himself on people or to attract their attention, in order to raise self-esteem or to develop a social relationship; he turns the initially stressful experience of social isola-

* From record by B. Wright.

tion into an "opportunity," and tries to challenge the others; or he may accept the isolation but try to make it constructive by doing something by himself; or he may turn his interest away from the activity of the group.

Sometimes a sequel is secondary to unsuccessful coping devices; such would be the case of the child who, after failing to resist aggression, isolates himself, and becomes uncommunicative.

Then he met Tommy who had another smaller gun; when Tommy saw Martin he suggested an exchange of guns and at once took hold of the gun in Martin's hand. Martin resisted a little but finally released his grip. This encounter almost froze him up, and once again he hid behind the expressionless mask of his face.

To be able to identify the consequences of a coping device might permit us to judge its success or failure in meeting the child's objective. But it is easier to make an inference as to the consequence of such a device than to find unequivocal evidence about the outcome: a feeling of relief may sometimes be inferred from the child's facial expression or subsequent behavior but often it is only the child who could tell.

If the situation is vivid or challenging and leads to successful coping, it seems that vigorous participation and self-esteem would be reinforced. If the situation is experienced as stressful and leads to successful coping, there might be room for more varied sequelae. One child may perseverate with the one successful behavior pattern. Others may be more willing to try something new in the next stressful situation. In any event, focal tension would be reduced and increased comfort would be experienced but it is not necessarily true that reduced tension would transfer to another stressful situation.

PART II ✻✻✻

CRISES

6

AN ACCIDENT

Up to this point we have discussed demands similar to those in ordinary situations—medical examinations or group events which are typically met by young children. In the following two chapters however we shall be dealing with crises: first, an accident in which a child was hurt; second, the sequelae of a severe illness. In both instances the threats experienced by the children involved body damage, pain, and changed relations with both the personal and impersonal environment. The accident is reported in detail by the child's mother.

When one is very young, an accident or operation to a body part involves pain, loss, and possible injury to one's sense of completeness, just as it does to adults. It is also likely to arouse anger and fear about new hospital procedures, perhaps an overwhelming anxiety about "what will happen" or "what will they do to me?" When a small child is hospitalized without mother, as recorded in the movie *A Two-Year-Old Goes to the Hospital*,[1] we see how drastic an experience this can be. Records of disturbed children often contain a history of such traumatic illness or operation experiences, frequently made more over-whelming by the added trauma of separation from the mother.

In the experience to be described, the mother was allowed to stay with the child for much of the surgical work, and being a profession-ally trained person who knew the implications of such experiences for children, she made full notes each day. Her record shows how the child and his mother experienced the accident and its treatment, and the methods used by each of them to handle each phase of the experi-ence. I shall present the record with minimal interpretation, simply organized and edited from the mother's notes, and keeping her report in the first person; I have made no additions and no changes except for condensation, necessary disguise of the professional individuals in-volved, and toward the end some comments.

The accident *

On the afternoon of August 7, Sam, age three years and three months, and a visiting friend Lou, aged six, had been in the tub together. I took Sam out and dressed him and went on into the kitchen, leaving him in his room. Lou was in the bathroom, having closed the door because she wanted "pri-vacy." At ten minutes after six, Sam came running into the kitchen, crying, but not very hard. "Mommy, I hurted my finger." I picked him up, seeing the tip of the finger had come off (just below the base of the nail), covered the wound with Kleenex, and tucked his hand against my chest as I held him. Still carrying him, I went into the bathroom and found the little white bloodless tip, nail still attached, on the floor next to the toilet. Evidently Sam had opened the door while Lou was still in the bathroom and she had slammed it hard catching his left little finger so that the tip was amputated.

At the age of three it seems that Sam was aware of the event and the pain, but not precisely aware that the tip of his finger had come off. In the following account his mother's behavior is consistent with this assumption and she supports the global awareness of "hurt" with-out even saying anything directly to him about the loss of the tip of his finger.

I told Lou to go into Sam's room to get dressed, where her clothes were, since I would have to call her mother to come for her—that I had to take Sam to the hospital. (I kept the fingertip clutched in my left hand until turning it over to the nurse at the hospital.) I took him back to the kitchen, called Lou's mother, then I called my husband and asked him to meet us at the hospital.

After the calls, Lou said "Sam's just a big, big baby anyway." I told her

* Edited, organized, and minimally interpreted by the author on the basis of records by the mother.

he had a right to cry. Sometime along in here Sam asked me, "But why weren't you *with* me?" and I reminded him that he was big enough now so he didn't really want me with him *all* the time. (This is the same question he asked when he fell headfirst into the swimming pool.)

On our way to the elevator after Lou's mother arrived Sam asked to take his "little summer blue blanket" and we went back to his room for it. By this time he was no longer crying, but was patting me on the shoulder saying, "I like you, mommy." (I had previously explained to him that his finger had gotten quite a bad "bump" (his usual term for any kind of injury) and we would have to go to the hospital for a doctor to fix it up.)

On the way to the hospital, Sam was quiet, but not limp. I reminded him about going to the emergency room about four months before for a cut on his head. (Once he had had this injury fixed up there, he was quite proud of himself, and woke up in the middle of the night saying, "I'm *proud* of my Band-aid." He was wearing his "doctor's coat" when he was hurt.) I also reminded him that he used to wave to grandma when she was in the hospital.

There was a little delay getting into the emergency room; the door where I was knocking was no longer used, although the sign was still on it. Upon entering I immediately showed the nurse the severed tip, and the rest of the finger. The doctor—Dr. T—was talking on the phone, inquiring about the treatment for a certain kind of poisoning for a patient sitting in the room; following this he proceeded to care for this other patient. Sam was relaxed and quiet, clinging to me in such a way that he hadn't seen me show the severed tip to the nurse and I don't think that up to this point he actually grasped that the tip was off. Subsequently, through exposure inadvertently to various conversations on the part of doctors or others, he may have realized it—although he continued to refer to it as "growing new skin," which was the explanation supplied by Dr. H. at the beginning. The nurse had offered him a lollypop but he refused it.

Finally, after about ten minutes, I asked the doctor if he didn't think he should start getting a surgeon on call. He came over then, and on seeing the situation said, "Jesus Christ, why didn't you say something to somebody!" I assured him that I had told the nurse, and she reminded him she had spoken to him while he was on the phone. He immediately put the tip in a saline solution, and put in a call for the surgeon on duty.

By this time my husband had arrived, and helped in giving necessary information, etc. He also had the doctor put in a call for our pediatrician, Dr. M. All this time Sam was curled up against me like a little kitten—no crying—not saying a word, but alert to everything.

Dr. T. now insisted that Sam be laid down on the examining table (he always feels much better about any type of treatment if he can sit up) which meant that I had to forcibly hold him there; so he cried bitterly, as much from anger and fright as anything. I just kept telling him that the doctors were helping him. They isolated the finger with sterile dressings, daubed it with something, saying "Ouch, that stuff hurts," after putting in a shot of Novocaine, and they experimented with trying to put on the tip. Somewhere along here Dr. T was talking with someone on the phone, mentioning in his conversation: "This is beyond me—I don't know what to do with it." At this point I felt woozy for the first time and asked for smelling salts. (Twice they couldn't locate the paper cup they had put the finger tip in and thought it had been thrown out.)

The doctors finally decided that Sam would have to be admitted so the work could be done under general anesthesia. A big gauze bandage was put on the finger, which Sam and I jokingly called an "elephant bandage." There was considerable conversation about whether his stomach would have to be pumped since he had had some milk and cookies about 4:00. By this time it was about 7:00. Dr. T now called Dr. S to come to do the job. My husband went around to the admitting office to arrange the details there, and I waited with Sam in the emergency room. He was quite relaxed by that time and fell asleep on my lap.

Then Dr. M called in, checked with me, and talked with Dr. T, cancelling the arrangements with Dr. S (who he explained to me had just finished his internship last year) and arranging to engage Dr. H, who had been the chief of surgery at the hospital until last year. Dr. H was reached almost immediately, and agreed to drive right in from a suburb twenty miles away.

Dr. M, our pediatrician, had also given orders about the admission and various procedures. When I started to take Sam upstairs he woke up and I explained we were going up to the children's room where his cousin Johnny had been (for a hernia operation) a few months before. I also told him Dr. M, whom he knew well, was on his way to the hospital.

Upstairs, the nurse, Miss T, showed us to the ward—a long narrow room with about six cubicles, each with just enough space for a crib (blue), bedside table and chair. There were no other children in the ward at this point but it was obvious that two of the beds were occupied and we talked about the toys the children had in their beds, etc. The nurse was friendly and gay, but not demonstrative or aggressive and made no effort to "take over." She mentioned various procedures that would have to be accomplished—getting him into hospital pajamas, temperature, blood test, urine specimen, and a sedative suppository—but let me actually handle most of these details with Sam. In the meantime, his father was talking with him about the decorations in the room, etc., and Miss T also brought him a rubber 'Bugs Bunny." He made little protest about any of the procedures, except the temperature, which he always resists. A couple of times a volunteer—a sweet lady in a wheel chair—came in to talk with him, told him about the playroom, etc.

About this time I began to talk with him about getting him the big wagon that we'd been planning about for some time. His first comment was, "And I'm going to take Lou and Margie and Roy—I'll share it with everybody."

When all the routines were finished, I put him down in his crib and tucked his blue blanket around him, held his hand and chatted with him. A boy, Pete, about his age, was brought into the ward by his daddy, given a bottle, and his father was "talking" him to sleep. Sam and I played a little game about having to keep his bunny from squeaking so he wouldn't disturb Pete. There were a few questions—"Can I take my bunny home?" (Of course.) "Will we have to stay here all night?" "Will we have to come here every day?" (I answered to both—"We'll have to wait to ask Dr. M.") I made no effort to "prepare" him for anything since I still didn't know what the procedure was to be.

At about 8:45 the nurse, Dr. H, and a couple of other people came into the ward. Miss T told Sam, "I'm going to take you for a trip—choo-choo-choo," as she started to move the crib. Just as we got to the elevator, Dr. T remembered he hadn't checked his chest, so I helped him unfasten the pajamas and explained to Sam what the doctor wanted to do. Sam was quite relaxed, but announced indignantly afterward, "He didn't fasten up my pajamas!" I did this for him and the crib was hustled into the elevator. At the point where the nurse said he'd be coming back to his mommy soon there was a loud howl—the first real protest since we'd been upstairs.

As we turned away from the elevator, Dr. T and another doctor were at the floor desk. My husband asked a number of questions about what was going to be done and the other doctor was dubious about whether the "graft" (tip of the finger) would be used (since so much time had elapsed). He thought perhaps they might do a new "living" graft from the palm of the hand (a "pedical"), and I knew from my hospital experience that this required long months to grow. This really undid me, and the tears came for the first time. We did know by now, however, that Dr. H had cancelled the order for the stomach pumping and the general anesthesia. (Later, on one of the visits to Dr. M's office, I read the medical report from the hospital. It included the information that bits of bone had been taken from the severed tip, and that the nail had been removed before the tip had been re-attached to the stump.)

The nurse suggested that we wait in her private office and arranged for someone to bring us some tea. In a few minutes my husband left to go home and pick up some things—a fresh blouse for me, since I was still wearing the one blood-stained from picking up Sam, Sam's "jello bottle" (a comfort device he still used at times) and a couple of familiar toys for him, including his doctor's kit.

Before he returned, Dr. M, our pediatrician, arrived and visited with me for a few minutes, then went up to the operating room to see how things were going, explaining that he'd come right back and let us know. Soon my husband came back and we went into the kitchen to make the liquid Jello in the bottle. When Dr. M came down again, he said everything was going along fine. Sam was asking questions about why the oxygen tanks were different colors, etc. He said Sam had started to cry when he saw him but he had urged him to be a good boy and he'd get back to mommy sooner. Dr. M then went back up again to the operating room.

About 10:00 a bell rang and they told us that was a signal they were bringing Sam down. We went out into the hall to meet him at the elevator. As they rolled his crib out he looked around in a slightly bewildered way, then reached out his arms and someone said, "You can take him out." He seemed relaxed, and cuddled up against me. Dr. M. told us we could take him home, but Dr. H wanted us to wait so he could speak to us for a minute. While we were waiting, Sam had his Jello bottle. He showed us his new bandage which he said was a "fishy tail" bandage instead of the "elephant bandage" he had had on before. He told us he'd been all wrapped up in cellophane paper, and that Dr. H had put new skin on his finger.

Several people poked their heads in at the door, complimenting him and us on what a fine little boy he was, including the chief nurse from the operating room, who said she had never seen anything like it—the kinds of questions he asked, his interest in everything going on and the fact that when it was all over he had told her "Thank you!"

When Dr. H came in, he told us he thought there would be good results—that Sam would have to come to see him twice a week for several months, that he'd not be allowed to ride his bike or skate, or get the bandage wet, and that I should take him to Dr. M's office for penicillin the following day. We also had to stop off at Miss T's desk for a penicillin shot before we left. She kidded him about giving him a "pinch" and he made little fuss about the injection.

After we got home (about 11 P.M.), Sam seemed quite natural, and played for a little while before he was ready for bed. There was no evidence of any severe trauma.

The following day, we went to Dr. M's office about 10:30 for the penicillin shot. Sam asked to take his blue blanket, which he had never taken to the doctor's office previously. When the shot was administered he said "ouch!" emphatically, but there were no panicky tears. He was generally rather subdued, and much less active than usual throughout the morning. In the afternoon we drove to a special toy store and bought the big red wagon, which pleased him very much.

When we were getting ready to go to Dr. M's office the following morning, August 9, he asked me to take him in the wagon, which I did. He selected a flower from the bouquet in the house to take to Dr. M, and one also for his nurse. Most of the way to Dr. M's office, Sam was lying down in the wagon, with his blue blanket tucked around him. On this occasion he was given "bicillin"—to allow for longer protection over the weekend, and his protest about this was much stronger. (Dr. M had mentioned on a previous occasion that the "bicillin" injection was much more painful.) At this point Dr. M was assuming that no further injections would be necessary unless Dr. H specifically requested them, but Sam was supposed to take Achromycin by mouth for 36 hours beginning the following day.

After we had returned home, Sam said he wanted to take his wagon outdoors and "maybe I'll find Lou and I'll share it with her." There was no time for this, however, since we had to go to Dr. H's office in the afternoon. There Sam was tense, wary, but not panicky. Dr. H greeted him cheerfully, calling him "shrimp" as he had done before, and gave him several little trinkets—a tiny top, whistle, and puzzle. Mrs. A, his nurse-receptionist, was jovial and friendly. Dr. H had me put Sam up on the examining table, under a very bright light, and changed only the outer bandage. Dr. H explained that he would want to see Sam every Tuesday and Friday for a couple of months, at least.

During this entire first phase of the surgical experience, we saw that Sam was sustained by his mother's protection and presence, her promise of future gratification, games, his favorite familiar comfort devices, the Jello bottle and blanket, and other familiar toys, and rewards from the doctors. Both Sam and his mother were fortified by the father's early presence and active help in dealing with the admission procedures, obtaining the support of the familiar pediatrician, as well as his emotional support.

We saw that he was rather subdued and passive, during this phase. Perhaps we can say that he regressed in the service of maintaining control and cooperation. In view of his subsequent progress it seems important that his mother was comfortable in permitting this regression. Let us now go back to the record.

Sam's questions about the hospital experience

Throughout these two days following the accident Sam had had very little to say about any aspect of it. During the latter part of the second afternoon, however, he was very aggressive and provocative toward me—hitting and punching me repeatedly. Finally I asked him whether he was angry at me because he had gotten hurt, and he said emphatically, "Yes." I explained to him that I was very sorry about it, and would have prevented it if I could, but that I just couldn't be with him every minute—that really he doesn't even want me to be—that he likes to be off on his own sometimes—and he gets around so fast and is so busy that I can't possibly be right with him all the time, and once in a long while something happens that is just an accident.

This seemed to open up the gates, and during the rest of the afternoon and evening there were many questions:

"Why did Lou slam the door?" I told him that girls as big as Lou often like to have "privacy" (to be by themselves) when they are getting dressed. "When can I take a bath again?" "Why did they put my crib in a dark place?—I like my crib best of all." (But three years later he expressed strong resentment about the crib—"I was a big boy already"—as well as about having his legs tied down.) "Why did they put me where the bright lights were?" (He has always been very sensitive to bright light.) "Why don't they allow mommies and daddies in the operating room?" "Why was the nurse naughty—the doctor scolded her for bringing him *black* thread to tie up my hand?" "Did they say I was a good boy?" "When will I have to go to the operating room again?" "Will I be able to throw a ball again?" "Was Curious George (a story-book monkey who broke his leg and had to go to a hospital) in that hospital? Did Dr. H take care of *him?*"

During one of these conversations I asked him why he had cried when Dr. M had come into the operating room and he said, "Because I wanted him to go and get you."

The following day, August 10, was taken up primarily with valiant efforts to get him to take the Achromycin by mouth. After every kind of persuasion and approach had failed, he decided quite of his own accord that he would rather have the penicillin shots, and he spontaneously assured me that he wouldn't make any fuss about it. And he didn't. He went to Dr. M's office for five consecutive days for the shots. For several days, there was scarcely any objection at all, except for a plaintive, "tushies (buttocks) are very tender" by about the third day. Almost every day he took a flower for Dr. M and one for the nurse, and also I surreptitiously provided a small surprise for Dr. M to give him (which we had been doing consistently for over two years, as an alternative to the usual lollipop at the times of office appointments or house calls).

On the fourth day, Sam resisted the shot, protesting that he wanted to *"sit down."* Both Dr. M and I thought he was just fed up with the whole business, so Dr. M went ahead and gave him the shot in the buttocks anyway. After we had left the office, when I asked Sam about it he said he had wanted to sit down because his "tushy" was sore, and he thought Dr. M could give him the shot in his arm instead. The following day we mentioned this to Dr. M and he explained to Sam that his arms just weren't big enough yet to make it possible to give him the shots there. Fortunately, no more shots were necessary after this.

During the height of the struggle about taking the Achromycin, the first really strong reaction directed toward Lou was apparent. At a point when I was trying to persuade him to take the medicine, he said, "But *why* did Lou slam the door?" I again explained that she had just wanted to be by herself while she was getting out of the tub and getting dressed, that she had not meant to hurt him and it was just an accident. He then said, "When I get bigger I'm going to *slap* her. When I take her for a ride in my wagon I'm going to slap her." I reminded him that sometimes he had done things that had hurt somebody when he hadn't meant to, and I was sure Lou was sorry it had happened. Sam asked me if Lou's mommy had spanked her, and I said that I thought she had. Sam asked a little gruesomely, "And did she *cry?*"

From August 11 to 13 he asked the following questions among others; these were chiefly concerned with the condition of his finger, changes occurring in the process of healing, attitudes of others towards it, and steps ahead in getting well. We might infer that at this time he was himself aware of not knowing exactly what had happened, or what was going on, and wanting to clarify the real situation. Whatever anxiety was present did not seem to interfere with his pleasure at progress: "When will the new skin grow on my finger? There must be a brown scab on it now—" "Why did Dr. M come up to my room?" "Why did they put an 'elephant' bandage on my hand? [in the emergency room]. They shouldn't put such a big one!" "When didn't I have a sore finger?" "Is there blood in fingers?" "It's not as worse as it used to be—" "Why do somebodies think I have a *broken* finger?" "My finger's getting better every week!" "When will Dr. M not have to give me any more shots at all?" "When can I go in the water again?" "I'm proud of my bandage —why did he put a brown one on this time?"

By September 3 it became apparent that a new nail was beginning to develop—Dr. H saying that about ⅟₃₂ inch was visible, and he began to be quite optimistic about the final result.

Some of the helps to coping during early visits to the doctor

For the first visit to Dr. H, and several thereafter, Sam wanted to wear his white sailor suit—"because it's white like Dr. H's doctor's coat." He also wanted to take his blue blanket, which we rolled up like a sailor's bedroll, with a strap around it. After about the third visit, he didn't even bother to unroll it, and by August 27 he had decided he didn't need to take it any more. Also at the beginning, since he complained about the bright light, I suggested he could use his dark glasses if he wanted to. For the next five or six visits he took the glasses out of my purse each time and put them on, even though usually the bright light was not being used. The same day he gave up taking the blanket, he decided he could get along without the dark glasses, too.

Other ways of mitigating the situation during these weeks included

Supplying him with Stars and Stripes Band-aids from which he made his own selection of one to put on top of the new dressing, and an unlimited supply of Band-aids for use in playing doctor, helped him to make his passive experience an active one in which he could identify with the doctor.

Supplying him with a box of stars to put one each time on his medical chart when he felt he had done "the very best he could," provided tangible rewards for cooperation.

Keeping a bag of chocolate kisses in the refrigerator, which Dr. H and Sam shared when the dressing was finished.

Coloring book and crayons to use while awaiting his turn in the doctor's office. (He also used the crayons for coloring the new adhesive tape on his hand.)

Occasionally Dr. H offered him soda or lollipops—the latter always being refused with the comment—"They aren't good for your teeth." (His uncle was a dentist.)

At a point when Sam seemed discouraged about the prospect of ever getting through with the treatments, I planned with him that when the last bandage was taken off for the last time, we'd get a celebration present—a real engineer's lantern, with a white light and a flashing red light, which he had been wanting for a long time. This was an exciting prospect—he often asked when it was going to be time for the "celebellation" present.

Coping with separation from mother

At the visit to Dr. H's office on August 13, Dr. H removed the entire bandage. I held Sam sitting up, on the examining table, under the bright light. After he had finished treating and dressing the finger with a somewhat smaller bandage which Sam called a "pony tail" bandage, Dr. H mentioned to me that as soon as it was time to start removing the stitches, which he would do gradually over a period of time, he would not want me to be in the room with Sam. He was quite adamant about this, insisting that invariably children get along much better in such situations without their parents, that it would be much easier for him to do his work, and that the successful recovery of the finger was at this point much more important than any possible psychic trauma due to separation from me. He also stressed that it would bewilder Sam to have me be a party to the painful experience, a point which I felt had some validity. I also recognized that it would be inevitable for Sam to sense my tension and uneasiness to some extent, no matter how relaxed I tried to be. I therefore agreed to go along with Dr. H's procedure, but suggested that we establish the pattern immediately at the next visit, rather than having to instigate it at a time of special discomfort.

Before the next office visit I talked with Sam about the fact that sometimes there were things to be done in a doctor's office to help people that doctors and nurses could do faster and better if there was no one else around, and Dr. H had a rule that I had to stay in the next room while Dr. H was taking care of him. (Actually this was an adjoining room which was only partially partitioned off, so that Sam could *see* me sitting there, and most of the time I could see what was going on.) I told him that even though I had to sit in this other room, my loving him would be right with him. During one of these conversations about this I mentioned that this rule was like the rule they had at the hospital, when they don't allow mommies and daddies to be in the operating room. Sam's response to this was "But when I was a little tiny baby and the doctor was helping me out of your tummy, they let you be in the operating room with me then."

In working out the procedure with Dr. H and Mrs. A, it was our consistent practice to make it clear that *I* was the one who had to stay by *myself* —that I was not allowed to go in the examining room until Dr. H said I could. Repeatedly, Dr. H literally "peeled" Sam away from me, with Sam screaming and continuing to protest, "I want my mommy" while he was in the treatment room. There were many instances of differences of opinion between Dr. H and myself, within Sam's hearing, but I always made it clear that I thought he was a wonderful doctor, and I had a lot of respect for his skill.

The appearance of a fantasy helper

As an outgrowth of this separation situation a little elf named "Woody" appeared in Sam's fantasy. On August 22 Sam told me about him—that Woody was with him in the treatment room because I couldn't be there. In the next three weeks Woody turned up in many different situations and served many different purposes—sometimes a companion, sometimes a helper, sometimes a scapegoat:

> Playing doctor, Sam said to me, "You take your medicine and you won't have to have penicillin." "You'll have to stay in the hospital all day and all night." When I asked him how I could manage to do that he told me there was a little elf, "Woody," who would stay with me, just like it was at Dr. H's office—Woody was there with him because I couldn't be with him.
>
> At Dr. H's office he cried hard when leaving me and while soaking his finger—this was one of the times when he had gone to sleep on the bus on the way to the office. Before putting a bandage back on today, Dr. H held up Sam's two little fingers next to each other to compare the length. Later Sam asked about this, "Why did Dr. H *measure* my finger?" "Why is it pink at the tip?"
>
> I asked him why he had made a fuss at the doctor's office, and he said "Because Woody wasn't there—he was on vacation."
>
> Later, when we were making brownies he said, "Woody used to make brownies when he was a little boy—he told me that up at Dr. H's office."

The creation of such a satisfying externalized image to stay with him at the time his mother was forced to leave suggests both the importance of the strong support from mother, and the strength in his own struggle to maintain the feeling of support during her absence. Later he said to his mother one day, "You know Mommy, Woody was really you." *

For the first few weeks, the effect of the forced separation was apparent in various ways—Sam crying out in his sleep, "I want mommy to go with me." Also he was more apprehensive than usual about minor injuries, "Is it bleeding?" *When* is it going to feel better?" The incidence of "doctor play" was even greater than usual—for a while it was taking place in one form or another almost every day or evening, with various aspects of the accident and the treatment experience being reflected.

* Dr. Max Gitelson raised the question why Woody had to be a masculine image and suggested that this active, motoric little boy at a phase of asserting autonomy and initiative needed to identify with the active role which his mother supported rather than with oral aspects of the mother's support; hence Woody as a masculine supporting image.

Sam's further efforts to master the threat by questions and fantasies of retaliation

From August 14 to 22 Sam had asked some questions regarding the custom of shutting bathroom doors, slamming them, and the meaning of this:

(When I was in the bathroom) "Are *you* going to slam the door?" "Is Rod old enough to dress himself? *I'll* slam the door on *him!*" And the next day: "When I get big I'm going to slam the door on little kids!" (Why?) "Because *I'm* going to want to get dressed by myself!" as if he was feeling that "getting big" would bring both the wish for autonomy and the right to defend it aggressively. That this did not resolve the matter is indicated by his question a week later: "*Why* did Lou slam the door?" He added, "I don't like to get hurt." I explained again that she hadn't meant to hurt him, and reminded him that it was getting better every day. He then asked, "And there'll be a new nail?" I assured him that there would be (although at this point this seemed doubtful).

The same day he was apparently thinking about the doctor as aggressive: "Is Dr. H going to make you stay by yourself today?" I explained again that Dr. H could do a beter job if I wasn't there, and that it really was a job just for doctors and nurses to do. I also again assured him that it was getting a little better every day. He then thinks of his own pediatrician, Dr. M, as identifying with him and the progress with his finger: "When the new skin grows on my finger, won't Dr. M be happy?" (I asked him if he would like to stop by at Dr. M's office to show him the new skin when it was all finished, and he said happily that he would.)

He had many feelings about the bandages. "What does Dr. H do with the old bandages? I'd like to have them." "What is Dr. H going to say when he sees this new adhesive tape?" "I'm *proud* of my bandage."

Several days later he again asked, "Is Dr. H going to make you stay by yourself again today?" (Yes, etc.) (This was the first time that Dr. H started to remove a few of the stitches.) He screamed as before, "I want my mommy, I want my mommy," and also—to Dr. H—"You're hurting me, you're hurting me *right now.*" Later, at *my* doctor's office where he has always been quite at ease, and able to stay in the waiting room by himself without any difficulty, he cried hard the entire time I was in the examining room, but this may have been partly because the usual familiar nurse, whom he adores, was on vacation.

Evidently the experience of being alone without mother, in a medical setting, even though nothing was to be done to him, aroused anxiety reinforced by the real pain he had experienced shortly before.

Escape

After he had become somewhat accustomed to the treatment procedure, there were two or three occasions when Sam fell asleep on the bus on the way to the doctor's office. It was hard to tell how much of this was genuine fatigue, and how much an escape mechanism, but in any event it made the handling of the situation more difficult, since he would be clinging and cranky on being awakened, and in the treatment situation he reverted back to the pattern of anxiousness and protest. On one occasion, therefore, I took him to the office in a taxi, explaining that it was on purpose to get him there without going to sleep, so it would be easier for him when we got there. This device worked, and did not have to be repeated.

Questions about the doctor's technique

Beginning on about the fourth office visit, Dr. H began to remove the stitches, a few at a time, and this process continued over several visits. At times, the treatment procedure also included soaking the finger in peroxide, with or without the old bandage, to loosen up the dead sloughing-off skin. Bits of this were removed, and the tip painted with gentian violet. (Later, Dr. H also snipped off bits of new skin in shaping the tip, but since there were no nerve endings as yet this caused practically no discomfort—just a little bewilderment.)

August 23 to September 3 Sam's questions, observations and remarks were often concerned with details of the doctor's technique which he talked over with me:

> At Dr. H's office, Sam showed me where Woody was sitting right beside him on the examining table. This time his crying was much less intense, and he became more interested in finding out why certain things were being done. He also asked why Dr. H had used black string in tying up his hand in the operating room. Dr. H explained that the black sutures show up better against light skin. Sam suggested that he'd like red string better.
>
> While Dr. H was removing a few more stitches, Sam protested vehemently, "Stop, you're hurting me!" Dr. H joked with him about whether he wanted to take the little bits of sutures home and plant a suture tree, but Sam would have none of this. When Dr. H challenged him, "Tell me, am I really hurting you?" Sam said, flatly, "I'd rather tell you that some other day."

In the next days he asked several questions about bandages such as:

> "Why, when Dr. H. changes the bandage, do they call it '*dressing*' the finger?" "Why, every time I cry at Dr. H's office, does Mrs. A (a nurse) come in?" "You know when Dr. H took the bandage off today you could see the pink skin around there!" "Why did they use black thread?" "Why did

Dr. H want me to soak it?" "When will the bandage be off for the last time?"

"When that nice nurse gave me penicillin why did she call it a 'pinch'?" "Why doesn't Dr. M make you stay in the other room when we're at his office?"

Interestingly enough, a few days after the fantasied autonomy that would come when he was "big" (cf. p. 126), Sam began to feel more independent, judging from the following incidents:

> One morning I had washed Sam's blue blanket, explaining to him that it would be dry in time to take it to Dr. H's office. Sam said, "As a matter of fact, I don't really need it." Similarly, after we had started out of the house, I realized I had forgotten his dark glasses, and when I mentioned this to him, he said, "I can get along without them."
>
> A few days later, as he washed his hand himself with the Carbona and alcohol he said, "Now I can do it all by myself! Do you appreciate that? What would Dr. H say?"
>
> At Dr. H's office: Mrs. A arranged for him to soak his finger while waiting for Dr. H to arrive. While he was doing this, Sam was coloring in a coloring book with his right hand . . . "Soon Dr. H is going to have to put up this other part of the examining table—my legs are getting so long!" "Why does Dr. H put the medicine [gentian violet] on it every time?" (To Dr. H.) "You're so gentle!" (When Dr. H was snipping the skin) "Don't do it so hard!" As we were leaving the office, to me, "Mommy, I only fussed one tear!"

While Sam's mother supported his control of tears in this situation, feeling that screaming would make the treatments hard for the medical personnel to manage, she was under ordinary conditions extremely accepting of Sam's outbursts and had as a matter of fact been considered by some observers to be too tolerant of Sam's regressions.

But he still felt the need for some realistic protection:

> "Soon I'll be going to school—you'll have to tell the kids not to bang my hand."

There had been much discussion of "new skin" but Sam was aware that bone was involved:

> "When does the *bone* grow back?" "Do animal doctors have pictures of animal bones and muscles in their offices?"

Managing the precautions against further injury or infection

For about the first two weeks, the dressing included a small soft metal splint around the tip of the finger, which was then covered by a tubular knit bandage slipped on over a metal device which was then removed. Sam was fascinated with the mechanics of this procedure, and tried in various ways to imitate it at home.

When the metal splint was no longer used, the only covering was the initial gauze bandage, and the layered tubular bandage, which was sometimes white and sometimes brown. This was anchored by an adhesive strip around the palm of the hand. This latter part we sometimes had to change at home in between the office visits.

Since there was only this minimal covering (in order to provide for maximum circulation) it was necessary to exercise considerable precaution against the finger's getting bumped or wet. In regard to the first, Sam developed a kind of instinctive self-protection—even to the extent of being able to turn somersaults using only his right hand for support—his left hand being tucked behind his back. I tried to avoid having to caution him except when absolutely necessary, which meant a certain amount of environmental management—not getting involved in situations which would inevitably be too hazardous, but substituting activities which were equally inviting—such as trips to Central Park, ferry boat rides, etc.

In regard to keeping the bandage dry, I found a plastic mitten from last winter, from which I removed the flannel lining, and for fifteen or twenty minutes at a time he wore this in order to engage in some of his favorite activities—painting the fences in the park with water, playing in the bathtub, finger-painting, etc. However, the length of time of wearing it had to be carefully limited in order to avoid having his hand get wet from perspiration, thus causing maceration of the tip, and on very hot days it could not be worn at all. He was cooperative about this, almost always remembering to come and ask me for the glove when he wanted to do something requiring it. On one very hot day, when we had gone with friends on an outing to Lake Sebago, he let me hold his hand for three-quarters of an hour, so he could play freely with his right hand at the edge of the lake, even up to his knees in the water, with his friends. He also soon became very constructively involved in the home care of the finger—cleaning the area free from adhesive tape with Carbona, washing the whole hand with alcohol, and helping to change the adhesive tape.

Coping with friends' curiosity

One of the complicating factors was the frequency of comments and questions regarding the bandaged hand by neighbors, friends, even total strangers and casual passersby. "What happened to your hand?" "Did you break your finger?" "What did you do to yourself, sonny?" I usually tried to pass these off as casually as possible, saying there had been an accident, but that the finger was getting better all the time. Often Sam would seem to be ignoring the inquiries, or would just "clam up" completely. The most distressing situation occurred with a four-year-old acquaintance who was extremely persistent—asking one question after another, ending with "But is it OFF?" Whereupon I suggested that he feel it himself, which Sam willingly let him do. On

September 14, when a friend of mine asked him about it, he spat at her. As far as I can recall, the first time he gave a direct answer to such an inquiry was on September 18, about six weeks after the accident, when a waiter in a restaurant asked him what had happened and he said, "Lou banged the door on it."

During the early weeks, Lou's mother and I agreed that it would be best for Lou if the children were not together much, in order to avoid having Lou too constantly aware of the condition. Their relationship had been quite recent, so it was not awkward to do this. With other people generally, he has been quite ready and proud to display his little new finger. It is still about $\frac{1}{16}$ of an inch shorter than the right finger, but this is scarcely noticeable.

On October 14 he met Lou for the first time after the bandage was off; she was on her way home from school. After mutual greetings, Sam held up his finger and showed it to her, without saying anything. She made no comment then but a moment later asked him, "Do you *like* me?" He replied, "I don't like the thing you do to me." I assured her that we all loved her, gave her a big hug, and swung her around. She picked up Sam, gave him a big hug, and a big swing around. For about five minutes then, they went through this same routine—Sam would run off about fifteen yards, turn around and rush back, and she would pick him up with a swinging hug.

Factors in Sam's coping with the accident and the hospital experiences

Sam's mother noted several factors in Sam's orientation to the hospital experience which helped him, in addition to "Woody":

His own recognition that this injury was something that needed special help.

His basic confidence in people generally.

His confidence in Dr. M. (He had finally overcome his infantile panic regarding check-ups—no more tears but a loud "ouch" instead for shots.) Also the fact that Dr. M. had always been utterly frank with him, never telling him something wouldn't hurt when it did, and had always welcomed my participation.

His familiarity with the hospital and with medical techniques: first, his own previous experience in the emergency room, and awareness of Johnny and grandma having been in the same hospital. (Also possibly the fact of my having been in a hospital last spring—although not the same one.)

His familiarity with the story of "Curious George Takes a Job" in which a monkey breaks his leg and has to be taken to the hospital.

His familiarity with the experience of a four-year-old friend—Robbie, who had a tonsillectomy last spring—which included several readings of Robbie's book about "going to the hospital."

His thorough assimilation of and familiarity with many procedures and accoutrements of the medical profession through playing "doctor and nurse" since the age of two, including the use of hypodermics, stethoscope, masks, white coat and hat, etc.

Previous reactions to body intrusions, injections, pain etc.

While the factors mentioned above were helping Sam, other experiences contributed both anxiety and ways of managing it:

His reactions to injuries and attitude towards treatment, and manipulations of his body have had a long history; Sam has had "mixed feelings" for a long time about personal attention involving contact with his body; buying shoes, haircuts, treatment for scratches or bumps, medical checkups, even face washing! When he's been upset and unhappy or uncomfortable and he has been crying, he has often said, "Wipe my tears." But when crying from frustration or anger he has often been fiercely independent, saying, "Leave my tears alone."

He didn't need any haircutting till he was almost two. At that point he was so resistant and fearful that I sat in the barber chair and held him on my lap. He didn't fight it, but was stiff with uneasiness. This same procedure was necessary for at least the next two haircuts, although he was more relaxed each time, finally deciding that the clippers "tickle"; and by the time he was three, he actually enjoyed the experience, telling the barber just what color of "smelly stuff" he wanted, and spontaneously giving him a kiss when he was through. Although there was from a very early age an unusual sensitivity to newness in environment (physical and human beings) there was also a noticeable lack of specific fears, and an exuberant use of many new experiences—getting acquainted with animals (putting his whole hand in the mouth of a calf, at two and one-quarter); relishing climbing, jumping off steps, or into the pool to his father's arms.

For as far back as he was able to talk—twenty to twenty-four months—he usually refused, or tried to refuse, any treatment for scratches or injuries, insisting, "I want it to get well by itself." For bumps, he used to say, "Put a little water on it," but we haven't heard this recently.

During the weeks before he was two, he had repeated attacks of sore throat, with high temperature, for which penicillin was consistently given. At one time his panic reached the point where he used to scream whenever the doorbell rang, or start crying two or three blocks before we got to the doctor's office. But once the injection was over, he has always immediately relaxed and has been friendly and affectionate with the doctor. (I have always provided a little toy for Dr. M. to give him.) I remember vividly once, before he was two, when as we accompanied Dr. M. out into the hall, Sam gave him a kiss, then literally pushed him into the elevator.

It has never been possible to give him any medicine by mouth no matter how tastefully flavored or disguised. As a corollary to this, we had practically no problem of his putting inedible things into his mouth. As a young baby he would spit out anything the least bit unfamiliar.

Sam was an infant of high sensitivity and alertness, intense affective response, and strong autonomy. At three months he was observed by LBM to be uncomfortable in a strange environment even when his consistently supportive mother was present. His excellent coordination made it possible for him to control (pushing away, avoiding, etc.) unpleasant or unwanted stimulation very early.

Once during the winter before he was two years old, I tried in desperation to give him forcibly some cherry-flavored Achromycin. This resulted in nightmares—"No, mommy, no, no!" until we spent fifteen minutes one midnight dumping the medicine and washing out the medicine bottle with great flourish.

On the occasions when something painful has bothered him, however, like a splinter in his finger, or something stuck between his teeth, he has come voluntarily for help. Evidently Sam had worked through many anxieties regarding threats to his body before the accident and this fortified him at this time.

We can now review further reports of his experience to round out other aspects of his coping efforts and his mother's ways of helping.

Mastery through his relation to his doctor

Dr. H.'s technique of requiring Sam's mother to stay outside probably provided a better chance to develop a relationship between the doctor and the child than would have been possible if Sam's mother had been present throughout. This was reflected both in Sam's remarks to the doctor at the office and in his comments and questions about the doctor at home, late in August and early in September:

"What is Dr. H going to say when he sees this new adhesive tape?" "I'm *proud* of my bandage." At Dr. H's office: Mrs. A arranged for him to soak his finger while waiting for Dr. H to arrive. While he was doing this, Sam was coloring in a coloring book with his right hand. . . ." Soon Dr. H is going to have to put up this other part of the examining table—my legs are getting so long!"

At Dr. H's office (to Dr. H) "You're so gentle!" (In connection with the snipping of the skin) "Don't do it so hard!" "One day I made a little river down the examining table with the peroxide. Did you like that, Dr. H?"

"Why did Dr. H say, if you see me running down the hall you should stop me?" "Why does Dr. H always call me 'shrimp'?"

As a result of his increased interest in Dr. H., he may have felt some conflict regarding loyalty to his pediatrician, Dr. M.:

"Dr. M just *watched* me in the operating room—he didn't take care of me." (I explained to him that the fixing of his finger had had to be done by a surgeon, and that Dr. M had called the best one he knew.) Later he said, "Dr. M was just watching me, not taking care of me—why not? Dr. H is bigger than Dr. M!" "Why did M send for Dr. H? Why isn't Dr. *M* a surgeon?" During the night, Sam apparently dreamed about Dr. M since he asked, in a half-awake state, "Is Dr. M going to bring me a surprise? You said he was coming."

As it developed, this relationship with Dr. H. meant so much to Sam that as the time of termination of treatment approached Sam wanted assurance of the possibility of some visits, to overcome his distress at separation from his doctor:

"When I'm all through at Dr. H's can I go up just for a visit?" At this same period he made several comments about Dr. H's good qualities: "Dr. H is a very sweet doctor—he takes those stitches out very fast, and very gently."

One day at Dr. H's office, while we were in the waiting room, there was a small baby being taken care of in the treatment room. Sam heard the baby crying, and saw the mother in a distant room; he commented about this saying, "I guess Dr. H understands that I like you—that's why he lets you stay in the room next to me." Another day he asked *"What* did Dr. H use to be?" (chief surgeon) "Why?" (Because he is such a good surgeon, don't you think so?) *"Yes,* he took those stitches out so gently."

We have seen that during the entire two months memories of various incidental aspects of the accident and of the hospital procedures came back which Sam wanted to clarify or check by asking questions; his ability to express precise questions and to assimilate answers evidently continued to contribute much to his capacity to master the experience. After the development of a more direct relation with his doctor, many of the questions and thoughts pertained to him:

"Does Dr. H like me to put on these Stars and Stripes Band-aids?" "That's what makes my finger grow so fast—those plastic ones just protect you slow—Stars and Stripes go very fast—twenty miles an hour!" "When Dr. H tied up my hand that dark string *hurt*—that's why I wanted to know why they used *dark* string. What did Dr. H say about it?" "Some day I'm going to take Dr. H a present." "Why did Dr. H use to put purple medicine on my finger?" *"What* was Dr. H?" (chief surgeon) "Chief of *everything?—All* the floors?" "Dr. H is a very good surgeon—very fast taking out stitches— some surgeons are very slow."

In talking with someone on the phone, I mentioned something about someone having been lonesome. Sam commented parenthetically, "I was lonesome in the operating room."

"Why did we go to the emergency room first?" "Why do doctors put new skin on sore fingers? That's just temporary new skin; then the real new skin grows under the brown scab." "Why did the doctor [in the emergency room] dab the whole part of my hand with medicine?" "Why did they take my tem-

perature *before* they took me to the operating room?" "When did I have to
have penicillin for my finger—when it was *bleeding?*" "Why did Dr. M wear
a *green* coat in the operating room?"

He also ruminated about his mother's feeling about the accident
and his recovery:

"Were you unhappy when I hurted my finger? Did you like to stay in
the room by yourself?" On the playground, when a four-year-old boy wouldn't
get out of Sam's wagon, Sam bit him quite hard on the nose. When I scolded
him for this, he asked, "When I got my finger pinched, did you feel badly?"
At another time he asked, "When you saw the blood coming from my finger,
were you unhappy?" "Are you *proud* of my new nail?" (Of course, and I'm
proud of how good you've been about doing everything the doctor told you
to.) "Is that why the nurse came down from the operating room to talk to
you?" "Why did you say, 'Lou, go in my room and get dressed'?"

In contrast to his earlier identification with what he felt was Lou's
aggression, he began in October to think of other solutions:

"Why didn't Lou want me where she was?" "Next time I'll just knock
loudly on the door."

Use of play and reversal of roles

For the first weeks Sam was preoccupied with the reality aspects
of the experience, but by the end of a week he began to play with various aspects of the experience—playing doctor, first being doctor to "Mr.
Bear" then reversing roles more boldly as he gave his mother penicillin
shots, playing that she would have to stay in the hospital all day and
all night, as we saw above:

(Playing doctor) "Mr. Bear won't take his medicine—he'll have to have
penicillin. He has a fever—he has to stay in the hospital all night—the sailor
has to wait for the doctor—Mr. Bear was here first and he has a fever!" (He
handed out masks for both my husband and me to wear, and in response to
question, said that six doctors and one nurse in the operating room had worn
them.)

(Playing doctor) Saying to me, "You take your medicine and you won't
have to have penicillin." "You'll have to stay in the hospital all day and all
night." When I asked him how I could manage to do that he told me there
was a little elf, "Woody," who would stay with me, just like it was at Dr. H's
office—Woody was there with him because I couldn't be with him.

This continued, with fantasy approximating the details of his reality experience more closely as he bandaged his mother's fingers, and
"sewed" up his father's fingers:

(A month after the accident) In the evening, while he was playing doctor, Sam used me as a patient and bandaged up two of my fingers, fastening on bits of Kleenex with adhesive tape, then snipping off pieces from it. "You like that bandage? How is your finger? Now I have to put on a finger lid."

Later, playing doctor, he asked if he could use a big spool of black thread for operating room thread. Given permission he took it over where my husband was sitting, and in an elaborate fashion tied his hand around and around with the black thread, asking him, "Does this hurt?"

He could also use fantasy to take his doctor-role into the hospital on a day when he had not wanted to go:

"Do we have to go to Dr. H's today?" (Yes.) "I don't want to." (Any special reason?) "No, do I have to go to the operating room?" (No, no more.) "I don't like to be in the operating room by myself." I recognized that he felt this way, and went through the usual explanation of why it had had to be that way. He went on then to other questions—"What's in those little green jars?" (at Dr. H's office) "Why does Dr. H have two garbage cans?"

He decided he wanted to wear his doctor's coat to Dr. H's office, and was pleased and proud about all the attention he received in doing so. There was no fussing at all—he chatted with Dr. H about Woody being there, and asked him the questions he had asked me previously, about the jars and garbage cans.

"That's Mr. Bear's sore paw. I'm going to put a new Band-aid on it. Can I throw this one away? Mr. Bear wants the other kind."

And in October, after he had started nursery school, he used fantasy to work through some residues of feelings about medical treatment:

He made a clay "bandage," which he put first on his own finger, then on my finger, then took it off and smashed it.

Realistic participation and self-help

His mother and the nurse allowed room for his interest in active participation in the treatment procedures:

(Washing his hand himself with the Carbona and alcohol.) "Now I can do it all by myself! Do you appreciate that? What would Dr. H say?"

At Dr. H's office—there was a little fussing this time. I had taken him in a taxi so he wouldn't go to sleep on the way. Dr. H had been delayed, and Mrs. A had put Sam up on the examining table and started soaking his finger while waiting for Dr. H to arrive. Sam was quite pleased that she let him cut off the old adhesive tape himself.

One day Dr. H again snipped a little of the new skin in shaping the tip, and Sam made practically no complaint at all. Dr. H explained that there were no nerve endings in the new flesh as yet. He felt that excellent progress had been made. Getting ready to put a new Band-aid on Sam's finger, I let him snip off the end of the wrapper (with a small pair of real bandage scissors which he has had in his doctor's kit for a long time), "I cut it open—wasn't that wonderful!"

But his mother also had to set limits to some of his efforts to manage for himself:

Dr. H said there was only about 1/8 inch more for the finger to grow, and he put on only a small round Band-aid, which I was to change as often as needed. He said there was no reason to observe any precautions any more— that the little Band-aid could be changed as often as it got wet or dirty, and that it would be quite all right for him to be in nursery school. From this point on, the office appointments would be only once a week, and in another two weeks or so he would be discharged.

Shortly after we returned home, the house seemed very quiet, and looking for Sam, I found him in the big bedroom, industriously trying to change the Band-aid, and snip off the corners of it himself. I explained to him quite firmly that this was a job just for grownups, and he agreed not to do it again.

When I saw him fiddling with the Band-aid, he hastily assured me, "That time I was just *checking* my bandage."

Defense mechanisms

We have seen a variety of defensive operations carried out by both Sam and his mother, many of which helped him to tolerate and to work through this stressful experience. Initial hiding or glossing over the actual loss of part of the finger implies denial. Here we are reminded of the adaptive use of denial by severely burned patients studied by David Hamburg.[2] Temporary denial can serve to reduce the size of what has to be faced, until some aspects of the reality have been sufficiently modified to make the actuality bearable.

Some of Sam's questioning may be seen as a tension-release device, substituting for action which was restricted; however we should not lose sight of the direct contributions to cognitive mastery resulting from many of his questions.

What is most important is the fact that Sam's combinations of direct coping devices and defense mechanisms supported his cooperation with the necessary and often painful treatment he had to bear. Whether another three-year-old boy could have managed with less elaborate efforts is hardly relevant to Sam's approach. He evolved his own combination of ways of managing the stress.

We have seen a number of instances where Sam's turning from a passive to an active role took the form of turning his experience of being a victim into fantasies of being the aggressor: "Next time Lou

slams the door I'll just give her a great big pinch!" But as healing progressed the theme of retaliation changed to an attitude of prevention:
"Soon I'll be going to school—you'll have to tell the kids not to bang
my hand." At the elevator, as we were seeing someone off, "Did he
close that door slowly? I wouldn't want him to knock off that little new
nail!" "I'll never get Lou angry again. I would just knock on the door
as loud as I could so she wouldn't knock off that little new nail."

Evidences of the trauma, limited as it was in comparison with
what it might have been, came out indirectly through displacements:
at times Sam tended to avoid certain associations with his injury such
as a hospital not his own.

Passing another hospital, Sam said, "Let's get out of the way of this hospital." Nearby, however, was his hospital, and when I asked him if he'd like
to see the room where he had been, from the outside, he was quite interested, and intrigued with the effort to locate the room.

When the tip of the wing of a small airplane broke off, Sam was very
upset, quite out of proportion to his usual reaction in such a situation, crying brokenheartedly, and trying desperately to find it "So you can put it on
with Duco." It just couldn't be found. I told him it wasn't like his finger,
that this really didn't matter much, that the airplane could get along without
it. He decided then, "Maybe Woody can find it."

The feelings of mastery, control and progress

More conspicuously, he did not avoid situations which might lead
to an accident or because of association with the experiences connected
with it might have been expected to stir up anxiety:

At Central Park, Sam was in the wagon, Mark was pulling and Robbie
was pushing. Going too fast around a downhill curve, the wagon tipped and
Sam fell out on his head, getting quite a scrape on his forehead. His first
reaction was an anxious inquiry, "Is there any blood?" "When will it stop
hurting?" Within a few minutes, however, he was boasting (with a little sales
talk having been introduced), "I turned a somersault right out of the wagon,"
and suggesting, "I should have given Mark a ticket for speeding," (although
he was the one who had urged Mark to go faster).

Tonsillitis: he was again given penicillin shots and did very little fussing.

Two months after the accident, when Granddaddy was in the bathroom,
Sam started down the hall after him. I suggested that he'd better not disturb
him, and Sam said, "I'll just knock on the door—that wouldn't make Granddaddy slam the door on my finger."

Sam had made so little fuss during the initial visit to the hospital
that doctors and nurses had commented on how well he had done.
Later experiences were more painful and more disturbing; he ex-

pressed his feelings of distress vigorously at times, but also kept a goal of control and a self-image of one who can master crying. Here we shall review in sequence examples, some of which were quoted in other contexts above:

"Is Dr. H going to make you stay by yourself again today?" (Yes, etc.) (This was the first time that Dr. H started to remove a few of the stitches.) He screamed, "I want my mommy, I want my mommy," and also—to Dr. H— "You're hurting me, you're hurting me right now."

At Dr. H's office, Sam showed me where Woody was sitting right beside him on the examining table. This time his crying was much less intense, and he became more interested in finding out why certain things were being done. He also asked why Dr. H had used black string in tying up his hand in the operating room. Dr. H explained that the black sutures show up better against light skin. Sam suggested that he'd like red string better.

"Do we have to go to Dr. H today?" (No, tomorrow—why, would you like to go today?) "Yes, I don't cry any more!"

"Did Dr. M come down from the operating room and tell you what a wonderful little boy I was?"

But his image of self-control and self-esteem related to it did not interfere with a clear and realistic awareness of his negative feelings— and relief that the painful process was gradually coming to a conclusion (a month after the accident):

"Do I have to go to Dr. H's today?" (No, not till Friday.) I asked whether he was glad he didn't have to go and he said, "Yes," in a half-hearted way. I suggested that maybe in a way he had begun to sort of like going, and he said, "I do, but I'm glad when I don't have to!"

Triumph and pride

His delight at progress was whole-hearted, and spontaneous, apparently unshadowed by anxiety about the experience as a whole.

"My finger's getting better every week!"

When it was time for Sam to go in, he pranced into the office and jumped up on the examining table with alacrity. Dr. H mentioned that we could now leave the Band-aid off entirely at night. That night Sam woke up from a sound sleep, sat up in bed and said, "See my little new nail!"

Part of the dark, gentian violet-colored tip fell off. Sam was quite elated about this. "The temporary skin is gone—now it's just the permanent new skin!"

The last bit of dark spot fell off. "It's brand new!" It's just as good as new! We won't have to go to Dr. H any more!"

The last visit to Dr. H was on October 4; there were to be no more Band-aids; instructions were given regarding using an emery board to keep the nail smooth, and a little cold cream at night to soften it. Also we were asked to return in six months "just for a visit." We were advised to have him "practice" on a toy piano to exercise the finger. At the earliest opportunity, we went to get the "real engineer's lantern" which we had planned some time before as a "celebellation" present when the last bandage was off. On several occasions subsequently, when someone admired the lantern, Sam would hold up his finger proudly.

For the finger itself the episode was finished. When I saw Sam four months after the accident he seemed unconscious of any difference in his fingers, but showed me the remade finger casually at his mother's request.

However, when he started nursery school several weeks late, he required his mother's presence for several weeks, probably longer than would otherwise be necessary—suggesting that some persistence of separation anxiety was involved. The likelihood that this was anxiety about separation from the mother-as-protector, not mother chiefly as love-object, is indicated by the fact that at the time of permitting his mother to leave him at school he insisted on wearing his holster and gun every day.

At the age of five when telling me about his kindergarten "gang" he mentioned a big one, a wise one, a strong one, a fast one, a silly one; "and I'm the brave one." Many other experiences undoubtedly contributed to a self-image centered on courage, but the success of everyone involved in this crucial event in helping him to master a potentially disturbing experience probably played a major role in helping him become a "brave" boy. His mother reported that before the accident he met challenges eagerly: "It's my birthday, that's why I can climb so high!"

Some aftermaths

In 1958 Sam's father became suddenly very ill while the family was on vacation in a somewhat isolated vacation area. At the age of five Sam had to be left alone at a motel to play around under the casual supervision of strangers, while his mother spent long hours at the hospital necessitated by the shortage of nurses and the nature of the father's illness and needs. After a few days, the entire family was suddenly removed to a large city two hundred miles distant, to provide more adequate medical care for the father. Relatives joined them to help in the total situation. Under these strange conditions Sam was understandably anxious on arrival at the new hospital at letting his mother go; he clung to his mother, angrily demanding that she stay with him. After his mother explained to him the necessity of seeing the doctors, he sullenly at first, then more positively, accepted his aunt. At night in the strange hotel, since again it was necessary for his mother to stay with his now paralyzed, mute father, Sam permitted his aunt to sleep in his mother's bed, after protests that it was not fair for mother to leave him so long. Huddled in a heap with several teddies, refusing all routines, help, comfort, or other physical contact from his aunt, he could not go to sleep until, after some hours of stories, he dropped off to sleep exhausted. Every couple of hours he woke crying, but relaxed and slept again after his aunt told him she knew he needed to cry, it was frightening to have his father so sick, and to have his mother away so long. Once when he woke crying and his aunt asked whether he wanted her to be close enough to hold his hand, he said concisely, "Stick around, but not too close."

In the morning he responded to suggestions for a boat ride, drawing pictures—for which his ideas were prolific—and for hamburgers at lunch. Gradually through the next days he accepted more comfort, while continuing to protect his right to a share of his mother, which he enjoyed as soon as she was able to leave the hospital. The periods of sleep at night grew longer, although even at the end of a week he still wakened crying.

Despite the fact that during the episode he appeared to enjoy the activities planned by his aunt and other relatives, months after his father recovered and the family returned home he complained angrily about having to stay with his aunt at that time.

Obviously here are multiple elements—a deeply anxious disturbing situation for all members of the family, adults and child alike; Sam at first, still close to his mother, needing her, and doubtless involved in the usual five-year-old rivalry with his father, the more acute because of the lack of siblings. Other ripples we can guess at, from his own hospital experiences two years earlier.

In 1960, when Sam, now six years old, was visiting some friends, he accidentally pushed one of them, a boy also named Sam (T.), as they roughhoused in a double-decker bed. His friend fell on the floor, receiving a cut that required a trip to the emergency room of the hospital. Sam T.'s mother completely accepted the fact that it was an accident and unintentional on Sam's part.

Sam T. was very proud of his stitches, "and there was some kidding around about "The Stitch Club"; another boy in their class had had to have stitches for his forehead.

Sam's mother's report went on:

In talking about this, Sam asked me how many stitches *he* had had for his finger—I told him I didn't know exactly—but there must have been at least twelve or fifteen. He said exuberantly, "Boy—I guess I still hold the record for stitches."

At bedtime Sam seemed thoughtful and preoccupied; soon he was telling (me) about the incident in great detail. He mentioned that he had bumped his head too, but it hadn't amounted to much. Franny had taken Sam T. to the bathroom and Sam had thought at first that Sam T. had just gotten a bump, too. When Franny talked about having to go to the doctor, and getting stitches—Sam was worried about how Franny and Sam T. were feeling about *him*. I said they seemed to understand that he hadn't meant for Sam to get hurt—and Sam assured me they were just playing. I said maybe now he understood better that Lou hadn't really meant to hurt him, either (when his finger was caught in the door at three), and he said, "Yeah—" (thoughtfully).

Later when I was cutting his nails he asked how old he had been when his finger had been hurt. As we talked about it, the subject of his feelings about Lou came up; I said something about anybody naturally feeling angry about being hurt, and he said "The trouble is when something like that happens when you're *small*, it's so much *harder* to understand that it wasn't anybody's fault." I agreed with this, and we talked about how most anybody naturally feels somebody—or something—is to blame, like the time (when he was four) when we were visiting and he bumped his head hard on the coffee table—and both the little girl and her mother "spanked" the coffee table. I think there was some element in his remark of feeling a contrast between his feelings about Lou—and the total lack of any hostile feelings towards him from Sam T. regarding his accident.

Sam was tremendously set up by the fact that his two bottom teeth were finally loosening—he was about the last one in his class to lose them and he'd been a little troubled about the delay. But he was a little uncertain about whether he wanted to put them under his pillow when they did come out—he had understood that the tooth disappears when the dime is put there "And I'd like to save *my* teeth for souvenirs!"

Later, Sam's mother reported that his reactions to actual loss of his first tooth were complex.

He felt proud to be able to finally join the club of those who were losing their baby teeth, but he was anxious about the prospect that it would disappear from under his pillow when the "Blue Fairy" left the dime. So instead, he carefully put it in a jewel box, putting this inside a "strong box," and putting this inside his metal combination safe. The next night, wanting to get it out to show the baby sitter, there was real *panic;* he *screamed* when it wasn't there (having forgotten he had already taken out the box earlier). After it was found, we talked a little about how baby teeth are *supposed* to come out, so that new teeth can come in just naturally. His response was primarily in terms of "how much is 32 times 10—$3.20, *right?*"

Here we infer that the repression of the anxiety or concern about loss of a body part in connection with his little finger, loosened by memories stirred by the accident to his friend, along with conflicts about his anger to the little girl who slammed the door which caused his accident, and anxiety about his own role in Sam T.'s accident—all no doubt reinforced by the coincidence of names—lowered thresholds for anxiety about loss of his tooth. Since other children accepted this loss of teeth and he himself had looked forward to it, the displacement is dramatic.

Here we see, all in all, the variety of factors entering into the qualities of an experience, how it is met at first, and re-experienced later, and how reverberations from a situation handled well at one time can swell into a flood tide which rises to panic and sometimes at a moment when we do not expect it.

By the time of loss of his second tooth, this tooth-losing business was old stuff and Sam was completely matter-of-fact about it.

Sam has erected a strong bulwark against fear. After these events his mother reported:

I think it is likely that the closeness of his relationship with his "best friend" (the "wise one," who is big, but markedly lacking in physical aggression) represented part of this bulwark. When his need for other friends came up last year he exclaimed, "I need another dependable friend."

One day when I picked Sam up after school, he told me he needed to have a hood that wouldn't come off so easily; some of the kids had been throwing hard snowballs, and he was trying to defend himself—they got him down and took off his hood and rubbed snow in his hair. I told him that ordinarily that wouldn't amount to much, but since he just had a fresh cold (we had even wondered whether he should go to school) it didn't seem like such a good idea, and hadn't his teacher done anything about it. He explained that his regular teacher had left to go to the doctor (broken arm a few weeks ago) and the one who was helping out in her place didn't seem to be there just then and Mary, the new student teacher, had seemed afraid of the kids— "And besides—I wouldn't want to risk my reputation of being 'fearless Sam.' "

And I wonder about all of this having something to do with his disinclination towards fishing and hunting: "I'd rather go down and make friends with them [the fish]." He felt bitter about his fifteen-year-old friend Eddie shooting rabbits, squirrels, deer. "Why doesn't he make up his mind. Does he want to be good to them, or does he want to hurt them?"

The professionally oriented reader will wonder about still later sequelae, and about the view of this experience which Sam had when he was older. Sam is still a young boy, and we cannot tell what later experiences may further elaborate the residues of feelings about these early events.

Some clues come from some drawings and paintings made in his seventh and eighth year. Paintings were typically well organized, color-

impressed by the courage, strength, realism, and sparkle with which she managed her handicap.

As she came into the room with my usual arrangement of five piles of Miniature Life Toys in a semicircle on the rug, and was told that she could "do anything she wanted to with the toys," she smiled, walked on her crutches past the housekeeping toys and the cars to the sofa at the far side of the rug near the tame and wild animal piles and the soldier pile, and pulled herself to a sitting position near the end of the sofa as she looked down at and looked over all the toys, simultaneously surveying them and handling her body adjustments. Still sizing up the toys she removed her crutches and took off her jacket.

Sliding herself slowly down the edge of the sofa to the floor, she quickly began an intensely active, often excited hour. She could not handle the toys freely while sitting up, nor could she reach in different directions as she wished to do. So we watched her worming and wiggling her way ingeniously from one group of toys to another as she lay prone on the floor.

In this first opportunity to play with many toys of a very wide variety, her choices, her fantasy, her affective expressions all gave indications of her image of herself and her feelings about other people, including the experimenters, who maintained what for such a vocal little girl probably seemed a strange quietness and passivity on the sidelines. Before long her pale coloring changed to a flush which remained much of the hour.

She reached for a toy snake first. This is very unusual for preschool girls, who generally start with housekeeping toys and come to the "boys' toys"— cars, wild animals, soldiers—later, if at all. In view of the fact that her own prone position and worming movement was in fact snakelike it does not seem far-fetched to assume that this was in some way how she saw herself.

But she evidently had much ambivalent feeling about this role; as she picked up the snake she exclaimed in a raucous, mocking, playful voice:* "I know what that is. A snake! He's a snake! I don't like real ones . . . but I like play ones!" (In Kansas, children do not see snakes solely in zoos; and the small city of Topeka had been spreading into the countryside so rapidly— growing 50 per cent between 1950 and 1960—that snakes could still be encountered in one's back yard, and children were warned against the rattlers and copperheads still appearing occasionally in the woods or along the road. At this point we could not tell what reality and what fantasy elements might have most weight.)

Next she handled the elephant and the giraffe, both of which she commented upon: "Aaah . . . elephant! Aaah . . . that's a giraffe. . . . Tiger. . . . That's a silly thing! I know what I'm going to do! I'm going to make a zoo! . . . 'Nother snake, 'nother snake. I know what this one is—an alligator. I don't like real alligators because they bite. They've got two sharp teeth. They fight the snakes! I'm going to kill 'em! I killed 'em! I killed that one. Going to fight the alligator."

* In this verbatim protocol, records of two simultaneous observers are integrated. Details of her varied movement patterns are omitted here in the interest of brevity.

"Gonna' swat him," she exclaimed, with expressive nonsensical burlesque vocalizing. "I know what . . . this one is going to eat the alligator up . . . this one is going to eat the alligator up, too! The alligator doesn't like it. . . . But we're doing it! The snake will do it, too. Everybody's going to get on top of him. Do you know where the alligator is? (underneath?) There and he's already dead." She seemed to be expressing a vigorous anticipation of triumph over the aggressor.

There was more vigorous aggressive movement of the snakes and the alligator which ended up in piling all of the animals in a heap. Having done this, she sorted through the pile and pulled out the alligator. Her attention shifted from this fantasy as she asked me, realistically and in a more matter-of-fact voice, "Do you want to see how much I can pick up?" Adding, "I can carry more than one thing," Susan grabbed the entire pile of animals between her hands. (No other child had done this. Other children who want to show what they can do usually exhibit large-muscle achievements.) In this situation where she could have been overwhelmed by what she could *not* do, Susan focused her attention and ours on what she *could* do, after finding ingenious ways of handling the opportunity provided by the toys, and after playing through an attack on the aggressor to the point of triumph.

Susan now more or less slid and wiggled over to the pile of soldiers. In front of them she lay down on her side in a more restful position saying, as she picked up one, "I know what I'm gonna' do, I'm going to line them up . . . line them up." Here she continued to express her capacities for control.

"Sh . . . sh . . . sh . . . He's sitting down. He's walking. That's a little boy that hasn't got a gun. This one's got a flag in him! Boop, boo, boo, boo. P-s-s-sp-s-s-s—There!" Susan named each toy as she picked it up and made some comment about it, interspersing expressive sounds, most of which conveyed vague aggressive feelings, at the same time that she expressed preoccupations with object loss and possessions.

She made a double row of eight soldiers, not too neat, and added more soldiers to these rows. "Oooh, there's a cowboy, no, an Indian. I don't like real Indians that are bad! And another Indian. Scrup scrup . . . scutzh, psst, sput, puck, spat. He is going to lay down, that one [laughs] put this here; I [going to?] knock [ed] them all down (3)* scrup, scrup." Here, while continuing her theme of control by organization she introduced moralistic concerns of goodness and badness, quickly demolishing the bad.

She fingered the toys . . . she would like to be more active then she is. "Oooha band! (She elongated the vowel sound.) Boom, boom, he jumped on top of the other one. I'm going to chop 'em, gush, gush, I'm going to make 'em dead. He's dead (2) I killed 'em. What did he do? He got killed." As she said this, she hit a soldier with the long piece from the Lincoln logs.

After disposing of bad ones (impulses?) she transferred the conflict to a peer-group, possibly among siblings. Still identifying with the aggressor freely she demolished the adversary. All this was quite boy-like. The themes of mastery, good-bad people, aggression, and her ways of supporting mastery by spe-

---

* The numbers in parentheses refer to the number of repetitions of the phrase.

cific overt acts of triumph suggested the force of her conflicts, and the chan-
neling of aggression into a strong determination to win. At the same time she
projected onto others—the other sex—in terms of weakness, or loss, the disability which she actually experienced in herself. Her use of projection evidently helped to conserve her own energy for her efforts.

"Now they're going to go someplace in this. Where do you think they're
going? (LBM: You tell me.) "Ul-ul. . . . They're going to back into this . . .
Giddy-up (3) Giddy-up horsie. This horsie he doesn't want to stand up.
Boopuupuuoopee." Susan rolled over and again picked up the elephant from
the wild animal pile. "Do you know where the elephant is crawling? Up here
. . . he crawled up, he crawled up in here . . . (The) elephant (s) can do
tricks. (She crawled the elephant up the sofa.) You stay there. . . . Oh, a
snake again. He's peeking in the tail."

She acted out with the toys dramatically, and talked in a dramatic voice,
with playful emphases and made-up words at times—an element of "putting
on a show." Very flexibly she played out locomotion problems—the horse
"doesn't want to stand up"; the elephant (she was large for her age) crawls.
Her reference to the snake peeking suggested that she had some of the voyeur-
istic impulses also frequent among young children, and perhaps intensified
in Susan by her restricted opportunities for exploration.

"Bang! I shooted her instead." Susan had found the small gun among the
soldiers and leveled it to shoot me, probably because of the note-taking (our
"peeking") and her sensitivity to our observation of her. "Dum, dum, dum.
. . . He can't find his gun! And I got his gun . . . bloopbloop." She made
a face at me in a slightly show-offy way. "That's a silly looking face!" commenting on herself. (When the gun was coyly leveled at me) I asked playfully,
"Shall I be dead?" Susan pointed the gun instead at AM. She held the gun in
her right hand, balancing herself on her left hand in a sitting position. This
was a child, we can assume, who had been examined by many physicians and
nurses, often under painful conditions; probably she had often felt like
attacking those who "invaded" her body domain, and this situation of being
observed by two examiners reminded her of others.

There was a partial crawling, partial shifting or sliding to the pile of tame
animals now where she turned over on her back. She picked up the gray
mouse, again with a slight scream, saying, "Ooop! We've got one of these
things at home." She rolled over and examined the rabbit, took two pieces
of fence and managed to fasten them together, saying, "A fence! Got to go
like this . . . (4) push," verbalizing about her effort. She continued to try
to put the fence pieces together, but this was difficult from a position of resting on her elbows. "There! Going to make a fence for Chris . . ." "Whoop,
whurrrr . . . the fence fell, that horse fell. Whop, poop. That man is dead.
Then the steer comes along, then the Indian. Giddy up (3) fight the cowboys."
There was a great deal of excitement in Susan's tone as she talked about what
she was doing, now engaged in a dramatic conflict in which controls (fence),
the good (horse), collapse, and other good ones (cowboys who take care of
cows) are attacked. At times she used very deep, perhaps masculine, tones. At
other times, she sounded like a little girl. She seemed to enjoy rhyming non-

sense sounds which lent humor to her style and quite frequently interspersed them with her fantasy; her repetitions were made rhythmically as if she enjoyed the sensory experiences of sound she could make in this way, and felt free to indulge in whatever fun she could create for herself, while at the same time expressing her ambivalent feelings.

"This! . . . a dog! . . . Boost . . . !" Now she dropped her dramatizing tones for a normal voice, referring again to the rubber mouse, "We've got one of these things at home. Daddy had it in his coat pocket and when he took it out mommy was scared." In this way she brought herself back to simple realities of home life, with a flexibility which showed that even at peaks of emotionally intense fantasy she could keep control and shift to matters close to reality at will.

She pulled herself to the town toys, getting there quite easily, lying on her stomach, waving her legs in the air, absently; she had motion from the knees when her legs did not have to support anything. She started to put the ladder on the fire truck. "Booey (3) oh boy, policeman. Oop, a lady!" (in a mocking voice).

She balanced herself on her left arm while she reached with the right arm. At times she ingeniously supported the weaker arm by resting it on the other hand.

Excitedly she noticed the car and the airplane. "Oh, a car! Oh, a fire! Gotta' wait for the truck to go by." Now she selected an airplane: "Zoom, (3) it's going up in the air and then it's going down and it's landed." Susan moved the car and the fire truck appropriately and realistically, paralleling her words. She picked up the airplane as she said, "Zoom," kept it on the ground at first, then up, circling as far as she could from her position. In these various ways she expressed her awareness of problems of movement, and the excitement she felt at ideas of total freedom of movement.

Next, she pulled herself to the housekeeping toys, walking on her knees. She noticed the small radio first. Once again she immediately indicated to me that she knew exactly what she was going to do, "Mmm, I know what I'm going to do. There's the kitchen. This will be in the kitchen. The ironing board is in the kitchen here." (Sang a bit.) Again she supported her right hand by holding her left hand against it. Her resourcefulness in using the available body muscles and parts to support or substitute for the weak ones was illustrated in many ways in our later contacts with her.

"They need a chair to sit down, then footsie. A chair will go in the kitchen right beside it . . . over here . . . for to sit down to play . . . and then . . . what's . . . what's . . . what's . . . what's footsie." This constant verbalization may also serve as a substitute for action.

"Another ironing board! Going to put another one here . . . a clothes hamper . . . don't need a clothes hamper yet, oh, don't need two of these." She tossed the second ironing board and the second clothes hamper into a pile. She set up one ironing board with two chairs in front of it. Beside the ironing board stood the refrigerator and to the right of them two chairs with metal frames. "Now we put this over here . . ." She pulled things selectively out of the pile, after periodic pawing and looking through it.

"Pottie, pottie chair, pottie, pottie, pottie. Now the woman! (Dramatically) Now we'll put the pottie right there, we'll put the bathroom right beside the kitchen, with the baby things in it. Put the (baby bathinette) in the bathroom, oh, the tub . . . in the bathroom . . ." Susan picked up a small girl doll, saying: "She's going to wet in the pot! No, she isn't . . . !" She started to, but did not put the girl on the toilet. "Oh, this one's going to . . . she's going to get in the bathinette to wash! No, she isn't . . . (we're) not going to use her (yet)." Each time Susan started to pull the girl doll in the proper position, then changed her mind and finally left the doll in the pile of toys. We did not know whether this episode reflected a momentary impulse to go to the bathroom herself, or followed naturally in the review of things that happen in the home. But later there was some evidence that she suppressed a need to get up and go to the bathroom.

She set up the radio in the kitchen. "Now this will go in the kitchen so they can listen to the radio . . ." and she began to sing again as she manipulated the various objects.

Now she pawed through the toys, wheeling the stroller briefly, seeming to be considering what she wanted to do next. "Nowwwww what?" (4) She was lying on her stomach with her legs bent at the knees, heels together in a sort of swimming position.

She tried to stand up the two-legged green sink, then put it back exclaiming very dramatically "We don't use that!" By contrast with her own resourcefulness in finding ways of giving herself physical support, she made no effort at all to discover how she could succeed in helping the (inadequate) sink to stand, but rejected it instantly as if devaluating any inadequate object. "Oh, poof! The couch. Now I'm going to make the living room. Here's the other radio, right here. This chair goes over by that (sofa). This will have to go in the bedroom, right here." I haven't got to the dogs yet. Don't need these . . . the piano, (we) don't need the piano for a minute." She was swinging her legs.

"Next, the bedroom. . . . Now the dining room."

"First the table up here in the dining room, kinda there. Duddle, da da do." (Half singing a nonsense song, she brushed her hair back from her face as it slid across her eyes. She was again supporting the right arm with the left arm as she reached quite far out in front of her, lying almost flat on the floor.

"Where will the piano go? The piano goes right here. That's where the piano goes." She scrutinized the housekeeping toys briefly, resting her chin on her right hand. She found the grandmother doll, saying, ("The grandmother, yup,"). The grandmother was laid back in the pile.

Susan was quiet for several seconds, leaned on her elbow, seemed to be thinking what to do next. She passed gas, then after a pause resumed more quietly . . . "Baby . . ." Clucking . . . picks up the broken bed . . . "Inside the bedroom!" Then she started lining up the beds, saying, "Another bed, another bed, another bed." She set up two beds side by side with a cradle placed next to one of them. She was wiggling, swinging her legs, leaning on her elbows, through all this. Her legs often swung in a dangling fashion behind; she turned on her buttocks with more trunk motion than most children, twisting, to rest on her left elbow as she set up the bedroom. She located a chest of drawers, set on one side of the bed, and moved the mother's bed slightly. She looked up quickly when she heard a sort of squeaking noise upstairs.

Again she was singing as she half crawled, half pushed herself about to better reach the things she wanted. The left leg was resting on the right leg, which was bent at the knee. Susan rolled over, swinging her trunk to the right, and turned on her back to pick up a pink blanket, folded it and placed it on a third bed in the bedroom. "There is another bed!" In arranging the bed, Susan had knocked over the dresser. "Poop! Fix this up. There!"

She swung back to the left, rose to her knees and swung to sitting on her buttocks with her legs back, to reach the toys. As she sat, she supported herself at first with her hand, but as she continued to sit, she maintained the position without the support of her arms. She swung to a prone position, then a side position, then back to her knees and sitting on her fanny. Her legs were curled under and back. Evidently she got tired and uncomfortable in most of the positions available to her, and handled her discomfort by shifting her position flexibly.

She now put the stove together, after setting up four beds in the bedroom. Other preschool chlidren often set up beds in separate bedroom areas; the fact that she put beds for the two children in the same room with those of the parents suggested that she felt a need to deal with a sense of isolation or distance which resulted from her limited mobility, or her feeling of being different from the rest of the family, doubtless evoked by the passivity of the observers in this situation.

She sat back and pushed her hair back from her forehead, then crawled across the floor, pulling her skirt up out of the way. She was able to progress two or three steps before she needed to balance herself with her left hand. She sat, resting on her left hand, using her right hand. She pushed with her left hand to sitting position, then to kneeling, then to prone position. Her play had been so active that her shoulder strap was unbuttoned and her blouse was pulled out of the skirt. Susan did not attend to these things at this time. She was again interested in seeing what was available in the housekeeping toys. "Get these two chairs. Another potty. We need another. What's this? (the lamp base) This is going to be perfume in the bathroom, no, in here. (on the dresser in their bedroom) Oh, I fix my stwap, strap." (Susan first used the infantile pronunciation of the R in the word, but immediately following, said it correctly.) She was up on her knees, and looked up at AM as she buttoned the strap.

She heard voices upstairs but listened only a moment . . . "Booboooo." She picked up the blue mother doll and looked carefully under the skirt, saying, "Oh, souffle," in a deprecating tone of voice.

There was still a lot of movement; she took several creeping steps on her knees and was then forced to maintain her balance by the use of supporting hands. She picked up several chairs, "These chairs. Bring them over to the kitchen. Going to put these chairs in the kitchen." As Susan set the table behind the couch, the refrigerator fell over. It seemed to demand considerable effort to set it up again and we had the feeling that Susan was definitely becoming quite tired. One could occasionally note a slight tremor of the hands now, and as she walked on her knees, she seemed more effortful and awkward but still much like normal children in her active outgoing direct attitudes; there was no self-pity.

"Going to make a picnic for 'em in a minute. (4) Going to get these three things—take a basket!" She added two chairs at the north end of kitchen . . . two chests to dining room.

"We don't need anymore pottie-chairs . . . we need another sink, though. Have to fix (up the chair here). (the kitchen.)" This time she changed her position by pushing with her heel and sliding backwards. She crawled away, then back to the housekeeping toys. She set up the sink behind the bathinette and almost as though she expected something else to fall, said, "Boop . . . what fell down? I hope nothing fell down. Nope, nothing fell down!" Still, or again, she tried to fix the stove and set it beside the ironing board. Here we see her active effort to repair damaged objects as well as her ingenuity in providing support for the two-legged sink.

"Foof-bou-do . . ." Susan put a small object in the back of the refrigerator. She hunted again through the toys, ignoring sounds upstairs except for momentary listening. She set up a pink rocker in the kitchen, "This will go in the kitchen where they rock the baby—to sleep . . . Pirsl-gun-der . . . pirsl-gun-der . . ." She crawled over to the housekeeping toys on her knees, and picked up a washing machine. Incidentally she found a small Santa Claus. "Now it's nighttime, time for Santa Claus to come. And he will go here, and he will go here, and he will go here. I made a house! And Santa's coming. Look! He's behind here . . . and he's flying back. Hee, hee!"

Her thoughts of sleep, and (dreams of?) Santa Claus (delightful future gratifications?) come in the context of the increased fatigue we noted just above; this suggested that she kept on trying as long as she could, and when her energy gave out, realistically gave herself a chance to rest, full of hopes and fantasies for more gratifications.

Comments on the play session

In this setting Susan was not deterred by her handicap; she made an instant contact both with the situation and the people in it, seeming to integrate an observant receptiveness with a rich capacity to respond at many levels, and with many intellectual and emotional nuances. She surveyed the situation rapidly before using its resources actively. It seemed as if this kind of situation, free from the stress of competing with other children, and with minimal frustration by her limitations evoked a quick eager response.

Some children used the toys, almost ignoring the adults present; others made the experience a social occasion, preoccupied with the adults and unable to get deeply involved with the toys. Susan used both, but without large ambitious integrations of the toys; she shared her feelings through the toys and used them to act out some of her problems. She communicated her progress to the observers, maintaining constant contact through comments on her feelings, plans, and actions, and through her varied emotional expressions; she showed her competence, and accepted help when she needed it, immediately regaining autonomy and keeping it after being helped, without regression to helplessness at any time even when she must have been very tired. The maintenance of her autonomy seemed very important, and was, expressed in her varied ingenious motor efforts, wriggling and pulling herself about, moving on her stomach, supporting her weight in resourceful ways.

Perceptually she was quickly oriented, and sorted out what she wanted to use; she used the snake as a point of departure, perhaps repressing her embarrassment at some sense of ignominy in having to crawl in such a snakelike way.

Five-year-old children often emphasize their knowing, in contrast to the three-year-olds who typically ask, "What's this?" "Where does this come from?" In contrast with some children of her own age she did not bother with details, nor was she as preoccupied as we might have expected with such questions as whether or not things can go, although she was delighted by movement and concerned with falling and her selections and rejections of objects were influenced at times by whether the object could stand alone. (She could not at this point.) While her initial choice of the snake seemed to be influenced by the fact that it does not stand or walk, but crawls as she was doing at the time she chose it, its conflict with the orally aggressive alligator, suggests that it was not only an expression of a problem of movement, but a vehicle for playing out conflict with superior creatures, perhaps authorities.

Her first emotional expression, "I am five!" with typical pride for this age level, might imply that what she is felt more important or as important, as what she was able to do, and her identity as a five-year-old, as a person, was more important than her illness and its effects. She made clear explicit distinctions between reality and fantasy as many five-year-olds do, especially with the comment "I don't like *real* ones" (snakes, alligators, etc.), and between her ability to cope with such threatening things in fantasy as compared with reality. Fantasy was for play, excitement, fun, release and was a major coping resource. Much of this—her concern with five-year-oldness, with authority conflicts, with sex-role, and her capacity to play, and to move and get around as much as possible is normal for her age: it is evidence of ego-strength that she could be so five-year-oldish, when she had been cut off from so many normal developmental experiences after her illness.

Susan's range of emotional expressions also reflected her ego-strength. Sometimes a humorous mischievous smile, half shared, half secret, spread across her face; at other times, expressions which had a quality of childish burlesque, clowning, or show-off seemed to push their way out almost in spite of her expressed feeling that they were silly; or a fishy embarrassed smile; or a twinkling, warm smile of rapport; or a half-playful hostility; only anxiety seemed to be hidden by a mask of pale, sober, steady looking. Even here she did not completely hide or withdraw herself. But she never openly admitted fear, or uncertainty about her uncertain future; she ascribed fear to her mother, in reaction to the conventional stimulus of a mouse.

At the same time that she used so much vague squawky expressiveness, Susan also used objective, realistic or conventional patterns to express hostility or fantasy and other non-realistic devices, with equal ease.

At the age of five she was an emotionally vivid child, whose responsiveness appeared to flow in many directions—into autonomic reactions through skin, into primitive expressive vocalizing, into resourceful motor efforts carried beyond the point of fatigue, into fantasy and play constructions, and a sustained vital communicating contact with the experimenter. Affective expressions were at times controlled, differentiated, and well channeled, and at times primitive and diffuse.

She used objects spontaneously in varied ways, occasionally exploring them, frequently combining them as she acted out fragmentary fantasies with them, or organizing them in more or less conventionally appropriate ways; generally simple organization provided the stage setting for additional activity and was thus functional; there was order without inhibition beyond the tendency to keep different classes of objects separate. Objects gave realism and content and the opportunity for action to her fantasy which appeared to be a major way of handling her vivid emotions.

She was subjectively involved in relationships with people, and in her fantasies; the latter were more directly acted out, "I killed 'em," than similar fantasies of other children (the typical way of playing out was to say *he* killed him, if the child said anything at all); thus she gave an impression of intense personal living through a wide range of feelings—joyous, angry, zestful, playful ones predominating; this fantasy life was something to be shared and she used it to enrich her contact with people as well as to deal with her feelings. The fact that she used fantasy partly as a temporary substitute for reality or within a framework of reality boundaries may explain why she was able to carry her fantasy to such peaks of exhilaration without becoming disorganized or confused.

Susan appeared to identify with the crawling snake, and the elephant trickster, perhaps even with the orally aggressive alligator if we take into account her aggressive vocalizations; also with the cowboys who are threatened by bad wild Indians, the horse that falls down, and with the soldiers that will threaten human beings, and with the bad Indians who fight the protector cowboys and the wild fire truck that can bump conservative trains and make them park way down the track, and finally with the free-flying airplane that can go where it pleases.

We can see that a major problem was the realistic one of hampered movement, and a major longing was the desire to be able to move in a carefree way. Her capacity to elaborate this in fantasy gave her the manner of a free spirit, positive, vital, and undaunted. We also saw the feelings that underlie this longing for freedom: she was anxious about falling and her inability to stand alone.

Anxiety and frustration were handled in many ways: by mobilizing her capacities for mastery, triumph, aggression, realistically and in fantasy; they were projected to others; they were balanced by gratification; food, picnics, and perhaps other excursions, being cared for, and the multiple fantasy gratifications associated with Santa Claus and story satisfactions; glowing, shiny-eyed, zestful feelings accompanied her fantasies about things like this.

Susan had, then, several levels of coping problems. We may assume the normal problems of her age, of accepting her sex-role, her likeness to mother and difference from father, and the different love for a father as compared with mother, and the problem of accepting adult authority. In addition she had the problems connected with her illness: her actual physical handicap; her anxiety about falling and perhaps about adequacy; her angry feelings about threats or scolding and her feeling about her angry hostile retaliation impulses; her need for gratification.

We can see equally well several levels of coping effort: her efforts at mastery and control, both in reality experiences and fantasy, which she used for conceptualizing her problems through cognitive and motor skills; her expression of anger, embarrassment, releasing her feelings of retaliation; her shutting out of anxiety and despair, denying the bad, projecting fear; her reaching out for satisfactions including fantasy gratifications as well as real ones, which helped her to accent the positive; her absorption in present stimuli and use of objects and people for a vivid life now; this included use of stories belonging to her age level which universalized and also gave distance to her problems.

Limitations might result from these coping efforts: She might limit her originality by keeping emotional areas too separate, so that she could not integrate ideas and objects from different sources as many of these children did. Perhaps she needed to do this; if she had sensed and accepted the doctor's original view that she would always be a bed patient, she might have been overwhelmed by a despair which in itself would be paralyzing. At this point we may ask: What price realism?

Susan appeared to use her energy to the maximum, and ignored her difficulties except when she was actively coping with them. When angry feelings welled up she expressed them and balanced up her attack on the outside world with constructive efforts. When frustrated feelings threatened to get the upper hand she reached for dependable satisfactions which she could find both in reality and fantasy. In this way she refueled the motivating engines for further efforts, strengthened herself to carry on, and reassured herself that the efforts were worthwhile. Balancing frustrations with gratifications and compensations and continued efforts at mastery were central to her coping style.

To her the world was both depriving and rewarding, both threatening and satisfying; she counted on her ability to know what she was going to do to get enough gratifications to carry her through. Thus she could express, deny, compensate and, above all, handle both her environment and most feelings with flexibility and a range of levels of control.

At this point there were some questions: What else did she do with the obvious facts of incompleteness, of defect and damage, of an uncertain future? We saw her aggressive defense against threats like the alligator; she assigned fear about a mouse to her mother (this might be realistic, or a projection of her own fear of small uncontrollable things that threatened her insecure stance). But these did not deal with problems of anxiety about herself, her place in the world. We might say that she confined her expression of anxiety to external objects, and at a deeper level controlled it by repression so that it did not overwhelm or paralyze her or interfere with experiences of joy and gratification.

As a help in giving a wider dimension to the observations of Susan, let us have a look at Baljeet Malhotra's impressions of Susan at the party as they appear in summary:

With a gracefully regal quality about her, she is princesslike, majestic, and queenly. She is a resourceful child who seems to be quite able to cope with immediate problems. She has a great capacity for different and soft shades of enjoyment, a sensuous quality. I would imagine her very capable of strong emotions, too. She brought the tiger to "kill" Alice first, then to "kill" me; the strong emotions are rich and deep and in this way have something in common with the soft qualities I mentioned first.

She is handicapped, but there is a life, energy, desire in her to participate in the world. Since she can't participate because of her disability, she creates a lively world around her and lives through her environment; and this life through the environment is sustained by her very vivid imagination. She reminds me of a fine mogul emperor (Bahadur Shah) imprisoned by the British who played chess constantly, recreating the war and "winning." This living through gives a strong satisfaction; she is able to draw satisfaction from persons, social situations, toys and animals, too. Since there is no bitterness, being an outsider does not seem to create too many conflicts. Toys and other things come to life for her but in a different way from some other children. Here coming to life has a dreamlike quality; everybody rises up but the player as well as the observers never feel that it is reality, though it serves the purpose of reality.

Her relation to adults and also to peers is a very pleasantly accepting one; her physical disability puts her in a position of receiving. She does it graciously but at the same time she can give. For instance, at the party she made a necklace for another child, picked up a fallen spoon for Gordon Spencer and handed it to him.

If she had not had this disability, I could imagine her as an active, dominating, leader-type of child. She seems to have the quality of giving to and at the same time taking from others.

In a more concrete way, Mrs. Smith conveyed a similar impression of Susan at an earlier party the previous year:

Susan appeared happy and excited, I thought, from the moment she arrived until she went home. Even when the other children were climbing and running and jumping, she would stand and watch and then show us how *she* could walk on the watering hose. She took great delight in the doll and asked me to help dress and undress her, take her to the doctor, give her an operation, etc. There were times when she looked a little dreamy, especially when she was taking her rest on the cement slab that GH had cushioned for her with a nice thick warm blanket. The musical doll was going and she had finished her play with the doll momentarily and the other children were nowhere in sight. It was quiet except for the tinkling notes of the doll; she rested her chin in her hand and rather smilingly looked at the sky. I asked her what she was looking at. "The smoke," she said, and sure enough as I looked some smoke was rising evidently from the roadway over the embankment from a bonfire of some sort. We talked of the blue sky, the leaves turning, and summer being about over, and somehow I felt very close to her in the little short silences in between our bits of conversation. At this point LBM called me to help with something else and I excused myself.

I thought Susan seemed very much at ease although once or twice I noticed her hand trembled a little bit. I thought she particularly enjoyed the beads and clay as this seemed something she could do along with the other children.

A few weeks earlier she had been more carefree in dealing with intelligence test demands as set by Dr. Moriarty:

Susan's clear-cut features, smooth, clear skin, sparkling green eyes, rich, melodic voice, and charming, gay effervescence made her entirely charming and delightful to examine. There was a steady stream of conversation, centered around test performance but interspersed with many colorful and dramatic recital of trips and activities, and of her fondness for color and beauty in feminine apparel. Her physical handicap necessitated taking the test in a recumbent position of examiner's divan, but aside from occasional awkwardness in manipulating test materials, this in no way interfered with test performance. Susan was ingenuous in handling her body, varying her posture to fit the occasion. She sometimes moved slowly, but always gracefully, deliberately, and with excellent coordination. Aside from two brief references to physical handicaps, during which times she mused in a rather depressive way, she was uniformly happy and very much at ease.

Susan seemed to think of each of her sessions as a gay adventure, in which the examiner and the parallel observer were included as friends and allies. While she was aware of physical limitations and usually adhered to established rules, she sometimes side-stepped them and then would ask for the examiner's promise that she would not tell her mother how much she had been sitting or standing. The tests themselves were stimulating and interesting to her but details of her own full life were even more fascinating to relate. Her eyes often widened with delight; her whole body quivered with excitement and her voice took on rich, resonant and dramatic overtones. There was great pride in her achievement, expressed in happily pointing out time and again that examiner must be surprised that she could do so well. Cathexis was perhaps greatest for her vivid and colorful use of words which was greatly intensified by varied intonation and sound effects. One felt she liked to impress, but that beyond this there was tremendous personal satisfaction in hearing herself and in relating warmly to the observers.

Aside from aforementioned references to physical handicaps, Susan expressed little anxiety. Most of her movements were purposeful and only toward the end of the test when failures were piling up did she manifest any tendency to indulge in occasional nose-picking and finger-sucking. When finger-sucking occurred, there were smacking sounds and pleasures were obvious. She could unashamedly find pleasure in regressive behavior when self-esteem was at a low ebb. Anxiety never took over and recovery was rapid.

Reactions to success, failure or difficulty

In response to *success,* she showed pride in accomplishment: Susan was wide-eyed with delight as she described coloring skills, pointing up how she had progressed from scribbling to making realistic drawings, how she now made even strokes, stayed within lines. She also stressed her superiority to sister. "Do you know what? I can stay inside the lines. That little kid goes outside the lines."

When confronted with difficulty or failure, she offered response tentatively in a questioning voice, then repeated it firmly after the response was confirmed. She commented on minor awkwardness or error casually, but covered her productions so the examiner could not see (diamond).

Short, popping sounds seemed to offer affective release and to screen off potential frustration (when she went off the line in Maze tracing, and when excitedly describing picture absurdities, which seemed rather difficult for her, and in response to her failure to tell how two different objects were similar).

She usually ignored errors, but sometimes they seemed to be alleviated by the above-mentioned sound effects or by relating tales of personal experiences. A fleeting disappointed expression would evaporate as she spoke dramatically. Sometimes she spoke very softly when unsure (comprehension), or teasingly told AM, "This time I'm going to whisper, so you can't even hear."

She set self-imposed time limits, implying that she could accomplish a set task if unhurried. She was markedly disappointed when she failed to meet her own time limits. At times she initiated guessing games, which seemed to be used to deflect AM's attention from an inferior response (reversing digits).

She licked her fingers and picked her nose as failures piled up at the end of the test. Smacking sounds and smiles indicated enjoyment of regressive behavior which screened her ebbing self-esteem.

From these relatively brief sessions we could not learn what she was like in real life situations. We have hints of some ways in which she handled her own intense feelings and wild impulses, through excited vocalizations and manipulations. But we do not know with certainty whose aggression she feared, or how she dealt with aggression from others, handicapped as she was at that time. We do not know whether her tendency to ignore babies and the nurturing side of feminine interests implied that she feared or felt that she would never be able to function as a woman. Nor could we learn from data like these what long persistent characteristics or experiences of her infancy helped her to meet this threat so gallantly and mobilize all her energy so effectively. How much evidence was there in infancy of her zest and deep involvement; her quick, clear, perception; her motor ingenuity; her emotional nuances; her ability to play, to combine objects; her resilience and ability to recover from angry feelings, balancing them with constructive efforts? How much evidence was there of the trust that must underlie her quick contact and steady communication, and her quick ability to use the objects of her environment freely in ways which give her great delight? Perhaps most central for understanding her coping resources: Did she, in infancy, show the autonomic responsiveness and wide variety of levels of emotional expression from delight to anger with varying degrees of control and of defense; and the marked ability to shift, and to accept and use comfort and gratification which I found in my hour with her? And along with her own resources, what kinds of support in coping from her mother and other members of the family helped her to develop the resourcefulness, hope, and courage which are so impressive?

A full study of these and other relevant questions is not within the scope of this book.

SOME PROCESSES
OF MASTERY

IF WE FOCUS TOO EXCLUSIVELY on specific coping devices and defense mechanisms, it is easy to miss the process of mastery, which involves the parallel and successive use of different devices and resources, according to the cognitive, affective, and motor levels of integration in response to each new challenge. First, then, we shall look at relatively simple examples of different ways in which different children achieved mastery as we observed them in our research setting; later we shall focus on the more complicated aspects of mastering fear and shyness as recorded in records of behavior at home.

In Mary Shirley's records (pp. 48 ff.) we saw children's fears about examining sessions reinforced in some instances by their experiences. The process of change of attitude in a new situation from doubt to a spontaneous positive response can be seen under favorable conditions; with Ronnie these favorable conditions included the presence of his family, mother, younger sister, and brother, and a flexible, understanding examiner. Ronnie was initially suspicious of the intelligence test but ended with a strong attachment to the examiner, and came eagerly to further testing sessions with her. The following record* shows in detail the steps he went through:

At the age of four years and one month when first confronted with the intelligence test, Ronnie cautiously and slowly allowed himself to be involved. At first he almost entirely averted his head when AM was presented to him. He promptly sat in the designated chair, but remarked, "I don't want to do these things now." Unlike his younger sister who approached and was interested in test equipment, Ronald looked uninterested and neither moved nor spoke.

Dr. Moriarty flexibly tried a series of maneuvers to help him get started with the test. When she asked him to draw, he shifted responsibility, suggesting that his mother draw a picture. His mother reassured him, and said she would stay with him. His younger sister accepted drawing paper and a doll, and comfortably sat on the floor to play. His younger brother became restless and noisy; thereupon his mother said she would take the younger children to an adjoining room since one could not tell what the baby would do next. This explanation must have seemed momentarily logical and satisfactory because Ronnie then agreed, "O.K., I'll stay a little bit." He began to color, but in a few moments left the room to seek his mother.

Dr. Moriarty gave Ronnie a few moments with his mother, then joined the family where the younger children were playing happily. Ronnie stood close to his mother who had one arm around him. She was telling him, "You know what we talked about. You wanted to 'go to school' and to be able to tell your father about it." She also reminded him that he would enjoy telling his playmates about his "schoolwork." AM smiled, but did not urge Ronnie. With these reminders and support from his mother he decided he would go back to the examining room. Again he avoided AM's direct gaze. But he now began to show some interest in performance materials and was obviously mildly pleased with success on several tasks.

However, greater difficulty soon brought out verbal resistance: "I can't make that," although he continued to try. When the difficulties continued, he protested, "Oh, oh, I don't want to. I want to go sit on the stairs." Instead, he walked over to a window and looked out, not removing himself so far from the situation; he was near enough to watch AM. Evidently he was sufficiently caught by the test possibilities not to detach himself completely. When he was shown the tiny toys to be hidden he came back with increased interest; but he made it clear that he did not want to close his eyes when asked to do so. He had to remain vigilant and he had his own ideas about what to do with the toys. "Why don't you make a train? I saw car wrecks on TV." He was able to delay his own plans, however, and acquiesced in the test demands. He was not reprimanded for peeking, and consequently "spoiling" the test, but he immediately arose, saying, "I don't want to" and rejoined his mother.

The test situation was by now exerting a real pull. This time AM did

* Based on the record by Alice Moriarty.

not follow him and in a very few moments he was back of his own initiative and now appeared more willingly to comply and more interested.

We had the distinct feeling that Ronnie would not be pushed. He had to find out for himself that the session was permissive and there was in reality no cause for alarm. His voice became louder and clearer now and testing went along smoothly for some time.

But when he found it difficult to identify people in some of the pictures, he suggested returning to play with cars (keeping a contact with test objects, not retreating from the situation as he had done earlier). AM left the cars on the table, and went on with the test questions. Every now and then he made comments such as, "The car is sitting up on the train. Now, it can't drive, can it?" This activity and the fantasy it involved did not interfere with testing.

As he felt more and more comfortable, he began making more spontaneous comments, such as, "I should have brought my watch along." He also asked for specific items which appealed to him, as "Pretty soon, would you show me these?" (beads).

Growing more and more free he began to examine the equipment more carefully, investigating shapes and textures; he asked how things were made, suggesting changes in procedure and spontaneously made verbal associations with past experiences.

By this time, about an hour had elapsed and he was offered a choice of more drawing or stopping. He decided to tell his mother what he had been doing and then spontaneously returned to color. When AM joined him after a few minutes, he was talking in an animated, interested tone as though he had fully accepted and enjoyed the session. He then decided he would like to leave.

The warm feeling about the experience was expressed in the car on the way home. Ronnie enjoyed the status of his special relationship with AM and stood directly behind her, patting her head. With an air of benevolent authority, he made suggestions about the seating arrangement and passed out gum to his sibs. When his sister found a small metal ball on the floor, he promptly asked AM to decide what to do about it, ignoring his mother's comment that the ball did not belong to the family.

He continued to stay close to AM and looked to her for help in getting on the merry-go-round horse in the store after he bounded out of the car when treats were suggested. His spontaniety was complete, just getting on seemed to be pleasurable and when AM's dime also provided a rocking movement, he was completely delighted.

By the time they reached his own house, Ronnie found it a little hard to separate; he asked in a tone which was more than polite if AM would come in to play with him. He seemed to accept her refusal since it was nearly noon and ran off to greet several friends to whom he obviously talked about his recent experiences. Since the mother had carried considerable equipment to care for the two younger children, AM helped her into the house. In a moment or two, Ronnie bounded up again inviting AM in. She substituted the suggestion that he come back to play with her another time. He was agreeable, but obviously disappointed as he said, "I'd rather you came in, so I could sleep with you."

The father appeared then and Ronnie immediately began telling him in a very enthusiastic way about his experiences. It was undoubtedly an asset for future relationships with AM that his mother's promised satisfaction in telling both playmates and father about his experiences came about so soon after the session, reinforcing the progress he had made in coming to terms with the new experience.

The steps by which Ronnie overcame his diffidence in this situation were evidently emotional, in contrast for instance with Donald's slow appraisal of the new situation at the party (pp. 100 ff.). It was clear very early in our contact with Ronnie that he was both fearful and gallant and that any relationship established with him needed to be based on both his own understanding, and measures to increase his confidence. He definitely responded to warmth and support, but coaxing or urging would have been of no avail. To achieve security as well as understanding in the situation, he first avoided contact and involvement, and controlled the expression of his feelings. He relied heavily on his mother's support and help, staying with AM only because he was assured that mother was close and that he could go to her without interference whenever he wished. Gradually, he was able to shift from mother to AM for the same kind of help and support, but his own pleasure in mastery and success played a big part here. Confronted with test difficulty, he backed off, verbally resisting, but not as completely shutting off the relationship as at the beginning. As he felt freer he expressed his own wishes, including his own uncertainties and his need to see and talk with his mother, but he came back of his own accord. Increasingly, he took a more active role in testing, and both speech and movement increased in vigor and intensity. As this occurred, he indulged in his own fantasy, explored and examined, sought to learn more about how things work and are made and began relating experiences to past activities and feelings. By the end of the session, he felt so confident and comfortable that he asserted himself socially, expressed delight with equipment and real warmth toward the examiner. He took a great deal of pleasure in relating his experiences to his friends and to his father, apparently acquiring status with his friends and glorying in a sense of accomplishment in his capacity to handle the situation as he confided in his father.

In the following carefully observed and recorded sequence during his second test session he moves from refusal with an initial attitude of "I can't," through the pleased discovery that he is able to do some things he did not know he could do, to a final casual stage of taking it

for granted that perhaps he can accomplish the new task. Very important in this progress is the warm rapport developed with the examiner during the preceding session reviewed above.

Sequences in Ronnie's second session*

When Alice Moriarty asked Ronnie to draw the plain cross he did so, slowly and deliberately, but when asked to draw the starlike cross (next step and more difficult) he refused, saying "can't do," and quickly turned his attention to something else.

But he was sufficiently interested to respond when AM asked Ronnie to copy her "bridge" made with blocks; he did this slowly and deliberately. Again when he was asked to attempt something that seemed too difficult, to copy her six-block pyramid, he quickly said, "No. I can't. I'm *sure* I can't!" As she encouraged him, he said "Uh-uh [meaning no] I couldn't, I'm sure I couldn't." When she encouraged him further, saying, "Want to try?" he took the blocks and said, "Linda and me build at home like this," and built several structures although none were exactly like AM's. He seemed to recognize this, so he built the original three-block bridge and said, "I can make one like *this,*" as if reassuring himself about the thing he could do.

He protested again when he was asked to try the first button test, saying, "I can't button. I can't make it. I can't." AM offered it to him and he took it in his hand but still said, "I'm sure I can't. I bet I can't." As she encouraged him he was reminded of a similar task that he could manage and said, "I can button my *coat.*" He then began to try, verbalizing his method: "I have to put my finger in," and put his finger through the button hole in order to get hold of the button. "I don't—think—I can—" he said very slowly as he worked. However, he did accomplish the task, but immediately pushed the finished product away very determinedly, saying he didn't want to do "any more" (buttons). He no doubt saw the next button test in the box and seemed to feel that he had reached his limit.

Despite the fact that he eagerly anticipated the next test (matching cards) his self-doubt was aroused by the specific instructions and he said, "I don't think I can." He was interested in the designs on the cards, but made no effort to "match" them up. In fact, he suggested that AM do the matching. When she persisted with her suggestion that he do it, Ronnie said quite emphatically, "I can't, Mrs. Moriarty, I can't!" When she ignored his refusal and handed him one of the cards saying, "Where's this?" he sighed very deeply but took the card and said, "Now, I *will* find one like this," and did so. As he initiated none of the matching on his own, she continued to hand him cards, encouraging him all the time to find the proper one. When he succeeded he exclaimed, "Boy!" enthusiastically, "we got nine points, didn't we?" Finally he was finished and said quite happily, *"I got all of them, didn't I?"* (He matched ten correctly.)

Ronnie continued to alternate between initial alacrity and protest when

* Record by Marie Smith.

difficulty arose. He did the two-piece puzzle very quickly, but with the three-piece when he got two pieces together and began to have trouble with the third, he said, "I can't, I'm sure I can't." He began to put it back in the box, but when AM suggested that he fit it together in the box he said, "O.K.," and put the first two pieces together as he had before. Then he saw where the third piece went and laughed happily with AM at his success and again smiled happily and proudly when she chided him about saying he "couldn't" when he "could." With the four-piece puzzle he again got two pieces together rather quickly, but when he had difficulty with the third piece said, "I can't put this together, Mrs. Moriarty," in a very discouraged and unhappy tone. When she continued to encourage him Ronnie got the two remaining pieces to fit together. When she praised him and asked, "Can you get it *all* together?" turning the pieces around so that it was right-side up, Ronnie slowly slid them together and looked almost unbelieving as he began to realize they were in place. When AM praised again, Ronnie put both hands to his head stroking his hair in a downward motion on his forehead; he sighed deeply as if he might have just passed a great milestone in life and then said "O.K., where's something else I can do?" It was almost as if he suddenly realized there were many new horizons that could be conquered.

Hope now displaced doubt in his approach to a new test. As AM got out the Mare and Foal test and arranged it in front of Ronnie, he asked for the first time with a positive expectation, "Maybe I can make it?" He went ahead eagerly, did not appear tense, and seemed to be working almost confidently. He put several pieces in correctly, had a little trouble with one and said, "I don't know where it belongs," but did not give up and kept on trying to fit it into several places. When he found the correct place he said very matter of factly, "It belongs right here." Although this last puzzle was much more difficult than the preceding ones and he had done it all by himself, there was much less elation at its completion than with the previous ones. Instead, he had already turned his attention to the picture on it, casually taking his success for granted.

Mrs. Smith, who recorded this sequence commented: My mother used to say that there were four stages of learning or development (paraphrasing the folk wisdom regarding steps from infancy to age):

1. The child knows not, but *knows not* that he knows not.
2. The child knows not, but *knows* that he knows not.
3. The child knows, but *knows not* that he knows.
4. The child knows, and *knows* that he knows.

These sequences seem to take Ronnie through the last three of the above stages. We also see the subtle shifts of feeling about effort which accompany his changing perception of his capacities, and his actual mastery of the task. For some time he was very dependent on adult pressure and encouragement but as he experienced success he was proud of his mastery, and also developed increasing capacity to keep on trying, and increasing autonomy in doing so.

Steps in mastery of a motor challenge

For one child an intelligence test task is a demanding new challenge—for another, new physical feats are more disturbing. At the party, the "jumping board" was supported about eighteen inches above the level of the ground, easily crossed, and often jumped on by the other children. To Darlene, who had a slight orthopedic difficulty which caused awkwardness of motor coordination, the jumping board evidently seemed hazardous and she doubted her ability to manage it. By slow repeated efforts she gradually came to a triumphant mastery of the challenge. The sequences here are not unlike what one can observe in watching children learn to dive, or to handle gymnasium apparatus.*

When LBM asked Darlene and Diane if they would like to go on the jumping board, Darlene began to twirl her hair, and somewhat apprehensively said, "I don't know how to do that." At the same time she seemed interested and curious about it. LBM, Diane, and Darlene walked toward the board with Diane in the lead. Diane walked across, without hesitancy and with complete confidence.

Darlene watched her with interest and concern; she agreed to take her turn despite her uneasiness. With great uncertainty Darlene now mounted the steps one at a time and walked cautiously, feeling her footing and taking very small steps. She walked to the end of the board but was afraid to jump off. Although MS encouraged her to jump into her arms, Darlene was quite firm in her refusal, turned around and walked slowly back across the board, going down the steps one foot at a time.

A second time MS tried to encourage her but Darlene ignored the support; instead, she walked away toward where Diane was standing and watched as a boy ran boldly across and made a flying leap as he jumped off. When he did this Darlene made a guttural sound which seemed to reflect a good deal of inner tension with respect to this daring motor activity. She appeared even more anxious. MS thought it was merely because she wished she had the nerve to do the same. Darlene put two fingers in her mouth and laughed in a nervous way. She moved away and responded quickly to LW who offered to put on her name belt. BW felt that as the distance between Darlene and the jumping board increased she relaxed markedly; instead of nervous laughing she struck up a very free conversation with Diane.

A third effort was made to encourage her when her attention was directed to the board by the activity of others: she watched from the sidelines, keeping a safe distance. Three other children were having a wonderful time running, jumping, and whooping. She followed all this with mounting apprehension; her fingers were in her mouth and she rubbed her eyes in a nervous

* Recorded by Beatrice Wright.

tired way. When adults suggested that she join in the jumping board play, she resisted, shrinking back bodily. Finally she said simply but with conviction, "I don't like to," and wandered off. She walked over and stood close to Diane saying to an adult, "I like to seesaw," as if to turn her attention to a preferred activity. But there was no seesaw. Darlene went over and sat on the concrete bench; she seemed unable to keep her eyes from the jumping board although she could easily keep her distance. The boys were still jumping. Darlene said to LBM, "Them silly things make you feel silly." There was further conversation about something else but Darlene was primarily concerned with the jumping board and still couldn't keep from looking at it, though even the watching made her tense. She fingered her shoe nervously and then put her fingers in her mouth.

Finally she turned her complete attention to the jumping board. When Ray walked by, she asked him his name. Diane went to the jumping board and now the adults urged Darlene a fourth time, pointing out that they would hold her hand, she didn't have to jump, and so on. Again she said, "No" in a straightforward way, but with some apprehension, adding, "They all jump and fall." But the physical distance between Darlene and the jumping board now gradually narrowed as she continued to watch the performances, evidently with intense interest, and a wish to try it, along with increasing awareness of what was involved.

Suddenly she said to MS, "Can I jump? I can jump." Then she added, as if the full realization of her commitment required precautions, "Not with those two boys." (The boys were still jumping.) MS assured Darlene that all the other children would go away.

In this phase of positive effort, Darlene had the board all to herself. The threat of distraction or possible tripping by other children was removed. Simplifying the goal and keeping the first attempt within her range of confidence in mastery, she literally crawled up the steps on hands and feet, and walked across, very cautiously; when she got to the end she was not willing to jump into the adult's arms but instead she stepped off the board holding onto the adult's hand. She did not spontaneously go back to the board but willingly agreed to do so again upon suggestion. As she approached, a boy bounded by and Darlene recoiled. When the board was clear she climbed the steps, in a more mature way but still one foot at a time. She walked across with somewhat greater assurance but would not really jump; she stepped down and said with obvious delight, "I jumped." The viewing adults made much ado over her performance and she spontaneously returned to go over the board again. She did this several times, making grunting and pleasurable noises.

She was distracted now by some tricycle play, with much racing around, and this seemed to create tension—she stood watching, fingers in mouth, close to Diane as if for protection. Later she moved close to GH. MS encouraged her to go up the jumping board again but she resisted. GH encouraged her and she complied. Darlene seemed definitely more secure on the board than she did earlier. She still went up the steps one foot at a time. She easily stepped down from the jumping board at the far end. The next time she went she was not willing to step off without help from GH. Now she chose to jump (or rather step) into GH's waiting arms rather than MS's. The next time she insisted on the supporting arms of MS.

On the final round, however, she was able to jump off by herself, not in a free sweep, rather by a constrained steplike movement. But she was gleeful and ran around to start over with anticipation. Pleased chuckles accompanied her efforts. She now had the scene all to herself, and traversed the jumping board again and again. She was so absorbed with it, that she didn't notice a roaring plane overhead. She exclaimed for all to hear, "I jumped! I jumped!"

Steps in Darlene's mastery of the motor challenge

In this sequence we see certain steps toward mastery very similar to those we saw in Ronnie's first record: self-doubt, a need to distance herself from the challenge; after removing herself from the tension area, mobilizing her energy for a new try. She, like Ronnie, needed to measure her own readiness, to be allowed to make the decision herself at her own time. In this situation, much more time was required for watching and perhaps visual mastery, acquainting herself with the nature of the jumping board and the way other children used it. She was able to verbalize her feelings, her embarrassment, feeling "silly," her anxiety about falling after the jump. Her initial retreat was a clear example of "strategic withdrawal" or withdrawal as used by a vigorous child in preparation for subsequent participation.

It was just after she had openly expressed her anxiety that she drew closer to the jumping board, and suddenly experienced the conviction that she could jump. Once making the attempt on her own decision she was more free for further tries, moving now through sequences of limited goal (stepping off), more ambitious goal (jumping with help) until she finally accomplished the jump autonomously and with practice perfected it to a triumphant finish.

Her resistance to encouragement and help during a period of coming to terms with the challenge, followed by the ability to use help—help which respected the child's right to determine his own timing and readiness—led to the experience of capacity which was followed by autonomous effort and mastery. In this sense, the resistance to being pushed faster than she could manage, and even her strategic retreat, can be seen as expressions of the ego-strength shown in her subsequent mastery.

The role of aggression in mastering fear of the new

The threats experienced by small children in a situation which to the adult is innocuous or pleasing may evoke an aggressive coping sequence. Adults who feel variously secure in their intentions not to harm a child, or justified in whatever discomfort they may cause a child, often have difficulty sensing such threats, imagined and realistic, which children feel in many new situations. What these threats may be is hinted in Karen's uninhibited explorations and provocations.

When we look at Karen's responses to some of the new experiences in detail, we see that her efforts to understand, to find out, to be clear about situations were impressive features of her behavior from the beginning of our contact with her. This applied to things, people, relationships, and limits. Until she came to the test situation, curiosity was the response most vividly highlighted. When she was picked up to come to the testing office at the age of five years and three months:

> She crawled into the space behind the back seat of GH's car, and asked numerous questions about various objects in the car; when we left the car to go to the testing office she asked why GH would not join us, where she would be, and whether she would return.
>
> On the way to the room she asked, "Can I color?"
>
> When we entered the room, she asked about furnishings in the room, what the radiator was, the function of water, and the process of making steam.
>
> As she worked, her questions sometimes involved a sense of order and convention; how should the crayons be put away? But in addition she asked questions about things and questions about AM's personal belongings, such as her watch.
>
> She kept looking up at AM as though to figure out what the test was all about. She also constantly observed—watching and inspecting the test blank and AM's activities.
>
> On the trip home, she explored AM's car, opening the glove compartment, crawling from front to back, getting acquainted with the whole car.
>
> In subsequent test sessions, Karen tended to be very curious, and implemented her curiosity both by exploring physically and by asking numerous questions, which seemed to be evolved from a real need to know and understand rather than from any effort to delay or to avoid the test.

Both orality and aggression emerged as she was confined to the demands of the test itself.

> She made abortive movements as though she would color on AM's watch. Her speech and movements had a teasing, testing quality. She also made quick jabbing movements, bringing her sharpened pencil very close to AM's face, licking her face.
>
> Drawing, she soliloquized, "It's a cockroach with mean snakes on it. I'm going to get these crayons and let them bite you. They don't like to have you around." She extended her aggressive intentions to MS and GH.
>
> She drew over the test blanks.
>
> She kicked the chair almost constantly as she drew.

She pressed so hard that the pencil broke.

She threatened AM playfully, "I'm going to lick you." (spank)

She interrupted the test—Identification of Pictures—with "leaves for the snakes. Make some snakes."

On the Objects from Memory Test she said, the dog is a "Wow-wow." "He said, I like you. The shoe is going to dance by the dog. The dog steps in his daddy's shoes. You get out. You've knocked the car over." (There was an active quality, with movements accompanying her words.)

Following the reversal of roles, with AM closing her eyes at Karen's request, she picked up a doll, saying, "Dolly, were you hiding from me? I'm going to make your lips pencil-colored. I'm going to make your eyes and face and all of you pencil-colored." When she was not deterred, she actually colored very little on the doll.

She vigorously chewed on the doll's head when the Picture Identification Test was difficult for her.

She held the doll upside down by one leg. She commented, "She likes her games." She played out a toilet scene. Then she commanded the doll to sit down. "The puppy is going to bite, is going to mess that little girl's seat." (laughingly, knowingly)

She made growling sounds as AM asked several questions.

On the Comparison of Pictures: "The witch is behind the mother and behind the girl . . . a witch man, too. He's going to kill the man."

When she was asked the Opposite Analogies, she put her finger in her mouth and asked a question of AM. Then she retracted earlier aggressive comments, reassuring AM, "Oh, my snakes aren't really going to bite you. I'll fro' snakes at people." She then sagely announced that she would probably be hurt in turn and that this would be unpleasant.

She squeezed the sponge with unusual vigor, then colored on it.

She drew, saying, "There's a little tiny thing, like this. The kid is going to stick his finger in it." She decided there was a hole in a screen door. "He put his finger in it," an activity the mother dislikes. The child was spanked, she interpreted.

She hugged MS so hard she knocked her glasses off.

The sequence here was interesting: (1) Open questioning about things and people was followed by exploring limits. Her movements toward AM were distinctly aggressive, but not without some control. (2) Aggression increased in protected form through drawings. Then she actively defaced equipment. (3) As she became clearer about the permissiveness and harmlessness of testing procedures, she had the dog comment that he liked AM, but she continued to deface toys and equipment. (4) Then, she became indirect, projecting her needs onto the toys and fantasying aggressive releases for which she could deny personal responsibility. (5) She then verbally retracted her original aggressive intentions toward AM but showed more open direct aggression toward toys. Along with her retraction, she explained logically that control was necessary to avoid the unpleasantness of being treated aggressively in return. (6) In the end, aggressiveness fused with love appeared as vigorous affection.

She could shift aggression from people to things, make her feelings less direct by projective devices in active playing out and in fantasy, intellectualize her control of aggression toward people and find release in aggressive use of things, change aggression into more acceptable displays of affection. Mild degrees of aggression also appeared in her critical, resistive, and competitive behavior.

Here we have seen three children, each with a concern about mastery, each with doubts, making their respective ways toward success in dealing with the demands of the environment. The ways of Ronnie and Darlene were hesitant and gradual, Ronnie achieving pride in cognitive performance, Darlene in a motor achievement; Karen's way was rash and provocative, full of devices for testing the adult, reversing roles and getting the upper hand—methods apparently motivated by the need to master her feelings of smallness and weakness vis-à-vis the adults.

Other varieties of sequence patterns in the process of mastery

We have already observed sequences in the concrete details of behavior in dealing with new situations and difficulties encountered in the intelligence test and at the party. These sequences within a single session sometimes involved marked variations in the integration of the child's functioning:

In his initial activity with the toys, Ray seemed rigid and clumsy, bumping into things on the floor, knocking things down, moving stiffly and heavily with finger tensions expressed in nonfunctional curling movements and rigid control reflected in his deadpan facial expression. All this was soon relieved as the play session went on; his handling of the toys was skillful, there were more smiles, relaxation and better coordination. His pronunciation seemed clearer as well. The arrangement of toy and fantasy sequences lost their rigidity parallel with the loss of body rigidity.

At first there was also some rigid lining up, but later his play was dominated by his thematic intentions. He responded sensitively to texture, sound and bodily contact and after his initial awkwardness was seen to hold the toys softly.

Here Ray did not allow himself to be inhibited in his approach to the play session as Rachel had been; he managed to introduce his own pattern by very simple organizing devices. Success in this was releasing and calmed his initial anxiety, so that he was able to deal with the opportunity in an increasingly creative way.

In this group it was rare for a child to move as Vivian did by a slow process of barely discernible and very gradual increments of expanding positive motor response. This type of gradual improvement occurred in Roger whose speech seemed to improve as his relation with the adult progressed during the hour. When a child also combined passive, demanding attitudes, and self-assertive dominant ones we might find sequences moving from one to the other in alternating directions depending upon his relation to the situation at the start. With Cynthia we also found alternations from quietness to spurts of daring behavior as she broke through constricted moods. Several children in making a strong attack on a new situation as Martin did with the Miniature Life Toys, moved from fast talking at first to slowing down in a more relaxed way after fifteen minutes or so. With young children like Sheila sequences may be dominated by shifts in involvement, loss of interest, limited capacity for persisting with the problem, or a need for a new start with a fresh stimulus.

When Greg seemed to deny the lady at the beginning of his responses to the Rorschach, apparently because he associated her with sexual interests, and then accepted her at the end when he gave up the integrative efforts because with him integration implied union, we saw the relation between sequences and the level and methods of resolution of conflict shown by the child.

Thus, on projective tests, sequences were directed by shifts in the emotional response to the stimulus, especially by the point at which anxiety exerted a strong influence on the child's response. Dr. Kass commented, "Many of the children whose behavior became disintegrated in some way, or disoriented in some way also had a disintegration at a more primitive level, at a perceptual level or a level of speech in which the area itself was affected directly by the conflict. Now the perception or the verbalization is a rather strongly established function; and a level of anxiety may arise which can interfere with the functioning only if it becomes sufficiently high." He added that Barbie seemed to show an intermediate step; the sequences involving two steps were more complex and perhaps less susceptible to disintegration since a possibility for interposing controls was multiplied. The controls could be interposed at the functional level or at the level where anxiety entered in.

Uses of delay

In the MLT, initial delay occurred with many children and had different qualities and roles for different individuals as judged by what followed:

Diane: Initial delay and poised appraisal led to comfortable relaxed activity in areas of security and familiarity such as family life.

Ralph: Delay for selection, then mastery, motor release, and social inter-action.

Darlene: Delay in the interests of differentiation and clarification of own values, and preferences, then selective participation, within accepted guilt-free limits.

Barbie: Learning what the score is, mastering techniques for reaching it, making the process part of herself by intelligent assimilation of the possibilities of the situation, and what might be socially acceptable.

Donald: Delay for clarification, selection, then fantasy elaboration leading to idiosyncratic fantasy-laden action.

Sally: Hesitant autonomous appraisal, classification of objects, problem solving, with continued emotional distance, reserve.

Ronnie: Cautious protected appraisal followed by determined mastery of manageable threats, disintegration with unmanageable threats.

Vernon: Long delay with controlled affect, "understanding," leading to skillful construction.

Teddy: A short period of delay with initial rapid cognitive mastery through observation, differentiation, concept formation, "knowing," controlled affect and drives expressed through integrated fantasy.

While many children used delay for one or another kind of sizing up of a situation, this cognitive mastery could lead to quite different next steps: some were highly selective and narrowed the field of their activity while others were much freer in their use of the available areas and materials. In other words, delay facilitated well-directed control in some instances; in others it led to release.

In those children who continued to deal with the situation in a very controlled way, the motivation was in some instances the wish to avoid doing anything wrong, while in others control was oriented toward mastery within areas dictated by strong interests or preferences.

Thus delay as such did not indicate anxiety; it was often simply an indication of the child's need to orient himself before acting at all. In fact we can hardly evaluate the meaning to the child of his delaying tactics until we watch to see what he does next and how he does it.

Children who began by immediate activity differed even more widely in the apparent intent and effect of their activity:

Sheila: Seemed to express feelings of mastery by organizing a selected area, while keeping motor and affect scope limited; asserting her own goals masterfully.

Chester: Active exploration for appraisal leading to physical mastery, enjoyment, fantasy elaboration.

Susan: Limited her anxiety and depressive responses by denial, while starting quickly with rapid investment in the opportunity, accenting the positive potential; fantasy gratification.

Jo Anne: Asserted own dominance through verbal threats to the adult, finding scope for her own areas of mastery in motor and dramatic action.

Karen: Contacted and incorporated objects effectively, incessant seeking of sensuous contact, and evoking interaction.

Brennie: Reduced initial anxiety by fantasy and mockery, while quickly moving into action with flexible even fluid shifting of affective levels, cognitive content and goals, manipulation of adults for his own gratification.

Greg: Mildly anxious exploratory physical activity, embellishing the situation by fantasy, handling spots of deep anxiety through primary process integrations.

Terry: Hyperactive competitive mastery, loquacity, maintaining constant social contact, and projecting.

Lenny: Ingenuous impulsive barging in, alternating with anxious bewildered hesitation and slow clarification, then followed by integrated manipulation and enjoyment.

Trudy: Step by step expansion from safe areas of intellectual and manipulative mastery to broader areas of social mastery and relatedness.

Molly: Defended her own stance, asserting strong self-awareness, soliciting support, while also achieving mastery via struggle.

Martin: Fenced off a safe area, fending off imagined attackers by porcupine attitude, while achieving mastery at a fantasy level implemented by play constructions.

Daryl: Symbiotically relied on the "other"—mother, sibling or other familiar support, while elaborating hostility in fantasy.

Ray: Although quickly active with the toys, the quality was one of passive experiencing with pleasure, with impulsive uncoordinated beginnings; organized play of limited constructiveness at first, good integration later.

Action, then, could serve needs for orientation by selecting the first familiar object or by promoting wide observation through exploring and observing from different vantage points; or it could allay anxiety by moving toward a source of protection, or selecting a safe area; or it could lead directly to sensuous gratification; or it could be a first step in an elaborate sequence. Occasionally activity seemed to be merely impulsive and haphazard, or an expression of a wish to establish vigorous control of the whole situation before specific goals had been formulated.

Occasionally action led to retreat. Only Daryl in this group seemed to use a self-destructive type of retreat, escape, or avoidance; in most instances avoidance and delay were used for progress and increasing integration followed by more active ways of coping with problems.

Sequences through time

Over a longer period of time we see such sequences as these:

The initial resistance of seven months ago is now completely gone. She is now quite spontaneous, more actively integrative, less emotionally and motivationally flat and more imaginative, in short much more of a self-assertive, self-expressive and distinctive individual.

The aggressive coping methods so prominent a little more than a year ago were successful in leading to positive growth. This is still a vigorous, energetic girl who has a great ability to deal directly with situations but it is also one who has begun to be able to admit the social demands of the situation.

Observations such as these can lull our thinking into a comfortable belief in steady "progress" if we do not scrutinize more closely the content and sequences in all individual cases. Our assumptions regarding growth, whether they focus on physical maturation or on learning, tend to emphasize continuity in one direction, as if a child retained any progressive step in the same manner in which he retained a new tooth. Other longitudinal studies based on behavior records have already shown that a specific level of "adjustment" is not retained in this way —that a child may reach a level of good functioning in one developmental-situational setting only to lose his gains at the next turn of the road—and regain them again later. Throughout the life span people experience ups and downs, good seasons and bad ones, times that are hard, and times that are favorable.

In this sense, sequences through life result from the ebb and flow of energy, the phases of good bodily integration as against phases of illness, endocrine upheaval, or equilibrium disturbed by changed pressures from the environment. As the latter bring loss of excessive increase in stimulation and opportunities for gratification or demands to be met, the integrative capacities may be strained and new coping methods required.

Other variations related to different demands at different times and stages foreshadow sequences which are sometimes mistaken for development. Rachel, so overwhelmed and immobilized by the multitude of toys in free unstructured situations, was totally at ease in the pediatric examination which was of course familiar to her from her long period of medical care, and in the body-photograph situation which followed a simple routine supervised in detail by an adult. In the Witkin tests which involved practice sessions following specific directions, her easy, even proud cooperation suggested that she would manage school demands far better than the open-ended play sessions and party in which we saw her at first. But her difficulty in unfamiliar situations containing multiple stimuli left a question about how she would get along in future unfamiliar, unorganized settings. Rachel's extreme inhibition in free sessions in contrast to her alacrity and motor freedom in directed situations implies that she was gratified and at ease in the latter, and that anxiety was aroused by her sense of bewilderment and unsureness of what to do when she was not given specific directions. Here we can see that the relation of the environmental demand to the child's expectations helps to determine the differences in stress at different times and the corresponding differences in coping capacity in a given situation.

Molly's steps in mastering fear, pain, shyness, dependence

Another type of sequence in mastery of major developmental tasks through time can be illustrated by referring again to the records on Molly's behavior at home.

In dealing with coping behavior at home, we have a more or less constant setting in which the changing demands and capacities stimulated by growth in one child meet the changes in the family from month to month and from year to year. Molly's records are very explicit about the steps in her mastery of certain fears, pain and shyness. The fact that she is one of four children, with older sisters and a younger brother, and that her records start while she is still a two-year-old, make them especially interesting as an illustration of some processes in the development of mastery during the preschool period.

Steps in mastering fear of thunder*

A brief summary of the stages Molly went through in conquering her fear of thunder and the noise of a jet plane follows:

As a two-year-old, Molly cried many times and was completely terrified during thunderstorms or when a jet plane passed overhead.

A year later she was able to get into bed with her older sister during a thunderstorm and accept comfort from her.

At about the same time Molly began to reassure herself (and her baby brother) saying, "It's just noise and it really won't hurt you a bit."

A month after this storm Molly was again terrified as a jet plane flew unusually low overhead; she cried, and clung to her sister for comfort. A few hours later she repeated several times to herself, "Thunder really doesn't hurt you; it just sounds noisy. I'm not scared of planes, just thunder."

* Based on material in L. B. Murphy, Learning how children cope with problems, *Children*, Vol. 4, 1957, and material presented at the 1957 International Congress of Psychology in Brussels.

The next month she opened the door into her parents' room during a thunderstorm, saying that her younger brother was afraid (although he was really fast asleep).

Nine months later, at four years and two months, she was awakened from a nap during a thunderstorm, but remained quietly in bed. Afterward she said to her sister, "There was lots of thunder, but I just snuggled in my bed and didn't cry a bit."

Four months later, at four and a half years, Molly showed no open fear herself during a storm and comforted her frightened little brother, saying, "I remember when I was a little baby and I was scared of thunder and I used to cry and cry every time it thundered."

Here we see the two-steps-forward-one-step-backward process: (1) Overt expression of fearful affect and helplessness; (2) to actively seeking comfort from a supporting person; (3) to internalizing the comfort and the image of the comforting person, acting as comforter to herself; (4) to differentiating sources of the fear while still reverting to the need for physical comfort from her sister; (5) to projecting the fear to her baby brother (as a way of rationalizing getting the support she needed) and seeking a symbol of support (opening the door without demand for physical or other active comforting); (6) to combining actively comforting herself with formulation of a self-image in terms of pride in control and mastery of her fear; (7) to reaction formation, achievement of bravery and referral of the fear to her past.

Steps in mastering pain

While a concept of herself as brave seemed to emerge from these records of mastering fear of thunder, the development of still more conscious control and its relation to both her image of herself and the image she wanted to present can be observed in the records of Molly as she coped with pain. During successive visits to the doctor and dentist she developed from a very frightened screaming child to one of great strength, who could take the shots or the drilling without a whimper. Her basically active orientation appeared in the first note:

At the age of two years and seven months Molly poured medicine in the toilet stool after having taken a dose or two for a slight case of the hives.

A year later (age: three years, five months) Molly had a bad cut from a fall and it was necessary to have a few stitches. Molly cried all the way to the office and told the doctor, "I don't know you and I don't like you and I amn't going to let you touch me!" Mother talked to her soothingly but firmly. Molly continued to cry then stopped and said, "Will you stay with me and take hold of my hand?" Mother agreed. Molly allowed the doctor to go ahead. When he finished he gave Molly a dime. Later she proudly displayed cut and dime to everyone. Four days later when the doctor removed the stitches, which Molly had obviously not looked forward to, mother was surprised when Molly did not cry. When he finished Molly looked at him expectantly. Mother suggested they go but Molly hesitated and said, "I was good this time, wasn't I?" Doctor produced a dime. Again Molly proudly displayed her dime and told of not crying.

Two weeks later Molly was determined to light a match although she had been warned of its possible consequences. It burned the end of her finger and Molly screamed very loudly. Mother bandaged the finger and Molly continued to cry for a while. When daddy came home she said, "I made a match burn and it burned my finger real bad and I'm not ever going to make another match burn!"

Six months later at the age of four years Molly was able to take a shot from the doctor for an ear infection without whimpering. Molly was obviously disgusted with the too talkative doctor who talked about "how brave" she was going to be and mother felt she would have bitten out her tongue rather than shed a tear! But a week later Molly refused to take medicine and began to cry. Mother was firm and Molly took it but spit it up. Mother poured out another dose, obviously unhappy with Molly's actions. Molly looked at mother, evidently sensing mother's feelings, stopped crying and swallowed the medicine. About two-and-a-half months later Molly did not cry when being treated for pink eye, although mother knew it was painful. As they started to leave the doctor caught Molly's glance at a jar of gumdrops on his desk and he immediately gave her one telling her she was a brave girl.

At four years and four months Molly was able to keep from crying until she got home after a bad fall and cut she received while playing with some of her older sisters' friends. When she got home and was asked if it didn't hurt she began to cry and said, "It just hurts a lot, but I didn't want the big kids to see me cry!" A month later Molly was able to keep from crying (although mother saw tears in her eyes) when her "boy friend" and/or hero had gotten off the teeter-totter without waiting for Molly to reach the ground. Her mother commented that of late Molly doesn't want anyone to see her cry—much less her "hero."

At four years and eight months Molly was able to go to a new dentist without crying, although mother realized she was close to tears as they waited for the appointment. When the nurse added to Molly's anxiety by requesting that Molly go in without her mother, Molly looked at her mother in a "stricken way" but said nothing and complied. Her mother was amazed at the "stern stuff Molly is made of at times." That night at home to anyone who would listen she told, "I didn't cry a bit." About three weeks later Molly was able to have the dentist fill a tooth without crying. As Molly went into the inner office alone she looked back at her mother but went on in without saying anything. When Molly came out she was smiling and said it didn't hurt, but later she told her mother it really did hurt even though she said it didn't.

Nine days later when she had to return to the dentist for another filling Molly's older sister (who also had an appointment) accompanied Molly and her mother. Molly was given her choice of being first or last. Molly thought a minute and then decided to be first saying, "I'll be first—then I won't have to wait and think about it while I wait . . . it hurts more if you think about it first." Her mother was interested in the "maturity of her reasoning." There were no tears and again Molly came out smiling.

Here we see a combination of external rewards, self-esteem, and status in the eyes of both adults and children, combined with flexible support from her mother, contributing to the development of control which used stoical inhibition and temporary denial, along with active solicitation of reinforcement through telling of her achievement. Some observers have remarked that early pressure to control crying has increased in the generation since World War II. If so, the pattern is widespread; it was supported by "the big kids" rather than by parents in this instance.

Shyness to confidence

In the previous record we have indications of the importance of standards of older children for a child like Molly who had older sisters. In the following sequence of notes on Molly's progress from shyness to confidence the role of sibling relationships is still greater, with pulls from both her older sisters, and her baby brother.

From being a shy little girl with strangers she gradually became a leader. On the Halloween before she was five she prodded her sisters on to visit the homes of strangers for their tricks and treats; the preceding year she did not want to go out at all.

The steps in this development were as follows:

At age three years and three months Molly used the excuse of "helping mother take care of Jimmie (baby brother) for not accompanying sisters to Sunday School without mother. After her sisters had left she remarked "Guess I'll go to Sunday School next Sunday, but I just wanted to help you with Jimmie this time." Two weeks later she was still unable to go with her sisters but she stormed at her mother for not going. After her sisters had left, she complained "I wish I had gone—could I go now?" She was told she'd have to wait until next Sunday.

Two weeks later at a picnic it took Molly about ten minutes' watching of a game of tag before she was able to tag one of the children—and then ran behind her mother. Her mother noted that this was her "first overture on her own to a stranger." Another fortnight later she thought over her grandmother's invitation to accompany her home for a visit but then she used the excuse that her next older sister would be lonesome without her. After her grandmother had left, "I really wish I had gone now—could you take me to Kansas City now?" When she was told "no" she was somewhat disappointed, suggesting that she was approaching a time when she would be able to make such a trip.

Not long after this she watched some neighborhood children playing on the jungle gym for about five minutes. Then she got some cookies and offered them to one of the smaller boys. One boy accepted them and joined Molly in eating cookies. After the boy had finished his cookies he returned to the jungle gym; Molly followed and was soon climbing with the rest. At lunch she told mother how she had succeeded in making a new friend.

This ability to initiate relationships with children developed gradually, often supported by a gift which she used to arouse the child's interest:

At three years and seven months at a picnic Molly initiated conversation with a small colored boy and gave him the better part of a stick of candy. The boy thanked her and ran back to his own table. Two days later when a girl of eight came to play with Molly, Molly offered first puzzles and then crayons. When her guest was not responsive Molly offered her "sissy's doll house" and her guest responded at once. But about two months later two children, ages three and four, came to visit. When mother suggested they all go to the playroom Molly continued to play by herself for a few minutes but watched the guests out of the corner of her eye. Then with no conversation she offered each child a stick of gum. After a moment or two she invited them to her playroom where they all had a wonderful time.

Later that fall she used the excuse of keeping her mother "company" to cover up her own shyness in not wanting to accompany children strange to Molly who were taking her older sisters to play miniature golf. After they were gone Molly asked several times when they would be home. Mother felt that the strangeness of the children plus newness of the game (where Molly might have to expose her lack of skill) was the cause of her decision to stay with her mother.

Now nearly four years old, Molly used the excuse of needing to "watch baby for mother" to refuse an invitation of her sister's friend to leave mother in the basement of the school to go upstairs and visit Molly's sister's room. Again her mother felt that the strange situation with no big sister present was the cause for her refusal.

About four months later, although Molly had talked about going to Sunday School all week, when she got there she began to cry as her mother started to leave. As soon as her mother was gone she stopped crying and said, "My mother will come back for me when Sunday School is over. Are we going to sing this morning?" Two weeks later as Molly entered her Sunday School class she walked over to her teacher and said, "What are we going to do today?" There was no trouble when her mother left.

At four years and four months, although she was eagerly anticipating a ride on a school bus with two older sisters the last day of school, when they were going to a picnic, she hung back when a group of strange children arrived, saying she didn't "know any of those kids." After her sister pointed out several children Molly did know, Molly said, "W-e-ll, can I sit by you if I ride?" When she was assured that she could she went along and enjoyed the ride very much. This pleasure strengthened her wish to ride with the group so that when her mother offered to take Molly home in the car with her after the picnic, Molly preferred to ride on the bus with the rest of the group.

By a couple of months later she was able to wait on a customer at her older sisters' vegetable stand all by herself with no hesitancy, although she had to come to the house to consult her mother as to weight, price, making change, etc. Her mother commented that the loss of shyness was the biggest change that summer; she was now free to talk with new children or adults.

In the fall at a PTA meeting with her mother Molly hung back for only a moment when the rest of the children went out to play on playground equipment saying she didn't "know anyone." Then she added, "Well, I guess I'll go anyway—I guess I'll find someone to play with." Molly joined in taking turns with the other children and played without any apparent shyness.

At Halloween, she prodded her sisters on to visit homes of strangers, saying, "Well, they have their porch lights on—sure come on!!" Her mother noted that this was also a big change—the previous year she had not wanted to go out at all. "Now she just loves Halloween and wishes it would come more often."

After the preceding illustrations of Molly's drive toward maturity we are not surprised to see Molly grow from a somewhat dependent small child to a very independent one who wants no help unless absolutely necessary.

At age two years and seven months, Molly accepted help from a strange man in order to climb upon a fire truck which had been put in the park for the children to play on. She had previously asked her mother for help but mother was unable to comply because of holding baby brother and suggested she ask the man to help her. Two months later Molly frantically called to her mother, "Come get me, mommy, before this darn tree (Christmas) falls on me!" Molly had been warned by her daddy not to play beneath the tree because of its wobbly base. When mother rescued Molly and before she had time to scold her Molly said, "See, that's what my daddy told me—that darn tree will fall over." Mother decided Molly's own scolding was enough. The next day Molly asked her older sister to go with her, when they were uptown shopping, to see Santa in order to obtain a treat that he was passing out since Molly was reluctant to go by herself. Two months later Molly accepted comfort and love from her sister one night when she (Molly) became frightened from some unknown cause during the night.

But only four days later—she was now three years, one month—Molly screamed and kicked at her mother for picking her up when crossing a busy street saying, "I hate you, I don't need to be carried, I can walk—you leave me alone!" The next day Molly joined her mother early for breakfast telling her older sister to stay in bed, "Your breakfast isn't ready, yet," in order to have her mother to herself.

About three months later Molly told her mother when she became separated from her, that she was not frightened, but her mother stated she looked pretty sober when she found her and said, "You took an awfully long time." Mother also noted that Molly held very tightly to her mother's hand as they walked to the car. About two months later Molly asked her mother to remain with her "and hold my hand" when the doctor treated a bad cut on her face. This need for her mother's support under stress was balanced by her autonomy in safe situations: About a week later Molly got up in the morning before her mother. When her mother questioned her she said, "Well, I woked up and you were still asleep and I didn't want to wake you up so I just put on my shorts and came out to play." When mother questioned her about having some breakfast Molly said, "Yes, I have, I looked in the fridge and saw bananas and I ate two and drank some milk and ate three cookies." [Mother comments that Molly could dress herself at an earlier age than any of her other children and has always welcomed a chance to prove what a big girl she is.] The next month Molly wet her bed during the night, came downstairs, changed into dry pajamas, and put a big towel in the wet place in her bed. When mother questioned her as to why she hadn't called mother, Molly said, "I didn't need you—I can turn on the bathroom light and I know where the towels and pajamas are." [Again mother comments on how much more self-sufficient Molly is than any of her other children.] Mother also stated that it is a long way from Molly's room upstairs to the bathroom downstairs but this does not seem to bother Molly.

But at three years nine months, as we saw in the preceding sequence, Molly would not accompany her sisters and two strange girls to play miniature golf. (Mother felt this was because she had not previously played miniature golf and would not care to demonstrate her ignorance and lack of skill of the game in front of strangers, so she elected to stay home instead although otherwise she would have liked very much to have gone.) About five weeks later, although Molly was quite upset when she became separated from her mother while downtown, she was able to go to the family car and wait until her mother came looking for her.

At the age of four and a half years when her daddy tried to show Molly (who was having some difficulty) how to shoot her new toy bow and arrow she began to cry and said, "I'll learn myself—I don't want anyone to help me!" She was gone for about thirty minutes. When she came back she was smiling, "I can shoot my bow," demonstrating her new skill and said, "I didn't need anyone to help me—I can do things myself." About four months later (age now four years, nine months) Molly said she wanted something to do, "I don't want a little kid's thing to do—I want a grownup's thing to do." After a while she asked her mother to make some chocolate frosting so she (Molly) could "make some frosted graham crackers for dessert for lunch." After she had made them she hid them so that no one would eat them before lunch.

The reader will already have noted that the direction of progress from direct, primitive, impulsive ways of coping to more controlled, sometimes indirect ways in line with socially approved standards, appears in each of the areas of Molly's development we have sampled;

the directness and impulsiveness is expressed in different ways—screaming at thunder, throwing medicine in the toilet, hurling angry announcements of antagonism at the doctor, and sly evasion of situations in which she felt shy. Over and over again we find her moving toward a picture of herself as one who doesn't cry, who can manage for herself, who is in short a big girl and competent, but one who remembers what it was like to be a baby and cry, be impatient, and frightened.

The examples of older sisters, and of other older children, and of her boy friend, seem to offer even stronger pulls toward the modification of her infantile coping methods than the limits set by adults. She wants to earn the respect of the big kids.

Molly "learned" to cope in more acceptable ways, through example, identification, receiving rewards for controlled behavior, getting direct satisfaction from the results of her methods, and with the help of her own memory and insight into patterns which grow from baby feelings as compared with those expected of big people.

At the same time, through all the records it is obvious that this is no straight line development; Molly progresses and regresses and progresses again; her regressions come at times when her own frustration is most acute, or too many demands are made at once, or where she feels under some threat such as separation from her mother. Her times of progressing seem to come most consistently during periods of gratification and well-being, the afterglow of Christmas, the freedom of being able to be out of doors in the spring and summer. With her high standards and her perception of what it means to be "a big kid," her own capacity for improved control probably contributed to her increased security and maturity, and to her feeling of differentiating herself from her little brother, who now had the difficulties and problems with control which she remembered and understood.

If we now review the samples of processes of mastery presented in this chapter we are impressed by the complexity of many of the examples, a complexity which is surprising if we look at records of young children against a background of either laboratory experiments or theoretical formulations. In Ronnie's struggles with intelligence test tasks, Darlene's struggles with the jumping apparatus, and Molly's struggles with fear, pain, and shyness we have a complex interaction of aim (mastery), ambivalently fearful and eager feelings, resistance to or compliance with pressure from adults or older children and indifference to or reassurances by support from these others. The child responds with varying configurations of retreat and limitation of the pressure, evoking support, trying to understand, making an effort—with alternations of doubt and confidence for a considerable period

before near-mastery reinforces confidence and leads to the crystalliza-
tion and integration of perception, feeling, and behavior in the actual
experience of mastery and the pride accompanying it. In very few
children of this age did progress in dealing with the environment
come by smooth steps implied in the formulation, "aim and drive and
competence results in satisfaction." "Learning a new skill" or learning
to conquer fear usually involved an interaction between resistance to
the progressive step and active effort to move ahead.

PART III ❧❧❧

ASPECTS OF MASTERY

9

ORIENTATION AND
FAMILIARIZATION

WHAT HAVE WE BEEN SEEING as we acquainted ourselves with these young children's responses to new opportunities, challenges, and difficulties? Not just perception, learning, memory, and other familiar mental functions; defense mechanisms were used, usually in combination with one or another group of active coping devices. We need now to review some of these steps toward mastery in terms which express what is happening in the child's way of dealing with the environment. Let us begin with the problem of newness itself.

It is intriguing to see that the same things which are fascinating through their novelty, or through their unexpected qualities, can be terrifying through their strangeness under other circumstances, as if there were a sheer quantitative difference in thresholds involved. Often the threshold for delight and the threshold for fear (perhaps through the seventh nerve threshold differentiation) are very close together. The same surprising loud bang or slapstick which can be fun if it can be taken in stride (usually in an otherwise safe and familiar situation) can be absolutely terrifying to a small child if it is a little louder or comes a little quicker, involves a little more violent movement, or occurs in a situation when the child is already insecure for other reasons. What is terrifying to the three-year-old may be assimilated by the four-year-old. Loudness and suddenness are not the same dimension as strangeness but they may function the same way as far as thresholds are concerned—that is, the threshold for delight and threshold for terror being quite close together. There is also delight in being able to control the fear or other negative affect. As Charles Lamb remarked, "And if I laugh at any mortal thing, 'tis that I may not weep."

This is relevant to the Miniature Life Toy play situations where that which is in reality too big to handle can be reduced to manageable proportions. A fire truck, or an Indian with a tomahawk is a terrifying thing but if it is put into small dimensions and made so that it will stay still, and so that the child can manipulate it, he will have the fascination of the terrifying thing and at the same time mastery over it. He gets not only the delight of mastering the fearsome object but the delight of mastery of his own impulse system.

A closely related situation is the use of masks to make strangeness controllable. Where a mask concealing the face of a familiar person may be terrifying to a small child, pulling the mask on and off the face like a peek-a-boo may be a favorite game. The child soon finds that the strangeness can be controlled, or better still, that the strangeness is itself a function of that which can be controlled. The very fact that there is some real fear there gives the necessary excitement, and at the same time there is what Woodworth calls an "escape motive." A child gets himself into a predicament for the pleasure of getting out. Real titillation of fear gives delight if it is not too intense, and the relaxation and mastery components involved in escape guarantee an oscillation between two types of intense joy.

We have been following the distinction that that which is "strange" is a little on the negative side, although what we call "novel" is by implication interesting. But the references for the word "strange" in Bartlett's *Familiar Quotations*,[1] a good many of them from Shakespeare, contain no such sense of the negative. For adults, the strange is on the borderline between the acceptable and unacceptable, and very largely in terms of its relation to the ego—that is, what is ego-alien or ego-syntonic, or perhaps more simply non-me versus me. As things become a part of me they cease to be strange. Not everything outside of me is repugnant to me. It may have interest in a remote sort of way. The change in "psychological distance" which is related to the mask game involves the delight in the sheer transition itself from familiar to unfamiliar, and in this way is related to *déjà vu* experiences and what Titchener[2] called the attachment of feelings of recognition to objects which have not actually been experienced before. Perhaps the strange is a composite involving familiar and unfamiliar components so that it sets off both these groups of responses and thereafter involves ego nearness and ego distance at the same time. This would contribute to the bewildering feeling and perhaps titillate the impulse to mastery. Individual differences in children's delight or fear in relation to the strange may be partly a matter of what the child feels he can master, and also a question of what is a part of the ego or what can be made a part of the ego, as well as resultants of earlier pleasure or distress with new people or in new situations.

Ethologists report that certain newborn animals or newly hatched birds are quite without fear of the "natural enemies" of the species or strange animals until a certain age. Apparently the fear period or hostile reaction comes on suddenly and from then on is built into the individual's repertory by species mates around him. There is, however, the implication that without social reinforcement, the fear period itself is rather brief and that exposure to the natural enemy before or after this period entails no fear. This is reminiscent of William James' observations on the optimal period of expression of an instinct, the fact that it has to be stamped in at the right time or it will never function; a modern formulation of this is "the critical phase," as discussed by Spitz[3] and others.

From behavior records such as those available from diaries of infant development, it seems that the perception of strangeness (in people and places as contrasted with sharp sudden auditory or visual stimuli) dawns upon different babies at different times and in different ways. In our records and observations, and those of K. Wolf[4] and others, an anxious response to awareness of a strange person occurs at different ages in different babies; it is sometimes seen at the phase of marked development of visual perception at about eight weeks. I have also seen evidence of unhappy perception of a female figure as not-my-mother at four months, and differentiated responses to mother as compared with other women are also observed in the infancy records of Escalona and Leitch at this period. In other babies it is not observed until the age of eight or nine months, whence comes the term René Spitz has popularized, "eight-months' anxiety."[5]

Just as the baby goes through a multitude of experiences of feeding satisfactions, frustrations and adaptations, some of which in themselves involve phases of recognizing and coming to terms with strange tastes and textures, so, we must infer, new and strange visual perceptions of objects impinge upon his mind with different combinations of satisfaction and distress, gradually building expectancies for better or for worse, depending upon what he is able to make out of the experience and do with it. Thus strangeness in itself acquires its own colors and its own implications. Some mothers are alert to the baby's feelings of the new and the strange and greatly help him to "get used to" things, to find new things, new places, and new people satisfying.

There seems to be a continuum from the utterly new which is bewildering, or, if it contains some vague feelings of familiarity, becomes the merely strange, then passes through the accepted to the fully familiar and then on to the tedious. That which is to arouse us or deeply satisfy us must have elements of familiarity but also elements of challenge. There must be something to do. The utterly strange may immobilize us because it says, "Here is something to do," but does not give us any hint as to what to do. There is a challenge but no cue as to how to handle it. The first day at nursery school (or the first day at a new job) may have this quality, as we saw in Chapter 3. It may be that a process of perceptual structuring permits a gradually familiarized structure to take shape. Organized perception permits more adequate and satisfying management. Thus gratifying values and cathexis or investments increase through this increasing familiarity. From observation of children's increasingly deep involvement with practice of new skills until they are mastered, followed by reduction of interest after mastery is consolidated, we can formulate the following sequence: anxiety about the new strange stimulus-situation or demand gives way to interest as familiarization begins. Increasing mastery is accompanied by increasing zest, and gratifying repetition. As the activity and object become totally mastered—where there is nothing more that is new, nothing new at all—interest wanes. The child's attention is turned to a new challenge.

Strangeness in the locomotor period

The achievement of locomotion, first with crawling and then with walking, means a dramatic expansion of the spatial world of the child, both two-dimensionally and three-dimensionally, with both dramatic gains and dramatic losses. Instead of being dependent upon the wish or interest of the adult who transports him from one room to another, the child now explores on his own initiative, discovering not only new areas of space as he gets into new rooms, cupboards, chests of drawers, and climbs under, onto, around, and behind furniture which formerly constituted barriers, but he discovers new things, and the actual and manipulative qualities of things, in places that were already somewhat familiar to him.

During this period when so much is incompletely understood and when stimulation has not yet lost its excitement through the dullness of repetition, sensitive children are frequently exposed to the danger of feeling overwhelmed. Even for the child who has become very familiar with everything inside the walls of his own home and a few other homes such as those of close family friends or relatives, newness offers a challenge to knowing. The child constantly experiments in order to find out what to do with new things and how to do it.

After mastering the anxieties at first aroused by the new and the strange, these experiences may be exciting and be greeted eagerly. The extent to which this occurs differs from one child to another. For one child to whom newness has progressively brought new satisfactions, a strange new experience arouses fantasies of new opportunities and potential fun; for another, strangeness brings potential ogres in its shadows. For still another, strangeness is simply a question mark, something to discover; this child will let strangeness have a fair chance. He allows it to show its colors; he does not prejudge it. One child may march forward, ready to beard the lion in his den if need be, while another skips into newness as if it carried a rainbow's promise of a pot of gold. Still another is transfixed and immobilized, seemingly hypnotized by inscrutable forces inherent in strangeness itself. What a child does with the opportunities, challenges, threats, and question marks which his experience of newness provides depends not only on this experience but many other aspects of his personality, and many preceding experiences during his few years.

Thus the child's experience of any new situation away from home and with strange people depends both on the resultants of the earliest infantile experiences of getting used to new tastes, sights, sounds, and on the consequences of his own efforts to explore the world of his home and neighborhood during the locomotor phase. These results of exploration in turn depend on the range and quality of new experiences away from home and his feelings about them, especially the degree to which he has developed a sense of mastery and capacity to handle the typical demands and challenges which confront him.

The process of familiarization

We can say then that in the early weeks and months and years, part of a child's task is to develop a way of getting used to things, to develop an approach to the new which will help him to come to terms with newness, turn it into the familiar, and to master it. It is only as an adult that we can see in dramatic clarity the ways in which the satisfying elements of former experiences are used as threads to be woven into new ones so that continuities are felt and a bridge is made from the old to the new. In infancy and early childhood, before experiences and memories of them have accumulated, we have to assume that there is less to draw upon and that consequently this cannot be the only method of making the new acceptable.

What are some of the other steps in familiarization? As we watch the baby during the earliest weeks and months, we find an enormous amount of just looking and listening, as if the baby was trying to "get to know" each new object which attracts its attention. Very, very early this looking can even involve some rudimentary process of comparison. Milicent Shinn describes this in her exquisite and classic account of the development of a baby:[6]

> This was on the twenty-fifth day, toward evening, when the baby was lying on her mother's knee by the fire in a condition of high well-being and content, gazing at her grandmother's face with an expression of attention. I came and sat down close by, leaning over the baby, so that my face must have come within the indirect range of her vision. At that she turned her eyes to my face and gazed at it with the same appearance of attention, and even of some effort, shown by a slight tension of brows and lips, then turned her eyes back to her grandmother's face, and again to mine, and so several times. The last time she seemed to catch sight of my shoulder on which a high light struck from the lamp, and not only moved her eyes, but threw her head far back to see it better, and gazed for some time with a new expression on her face—"a sort of dim and rudimentary eagerness," says my note. She no longer stared, but really looked.

Orientation more and more comes to be a process that utilizes all of the senses, sometimes simultaneously. The small baby looks and looks and makes visual comparisons. A little later, the baby will touch and feel things, bring them to his mouth and taste them. We do not need to review here those aspects of this sensory motor phase which Piaget[7] has described at length. The processes of registration which he calls "assimilation" and of internal adjustment to the impressions registered which he calls "accommodation" gradually produce new structures that accompany the baby's experiential participation in the world and increasing familiarization with it.

But is this all? According to Wayne Dennis,[8] very little is needed for the basic developmental processes to go on, aside from elementary care involved in feeding, cleaning, and the like. But perhaps he underestimates the role of the stable dependable caretaker even when the caretaker does not stimulate the baby beyond each current level of development as the Dennises described. For when we look at babies who were brought up under hospital conditions which do not provide stable mother figures for each baby, we find bizarre and tragic results. Some babies under such conditions never become at home in the world, never get used to things, never achieve any degree of familiarization. In other words, the baby's eyes and hands and mouth cannot accomplish this by themselves.

Children's individual ways of looking and their background

Since the child's over-all bodily responses at the preschool period are so much less differentiated and so patterned and stereotyped by convention and habit, his looking attitudes are more intimately embedded in his bodily orientation than is true of older children or grownups. One thinks of the contrast, for instance, of the older child who spies a turtle or frog, a grasshopper or some other intriguing small creature or object and who reaches toward it both visually and motorically in a highly focused, differentiated response. This is quite different from Rachel's attitude of observant wonder and receptivity expressed in total bodily stance as well as visual orientation; looking at something unfamiliar or new and interesting, she appears to be drinking it in not only with her eyes but with her whole being.

The over-all orientation in infancy and the early years can include different attitudes—an active grabbing kind of visual and bodily orientation as contrasted with an absorbing, receptive visual and bodily orientation; these are both different from other kinds of looking which could be differentiated by some such terms as the focused *appraising gaze;* the wide-eyed, perhaps not quite comprehending *stare* (not the same thing as the wondering look); the *comprehensive taking-in-everything* glance, the *systematic survey* or once-over; the *searching look* oriented toward a looking for or looking into; the *double-level* look where the child has attention on something which partially engages his interest while remaining very observant from the corners of his eyes to other stimuli; and the reverse of this, the aimless or *inattentive gaze* while the child is absorbed in inner sensations—for instance, when a child was drinking a glass of lemonade while idly looking around as at the beginning of a party session. Occupied with a glass of lemonade he could take in other things, letting his gaze wander with no conscious direction and little evidence of structuring of any sort; yet what he had taken in during this period of inattentive gazing was often reflected in his selections after he rejoined the group.

These differences in degree of conscious focus, reaching out, reaching for, reaching into objects in the environment visually as compared

with absorbing, drinking in, or catching on the fly, also imply differences in the structure of the relation between the child's ego and the
environment, as well as the degree of cathexis of specific aspects of
the environment or the environment as a whole—the purposeful or
casual orientation toward the area being scanned and the child's attitudes toward the situation at the moment. Sometimes, just as "listening with the third ear" may serve a very definite purpose, so "an inattentive glance" may be a safe way of taking in while being overtly
preoccupied with something else; the child is protected from the overtures which might be made by people who would be aware of his
visual search if it were more active and explicit.

Aspects of orientation

In the very earliest experiences of sucking, drinking, and later
masticating, there is a constant association of these incorporating acts
with both motor and visual reaching out and bringing toward and
within oneself by sweeping activities. It is not fanciful to say that the
child assimilates the drinking-in act to the visual incorporation; later
on when the child, as we say, is ruminating, he may actually be chewing the cud of a visual experience, reassimilating it, chopping it up
more finely, absorbing it into himself. Bernard was observed to make
such mouth movements overtly when pausing to ruminate or reflect.
We can speculate that a similar process occurs with some other children. A factor of oral incorporation is very likely still involved in
visual assimilation long after the infant has developed differentiated
looking; this is partly a remnant of the early relatively undifferentiated
phase when looking and sucking at the mother's breast were often
simultaneous, partly a result of the many repetitions of oral gratification from objects seen. There is much to suggest that the visual external world is somehow fitted to the internal world by a process of
mutual adjustment. These scanning activities then are to some degree
in the active oral incorporation mode though they are, of course,
much more.

In the same vein should be mentioned the phenomenon which
Tolman[9] has called latent learning in which there is an exploratory
assimilation and digestion of the structured environment, making a
"cognitive ·map," before one ever becomes actively and motorically
involved with it. The animal solving a new maze for the very first time
acts as if he had already had experience with its motor attributes.
Thus, without having been rewarded or punished for right or wrong
turns, he knows what's what at the minute he begins; he has obviously
absorbed the world visually in some deep way which orients his motor

responses. The proprioceptive system has already been cued to the visual signals. This may of course also happen at the level of vegetative activities, but the evidence here is less clear.

Reik's concept[10] of "listening with the third ear" may involve, as Kubie suggests,[11] a question of freeing oneself both from the firm structure of the external world and from the somewhat less firm but equally commanding structure of the internal world; as Rapaport points out,[12] there is a small zone of relative freedom between the coercive pulls of the external and the internal structure. With some children and adults early orienting patterns lead to a sweeping searchlight activity which goes on all the time; we are always looking for something else at a less explicitly conscious level. When someone says "Could you have been looking for so and so?" we brighten up and say, "Oh yes." We do this even if we have not explicitly established a search set; we are all full of search sets highly structured through our lifetime as we look for things we do not know we are searching for. This is part of the result of early conditioning processes, and we have many delights in the discovery of external and internal patterns for which we were in a sense ready; we are particularly happy when something rings two bells, an external and an internal bell, at the same time.

Now we also observed the children's "inattentive searching." It is hard to believe that there is fully "inattentive" searching; but one may be searching or assessing one's own inside feelings or sensations really while pretending to search outside. This process underlies these bell-ringing acts of integration of the creative persons who find outside what was already inside from previously organized storehouses of rich experience, and who find resolutions to unsolved problems because the formulation of the problem was nine tenths of a solution. It seems to be likely that there is no explicitly defined content of awareness, but that there is awareness in the form of schemata at a deep or vague level which seek out and find schemata either in the outer or in the inner world which match.

It is easy to set all this in opposition to the explicit or conscious keeping of one's eye on the ball. This latter function may be a norm or ideal never realized. Even in pursuit movements of the eye the object is not perfectly fixated and when the object is stationary the only way the eye can work is to keep cutting back and forth like a sickle, with constantly varying angles which build up a compound picture of the object almost as in the television scanning process. The eye cannot really come to rest. Eye movement photography and electromilligrams of the eyeball show that it is constantly agitated. After all, the organism is built on relativity with respect to a fluctuating and unstable external environment and the "constancies" studied by Gestalt psychologists are instances in which the object—its size, shape, color, and so on—has a certain constancy, although the flux of information regarding it is almost pure chaos from which we have learned to extract a little order.

When a child is not apparently fixating the outer environment but is just casually moving his eyes around as if not noticing, he is inevitably registering a series of points, lines, surfaces, hues, etc., with reference to deeply organized inner schemata which may even be more effectively used because they have not been overfocused. If he had just been looking for his ball, as he stood by the upper end of the steps at the terrace, he would know relatively little about the shrubs and the fallen crab apples. The very fact that he got a rich composite structure of the yard and could use it more effectively than a hyperconcentrated child who had been dutifully looking *for* something could have done, points to latent learning. In addition to this, each part of the total has, as the Gestalt psychologist would say, a membership character in the whole which is only rarely seen by the sharply attentive type of analytical observation.

Developing a picture of reality

Our discussion of orientation already implies that many of these children were more reality-oriented than our usual picture of the "egocentric," "animistic," fantasy-flooded preschool child would lead us to expect. They were described by different observers as follows: "frequently makes reality testing remarks such as 'they don't really . . . do they?' "; "engaged in precise reality testing"; "clear about reality but adapts it to his needs, adapts forms to role and goals"; "does not repress or deny—accepts reality"; "utilizes reality evidence"; "offers realistic live-and-let-live solutions"; "despite her great capacity for fantasy, her reality testing is firm"; "has a realistic acceptance and estimate of the inadequateness of small people"; "has an easy ability to adapt reality to his needs"; "was able to accept limits and to stay within limits." Some children were described in stronger terms: Martin "keeps his ties to reality tight." Diane "sticks to realism." Roger had "an over-all tendency toward being limited by reality." Teddy was described as showing a "cautious clinging to reality." In these latter instances the children were not able to swing freely back and forth between reality and fantasy as most children of this age did.

Realism in the sense in which it is used by these observers—and these include observers both of the children's behavior and of their responses to projective tests—are implying objectivity, accuracy, and soundness of judgment in the orientation to and appraisal of the new situations, objects, opportunities, and frustrations to which the children were being exposed. Only once or twice did we find instances of children handling objects animistically, and very seldom was there evidence of confusion between fantasy and reality. Within the limits of their experience the children's thinking was logical and coherent. Unrealistic, bizarre responses occurred only in a few children and at moments when deep anxieties or conflicts constituting stress to the child were experienced.

We do not suggest that these observations, intensive as they were, involving some thirty hours of time actually spent with each child, and the independent records of six to eight observers on each child, can be used as a basis for universal generalizations about the realism of children from three to five years old. The factors mentioned as important in contributing to the orienting processes of these children doubtless had a share in developing their realism and objectivity. The goal of their orienting activities, along with familiarization, appeared to be the achievement of a workable picture of the new reality.

While mastery of reality was characteristic of most of the children, certain ones had striking idiosyncratic patterns of their own. Steven used the phrase "I wonder" many times, not with intense emotion, and it was not clear whether anxiety was involved in this. He could express surprise and perhaps discomfort or uncertainty with his question. In the MLT session his wondering seemed to come just from himself, to represent a genuine questioning or reflection, a verbalizing of uncertainty, perhaps gaining security through being able to feel himself as wondering or to accept himself as wondering. "I wonder" seemed to give dignity to a process of searching for a way, the lack of which otherwise might be experienced as failure. Since this occurred even more at a time when his mother was ill and had a miscarriage which she did not discuss with the children, it evidently also expressed his way of dealing with his vagueness and questions about what was happening.

The desire to solve mysteries connected with mother or both parents or their relationship seemed to underlie the drive for cognitive clarity with certain other children as well. But there was no evidence that this was the sole or dominant motive; we would find ourselves forcing things very far if we went beyond the assumption that these children wanted to see clearly, to understand, to relate things in order to master the world so that they could use it. Such integrative functioning was typically instrumental to the expression of play ideas, whether realistic or unrealistic, and to communication with the experimenter or with each other in social situations.

Yet the inference that this drive to cognitive mastery developed without a competitive drive of an acquisitive sort is suggested by the fact that a number of the children showed considerable ideational range and productive energy, even creative possibilities, while they were not oriented toward the type of achievement which expressed itself in high scores on the intelligence test. It is possible here to offer the hypothesis that there is a great difference between the child's investment in meaningful cognitive functions as compared with the more or less arbitrary demands and problems which an intelligence test presents, and that numerous children have capacities for well-motivated and useful integrative functioning far beyond what the intelligence test indicates. Such was Ray whose test scores never offered him an I.Q. much over 100 but who was capable of adapting reality to his needs, adapting forms to different roles and goals in play.

These children were by no means waiting to be told, and if an adult did not see or understand something which the child tried to communicate, or was skeptical, or doubted the observation of the child, many of the children would sturdily, not rebelliously, not defiantly, but directly and simply persist in trying to explain the item which had not been understood or grasped by the adult.

When a child's inferences, beliefs, and concepts have emerged from his own autonomous observation, they have been acquired along with a complex web of motor and affective orientations which make the concepts and conclusions part of him. This may have something to do with the spontaneity and ease with which the children drew upon their concepts and resources for solving problems, dealing with difficulties, meeting new challenges. The latter did not easily threaten their egos. The children did not feel in danger of losing face or losing status as do children whose ideas, assimilated from adults second-hand as it were, are closely tied to getting the approval of the adults. The ideas of these children, developed from autonomous orienting processes, were woven into the texture of their own independent motor, emotional, kinesthetic, and other sensory experiencing.

Adults are often too far beyond their first experiences of newness to remember the uncanny feelings, the confusion, the uncertainty these experiences evoked. So the paralysis, the long hesitations, and complex manuevers characteristic of some children's responses to new situations of even a mild and inviting kind may seem almost bizarre. Since the children in our study differed widely in the tendency to be anxious in response to the new and the strange, we looked for relationships between this and other variables, such as: difficulties in communication and in relating to others and the tendency to use inhibition as a defense. The children who enjoyed newness and discovery communicated easily, were quickly oriented, confident in their choices, definite in their attitudes, free to protest actively what they did not like. They responded comfortably to adults as people and had considerable social skill with adults, in addition to being cooperative toward the adults' authoritative demands. In other words we could say that newness presented less severe challenges when children felt secure about their ability to communicate with new people and to get along with them. The children who enjoyed new situations also tended to show more capacity to struggle, or determination and drive to mastery.

To what extent are we in any new situation deprived of something important at the same time we are offered a new stimulus? Discussions of sensory deprivation experiments have sometimes emphasized the role of novelty or strangeness in producing some of the disorganization seen in subjects of these studies. Here the strangeness consists of the absence of customary stimuli, patterning of stimuli, structure of time and activities during the day. The subjects have to accept a totally different style of existence from that to which they are accustomed. The nature of the experiments usually involves passivity and restriction of movement along with absence of visual, auditory, tactual stimulation.

With the children in our study, some of whose lives had been very restricted, newness involved no absence of stimulation, but rather absence of familiar stimuli, familiar surroundings, the familiar behavior of known adults. The absence of clear structure, customary restrictions, or expected directions, combined with a wide array of new objects, in a new place, constituted a special case of deprivation of familiarity. But this deprivation of the familiar does not seem to account for the startled or surprised or wondering expression seen on some of the children's faces, such as at the commencement of the MLT session; this may be better referred to as "strangeness shock."

Strangeness shock at some level is an experience any of us may have at any age. It is repeatedly experienced in the early months or weeks or even days of infancy in the simplest form: change in the stimulus situation. Our data include photographs of the frown on the face of a four-week-old baby who, after being nursed at the breast for the first month, was changed to the bottle.

Soviet experimental work on infants is more extensive than ours partly because of the much greater accessibility of babies under institutional care. According to Soviet research[13] on the orienting reflex, a neonate may interrupt nursing to listen to a sudden new sound: this suggests that attention to a strange stimulus or to any change in a situation has priority among the hierarchy of instincts over the urge to obtain satisfaction. From this point of view, one of the baby's most important tasks is that of orientation or coping with change or the new. As long ago as 1910, Peterson and Rainey [14] published results of observations on reactions of newborn babies to sounds. Fifty-five cases are recorded in which observers noted marked responses soon after birth to the sound of a rattle, a lip sound, or a voice in ordinary tones near the baby: at the fourteenth hour after birth, one baby reacted with a violent startle, "hands and feet thrown upward," on hearing the sound of a rattle. At the fifteenth to seventeenth hour after birth, several babies stirred, opened eyes, "started to cry or uttered a low cry" and two babies "stirred" or "cried" at lip sounds. These same reactions occurred at later intervals, as on the second to tenth days. Other babies on the second and later days stopped crying when hearing a rattle, lip sounds, or voice. Eight babies "fixed" their eyes on the observer's face and stopped crying or "seemed interested," or "looked fixedly with a pleased expression" . . . "made a little 'goo' sound," when talked to. In other words, from the earliest hours and days, a new auditory stimulus has an attention-getting quality for many if not all babies; different qualities of sound attract attention in different cases; fearful (startle) reactions occur in some instances; unmanageability or disorganization of response in others while in still others a sound counteracts expressions of distress (baby stops crying), or mobilizes interest, satisfaction, and an increased integration (fixing eyes on the observer with a pleased expression).

Phylogenetically, as we observe in David Levy's study of "The Strange Hen," [15] and as described in Lorenz's[16] accounts of fish and certain other species we find an immediate defensively hostile reaction to the strange intruder, as if strangeness per se must be threatening. Newness is for humans a challenge to mastery and stimulus for development, and after familiarity has turned to dullness it may be needed to sustain interest. But it has to be kept within the child's coping capacity especially when thresholds are too low in sensitive infants.*

Depending on the pace of development of different receptors, and of the integrative processes which underlie differentiation, alertness to the new and the strange occurs in response to more and more complex stimulus configurations.

Here we can profit from a glimpse of some relationships appearing in our statistical explorations of the relation of orientation and anxiety about the new and the strange to separation problems. The "separation problem" was highly correlated with "dependency" and also with anxiety regarding the new and the strange, shyness, poor

* According to Shirley, most premature babies are highly sensitive; disorganizing effects of new stimulation are a greater threat.

motor control, several variables dealing with illness, and with low enjoyment of intense stimulation (i.e., sensitivity) . Degree of disorganization in family life was another contributing factor. Naturally the children with separation problems (and who as a consequence clung to their mothers or other adults) were not those who made their presence felt with peers.

The child whose ego development has been handicapped by motor limitations, sensitivity, inner stress, or disorganization due to illness is more apt to be anxious about newness, to be realistically more dependent on the mother, and to have a greater separation problem as a corollary of this real need for the mother's assistance and support. The latter is the more necessary because along with the tendencies mentioned above these children do not easily find support from or satisfaction in other children.

This is worth emphasizing because recent discussions of separation anxiety[17] have tended to emphasize exclusively the instinctual aspects of the child's ties to the mother, while omitting the role of energy, orientation, motor skill, and peer relations in the development of mastery which can free the child from dependence on the mother. The role of previous traumatic experiences in new situations must not be overlooked either. Children who were able to deal with the environment fearlessly were able to leave their mothers at home.

A corollary of this is that we still need to think more clearly about the relation between the "tie to the mother," as an explanation for "separation anxiety"; the roles of both love for the mother as an object, and need for the mother as guide to reality, support, and need-gratifier during a phase of incomplete mastery of environmental challenges are important in relation to the capacity for separation. Among the children we observed, as the need-gratifying, supporting, and orienting roles of mother were replaced by self-sufficiency in the child, dependence upon her and separation anxiety decreased. But love, identification, and respect for the mother's roles persisted. "Mother told me" was a frequent device for opposing the authority of a new person by the tried and proved authority of a mother who did not have to be present for the many reasons mentioned above. The children who were able to deal with new situations were more apt to be free from separation anxiety and more eager about exploring new opportunities.

In our first discussion of responses to newness we drew largely upon the records of younger and shyer children in whom orientation problems were especially visible. By the time of the first parties at the end of a year of tests and other experiences, no situation which included our staff was wholly new, of course, and the children were nearly a year older than when we began. Still there were many new aspects of the situation—a new physical setting, new activities, new peers. In such contexts we could observe such variables as "openness to new experiences" and found them closely related to over-all level of activity; clarity of affective states, and forcefulness of affective expression; ability to elicit the desired response; use of motor skills for coping with environmental demands, cooperativeness; and level of self-feeling. The feeling aspects of the child's response to the environment emerge here, while orientation as such is a cognitive matter first of all, a necessary first step in dealing with the environment.

Processes of familiarization

For a young infant, familiarity is probably largely a matter of sight and sound, taste and smell, touch and texture, along with some simple level of patterning these, and feelings of pleasure—or at least feelings of "being used to"—carried by these sensory experiences. Helping the baby "get used to" new stimuli typically involves gradual exposure in a safe or (more than merely safe) satisfying setting of mother's presence and care.

For the preschool child to whom activity, communication, and skill have become important, familiarity still involves visual, auditory, tactual orientedness (also sometimes taste and smell at these ages) but even more involves the feeling of knowing what to do and how to do it safely, as we mentioned earlier. While mother's presence may still be necessary to guarantee safety, the problem of learning what to do and how to do it is primarily the child's own problem—whatever help he uses in accomplishing this.

These details are reviewed because the child himself often tries to cope with all of the unfamiliarity by holding onto some loved familiar toy or blanket, something which brings at least a little of the sense of at-homeness into the desert of newness in which he finds himself, something which can provide an orientation point, and an anchor for his feelings, something whose lovedness can mitigate the strangeness of the new situation. Familiarization processes use a bit of the familiar to facilitate greater at-homeness.

Here we see that even with a very young baby, some of what we discussed earlier is involved. The mother herself who is familiar and satisfying contributes something of herself to the new situation. What was at first new, takes on some of the quality of situation-with-mother-in-it. Some of mother rubs off on the new situation and as fast as this occurs, this situation is more safe and more acceptable.

They also use sensory, motor, language efforts to become oriented, to understand, to learn what to do, to succeed in doing it. The process of familiarization develops another dimension as fast as the child can add words. The phrases "What's this?", "Why?" and later, "How?" add names, rules, relationships and processes to what the child can learn by looking and listening, feeling, tasting and manipulating. Words provide a short-cut; answers can be found without exploring so much. Adults sometimes find a multitude of questions unreasonable but in actuality when one considers how much of life is new and strange to the young child it may be surprising that we are not even more flooded with them than we are.

By the age of three, we also find that individual differences in responses to and management of the new and the strange are clearcut:

We saw with Donald the long, long look, the total bodily immobilization while his eyes were alive with fascinated observing activity.

With Karen we saw the testing processes, through action, through questions, by which she made herself at home in the new situation.

With Ronnie we saw the need for maternal support and encouragement of the examiner which helped him to try new tasks and to experience new mastery.

With Darlene we saw the cautious self-timing and slow relinquishment of resistance to new motor efforts, measuring the effort of her capacity, not going beyond what she could manage at any point until she finally succeeded.

With many, if not most, of the children, whatever the process they used, orientation and familiarization required a considerable time before the child could use the opportunities of a new situation in a satisfying way. That this should be so seems obvious enough. Yet this need for time is too often overlooked when professional procedures are involved.

NOTES AND REFERENCES

1. Bartlett, J. *Familiar Quotations.* Boston: Little, Brown, 1946.
2. Titchener, E.B. *Textbook of Psychology.* New York: Macmillan, 1909.
3. Spitz, R. Anaclitic depression. *Psychoanalytic Study of the Child,* Vol. 2. New York: International Universities Press, 1946.
4. Wolf, K. Individual tendencies in the first year of life. In Senn, M. (ed.) *Problems of Infancy and Childhood.* New York: Josiah Macy, Jr. Foundation, 1952. See also the sequel in the 1953 volume.
5. Spitz, R. Anaclitic depression. *Psychoanalytic Study of the Child,* Vol. 2. New York: International Universities Press, 1946.

6. Shinn, M. *Biography of a Baby*. Boston: Houghton-Mifflin, 1900.

7. Piaget, J. *Origins of Intelligence in Children*. New York: International Universities Press, 1952.

8. Dennis, W. Infant development under conditions of restricted practice and of minimum social stimulation. *Genet. Psychol. Monographs, 23,* 1941.

9. Tolman, E.C. Cognitive maps in rats and men. *Psychol. Rev. 55,* 1948.

10. Reik, T. *Listening with the Third Ear*. New York: Farrar, Straus, 1948.

11. Kubie, L.S. *Neurotic Distortion of the Creative Process*. Lawrence: University of Kansas Press, 1958.

12. Rapaport, D. The autonomy of the ego. *Bull. Menninger Clin. 15,* 1951.

13. Sokolov, E.N. *Perception and the Conditioned Reflex*. Moscow: Moscow University, 1958 (expected English translation).

14. Peterson, F., and Rainey, L.H. The beginnings of mind in the newborn. *Bull. Lying-in-Hosp.* (New York), 7, 1910.

15. Levy, D. The strange hen. *Amer. J. Orthopsychiat. 20,* 1950.

16. Lorenz, K. The nature of instinct. In Schiller, C.H. (ed.) *Instinctive Behavior*. New York: International Universities Press, 1957.

17. Bowlby, J. Separation anxiety. *Intern. J. Psychoanal. 41,* 1960.

10

AUTONOMY,
HELP, AND EFFORT

WHILE THE EARLY ORIENTING PROCESSES of the children in reaction to
the newness of the experiences to which we introduced them dominated
our discussion at the beginning of the research, we were soon deeply
impressed by their active autonomy. These boys and girls were seen
at the age when, according to Erikson,[1] autonomy has come into full
flower and initiative is in the process of blossoming, as dividends for
the ego from the maturing of drives and their interaction with the environment. Here we also see the contribution of motility to the im-
plementation of the emerging interests, choices, preferences, and needs
of the child. This was especially impressive to those of the staff who
had come from many years of life in eastern metropolitan areas. In
certain cities many middle-class children may not leave the apartment without an adult companion until the age of seven or older, and
even in many suburbs the play areas around home are very circum-
scribed and limited by fences or hedges which a child must not
transgress. Such ecological factors interfere with the free flowering of
autonomous exploration as we observed it in these Kansas children.

The most positive responses were described in such terms as "full of initiative," "she goes where she pleases, eliminates what she pleases, assumes that the world is at her disposal; she chooses to stay, to move, and so forth; she asserts her own thoughts and her feelings and sets limits to the adults." While freedom of motility and the freedom to express ideas in movement were impressive, even more so were the independent attitudes seen in dealing with the environment, whether or not gross motor activity was involved.

The strong, autonomous attitude of Chester expressed itself in a variety of ways: in proud self-assertion, structuring a total situation in his own way, braving threats, maintaining controls which he imposed on himself, sustaining relationships as he liked and also terminating situations decisively, always maintaining a manner of proud self-control and self-assertion.

Self-confidence, energy and forceful assertiveness were typical of Sheila. Brennie, Patsy, Susan, and other children could structure each situation spontaneously in designs of their own liking. This capacity to structure a situation so as to maintain their own feelings of confidence and to utilize maximally their own skills and resources, went along with an ability to admit their own limits, substitute one activity for another, shift roles, select or reject materials. We shall discuss some of these operations further.

Thus behavior which from an adult point of view may be referred to as escape, avoidance, or distancing can, as we saw in Chapters 4 and 5, serve useful preventive or preparatory values. This was especially true for children who were struggling to maintain their own integrity and control, and who did not want to be overwhelmed by situations beyond their coping capacity. This autonomous self-protection is part of the whole range of autonomy expressions.

Ray watched the adults "with a questioning, mischievous, half-defiant gaze that seemed to say 'You can't make me do anything I don't want to. I'll decide when I am ready to decide.' " Sheila insisted on autonomy at all times as if to say, "I'll do it my own way," and Sally consistently stuck to her own view under challenge from adults.

Susan typically had strong ways of dealing with pressure in situations, mastering them without yielding, and Jo Anne's attitude was generally one of making herself at home, deciding where she would go and what she would do, just as Greg determined his own path and chose what he would pay attention to. Standing firm in the midst of surrounding pressures including those from adults, emphatically announcing, "I don't want to," turning back interference, resisting help as in opening boxes of play materials, asserting one's own ability to manage, were other expressions of the drive to autonomy typical of many of the children.

Children who knew exactly what they wanted to do could dictate decisively which of the test procedures they would accept and which they would by-pass. They might dispose or shove away, scatter, dump, or hide unpleasant or unsatisfying objects; discard an unworkable suggestion in order to proceed with a new approach in Moriarty's tests; or, in the CAT, shut out things not easy to take; refuse to go along by asserting "I don't wanta any more" or sometimes more indirectly by trying to procrastinate, thinking up acceptable reasons for termination or getting rid of certain toys. After the fourth CAT card, Sheila disengaged herself from the situation and refused to be induced back. Other children impatiently refused, or objected to repetition of questions or refused to elaborate or qualify when probing questions were asked.

In the MLT session the children could use their initiative in the interests of self-protection even from threatening fantasies. Terry threw away the snake saying, "I don't want these snakes biting me here," and Steven disposed of a broken animal's head; such forceful elimination of threatening or unwanted toys was not unusual.

These ways of ignoring, refusing, devaluating, rejecting, declining invitations, or discarding objects went hand in hand with forceful, positive expressions of wishes such as "I want to make it this-a-way," or "Do you have something else? Don't want to play with these." The same child who could be very positive in suggesting a change in the test could also hide the colored cardboard circles instead of matching them. Sally, Ronnie, and Daryl all tended to force objects into position when they seemed recalcitrant, although none of them were deliberately destructive at any time.

These expressions of autonomy were more vivid at the preschool level than in latency when girls, especially, acquired polite conforming patterns which often masked if they did not block the spontaneous initiative and independence of the preschool stage. This was in line with what we expect in this culture, where the beginning of school implies a capacity to accept authority, rules, and group patterns.

Because of the vividness and clarity of such behavior at this stage we focused special attention on it, and Dr. Moriarty made a detailed study of expressions of autonomy during the intelligence test session,* which is worth presenting here.

---

* The following discussion of autonomy expression in the intelligence test situation is based upon Dr. Moriarty's discussion of this in Coping patterns of preschool children in response to intelligence test demands. *Genetic Psychol. Monographs,* *64:*3-127, 1961.

Autonomy expression in the intelligence test

In this situation, autonomy increased with specific demands after newness had worn off, and reached a high point with performance tasks in contrast with tests requiring merely verbal answers with many children. Only two inhibited girls remained passive when they encountered the demands for active performance. But when facing difficult situations six children reacted very passively, relinquishing initiative shown under other conditions. Still, half maintained a high level of autonomy; these were capable of making their wants known and were in no sense cowed, bewildered, or overwhelmed in situations involving difficulty.

There were some sex differences: girls behaved more autonomously in response to verbal demands, boys with demands for performance. It is relevant here that girls develop speech earlier and understand and utilize it more proficiently; while boys are usually found to be better with motor skills. Confronted with difficulty, a larger number of boys became more active in expressing autonomy, while girls tended to become more passive.

The effect of difficulty on the readiness to express one's needs independently was interesting in that the group was roughly divided into those behaving more actively and those behaving more passively. Only three children stayed at the same level of autonomy expression. The two inhibited girls mentioned above behaved in a markedly passive manner throughout the tests, and stress was probably not markedly greater when test items were difficult than at any other time since tension was always high, and the very fact of responding at all to a relative stranger who imposed a series of very specific demands was an intensely distasteful and unrewarding experience for them. By contrast, Gordon, on the other hand, never markedly passive, consistently behaved with a moderate degree of autonomy.

Our data suggest that when boys (in this subculture) are confronted with a difficult cognitive challenge they are likely to be stimulated to increase their own overtly expressed autonomy, whereas girls are likely to retreat to a more passive position. It should be pointed out, of course, that some of these shifts in rated level of independence were small and might easily be reversed in a differently organized or free situation.

These ratings must be considered as they are related to and balanced by other variables. Boys who are highly autonomous are also likely to be among those most willing to cooperate with authority demands, who relate most positively to the examiner, who quickly grasp the implications of test instructions, who comfortably ask for and accept help, whose own self-feeling is positive, who realistically accept their own limitations and who, while they may have certain tension in the testing situations, are not overwhelmed or flooded by tension. At the same time, these overtly autonomous boys seem to have good motor control and tend to be bright. The picture of high autonomy in girls is similar.

Accepting own limits

Since the ability to accept one's own limits (implying clear awareness of them) is related to autonomy, and to setting limits to demands from adults, we can look at this now. Children, as well as adults, vary markedly in the extent to which they can evaluate their own skills and openly or realistically admit wherein they fail to meet either self-imposed or adult-imposed standards. Some children were able to admit casually in the intelligence test, "I don't know," "I can't do it best . . . it's a little hard for me," or "I don't know how to make a foot, but I'll try." Sometimes limits were simply stated clearly: "I know I can't," said Sally when confronted with the demand to make a story about a CAT card. In other instances a child accepted his present limitations but consoled himself by looking forward to success in the future. In many instances a child would go as far as he could possibly manage but would simply not push beyond the point which he felt was impossible. Sometimes he would document his clarity about what he could do and what he could not do: on the buttons in the intelligence test one child said, "I can't. I'm sure I can't. I can button my coat. I have to put my finger in there," explaining circumstantially exactly how it worked. At other times, failures or near-failures were recognized but minimized by pointing up other successes, as "I can't draw both, but I can sure draw one," by offering substitutes, such as "Do you want me to do something I can do?" or excusing oneself on the basis of inherent difficulty or lack of experience, as "Mother never told me." This contrasts with the responses of some other children who stood their ground by simply ignoring an obviously poor response to a specific test item, by repeating the wrong response, by failing to remark about failure (with no obvious tension), or occasionally completely and openly denying a failure, as when one child, after marked confusing in color-naming, said, "I can name colors." Other children dealt with difficulty by disposing of unmanageable materials by carrying off drawings, stuffing buttoning material in a pocket, or physically pushing, squeezing, crumpling, biting, mutilating, or roughly handling test materials.

Those who were rated high in the capacity to accept their own limits typically dealt with the problem at a cognitive level, whereas those who were rated low on this continuum coped with the problem on a largely affective basis in which insecurity was often expressed by aggressive behavior toward the test materials. From an adult point of view, the former behavior appears to be more effective, but from the child's point of view, the latter behavior clearly served the positive value of concealing failure and thereby protecting personal integrity.

When we rated our children on a continuum set up to measure the objectivity with which they overtly recognized their own limits, half of the children were initially open in accepting their limits. Half of the children in some way tried to conceal limits from the examiner by minimizing, ignoring, or denying their existence. Probably, in some cases, it was equally necessary from the point of view of integrity of self-image to conceal from themselves a full awareness of limitations in or effective functioning of skills. When specific verbal demands were made, awareness of limits increased slightly; with specific demands for performance objective evaluation of limits was still greater, particularly with boys. Correlation coefficients suggested that the boy who could be most realistic or objective in regard to real limits was also more cooperative toward authority demands, more able to utilize or demand help, more adequate motorically, more able to express his own needs independently, more quickly oriented, tended to be slightly older and was relatively free of tension. In other words, the boy who could be more objective or more clear about limitations in himself tended to handle the testing situation more positively.

Since the testing situation offers only one kind of cognitive challenge, the behavior it evokes can be assumed to be similar to responses to cognitive challenge in daily environmental demands as well. We expect that the child who is realistic in regard to himself is more free to see external life situations realistically and hence to mobilize resources to meet challenge or stress in a more direct, and presumably more effective manner, in turn probably increasing the capacity for objective self-evaluation in the future.

Our data are less clearcut and precise for girls, but the fact that correlations followed a similar pattern (although not quite meeting standards of significance statistically) suggests that our hypothesis probably holds up for girls, as well. In one variable, capacity to ask for or accept help, the correlation with recognition of limits was significant at the five per cent level. Girls who can be realistic in regard to personal limits are likely to be more ready and realistically more able to utilize the help of an adult, as we would expect.

Controlling stimulation and demands from the environment

One aspect of autonomy is the *capacity to set limits to demands and pressures* from the environment. We illustrated in earlier pages the tendency of many of these children to give themselves a slow warming-up period, and time for orientation and familiarizing themselves with the new situation. This process of cognitive familiarization and probably emotional familiarization (or getting the feel of things) as well, in itself played a part in protecting the child against overstimulation, giving him a basis on which to select those aspects of situations, especially the free and unstructured ones with which he would deal.

Beyond this we saw certain children protecting themselves against overstimulation in other ways. For instance, one boy retired to an area in the garage when he arrived at the party; thus he did not expose himself all at once to the many people and the wide spaces in the party setting. As he narrowed his spatial range, he also narrowed the range of human beings and objects to which he had to familiarize himself at one time, and gave himself an opportunity to assert his areas of mastery by making a tall building with some blocks. Another child narrowed his range, mastering as it were a piece at a time of the new situation, and delayed involving himself until after a survey which included a series of such pieces.

Other children were described as "being able to keep the situation within the range of comfortable tolerance." Sometimes a child would manage this by communicating or admitting his limits, rejecting a demand or a challenge which he felt he could not meet or, as we have indicated before, suggesting that the task be divided; or shifting roles and assigning a more difficult task to the grownup. The substitution of an activity which he could handle successfully for the one in which he knew he would be unsuccessful was another constructive way of making a situation tolerable and managing his own limits.

Delay

We noted that another factor in autonomous dealings with the environment was the capacity for delay. This capacity for delay was seen to be important in the interests of clear perception, economy of manipulation, adequacy of problem solving, development of plans or fantasy solutions, and the like. Children like Vernon, Teddy, Rachel, all of whom had a tendency to respond to new demands with delay or with caution showed by their subsequent behavior how this had contributed to their capacity for integration and served as a preparatory period during which appraisal or course of action or an emotional orientation which would free them for action had been going on.

With Donald the use of the period of delay for emotional assimilation of the situation as well as perceptual mastery of it seemed to be implied by the gaiety if not raucuous delight with which he went into action when he got ready. With Vernon there was little evidence that emotional orientation or assimilation was setting the stage for spontaneous emotional expression, since the latter was seldom observed. Rather, there was much evidence from infancy on that he used delay chiefly to reach clear perceptions, and for the preliminary integration of anticipated perceptual motor acts. With Teddy we might speak of the use of delay in conjunction with his capacity to attenuate aggression and to use homeopathic releases or small sluiceways. (This inference was confirmed at a later age when Teddy made the following response to the question, "What would you do if a boy much younger than you started a fight with you?": "Well, do you mean, what caused the fighting? What type of fight?" "Well, any kind." "I mean in anger or play or what?" "Well, just tell me what you'd do regardless of whatever it is." "Well, I suppose I'd just hold him back with my hands or hold his hands." "That's assuming it would be in anger?" "Yes.")

Delay then is used in various ways depending upon the patterning of the child's response to stimulation, the discharge patterns which the child has developed, and the processes through which he needs to go between his initial awareness of an external demand or stimulus to his integrated dealings with it. Delay in one case can prevent the arousal of intense emotion, whereas in another case it can facilitate the integrative process which leads to the expression of intense emotion which has been aroused.

Whatever the pattern, delay generally went along with autonomy of appraisal, independent structuring of the reality situation, and the integration of body movement or physical response with the child's evaluation of the demands and opportunities present.

Preventive coping

Half or more of the children used devices aimed to prevent troubles of one sort or another; self-warnings were paralleled by warnings to the adult: "Why don't you watch where you're going?" One child explained in advance why he would be unable to do certain tasks. Another was described as an "averter of near tragedy." Sheila, generally so forceful in moving into situations, warned, "Don't get the water on the doll. It might get on its dress." At times the forthright Jo Anne would dodge a real showdown; the well-balanced Barbie often appeared to be using her competence to guard herself, while another girl was able to size up situations, anticipate, predict, and avoid consequences of behavior. Chester's control at times had the value of avoiding troubles, while Teddy, aware of his mother's time orientation, reminded the experimenter: "You'll have to take me home right after eleven-thirty."

Retreats to shelter and safety, leaving the field and similar operations had this preventive value for certain children. Jo Anne was able to threaten a departure, saying on the way to her first MLT session: "If you give me trouble I'll go home."

Certain children carefully poised the blocks on the Bonhop Play House roof in such a way that they would not fall through and perhaps be broken by the fall or break something else.

Sometimes prevention suggested the possibility of a phobic pattern or a need to cope with low thresholds for fear, while with one or two children there was evidence of diffuse and chronic anxiety underlying preventive operations.

Some of the children even expressed preventive concepts in response to the projective tests. Janice described the animals as "all holding on to keep from sliding off the mountain," and it looked as if her tendency to interrupt certain play units resulted from a need to prevent the revelation of feelings or behavior which might be disapproved. Protection against rain, hunting for guns, "just in case war comes," as one boy did, detonating bombs, and conquering a threat to the part by safely integrating it into a new and larger whole, had preventive values for several children.

Avoidance

Passive children used avoidance techniques as we would expect, but so did most active children, under certain circumstances. That is, avoidance was a normal device when appropriately used, and one expression of the child's autonomous control of stimulation.

The precise stimulation or threat to which each child responded by avoidance varied from child to child. Patsy, Greg, Roger, and others avoided very specific stimuli, threatening ones, figures implying a mother-child relationship, figures or situations implying aggression or stirring up guilt feelings. While Steven tended to avoid threatening situations on the CAT in general, in particular he seemed to avoid telling or thinking about what daddy would do if he got mad, in contrast to, for instance, Sally.

Certain children avoided dangerous interactions between people in MLT play or in response to the CAT cards. Others avoided areas which invited letting go of impulses whose expression could arouse guilt or anxiety about guilt. Janice avoided involvement, effort, thinking, concentration or deep absorption at any point, while in a somewhat similar but perhaps more sweeping way Cynthia seemed to avoid all cognitive ambitions.

The manner of avoidance also differed from child to child, varying from merely withholding active vigorous response to averting the head or turning one's back on the experimenter in the MLT session, actually leaving the room as Ray did, or refusing to come to certain sessions as Sally refused to come to the body photograph session. We can say that in this instance we saw an example of avoiding a situation which she felt would be overwhelming.

In such instances we can see avoidance functioning as preventive coping; for the small child who had such a limited possibility for controlling the environment such efforts at prevention of breakdown under stress may at times be the only ones available to the child.

Escape

At least a third of the children used various escape techniques—going out of the field, moving from one pattern to another, putting distance between themselves and the situation or the stimulus, being evasive, using disguises, hiding, engaging in pseudo activity or superficially going through motions trying to avoid investment or avoid risk through being noncommittal. The question as to whether these techniques interfered with or assisted good coping, however, was a matter of the circumstances under which they were used, what the child did next, whether the evasive, distancing, or escape techniques actually resulted in a retreat from the situation as a whole or were used by the child to assemble his resources for a more positive approach later.

In other words, escape techniques were sometimes simply a form of stalling, delaying, self-protecting device which subsequently led to more active and positive ways of dealing with situations. Even Jo Anne—who was generally very effective and could in one way or another deal with most of the situations in which we saw the children—used escape concepts and techniques on occasion as simply one type of coping method among a wide range of devices.

Other active children retreated, evaded, or escaped from a threatening stimulus at times, evidently when confidence in their usually active approaches failed them. It will be no surprise that passive children like Vivian and Martin were among those who also expressed fantasies of escape, running away, withdrawal, and so on (in MLT or CAT sessions). However these were not the only children who entertained such fantasies. Gordon, often very active, repeatedly showed a tendency to fantasy escape. Patterns of escape can appear then either as a dominant technique in the coping approaches of certain children; or as part of a very wide repertory in some of the most versatile, resourceful and outgoing ones.

"Negativism"

Some of the patterns we have already described are similar to those which have been often discussed as "negativistic" in studies of the behavior of young children.[2] Refusals, protest, passive negation, "silence is dissent," withholding all response, objecting to repetition, attempting to terminate the test, scornfully rejecting materials, and other protests have been offered as evidence of negativistic tendencies in preschool children. In our group we found such behavior among some of the most active children like Sally, and Terry. When Sally refused to come to the photography session; she remained indifferent to the pleas of LBM, MS, and her father's reproachful, "Daddy's ashamed of you." She showed "no sign of feeling ashamed or guilty, merely determined not to yield to pressure."

With a similar refusal to be moved by guilt, Janice was "not willing to surrender her autonomy or bury her aggressive impulses in order to be assured of love but merely tames or ties them down, with an appealing integrity in her struggle."

These methods were, again, simply a few among a variety of ways of maintaining their own stance, demanding that the environment come to terms with their preferences, abilities, limitations, and capacities.

The fact that children were typically realistic about their own limits often put such behavior on exactly the same level as the behavior of an adult who makes his own choices, accepting here and rejecting there. It is evidently merely because adults assume that children should meet the demands imposed on them that we use the term "negativism" to describe their refusals, whereas we think of ourselves as merely independent in doing or saying the same thing. A genuinely negative orientation probably occurred only in Darlene who tended to make her differentiations in negative terms, in Martin whose rejections tended to express hostile attitudes, and in Daryl who rivaled Martin in the diffuse, suspicious hostility which had dominated her outlook.

Inhibition

Inhibition played a varying role in the test situations. Children who were quite capable of being very spontaneous under many circumstances when they felt familiar and at ease in a situation, were also capable of being very inhibited as, for instance, in response to the utterly strange Rorschach cards. The reactive and situational nature of this inhibition readily became apparent as the children opened up and expanded either later in the same situation or in other more favorable ones. This restriction is not the same as the quiet taking-time-out to survey and look over a new area as at a party or play situation. The strangeness of the Rorschach cards, small and delimited as they were, did not permit the accustomed pattern of large-scale free visual exploration and appraisal. The very confinement of the situation itself probably contributed to the restriction which appeared in such active children as Jo Anne at the outset.

Inhibition was typically not global but appeared in certain situational contexts and applied to certain aspects of the child's response. For instance, Cynthia was initially inhibited in over-all bodily activity but was able to maintain a friendly outgoing verbal contact. Her moderately spontaneous conversation was "mostly of a soliloquizing kind" in which, however, she expressed her associations and reactions to the tests and toys. Her brother Roger appeared to be freer from inhibition in the locomotor area: while playing with Miniature Life Toys he would take animals for rides as if the area of animal life were freer from the inhibitions resulting from the policed areas of life.

The children in many instances tried to maintain their own freedom and spontaneity by such operations as seeking security in reality (Karen in the CAT); being most secure in manipulatory activities with objects and with clay (Teddy); keeping a contact with solid ground (Vernon); liking to feel related to his environment at large (Lennie); being more at ease in handling furniture; trying to consolidate her grasp of functions (Sheila).

Somewhat atypical was Vernon, a quiet, contained, highly competent but relatively inexpressive infant when first seen. He turned away from tests, yet he did best in making fine discriminations. This suggests an early pattern of shutting out, doubtless leading to inhibition (partly from others' response to his social isolating tendencies) rather than the reverse where inhibition leads to shutting out. Always with Vernon testers had an impression of conscious control. At the age of four, extreme inhibition (constriction, withdrawal into a shell, clamming up, tending to become rigid, staring wide-eyed but without actively looking at something), seemed to lead to control of or reduction of stimulation. He required a combination of time for orientation and acclimatization, along with an especially stimulating appealing challenge. This extreme shyness of one of the most intelligent and sensitive children however was not the typical pattern of inhibition in the group.

We could say that for most of the children a process of seeking their own level, finding their own dish, sorting out the opportunities available in the environment until they came upon those which fitted their own resources and strengths, was necessary in order to pave the way toward maximum freedom. Few children could freely move into all the situations with equal spontaneity and assurance that something in this situation would fit their interests and capacities. In other words some sort of security operations involving temporary inhibition were involved in attuning the child to each situation in many cases.

Withholding

Similarly a considerable number of the children used techniques of ignoring, shutting out, turning away from, holding out on the adult, not committing oneself, not giving, and other withholding techniques. Actually when we see this was true at times with some of the active children as well as with Vernon and others, we can see that such techniques were again part of the repertory of many children of considerable strength. These methods could serve the children well as ways of protecting them against risks, and in none of the instances we mentioned except that of Vernon was there any danger at all that such shutting-out methods would result in any over-all inhibition of the child's ability to cope further with the situation. The child's own confidence in his ability to hold out against the grownups for a time when necessary may indeed have contributed considerably to his confidence and to his basic sense of ego-strength.

Probably such operations of shutting out or refusing are at such a conscious level that they are under clear control by the child, which contributes to keeping them flexible, and makes it possible to move on to a more receptive approach after a period of cognitive mastery.

Less conscious and more deeply rooted in the child's character and less flexible in the children in which they were seen were tendencies to stick to general concepts or to avoid responding to concrete stimuli.

Darlene stayed with undifferentiated responses perhaps because they seemed safer; perhaps because separating things, sorting them out, differentiating, was at an unconscious level associated with anxieties about separation and conflicts about relationships: of all the little girls, she had one of the most conflicted relations with her mother. Sally, who also tended to stick to more abstract and general forms, remained vague about details and avoided any commitment to concrete things. Here again this pattern may have been part of a deep psychodynamic constellation involving a conflict with her mother who had always been rather disappointed at Sally's tomboyishness and perhaps a conflict about her father with whom she was more identified than with her mother. Interestingly enough, while not able to deal with details on projective techniques, when dealing with real objects she was an expert fixer, and could put things together; she was more skillful in manipulating toys than most of the other girls, having developed a pattern of watching her carpenter father like the boys who hung around while their fathers were using tools to make things.

Help

Autonomous children also seemed more ready to respond to offers of help. This tendency seemed to go hand in hand with "positive expectations" and high self-regard, not loss of self-esteem. Here again, the data from the intelligence test situation are especially useful. The readiness to ask for, or to openly enlist help in clarifying directions, or to seek assistance, support, or reassurance in motor execution of a task, implies an awareness of the demands of the situation, a recognition and acceptance of one's own limitations, and freedom to approach an adult with the expectation of receiving help. Seeking help usually took the form of direct verbal request for clarification of directions (as "Do you mean," "Shall I put it here?" or for assistance in responding, as "Did you make it this way?" "Show me again," "Can you read it over?" "I remember you took a square one and then a round one . . . was it first this?"). Sometimes seeking help involved need for reassurance, confirmation, or reality-testing as to accuracy: "Is that right?" "I think I know, but I don't know if I know," "I might not know what it means. I gotta think first," "I don't think I know everything . . . do you?" Requests for reassurance were sometimes non-verbal, quite subtle, and could be inferred only from wistful, appealing, or questioning facial expressions or slight bodily movements. Requests for physical help were numerous, particularly in the younger girls, and often implied sharing responsibility or a sort of "we're in this together" attitude. ("I wanna put the big ones in. *You* put the little ones in." "Help me, so it don't break." "Will you hold the paper while I cut?" "Will you cut it for me? I can't do it very well.") This readiness to relegate the adult to the lesser jobs suggests feelings of autonomy. Most children who directly sought help were equally able to accept unsolicited help, such as steadying a paper, opening a door, putting on wraps. Some children, who never asked for help, accepted offered help without comment.

Differing from these children were those who refused help altogether, by seeming not to notice that help was offered, by moving away, or sometimes verbally refusing help. These children tended to remain more aloof, refused to be involved, and held to an independence which chiefly served to maintain distance. This behavior was distinctly different from the behavior of the first group whose independence was evidently sufficiently well established to allow temporary and voluntary departures from it when reality factors demanded it.

Slightly more than one quarter of the children sought help initially and another third of the children could accept offered help in a new situation. Somewhat more than a third of the children rejected help initially. Requests for help increased with specific test demands and conversely, rejection of help decreased. This would suggest that it is easier to ask for help from a more familiar adult and that requests for help were geared to the objective need for it. Only five children continued to reject help when faced with difficulty. These included very retiring children like one child who refused to be deeply involved at any time, and more autonomous children who seemed to feel that offered help was an intrusive reflection on their ability to handle the situation. It is interesting to note that two children, who were both very withdrawing initially, were able to relax their guard against involvement after they had accepted the test situation even when objective difficulty arose. One child who was very independent much of the time was also capable of modified dependence when the situation demanded it.

On the average, boys capable of utilizing help were among those who were quick to orient themselves to cognitive challenge, relatively free of internal tension, more capable of expressing independent needs, more overtly aware of limits or personal need for help, who responded more positively to the adult as a person, and were more cooperative to adult demand.

For girls, these relationships followed a similar pattern, but were less striking. Those girls who were most ready to seek or accept help were among the more independent children, the more openly accepting of their own limits, the more positively reactive to the adult.

Dependency in other situations

We have seen many indications of the autonomous attitude of most of the children in situations which they could comfortably master. When they felt adequate to a task or opportunity it was not at all unusual for a child to refuse help, saying or implying that he didn't need it, that he didn't want help from the grownup, or that he thought the grownup didn't realize that he could handle the situation by himself.

Some children who were often very autonomous and spontaneous were insecure in facing certain new situations and under these conditions depended upon the adult to provide structure and guidance.

Children who were gladly autonomous as far as they were able to manage situations were still generally able to ask for help after their own efforts had not succeeded. For instance, Roger "initiated direct contact when he came for help with the musical jack-in-the-box which he had wound and wound but it would not pop." Ability to accept help when it was needed while being autonomous as far as possible—being even proud of accomplishment but actually needing to feel helped after having made an independent effort were variations of this pattern. Ronnie accepted help just as long as he needed it and then refused any more. Two other boys relied on mother for support or help in figuring things out, although they could move ahead into new situations when mother was not there.

In one instance however, alternating between being a helpless little person and a businesslike grownup was rather an expression of a conflict between the drive to grow up and a longing to remain little, which was expressed in dependency not only in relation to realistic needs for help. Reversing roles was a method used by some girls in the process of denial of dependency and infantile needs. The Rorschach test for one girl gave evidence that dependency could sometimes be accepted momentarily as a defense against aggression, or against a derogatory view of women, although in general she tended to deny dependency needs.

One girl defended her autonomy with some evidence of feeling guilty about dependency, while another appeared to glory in her competence, to be eager to demonstrate it on every possible occasion, and to fend off adult assistance as far as possible.

The capacity to accept help, freedom to ask for it or reliance on it was in many cases part of the over-all picture of the child-adult relationship which included the child's expectation of operating in terms of permissions and limits, giving unquestioning obedience when it was demanded, while moving freely when the green lights were on—assuming that adults would satisfy one's basic needs when one could not do so oneself. One child showed some dependent trends which included wanting help, expecting to operate in terms of permissions and limits, yielding easily when an issue was presented, and accepting suggestions. Another child who was active in safe situations was described as showing a rather passive adaptation "in which she looks to others for guidance, direction and cues"; one child tended to seek help in narrowing the field, becoming more specific. A boy who had been the most "quiet" baby in our infancy records, could also organize materials well in a protected situation, but was seen in projective tests as "expecting care and help from others." Another boy who at the party showed outstanding leadership at other times indicated a wish for protection and shelter. Ronnie, whom we saw earlier as capable of enormous effort toward mastery (p. 163) was "responsive to external stimulation, capable of rapport, and anxious to maintain it." Rachel, whom we saw earlier (p. 35), and Susan, the child with polio, were able to use tender and loving care as an effective reinforcement of their own coping efforts; Darlene (p. 168) expected maternal assistance when she needed it.

More extreme forms of dependent behavior are shown by a few children. One three-year-old girl allowed herself to be carried by her mother into the car; one boy would not come at all without his mother, nor would he stay alone with a strange person without her; his repeated asking for help was thought to be "an expression of inadequacy feelings resulting from the chronic feelings of frustration he appeared to have." Another boy, although full of spontaneity and motor initiative at the parties, seemed to the Rorschach tester to be "passively, receptively oriented and more demanding to be given unto than readily to give to others." In Vivian's (p. 83) case the need for support was generalized and included her way of leaning her head against the wall for external support, standing, leaning in a passive, silent way before she was able to start play with Miniature Life Toys.

Over and over again in the CAT, which includes a number of pictures involving size and power differences, we find reflections of the image which many of the children had of themselves as small creatures limited in their ability to cope with threats presented by big people. Actually, their energy, capacity for effort, and struggle in reality situations went far beyond what one might expect from the fantasy images.

We have been dealing with the child's capacity to use help in coping with external demands which he could not handle entirely by himself, and further than this his tendency to utilize, ask for, expect help at a deeper level as a reassurance of adult support; this involved coping with more persistent chronic feelings of need for the grownups, feelings of being little, of being exposed to demands which they might not be able to meet, feelings which were very strong alongside of the also strong feelings of vigor and satisfaction in functioning autonomously whenever they were able to manage by themselves.

It is not surprising that all the children who showed strong autonomy drives and initiative expressed their own self-sufficiency and refused help insofar as they could manage by themselves. However, we might not have taken it for granted that these autonomous self-sufficient children would be flexibly able to accept help when they got beyond their depth or confronted situations which they could not manage alone; yet many of the children mentioned over and over again as sturdily independent were equally able to reject help if they did not need it and to accept it when they did. They could be autonomous but were not compulsively so, and for them there was no conflict between autonomy and dependence.

Determination, persistence, effort

Over half the children were described at one time or another as being determined, firm, stubborn, or in some cases perseverative beyond simply effective persistence. Even mild Diane could stick to her own idea while Jo Anne, a generally assertive child, was able to put the examiner in his place by insisting, "Let me talk by myself." When the child's experience had differed from the examiner's, many children could insist on their own observation, perception, or knowledge of a situation: "Terry insisted that fire engine ladders go on the side, not on the top, as they were placed on the fire engine in this set of toys." Unyielding, persistent, determined effort was characteristic of Ronnie, Sheila, Teddy, and Roger, and some children even insisted on persisting with a difficult task beyond their own level of capacity.

With Martin, who was a child with many conflicts, this persistence alternated with a doubtful feeling that he might not be able to reach his goal, "I just about make it. It won't go on, I can't, I'll try," and in such instances the persistence probably has a value for the child in defending against his tendency to discouragement.

Persistence could take the form of repetition of effort in order to achieve mastery as with a child who resourcefully, insistently pointed to a tree outside the window when Dr. Kass did not understand his "pree" response to the Rorschach card.

We have seen Sheila's vigorous stance earlier (p. 82); her efforts with the Bonhop Play House included tackling one door after another after initial frustration with the first one which she failed to open. The quiet Vernon's capacity for persistence was also expressed in the sequence of structures which he made in his MLT play session.

With certain children a competitive orientation stimulated maximal persistence while with others the desire to maintain a firm stand (or a sort of obstinacy) vis-a-vis the grownup was more important than the objective goal orientation characteristic of the children described up to this point. Many of the children simply did not give up easily and while the most dramatic example was probably that of Susan's triumph over polio with the support of her ability to search for and hold to positive concepts, hope, and optimism, most of the children had the vitality to sustain their purposes to the point of mobilizing extra energy when needed, in the interests of reaching a goal. "Giving up" did not come naturally to them.

With several children the capacity for overt struggle, with grunting noises, reddening face, and tossing movements of the body, while for instance trying to pull out the Bonhop Play House from its box, or open the tightly bolted door, implied a total undifferentiated capacity for effort beyond what is ordinarily seen with adults except in vocations that are physically extremely demanding, in sports, or emergencies.

Minimizing or shutting out versus maximizing as an aspect of coping

We can see that many different devices may be used for quite similar purposes—that is, either maximizing the child's skill and capacity for satisfaction in use of the environment or minimizing stress of threats, pressure, overstimulation, and so on. The selectivity of one child has the purpose of avoiding strong stimulation that might be too much for the child to master, where the selectivity of another child has the value of sustaining a level of stimulation to a height which is satisfying for the child.

Perhaps in all cultures, certainly in ours, children sort out life in terms of those things that they don't see, don't hear, don't believe, don't pay attention to as compared with the things they take seriously, do believe, do look at, do listen to, and so on. With some children this is influenced very much by what they are encouraged to ignore or shut out; with others it is influenced by their own perceptions of what is undependable in the adult culture. In any case, this *patterning of what is attended to as compared to what is shut out* is part of the development of individual coping skills. As we saw, it has the effect of narrowing the stimulus exposure. This narrowing effect may be compared to the functioning of the stimulus barrier which Freud [3] describes as necessary to protect the organism from being overwhelmed by the great multiplicity of potential stimuli. The capacity to shut out can be helpful and protective to the child who would otherwise be exposed to conflicts or overstimulation, discouragement, or frustrations, if he allowed himself to respond to everything.

Individual differences in autonomy in infancy

Since the children differed widely at the preschool age in their capacity for assertiveness, exploration of the environment, and also their ability to set limits to pressures from the environment, to fend off excessive stimulation, and other expressions of active autonomous dealing with the world, we were curious about the development of this group of capacities.

In psychoanalytic thinking, autonomy is consolidated as a good outcome of struggles between the child and his parents in the phase of cleanliness training, which is usually emphasized in the second year of life in our culture. Initiative is expected to flower in the phallic phase, when sex differences in body parts are the object of new awareness. The children in this group were not being studied during the second year of life; all we know of that period of toilet training and its accompanying behavior and moods comes from the interviews with mothers a year or two later, at the commencement of the preschool study, and from subsequent discussions between the pediatrician and the mothers. On the basis of such admittedly limited data we found no close relation between autonomy as seen in the child and the experiences reported for the toilet-training period. It appears that constitutional factors and experiences in different zones were all involved in the patterning of autonomy in this group.

We did, however, find relationships between earlier aspects of the children's behavior, as recorded in infancy, and later autonomy. Ratings were made on the infant's tendency to protest, terminate, or reject unwanted foods, and also autonomy permitted by the mother. Significant correlations were found between these ratings and ratings of autonomy and the capacity to set limits to and fend off excessive stimulation from the environment at the preschool stage. Evidently both sets of variables were dealing with a generally active approach to the environment. It is possible that the development and reinforcement of this tendency in the first year of life is a major determinant in the outcome of training struggles in the next year.

Our explorations also suggest that a number of integrative functions of the ego contribute to (and probably are also an outgrowth of) autonomy. Among the girls—who show a wider range of degrees of autonomy than the boys because of the greater dependence of certain girls—we find autonomy in the sense of self-reliance and independence correlating highly with ability to organize and to provide own structure as well as the tendency to use environmental areas selectively. Other variables such as a psychically active approach, and speed of orientation, motor and visual-motor control, and having "coping concepts, ideas and solutions," (along with "knowing the score" which also correlated highly) can be seen both as implementing and as, in turn, increased by autonomy. The ability to synthesize thinking, affect, and action, and to integrate modalities, along with "competence" (implying such capacities for relevant action) can also be assumed to have this sort of circular relation. That is, a girl who is so flooded with feelings that she cannot think out what to do to meet a situation could be expected to be more dependent on her mother's solutions; relying on these in turn would avoid the effort to work out solutions of her own and thus interfere further with the development of autonomy.

A child with these synthesizing capacities has an additional advantage, in that social outlets are available to him which contribute to further strengthening of his own ego. Also, these expressions of, and contributing factors to, autonomy could be expected to facilitate the mobilizing of energy to meet challenge or stress, if indeed they are not prerequisites for this capacity which is highly correlated with autonomy.

In mental health attitudes and in much of the popular thinking in our culture we tend to assume that the quality of autonomy is a foundation for most other strengths of character and personality. In our analysis we do find it highly correlated with creativity and with satisfaction. Speed of orientation, responsiveness to stimuli, and specific coping devices such as "imposes own structure on a situation" appear to be related to autonomy. But we also find that the capacity to seek help when it is needed is related to other active coping operations and to autonomy as well.

We noted above that the range of autonomy for girls is wider than it is for boys, doubtless as a consequence of cultural differences in autonomy permitted and encouraged in girls as well as constitutional differences in drive and energy. Among the girls, autonomy as shown in the intelligence test situation is highly correlated with mastery drive, mobilization of resources, social skills, and ego functioning (as defined by involvement in own activity, determination, and directness of problem-solving).

Since ego functioning as defined above is close to autonomy, the contributing factors appearing in the study of the former are relevant here: other children available in the neighborhood, physiological factors, and aspects of equipment such as adequacy of vegetative functioning, motor and visual-motor control, weight, and chest dimension. This evokes an image of a well-built and well-functioning, well-coordinated child with good striped muscle equipment and freedom from gastrointestinal disturbances. Such a child has what it needs to be autonomous and does not have to use up energy in anxious or angry reactions to chronic inner distress. This child may also be expected to be autonomous, and is certainly likely to be more free from constraining protective efforts by the environment than a puny, colicky, or slowly developing baby.

Among the other contributing factors were age at sitting. Boys who sat alone earlier were more autonomous. We can speculate that those who sat up early may have done so as a consequence of more vigorous demands for exercise, for being held in the vertical position, and this may have been one expression of greater energy and drive. And further we note early sitting up provides greater opportunity for manipulation of objects, observing the world, developing skills, and outgrowing the passive orientation implicit in the supine and prone positions.

Other contributing factors for the girls included "child's living space, equipment in room" which implies that extensive early experience with objects free from prohibitions contributed to the expression of autonomy.

NOTES AND REFERENCES

1. Erikson, E.H. *Childhood and Society*. New York: Norton, 1950.
2. See the authors' review of these studies in Murphy, G., Murphy, L.B., and Newcomb, T.M. *Experimental Social Psychology*. New York: Harper, 1937.
3. Freud, S. Beyond the pleasure principle. *Standard Edition of the Complete Works of Sigmund Freud*, Vol. 18. London: Hogarth Press, 1949.

⚶⚶⚶ 11

DRIVES AND RESOURCES
FOR GRATIFICATION

WE HAVE SEEN MANY INSTANCES of the capacity to use old and new gratifications to tide oneself over periods of threat or loss. With Susan, especially, we saw the contribution of parents and professional people who made balancing gratifications possible. Her polio experience had occurred two years before we saw her so that we did not have concurrent records. However, reports by her mother and Susan's later detailed playing out of the hospital experience testified eloquently to the role of rewards, shared gay fantasies, toys, and expressions of love in sustaining her determination to survive and to conquer her disability.

The importance of the ability to enjoy and to expect gratifying exchanges with the environment was also visible in our records of getting used to nursery school, moving, and utilizing the opportunities provided by the parties. Capacity for development of new interests was present in children who responded to new situations expectantly. These optimistic expectancies and capacities for responsiveness underlie and motivate the development of skills. We were also impressed by the importance of the range of areas for enjoyment and gratification as support for coping efforts. The child who had a wide range of pleasure resources could more easily find or accept a substitute when frustrated, and awareness of this contributed to tolerance of frustration.

This range of resources for gratification, and also the depth of responsiveness typical of many of these children was more dramatically impressive by contrast with the "autistic" children whom I have observed in various schools for "emotionally disturbed" children. A fundamental characteristic of many of the latter is their inability to make any substantial response to, or investments in, the environment at all. They do not act like scared children; they are detached, uninvolved, unable to find delight in anything. At best, some apparently trivial object or part of the physical environment such as a door knob or a stick may be adopted by the child, who plays with it in an apparently meaningless, though usually deeply symbolic, way. We cannot discuss the many constitutional and developmental factors which contribute to such profound alienation. We mention them simply to show how fundamental the difference is between being able to enjoy many resources in the environment, and not being able to enjoy anything. Finding potential gratifications in new situations underlies the autonomous efforts to reach out for them and work toward them; it also underlies the flexible capacity to turn to another potential gratification when the first is lost, or when one is frustrated in one's first efforts to reach it. We shall discuss the flexibility of these children in the next chapter.

Origins of resources for gratification are complex; drive level in general may be presumed to be involved, and also the range of areas of pleasure in infancy, and the consistency with which a given stimulus provided pleasure. Even when a child found certain degrees of stimulation in a given modality pleasurable, when greater intensity or duration was a source of discomfort, tendencies to reject the latter might be generalized to include the former. For instance, Steve as an infant showed evidence of both pleasure and discomfort in tactile stimulation; by the preschool level he tended to keep his distance and avoid close contact except under rare circumstances.

Certain children showed tendencies even in infancy to respond with high drive toward many kinds of experiences; Roddie, Gordon, Sally and Brennie were responsive to objects, persons, and other social stimulation (voices, languages), as well as motor experiences. Others responded to a narrow range only, such as motor experiences. Several infants responded to objects more than to people. We cannot exclude here the possible influence, even in the first half-year of life, of earlier difficulties with people, especially the mother; four out of seven infants who preferred objects had teasing, depriving, mildly depressed, frail, or otherwise incompatible or unsatisfying mothers.

We infer then that the range of resources for gratification has a foundation in (1) a general level of drive in the sense of capacity for investment in the environment; (2) tendencies to respond to many versus a few types or modalities of experience with pleasure; (3) early gratifications and frustrations in specific areas leading to avoidance or to seeking of certain kinds of stimulation. So it is not surprising that we found the "range of areas of enjoyment and gratification" closely related to the capacity to cope with the environment and to maintain internal integration.* It is easy to see how the range of areas of enjoyment would contribute to the capacity to draw on substitutes and to be flexible in using the environment selectively and thus to forestall or to mitigate serious frustration and its sequelae of tense, angry, conflicted feelings. At another level, when we find the range of areas of enjoyment related to the capacity to integrate modalities, we have to think in terms of the importance of emotional investments as lowering the threshold for and easing the internal manipulations and experiments which lead to integrating processes. The relationships of two things in which one is interested may be perceived more spontaneously than relationships between things that have no emotional meaning to us.

Similarly, the expectation of pleasure often promotes the child's speed of orientation, and the cognitive responses which lead to insight regarding the uses and value of specific things. Thus the range of areas of enjoyment contributes to the reservoir of coping concepts and competence in dealing with objects in the environment.

When we came to the point of correlating† specific characteristics and tendencies of the children with our summary scores on "capacity to cope with the opportunities, challenges and frustrations of the environment" we found that the intelligence quotient did not correlate as well as these: the child's resources for gratification and his capacity for zest, pleasure, interest, and enjoyment of activities. In our group of children we thus found ourselves concerned about a few children with good intelligence quotients and other capacities—even broad competence wherever they choose to make use of it—who lacked the interest and urge which might lead to fulfillment through the use of their capacities. By contrast we were impressed by children of modest intelligence—no more than average—who found every experience full of interesting possibilities.

* See Appendix B for examples of correlations mentioned in this chapter.
† See Appendix B.

The resources of the child include not only the range and content of his potential areas of gratification but the appropriateness of affect, its quality and degree in the child's response to the environment. The majority of these children were neither "spoiled," demanding, nor bored—many aspects of life going to and from their homes, coming into new situations, were interesting to them. They were eager, curious, capable of enjoying new things; this was true even of the youngest children like Lennie and Molly, who were fearful of separating from mother or who were initially cautious in new situations.

The fact that in this study we were concerned with preschool children probably has much to do with the weight to be given to resources for gratification; at this age the environment is not emphasizing achievement and skills primarily. While competence was conspicuous it was closely linked to the children's expectation of satisfaction and the degree of eagerness in responding to the opportunities which we offered.

In giving our attention to the roles of zest, capacity for enjoyment, range of resources for gratification, we are of course concerning ourselves with some of the roots of character development of greatest interest to psychoanalysis—whether we call it drive level, strength of libido, or some other term referring to the degree of urgency from within as it becomes linked to the environment in a certain intensity of responsiveness. It is a matter of broad and deep investment in life, involvement with things and people, the capacity for immersing one's self in the environment and through one's interaction with it, molding it and being molded in the direction of greater satisfaction.

The deepest roots of this capacity to find the environment gratifying probably lies in the first and profoundest experiences of exchange with the environment, namely, in the earliest oral experiences and other gratifications in the first months of life. In the course of this chapter we shall give considerably more attention to this.

Areas of gratification

As we would expect of children at this age, oral gratification was high enough on the priority list so that most of the children looked forward eagerly to the ice cream or gum or candy which followed each session with the testers. In the first round of testing only Teddy preferred another treat—a "commie" (comic book); but at a later period he regressed to rely on oral satisfaction during a time of stress accompanying loss of his father.

Motor activity was also a source of pleasure. The children climbed and jumped off walls and did many other things for the sheer satisfaction or delight of the activity itself, directly satisfying innate drives; at the party and at the zoo Ronnie, Ralph, Sammy, Greg, and others spontaneously utilized the resources of the terrain for many varieties of motor fun whenever the adults were not limiting the situation by explicit directions or requests.

In our culture, zestful gratification accompanies early motor and verbal achievements as well as oral and other sensory experiences. To varying degrees in different subculture groups babies are stimulated by eager parents and siblings to sit up, pull up to standing position, creep, walk, balance, manage swings or walkers or kiddiecars; they also are encouraged to throw balls, spools, or other objects, to fit toys together. All of these motor and manipulative skills are greeted with greater or less excitement depending on the emphasis placed upon such accomplishments by the adults rearing the children. The natural gratification in activity thus comes to loom large within the first years of life, and mounts with the interest of adults. Of the fifty-four items in tests* through the seven-year age level taken by the preschool boys in this group, only sixteen were performed without overt evidence of gratification for one or more children; this was true even when the child did not meet the test standard for passing. The doing in itself was satisfying.

We can speculate that different resources for gratification have varied effects: gratification and pleasure in the process of the activity itself reinforces successful efforts, adding an extra filip to the satisfaction of reaching a goal or solving a problem. And thus the prospect of gratification adds extra motivation to coping efforts. We like not only to satisfy our hunger but to do so with food that tastes good. If the food does not look good or taste good, the four-year-old would, up to a point, rather go hungry. If it were not "fun" to do the tests and go to the parties offered by the Coping Project, the children would prefer not to bother with them.

We are emphasizing this point because those formulations of theories of adaptation which leave out the role of function pleasure seem to ignore many of the multitude of processes that go on in a child through a whole day. True enough, one has to eat to satisfy hunger and keep alive; but that does not account for much of the energy spent in a child's day. One may climb Everest "because it is there," but children behave as if much of what they do is done chiefly because it is exciting, gratifying, or most simply, "fun." Perhaps this is part of nature's extravagance or generosity—an extra guarantee that a wide range of sensory, motor, manipulative, or social experiences will be explored.

Closely allied to the range of resources for gratification if not part

* Both motor and verbal.

of it is the range of areas of competence and control, and achievement; here we are concerned both with the actual mastery and skill within the child's abilities, used for coping with difficulties, and also with the areas in which he has invested interest and energy, or which he most readily uses to obtain satisfaction. The coping efforts of the child are not always limited by the skills accessible at the moment; the former can stimulate both the development of new skills and new uses of old skills. We saw this at the party, as we noted in the records of Darlene (p. 168 f) and earlier with Ronnie (p. 163 f).

Satisfaction in and eagerness to master skills begins in early infancy; as soon as the child begins to use his muscles we see the practice of manual coordinations from the simplest waving of a rattle to complicated problem-solving efforts toward getting out of the crib, high chair, play pen, or harness in order to move around and in order to add more motor skills. Some of this involves satisfaction in the process; some of it, as in practice which does not directly reach a goal, involves delay in immediate gratification for the sake of greater facility in obtaining gratification later.

To be sure, when adequate skills are not yet available, the child may grab, whine for, wheedle, scream, in order to get what he wants, or he may bargain, ingratiate himself with the adult, wear down the adult's resistance, or play one against another. As fast as he is able to, he may use objects as means to ends, to help him reach his goal, or he may destroy obstacles to his goals, as for example when a year-old baby broke the posts of his play pen in order to get out. As his own competence in reaching goals increases and standards of self-control are raised, constructive methods supplant socially annoying or destructive ones.

Motility: resources for discharge and for dealing with the environment

As we have implied in our discussion of pleasure in activity for its own sake, locomotor difficulties, awkwardness, or heaviness in movement were rare in these children. Typically they were described as follows:* "Moving with the skill of a monkey"; "she seems to enjoy movement, skipping, dancing, whirling"; "he has many postures with easy shifts and a light quality"; "agile and athletic, she can climb, jump, run as easily as other people walk"; "she had great motor versatility, in the sense that she used a very wide variety of postures, lounging,

---

* Here we draw upon excerpts of descriptive phrases and sentences referring to motility in the preschool party and play sessions. The quotations used are from records on many different children and by different recorders.

squatting, jumping up, etc."; "daring and reckless in motor behavior"; "she easily shifts her position and changes the direction of her movement with even and unusual limber bending positions"; "capable of bounding movements"; "his easy locomotion, selectivity, interest in riding horses . . . were equally characteristic of both sessions." Here we see the ease of movement characteristic of children typically slender of build, agile and free from experiences of prolonged blocking of movement. With a few children, such as Lennie and Sheila, observers commented that "impulse seemed to move straight into action" or "achievement of perceptual clarity . . . led quickly to action."

As is typical for many American children but much less often seen, for instance, in India, motility is used by many of the children to let off steam; motor discharge through jumping, excited movement, or restless activity was typical of Terry and Roddy often, others less frequently. Of Roddy it was said, "His energy is on the high side; his tempo is slow to dashing quick; he moves over a wide area, sometimes with a jerky tendency to immediate discharge in activity . . ." With Jo Anne, too, we observe that it seemed for her "easier to do active things than the things that required sitting still."

Consciously or unconsciously, directly or indirectly, these children exercised, enjoyed and exploited their motor skill, maintaining and improving it by their constant use of it. There were only a few exceptions to this; for instance, Sheila, who was described as stomping and flat-footed, centripetal and earthbound, in keeping with her heavier endomorphic build; and Daryl, whose typically tense relation to situations was expressed among other ways in minimal movement, reaching as far as possible without moving her body.

At this age, acting out concerns and feelings, clowning or teasing or stimulating each other provocatively was another resource of motorically versatile children not available to those more inhibited or less skillful in the use of motility for coping or for expression.

For one or two, motor skill had competitive values—to Roddy being fast had the value of getting the most, while with Terry speed seemed to be associated with mastery and possibly with being grown-up.

Our observations of these children led to the suggestion that something about differences in coping capacity of children of different constitutional types might be learned by studying differences in the gratification from and uses of motor skill in endomorphic or heavy fatty children as contrasted with limber muscular children; comparisons are needed, also between the coping resources of children like this Kansas group who have maximum freedom for the use of motility from the time when locomotion is maturing, and young, urban, apartment-dwelling children who have more limited opportunities for development of motor skill.*,†

Manipulative skill paralleled gross motor agility with many of these children and appeared to reflect another aspect of freedom to explore and handle the environment; several of them had had an opportunity to watch and help fathers who were good at construction or fixing things. Two fathers were carpenters by vocation; four other fathers built new homes or major additions to the home during the period of the study, while still others did major redecorating and renovating work on their own homes. A daughter of one of these carpenter-fathers was outstanding in her interest in "whether things fit, and in doing things the right way. Fixing things and making things work seemed more important to her than nurturant activities." A son of another such father manipulated things unusually well. "He masterfully turned the Bonhop Play House around to get at it. He showed great originality, repeatedly doing things no other child had done—combining objects in original ways. He enjoyed things you can do something to, or with, especially winding things." With Susan, whose mother had many skills, manipulation along with expressiveness offered a major substitute for gross motor function pleasure at the period of paralysis after her polio.

This manipulative skill which was characteristic of so many of the children did not necessarily involve great creativeness or complexity of ideas, although typically in this group it did involve care and respect for objects; by contrast for instance with the eastern metropolitan group it was striking that rarely did any of these children break anything; at the same time the over-all level of imaginativeness and complexity of organization was probably lower than the other group when they were playing with the Miniature Life Toys. Their skill was most apparent with the larger toys such as the take-apart plane, pirate ships, play movie, that is, in handling structured objects with some degree of complexity. This manipulative interest involved not only skill

---

* Observations and a few case studies of the latter by graduate students in New York City showed intense and compulsive drives to activity in some vigorous children growing up in space-restrictive apartments.

† Mittelmann[1] has studied intensively the development of motility and its relation to ego development in both normal and schizophrenic children, following Hartmann's discussion of motility as an autonomous ego function. This is not the place for an extended discussion of Mittelmann's contribution beyond noting that he concludes that motility must be thought of as an urge, with its own energies that blossom during the phase of locomotion achievement. He also deals at length with affecto-motor expressiveness, its emergence in infancy and its role in normal development. Tragically, for the contribution he was in the process of making, he died before completing the study of various aspects of motility including its role in mastery of the objects of the environment.

and efficiency but deep interest and capacity for investment and satisfaction.

Affective expression of gratification

The capacity for joy did not seem to be closely related to any other basic equipment variable we observed: those who were most exuberant in one or another situations were very different children—mesomorphic, endomorphic, ectomorphic, in turn, on the Sheldon categories; from average to very superior intelligence on the tests; they ranged from youngest to oldest and included one only child. Their social backgrounds also ranged from top to bottom of the economic scale. On physiological measurements they were among the more variable of the group and perhaps reflected a tendency toward more antonomic responsiveness than could be experienced by the physiologically most stable children.

In the intelligence test situation Diane, Terry, Chester, Greg, Darlene (in the retest, not in the first test), Martin, and Susan were definitely gratified, proudly pleased, eagerly enthusiastic with many of their good performances, particularly if they followed difficulty, frustration, or uncertainty. Karen, Ronnie, Sheila, and Judy were less absorbed by test materials and less concerned with success in intellectual pursuits, but exceedingly gay and active on trips home, with toys and play equipment they saw in the stores where we stopped for treats. Ronnie was delighted with the merry-go-round horse, for example, at the grocery. Brennie was more cautious in the stores and seemed to acquire greatest pleasure from social contacts with clerks and even with passing strangers to whom he talked about a big, stuffed bear, following his initial caution in approaching and touching it. Roddy reached out for and gloried in the examiner's acceptance and fondness as he did, too, with Terry on the ride to the office for the body photographs. Teddy's joy was more contained except for one instance when he quite gaily and excitedly shared secrets with Mrs. Smith. Gordon was too concerned about knowing and not knowing to enjoy the tests, but during the ride home, he became playfully delighted with a slingshot. Only a few remained rather aloof and never gay.

Even here, we have to qualify, though, because among the aloof ones Daryl and Vivian were quite happy with the selection of coloring books and Vernon was amazingly loving, tender and warm with his baby brother at his own home following a rather tense test session; "his little face glowed with love!" On the trip to the zoo following body photographs, group interstimulation, zest, competitiveness, and cooperation were particularly striking with half a dozen of the boys. Even Vernon was having a wonderful time climbing the metal lion and the lifeguard's tower with all sorts of ingenious variations. (Only fearful Martin and Teddy, whose weight hampered him, remained isolated.) At the party sessions elation appeared first with Greg's antics on the climb-run-jump board, which stimulated other children, then with Donald's gay abandon in running and climbing, blowing the horns, etc., after his initial frozen period.

Affective range

Children like Chester, Ray and Diane were often warmly expressive, sometimes with a quiet glow, sometimes with more open delight. Within the group of openly emotional responsive children we would also include those who swing from one end of a scale to the other: "The impulsivity of her 'oh, oh, oh' reaction would suggest a kind of impulsive-repressive axis on which she swings from one to the other." With another child, "There were many reversals from affection to aggression, aggression to restoration, receiving help or protection to receiving aggression followed by retaliation." These swings of mood and quick open changes of feeling and impulse were particularly characteristic of girls like Karen, Barbie, and Susan, although boys like Donald and Ray also varied in emotional expressiveness along a very wide scale.

Sheila's range was different from that of the love-to-anger-range shown by the group of girls just mentioned; her typical affective tone seemed to be one of pride and confidence in her autonomy and ability to manage as when she proudly announced, "I'm a big girl." This strong positive self-feeling, however, could be abruptly shattered by two kinds of sudden events. The first was the experience of rejection or attack by someone or something she loved, as when she was scratched and abandoned by a cat she had been mothering. The second occurred when she had an accident and spilled ice cream on her dress, which spoiled its appearance; evidently feeling embarrassed and guilty, she burst into tears.

Thus at the same time we found not only wide differences in the range of gratification possibilities; we also found differences in freedom to enjoy expression of gratification. About one third of the children were described at one time or another as showing a "poker-face mask," "a guarded façade, hard to penetrate," "impassiveness," "betraying no affect"; "doesn't let out expressions of delight, glee, or surprise," "keeping a distance between acting and feeling"; "trying to avoid emotional reaction"; "repressing the need for affection, emotional involvement." This limitation of affective expression often, but not always, seemed to involve a limitation of the child's capacity for pleasure.

Such patterns of control, disguise, covering up, masking or repressing feelings were typical throughout our contact with only a minority of these children and even with them certain moments of deeply felt, delicately expressed feelings were shared with the adult at certain times. As Vernon's mother remarked, his smile "really means something." Among the rest of the children whose feelings were masked under certain circumstances were children who under other circumstances were among the most expressive and vivid of the entire group.

By paying attention to the contexts in which the children covered up feelings or expressed them openly, and the sequences that followed such masking or expressive times, we discovered some of the ways of coping with feelings which might be overwhelming, or which might commit the child to more involvement and interaction with new people than he felt safe in permitting. This is to be compared with the pattern of repressing or controlling feelings in the interest of coping with the situation. Most of the children who used a pattern of hiding, masking, or covering up feelings did so not as a fixed, rigid character expression but rather a pattern which was used at certain times and relinquished at others, permitting us to include it within the range of coping resources used by children of this age under certain circumstances.

Rather than covering up feelings in such a way as to totally hide them from the adult, some children partially inhibited their expressiveness. We see examples of this kind of attenuation in observations like the following: "speaking in soft, low, whispered tones"; "silent play with a highly charged emotional quality"; "giving subtle hints of very rich feelings beyond the immediate façade"; "avoiding open expression of a sad mood, but sighing deeply in the CAT and Rorschach"; "keeping affective interaction at a minimum"; "keeping a distance between acting and feeling." In such ways as these do we find the tester getting hints of feelings, sometimes with great intensity and depth, beyond the surface cover up or control shown under certain circumstances.

In still other instances we find descriptions of "minute, delicate, gradual expression of response"; "subtle facial expressions sometimes inscrutable"; "quiet ways of expressing closeness and perhaps affection"; here we find a level of emotional response more accessible to the observer but still delicate, and very controlled, however differentiated it might be.

Affect was sometimes expressed more through action and movement than through facial expressions: "Putting a soft teddy close to his

face . . . hinted a capacity for affection which I also felt in subtle,
warm smiles after he melted." "While she expresses her feelings less
openly than some children they are apparent in the shifts of pace and
mood during the play session, from excited, speedy running about to
calmer, slower movement around the room. While she is never effusive,
she is able to express how she feels about some things: "Dis is hard to
do!" "She has quiet ways of expressing closeness and perhaps affection,
gently holding the musical bear, leaning restfully against it in a softly
tender mood."

Similar patterns of expressing tenderness through gentle play with
a little furry squirrel or mouse or teddy bear, acting out love and enjoyment rather than expressing it through verbalization or more open
affective expressions was characteristic of several children. The ability
to respond to offers of comfort, to be replenished by a hug, or to express defiant or angry feelings through assertive ways rather than emotional expression are further examples of intermediate ways of experiencing or communicating feelings.

All of these various delicately conveyed, acted out, modulated or
indirect expressions of feeling were in contrast with the open, zestful,
free expression of delight and anxiety, the lability and spontaneity of
moods varying from uneasiness to a lilting gaiety, the obvious pleasure
in success, or frank discouragement with obstacles characteristic of
some of the children.

To round out this picture of range in ways of dealing with feelings,
we would include not only the variety of subtle shifts in facial expression as with Patsy from inscrutability to warm, resonant smiles, from
Chester's controlled responsiveness to sparkling and spontaneous
humor, but also a wider variety of expressions of affect through both
movement and verbalization as was characteristic of Terry.

Children who had some speech difficulty, such as Donald, naturally had trouble in expressing feelings through words, so it is not surprising that he turned affective energy into play with toys. This seemed
to give release as judged by the increasing warmth of his expression
to the experimenter after a play session.

Even flexible children (like Chester), who could express their
feelings quite openly and spontaneously under certain circumstances
and in more controlled and modulated ways in others, also tended to
repress intense feelings. Repression was by no means confined to children about whom the psychiatrist or other members of the team felt
concerned; on the contrary, it was used with other devices by children
who brought the widest range of resources to coping with the situations in which we saw them.

The capacity to handle feelings by direct, open expressiveness was no gilt-edged guarantee either of good coping capacity in terms of ability to use a wide variety of opportunities in the environment, or coping capacity in the sense of the ability to maintain integration. Greg, Susan, Karen, and others who had great emotional richness and expressiveness each had an Achilles heel or vulnerable spot associated with breakdown in situations where this point was attacked.

Children like Diane, on the one hand, who were able to cope with all the situations in which we saw them in the preschool period and were able to maintain inner integration throughout the period of our early acquaintance with them, were children with neither a strong tendency to repress their feelings nor an extreme intensity of emotional expression and relationship. Children with the flexibility to control their feelings when they needed their energy for problem-solving and effort towards goals, but who could also enjoy themselves very freely and express both negative and positive affects openly, were also able both to handle a wide variety of situations and to maintain their own inner integration in the situations in which we saw them. While intensity and range of emotional experience and expressiveness did not necessarily imply the highest degree of coping capacity either in external or internal terms, emotional range was important for creativity.

Affects and goals

We have already hinted that the relation between affect, action, control, and the capacity to invest energy in the effort to attain goals are very important in the coping orientations of different children. Strongly sustained goals were at this age not typical of children like Karen, Ray, Barbie, Brennie, Patsy, and others who showed the widest range of emotional expressiveness and used their affective wealth in handling people, or who showed some affect hunger and need to maintain relationships at a rich, active level.

By contrast with this group we can look at more contained or serious children like Sally and Teddy, who had a strong pride and forceful orientation toward reaching their own goals. Sally seemed to need to maintain her ability not to yield to pressure and her determination to accomplish what she set out to do by refusing to indulge in emotional expressions or interpersonal exchanges not directly relevant to her goal. Chester struck a balance beween emotional expressiveness and a laconic withholding to save energy for effort and for struggles. He could be stoical and brave in a soldierlike way at times, while at other times he was relaxed and gay, maintaining and stimulating social give and take with the adults by sharing zestful experiences and fantasies.

Chester could cope "by hyper-firmness to protect himself from being carried away by the stimulation" or could let go and float along with enjoyment of it. Similarly Sheila had forceful moods dominated by control and direction of her energy but these did not possess her so thoroughly as to exclude vivid times of warmth, maternal and tender feelings, or eagerness about new experiences.

With Cynthia we find a change over a period of two months: on the second test she was "more forceful, determined, expressed the feeling that she was 'strong'; she was more self-conscious and proud."

Why are we discussing the freedom and openness of affect expression, in relation to goal-directed energies as well as with resources for gratification? The careful reader could point to Teddy, a relatively quiet and contained boy whom we have seen here and also in Escalona and Heider's *Prediction and Outcome* where he was one of the most successfully predicted children. He was an outstandingly able and consistent child who seemed to get great satisfaction from his activities and interests although affects were moderate and he did not have the usual preschool child's spontaneity. His satisfaction tended to have a serious purposeful grown-up quality. Or the reader might point to Rachel whom we have seen both here and in *Prediction and Outcome* as a child who is extremely reserved away from home. At home she was seen to be very expressive and talkative, and it would not be sound to put her in the same group with Teddy who showed an early control and identification with adult ways. Such children whose marked control of expressiveness did not conflict with deep investment were exceptions. Typically the more inhibited children like Martin, Daryl, and Vernon showed parallel tendencies toward constriction of affect and lack of drive to utilize the gratifying potentialities of the environment as seen by other children. They simply did not seem to get as much out of life as the others. This was expressed in a narrowed range of response to potential sources of gratification. In Martin's case—and he was not alone in this—there was much less capacity, than with more open children to respond flexibly to substitute gratifications when the thing he wanted was not available.

If we pause to consider the probable relationships here, we can offer the following hypothesis: Feelings expressed can be shared. When these are feelings of satisfaction and delight, interest and zest, sharing them produces contagious responses in the other children and an active, positive feedback to the first child, who is then stimulated to more active responses, new ideas for utilizing the situation and for new goals. A positive chain of integrative, mutually stimulating, satisfying experiences is thus started. We can see this as the opposite of Gregory Bateson's "schismogenic process" in which the negative reactions of two individuals produce feedbacks which create increasing hostility and a deeper chasm between them. Shared pleasures bring people together and increase the gratification from their own relationship as well as increasing the ability of each to find new goals and new pleasures through which the partner can be stimulated. More concisely, this is the basic process underlying object-relationships. Erikson calls it "sending power."

The outstanding example of this zest-stimulating quality which led to the increasing range of pleasure both in terms of their reactions with children and in terms of his own gratification was seen in the record of Greg at the party; his gay and playful fantasies and games on the jumping board attracted other children and soon involved them in a group activity.

The drive to gratification

The drive to gratification, then, has to be seen not only as something within each individual organism, with deep roots in the most primitive interactions of the organism with the environment during the early oral phase of infancy, but it is also a positive interpersonal dynamic which produces widening ripples of response in others and also in the individual himself.

If the child can succeed in "making a good start" this in itself produces expectations of further satisfying experiences; also his joy arouses positive responses from the other people which contribute to the positive gratification-generating sequence of experiences.

The dramatic examples of hospital experiences with Susan, Rachel, and Sam, to which we referred earlier, illustrate how powerful the effect of gratification can be in limiting the reverberations of anxiety, fear, and the effects of the pain and frustration which contributed to them. We saw how Sam's mother consistently kept her eye on ways of providing compensatory pleasures and satisfactions at the time of Sam's potentially traumatic accident. In later play sessions Susan acted out in great detail the ways in which nurses provided direct loving, humorous, imaginative satisfactions during what might have been an overwhelmingly destructive hospital experience with Susan's severe polio.

Roots of resources for gratification

When we begin to consider the backgrounds of some of these different capacities for gratification, we think first of all of the quality of gratification provided by the mother. There is plenty of evidence of differences here, in the experiences of the infants in our study group, as Sylvia Brody has reported in detail. But our study of the records also quickly calls attention to what comes from the infant himself.

Oral demand level, like all of the variables observed after the first eight weeks or even the first four weeks, is a result, we assume, of initial tendencies to be hungry, a sustained capacity for intake, and discovery that demand leads to gratification.

Oral demands are closely related to the earliest goals. Sucking, rooting and feeding activities themselves involve not only instinctual motor coordinations but goal-directed efforts which are perfected during the earliest days and weeks. Long before motility has matured to the point where locomotion is possible, the baby may exercise considerable control over feeding operations, both in relation to obtaining gratifications and in relation to defensive operations against unwanted or imposed food. He does the latter by turning away from, spitting out, refusing to accept foods whose taste he dislikes or rejecting milk or food after he has had enough. His crying protests against something which is too hot or too cold, or at times when he has swallowed too much or needs to burp, can be included with the motor expressions just mentioned even if they are in responses of the mouth alone, as rudimentary actions involving early forms of or precursors to ego functions.

The mouth is thus the earliest zone for the development of patterns of gratification and by the age of two months in some of the babies in our sample, the expression of gratification to the mother for pleasant and satisfying feeding experiences.* The mouth is also the major first zone of ego function development[2] including the integration of some fairly complex patterns, the exercise of selecting and rejecting, demanding and protesting.

Patterns which begin as instinctive in the sense that they are essentially preformed action patterns utilized by the instinctual drive to suck, in feeding, are soon integrated into a wider spectrum of ways of dealing with the total feeding experience. We see babies who determine not only their own pace and rhythm of sucking, duration of sucking time, and frequency of feeding sessions, but also the posture in which they wish to be fed, lying down or sitting up enough to be able also to look around while nursing; and we have numerous instances of babies like Donald, who actively manipulate the breast into a position which facilitates the most effective nursing. Many babies while feeding keep their eyes glued to their mother's face and eyes, and explore her body with their hands and feet; in this process many forms of

---

* Visual and auditory responses occur from birth, but probably do not provide major gratification until about the age of eight weeks.

sensory and motor response participate in the reinforcement offered by the simultaneous oral gratification. It is these babies whose response to many aspects of life later carries the quality of zestful feeling that "life tastes good." Oral gratification is especially highly related to preschool strength of interests. This also implies that oral gratification in the first half-year reinforces the infant's capacity to respond to the external world in a strong and satisfying way.*

A positive correlation between oral gratification in infancy and security at the preschool level confirms what we would expect to start with, and what many analysts[3] have concluded from studies of adults. A positive relation to the later sense of self-worth and a comfortable relation to the child's ego ideal along with the adequacy of the child's self-image in the child's social milieu (self-esteem) confirms the hypothesis of Fenichel[4] and others.[5]

Adding these positive relationships to the negative correlation between infantile oral gratification and tension as rated at the preschool level, we can infer that oral gratification in the first six months tends to leave the baby with a good feeling about itself, free from chronic tensions which make it dependent upon constant stimulus feeding from the environment, and which blur its perception of the environment; along with this it is left freer for the development of clear awareness of self vis-à-vis others, and for maintenance of stable positive feelings about self.

Autonomy allowed in the feeding situation in the first six months by the mother correlates significantly with capacity to use substitute gratification and tolerance for frustration; also with resistance to discouragement, tolerance of temporary regression, ability to facilitate resilience by timing rest, ability to maintain internal integration.

The capacity to protest, resist, and terminate unwanted stimuli in infancy (including distasteful or surplus food) correlates significantly with the preschool tendency to control the impact of the environment, ability to restructure or cope by changing the environment, to defend one's position, self-reliance, self-awareness, to be able to maintain one's self-regard in the face of difficulty, and the ability to mobilize energy to meet challenge or stress. Evidently, psychically active approach is expressed in both "positive" and "negative" ways including vigorous pushing away, or against, active selection, capacity to imitate change, and also to maintain one's own self-regard.

While a detailed discussion of relationships between rated vari-

---

* While here I believe the early instinctual experiences have a dynamic contribution to later tendencies, it is also possible that early gratification tendencies are an expression of the same constitutional tendency as later strength of interests or zestfulness.

ables cannot be presented here, I believe that it will help us to obtain perspective on the role of resources of gratification and parallel capacities to look at some of the clusters of closely related variables. We find high correlations among the following: ego involvement in own activity, purposefulness of movements, resilience, ability to integrate modalities, confidence, pride, and courage.*

Investment of energy is central to some of those capacities but it is interesting to see that this is so closely related to (doubtless underlying but also perhaps supported by) the capacities expressed in "competence" and ability to integrate modalities, and also that the ego attitudes or feelings of confidence, pride, and courage are equally related. A child high on these variables is able to invest energy freely, deeply, and effectively. Positive ego feelings are probably in a circular relation, they are aroused by the effectiveness and in turn contribute to the freedom to invest energy purposefully with renewed increments of competence. Robert White[6] has discussed competence at some length and for further discussion of ego feelings we can turn to Federn.[7]

What seems important to note here is that the freedom to respond to different areas of enjoyment appears central to these: here if we put it in structural terms, ego and id come together—a free ego is on good terms with its id. But this is leading us now to the next section where we shall give further attention to the development of ways of coping.

The first six to eight months is the period during which the self is becoming differentiated from the environment (cf. Jacobson,[8] Spitz,[9] et al.); positive or negative sensations (leading to massive autonomic reverberations) from the feeding experience are associated with both the emerging self, and with the gradually differentiated environment. This is also true of other basic experiences—pleasant or unpleasant contact, auditory and visual experiences—provided only that they are strong enough to involve diffuse affective concomitants as does oral gratification, frustration or distress.

When our infancy observations dealing solely with children in the first seven months of life are compared with preschool level ratings of the same children based on observations by many different people, our evidence tends to confirm the hypothesis that basic patterning of the relation between the child and the environment and of the coping capacity of the ego is laid down in the early oral phase of infancy—in the first six months of life.† Specific configurations of oral drive, ways of incorporating gratification into the ego are thus, it is inferred, laid down during this critical oral phase. The hypothesis was developed

* See Appendix B for a discussion of correlations.
† See Appendix B, especially pp. 384-385.

by Abraham and elaborated by others; we are simply extending and confirming it.

Complex experiences of mastery over distress due to colic, frustration due to early difficulties in coordination, etc., may also provide triumph sequence patterns with an undertone of repressed frustration, anxiety, anger, as with Susan, Greg and others; these are important in later efforts to triumph over obstacles, pain, frustration, etc. (with the help of enough denial to support mobilizing and directing the energy toward mastery).

Later, massively reverberating stresses due to illness, pain, loss, especially when occurring during a critical phase (development of motility, speech, or psychosexual excitement, etc.) may change the positive patterns established during the oral phase. Our prime example of this was Lennie who had a good start at four weeks, but in the second and third years of life fell into a lake, had repeated high temperature illness, ear infections, hearing loss, and possible mild brain damage contributing to speech and motor problems. Even here, the good initial start evidently helped to sustain the warm positive approach which was expressed in his good relationships and his appealing "Can you help me?" So also, Rachel, the initially gratified infant later exposed to prolonged severe infantile eczema, hospitalization, flood, seeing the birth of a sibling in the next room, poverty, etc.; while she was inhibited by strangeness (*cf.* pp. 32 ff.) she was able to maintain internal integration so well at the age of four to five that Escalona has used her as an example of good ego strength.*

Probably the extent to which subsequent experience will change the orientation toward gratification established during the oral phase depends in part on the fluidity or variability of autonomic functioning, the stability and flexibility of the defense structure developed by the child, as well as the factors in the environment supporting or contributing to integration.

Gratification, available energy, and factors reducing these

Gratification may produce relaxation, decrease of tension, or a release and increase in energy expressed in covering more space, romping with more exhilaration, or in greater focus on construction or other activity; or in joy, delight, exuberance, smiles; ecstatic radiant expressions, increase in cooperation or persistence; decrease in importance of earlier or other frustrations or difficulties, and increase in the expectation of further gratification.

* Personal communication.

Along with the considerations which we have just been reviewing we can also add Dr. Heider's comment[10] that wherever the predictions regarding the development of a child were correct in their estimate of "available energy"* the over-all prediction was more likely to be in the right direction; she tested her hypothesis and came to the conclusion that this was the most important single factor affecting the accuracy of the conclusions. In connection with this we can recall again our observations that ability as measured by intelligence quotient did not seem to be as closely related to coping capacity in this sample of children as such factors as "resources for gratification," capacity for enjoyment, and other expressions of positive response to the environment and energy expressed in active dealings with it.

In Dr. Heider's phrase "availability of energy" she is emphasizing not only potential energy but energy which can easily be translated into effective action, use and enjoyment of the environment. When we look at children like Daryl, Rachel, and even Patsy, along with Martin, who from infancy had low energy or were easily fatigued, we find two interesting items: first, none of these children was rated as a high activity child in infancy; second, we find a limitation of overt expression of aggression; coupled with this limitation is the repression of hostility. Clinically, we tend to infer that repressed hostility and aggression deplete the energy of the individual and contribute to fatigability. But when we find the fatigability and low energy visible so very early in the development of the infant and when we recognize that differences in activity level, energy of sucking, etc., are actually visible within the first couple of weeks after birth, we are pushed to recognize the possibility that the lack of overt expressions of aggression, anger and hostility is itself to some degree a resultant of low energy. The low energy baby or child does not have the margin to spend in such ways. Hostile and angry feelings which would lead to expenditures of aggressive energy, are inhibited as a matter of economics. At the same time this is at a price, since the failure to work out, deal with, and come to terms with aggressive and hostile feelings also requires energy; thus the energy resources of the child are further depleted by this however much they may have also been protected.

This tendency for initially limited energy, which leads to the inhibition of expression of hostility and aggression, to produce a pattern that results in still further lowered energy, may have been neglected

* At this point some readers may raise the question what is the relation between physical energy and psychic energy? In terms of these children we find it hard to draw the line. At times when physical energy was depleted by illness, as with Ray and Tommy, we find decreased levels of cognitive functioning and of coping.

by Escalona in her predictions. For instance, Heider notes that Escalona did not predict Vernon's rather low energy reserves and the discrepancy between these and his average activity level; she also omitted Darlene's physical frailty and low energy reserve. In this case Darlene's energy may have been drained partly as a resultant of her aversion to stimuli of too great intensity, and the need to use her energy in cautious control in new situations in order to avoid the anxiety connected with disintegrative reactions to stimuli which were overwhelming.

Escalona also wrongly predicted that with Rachel stress would be accompanied by heightened activity; instead, this child reduced activity to a minimum, a pattern which may have been partly connected with a need to guard her energy but also with her severe immobilizing eczema and period of hospitalization. Her tendency to reduce activity to a minimum could then have been an internalization of a pattern which had been imposed upon her.

Dr. Heider also points to cases such as Donald and Vivian whose activity level was lower at the preschool level than was predicted on the basis of the child's rated activity level in infancy; in these instances the element of fatigability and other direct evidence of limited energy was not present but Heider inferred availability of energy evidently from the activity level during the preschool period.

Let us now have a look at Janice, the least well-predicted child, as an example of unsuspected energy resources:

Janice was imagined as a child notably fragile not only physically but also psychologically. It was believed that she would prove to be perceptually alert and that vision and specifically colors would be responded to with exceptional acumen. She was envisaged as a child more than ordinarily vulnerable to even minor stress. It was expected that—in the face of stress—behavioral regression would occur more readily than is age appropriate. In general it was assumed that both in terms of libidinal development and behaviorally (at least in certain areas) she would be found to be immature. Among the core assumptions was also one to the effect that withdrawal would be her dominant method of dealing with situations that threatened her equilibrium. Another behavioral pattern which was anticipated, was a tendency to deal with potentially overwhelming situations by reducing stimulation to manageable proportions.

In our focus on withdrawal tendencies, we clearly failed to see in baby Janice a reservoir of energy, a tendency actively to alter the environment in efforts to achieve satisfaction, which she proved to possess. Actually, Janice vacillated between withdrawal more extreme than had been forecast and a persistent, uncompromising, outwardly directed search for gratification or battle against conditions she found intolerable.

At another level Escalona commented:

> In retrospect it is clear that the behavior predicted would correspond to fixation at the anal retentive level of libidinal development. It was clearly expected that the problem of giving and withholding would be a major axis in her functioning, that stubbornness and passive resistance would be prominent, that for her a primary object would be to maintain autonomy rather than the striving for somewhat more remote goals or satisfaction obtained from mastery over components of the real outer world.

In contrast to this erroneous prediction, Escalona emphasized the fact that Janice provided a very good illustration of "oral greed."

> Janice relentlessly sought material possessions not because she valued having or using them. Rather she insatiably clamored now for this and now for that and never once seemed satisfied or even really pleased with what she got . . . she was described as among other things "a restless searcher for gratification" and all records make explicit that Janice seemed to derive no satisfaction from anything she did or had.

Escalona qualified this by a recognition of the role of oral gratification such as sucking her thumb in connection with many other oral defenses.

However, one observer saw more evidences of genuine satisfaction than are implied in the extreme formulation made above. Janice shared her pleasure in her bracelets and her pretty clothes on the way to test sessions, stopped to observe and enjoy small growing things in the grass, and gave certain other hints that under certain circumstances she was actually well able to enjoy a variety of things.

She appeared to be a deeply frustrated child. She had no room of her own at home, and lived in the midst of a disorganized family situation. The fact that when she was seen recently at the age of twelve she presented a very different picture, of a quite well organized and efficient child genuinely enjoying the activities at school, at her own church and her friend's church, hunting expeditions with her father and brother, and clothes, etc., suggests that the potentiality of real gratification along a wide spectrum of experience was certainly there but was masked by the tense and restless insecurity which may have been aroused more by the family situation in which she had no secure niche than in the deep core of her own capacity for gratification. It is this which we can put together with the "reservoir of energy," the "tendency actively to alter the environment in efforts to achieve need satisfaction" which was accurately recognized by those who reviewed the preschool data and which persisted throughout her first twelve years and contributed to the impressive progress which this child made.

Where did "the reservoir of energy" come from? Our hypothesis is that this reservoir was constantly being fed by the juxtaposition, on the one hand, of very realistic frustrations with the very strong feeling in Janice that gratification was something that was possible and that she could do something about achieving it. Now if we ask, what gave her such a strong expectancy that gratification was not unavailable and she did not have to be resigned to total frustration, we can go back to Escalona's own summary of her observations of Janice as a baby. Almost parenthetically she noted that "Janice was a very contented baby." We suggest that this experience of primitive basic contentment in infancy probably had something to do with the reservoir of energy which contributed to her capacity for progress. It is interesting to see that this element of energy related to the complexity of changes in drive level growing out of the degree of satisfaction in the child's exchanges with the environment is so central to the over-all picture of the child.

In our staff discussions of the way in which drives and affect work in the development of the coping capacity of the child, Dr. Walter Raine suggested that it looks as if something like the following is going on: The cognitive and motor—or basic ego—resources of the child contribute a major share toward determination of the potential skill, competence, problem solving, conceptualizing, and mastery potentialities of the child. However, the question as to whether these will be adequately or inadequately developed, will be used to make maximal use of the opportunities to which the child is exposed or will lie fallow, perhaps never achieving the development which seemed to be promised in the early years of the child's life, will be a matter of the depth, strength, persistence and vividness of the child's drives and affects and the ways in which he uses them. Thus we see children like Jo Anne and even Karen proving to be far more resourceful and productive in their use of the environment, although their intelligence quotients are just average, than children who like Vernon have high intelligence quotients but during the entire period of their preschool and elementary school years never seem to make much use of the rich resources they have.

Expectancy in relation to the range of resources for gratification

While most of the children had a wide range of areas of potential gratification, we nevertheless saw marked differences in their evident expectation that new situations would be pleasurable or "fun," that is, differences in optimism of anticipation, and also in the capacity to go after, seek, and control gratification resources. Whatever other problems they might have, the eager children did not approach new experiences with the assumption that they would probably be disappointed, nor were they blasé or smug or in other ways superior to or indifferent to what we had to offer.

By contrast, as we have seen, Martin, Rachel, Daryl, and a few others in our group approached some experiences with distrust. Where the first group discussed above seemed to feel the world was their oyster, and took gratification for granted, this second group did not expect much; and in the case of Martin, did not enjoy much.

Erikson[11] has pointed to "trust" as a fundamental orienting attitude which is laid down by the earliest experiences of satisfaction in the oral phase; in this period the basic expectancies surrounding interactions between the organism and the environment are built out of the infant's satisfactions and frustrations, and efforts to deal with frustration. We can think of trust as a general category which includes both the expectation that life will taste good, and other expectations that "my efforts to get satisfaction will be rewarded," and "when I have trouble, mother (or someone) will help me," or more passively, "life will taste good, and I can count on things I need coming to me, I don't have to struggle."

We saw the capacity for effort and struggle in Darlene, Ronnie, and in Susan par excellence (Chapter 7); we saw the passive expectation that things will come without effort in Rachel and Ray. Trust has to do with much more than being free to expect and to count on getting, however. The infant discovers that his preferences are respected: when he dislikes something it will not be forced on him; and when he has had enough he can terminate by his own decision; when he is uncomfortable his protests will be heard and the situation will be changed. In other words, the child learns to trust not only that the environment can and will give what tastes good, but that he can make his choices, his limits, and his protests heard, respected, and responded to.

Or he learns that he does not have much choice—he has to take what is offered. Or that it is of no use to protest, things will not change anyway. Or that good things cease or are terminated by the decision of others, not himself.

Each of these—and other—facets of trust and expectation has crucial consequences for the next steps of development, as our preliminary quantitative analyses are showing us, as well as our studies of the children at later ages.

Granted that it was true of this group that the highest degree of emotional expression did not guarantee coping adequacy, it is still of the greatest importance that a lack of emotional vitality was usually present in children who had limited or inadequate capacity to use the environment. Here we can offer the hypothesis that a moderate to high degree of emotional energy or capacity for emotional investment contributes to spontaneity in use of the environment. We could also suggest the further hypothesis that the peak degrees of emotional responsiveness can also contribute to use of the environment, provided these are balanced by adequate resources in other areas and not vitiated by points of extreme vulnerability.

What is involved here is different from the usual concept of "adjustment." The ideal image of a stable child able to cooperate with demands of the adult, to participate appropriately in the typical variety of situations in the culture, to be active and outgoing and at the same time self-controlled can be illustrated by only a very few of this normal sample and probably of any normal sample. Rather, we found many rough edges; times of spilling over; missing the mark; deviations sometimes due to their autonomous solutions to problems, or to defiance or impulsiveness. Like other investigators of larger groups of "normal" children we find problems, symptoms, difficulties—the expectable developmental trouble spots. But a major difference between these non-clinic children and a good many of the "cases" we see in clinics lies in the strong basic investment in or cathexis of the environment, the capacity to explore new opportunities for gratification and to use them for growth. These children could "keep on trying." A more intensive analysis of resilience in some of the children will be presented in *Vulnerability, Stress, and Resilience,* currently in preparation.

If this is what normal children are, our concepts for guiding those who live with them and those who want to help them might well include the ways of supporting interest in and use of the environment with the goal of increasing the children's resources during the few years before they enter the restricted world of school.

NOTES AND REFERENCES

1. Mittelmann, B. Motility in infants, children and adults: patterning and psychodynamics. *Psychoanalytic Study of the Child,* Vol. 9. New York: International Universities Press, 1949.
2. Hoffer, W. Mouth, hand and ego-integration. *Psychoanalytic Study of the Child,* Vol. 3/4. New York: International Universities Press, 1949.
3. Abraham, K. The influence of oral erotism on character-formation. In *Selected Papers on Psychoanalysis.* New York: Basic Books, 1927.
4. Fenichel, O. *The Psychoanalytic Theory of Neurosis.* New York: Norton, 1945.
5. Erikson, E.H. *Childhood and Society.* New York: Norton, 1950.

6. White, R. Motivation reconsidered: the concept of competence. *Psychol. Rev., 66,* 1959.

7. Federn, P. *Ego Psychology and the Psychoses.* New York: Basic Books, 1952.

8. Jacobson, E. The self and the object-world. *Psychoanalytic Study of the Child,* Vol. 9. New York: International Universities Press, 1954.

9. Spitz, R. Anaclitic depression. *Psychoanalytic Study of the Child.* Vol. 2, New York: International Universities Press, 1946.

10. Heider, G. See Escalona, S., and Heider, G. *Prediction and Outcome,* Chapter 10. New York: Basic Books, 1959.

11. Erikson, E.H. *Childhood and Society.* New York: Norton, 1950.

ᚡᚡᚡ 12

FLEXIBILITY

WE HAVE SEEN THE ROLES that orientation, exploration, reality testing, comparing, forming a cognitive map, selecting, narrowing the field, organizing, constructing, and creating play in helping the child to handle the problems of his environment. We have also seen the child's capacity for autonomous dealing with situations, including resistance to pressure from the environment and capacity to sustain effort toward mastery. We saw the development of the ability to control aggression and to use aggression to conquer fear. We also saw the role of resources for gratification in sustaining fortitude and resilience in Susan.

All of these resources are seen as functions which often involve the integration of cognitive, affective, and motor resources in a focused use of energy. In this chapter we shall discuss an attribute of functioning, namely, the flexibility of many of these children which was a manifestation of freedom in distribution of energy. It appeared in varied areas of behavior in many different situations and at different levels of personality functioning. To illustrate this point at a very basic level, I shall return to a series of brief notes on the bodily behavior of different individuals:

Steven's limber, relaxed body moved flexibly and freely through an area about four feet square, shifting from one position to another, sometimes crawling, sometimes squatting on his heels, sometimes one knee down, other times one knee up, poised on one foot or on tiptoe in a semikneeling position.

This flexible handling of the body was characteristic of most of the boys (along with the pleasure in activity described in the previous chapter), and obviously facilitated the child's exploration of an area, his handling of materials, and in general his use of space. Ronnie, for example, could shift or reverse his position or place and also his role and did so repeatedly.

Most of the boys could also shift the degree of their activity; they could be very quiet indoors and extremely vigorous and noisy outdoors. They could shift from loose or even wild activity to quiet control; from a level of high tension and excitement to a level of relaxed ease. Vernon, who seemed predominantly sober, restricted, and ungiving emotionally, was also controlled or inhibited in motor behavior in many situations, but at the parties where there was a large, free, open area for unrestricted exploration, he could run, climb, scamper up terraces and hills eagerly and with open laughing delight.

Girls varied in these aspects of motor control and flexibility; with some girls the range of activity levels was similar to that of the boys while other girls varied within a narrow range at the quiet end of the scale. Darlene showed marked changes in level of motor activity, suggesting periods of upsurging energy increases or releases of energy as if she had more energy in reserve than she used during her quiet, controlled period, or as if letting go of a constricted pattern of behavior untied much energy which had been used to maintain the control. Hence we found a statistically significant correlation between the motor capacities of girls and their coping capacity. With boys, the range of variation from one boy to another was too narrow for a significant correlation to appear in this sample.

Numerous children varied the intensity of their effort, and also the speed and tempo of speech at different times, depending upon their relation to the particular challenge of the intelligence test situation. We have already seen variations in intensity and speed of both bodily movement and speech which occurred especially when a child moved from success to failure, failure bringing retardation and quieting or soft slow speech with one child, or a renewal of bodily effort and higher, more forceful speech tones with another child.

This capacity to adapt one's self to objects, materials, and areas which could not be easily restructured, or to adapt the objects to one's self when they could be manipulated and handled, was especially well illustrated by the children's play with the Bonhop Play House. Some of them regarded it as a fixed object, as if it were nailed to the floor, although they themselves had removed it from its box. In such instances they would climb, lean over it, or move around it as we have already seen. By contrast, other children would pick it up, turn it upside down, turn it around from side to side, and deal with it entirely in terms of adapting it to their own position. This active dealing with objects in the environment on the assumption that they were mobile, that positions and organization could be changed, could be seen as one aspect of a capacity for restructuring the environment.

A different sort of flexibility is illustrated in the following note on Daryl:

> With the Bonhop Play House and subsequent games, ". . . she showed a tendency to either adapt herself to the objects or adapt them to herself; she could be competitive, could restructure the situation, . . ."

Comments on the flexible resourceful ideas of Gordon and others point to the connection between the possession of a range of ideas and the ability to be flexible in reaching solutions to problems: flexibility could hardly be possible without fertility in thinking up possible solutions, and a reservoir of ideas about possible ways of handling things. This is also seen in such comments as the following on projective test reports:

> Ideational range and flexibility are brought out here as elsewhere in her Rorschach. This capacity to shift from one aspect of the blot to another, to derive percepts, to entertain more than one possible percept for the same area, to reality test for the preferred percept, to document the secondary one as well, were typical of Jo Anne, other examples of whose flexibility we have already seen.

A flexible, imaginative use of materials implied a still wider range of ideas (beyond possible solutions for problems) from which the child could choose in his handling of toys and other materials.

Cognitive flexibility

We can also observe the child's ability to control his attention span, the depth of involvement which he would permit in a given situation, or the intensity of attention or absorption; some children were capable of deep attention, at times excluding extraneous stimulation, while at other times they could permit their attention to wander in a more casual way over the elements of a situation. Flexibility in these orienting processes was very important. We can see this especially when it is absent.

Vernon was a child with one of the highest intelligence test scores but in the Rorschach situation, which was evidently much more threatening to him than the specific concrete tasks of the intelligence test, he tended to stick to a stimulus in a stereotyped way, with a largely unproductive result. Even Sally appeared to be perceptually restricted and inflexible in her initial approach to the CAT, although she was a vigorous little problem solver in many other situations. This difference between the perceptual functioning of a child in one situation as compared with another was also striking in the case of Steven; in the CAT, while he could recognize, name, and identify places or objects in the picture, he did not integrate them or correlate different objects into an action pattern. Cynthia avoided getting involved in committing herself to materials or tasks in certain situations, and because of the lack of investment in the initial approach to the challenge, appeared to lack the perceptual clarity or integrative power characteristic of most of the children.

To the psychiatrist, many of these children appeared to be hyperalert in the session with him, while the same children were relaxed in situations like the zoo visit or party. We may ask, however, whether the intense alertness of these little people in situations which were strange and surprising to them should be described with the same term we would use to describe a chronically anxious adult whose hyperalertness is part of a vigilant orientation to life. With these children the acute alertness, perceptiveness, and eagerness to clarify the world appeared in general to be part of their flexible active investment in understanding and using the world in ways suitable to the different opportunities they found in different situations. With so much autonomy in their ways of looking us over and appraising the situations—with their persistent inquiring, exploring, reality testing, and coming to conclusions for themselves—it is not surprising that many of them had a high level of confidence in their percepts and showed a sincerity in their communication of observation, which contributed to the kind of ego strength that comes from the security of having seen for oneself. This security was probably an important condition of the tolerance, flexibility, and resilience which we saw in many of the group. While an initial approach to the situation might involve avoidance when a child felt threatened or faced with more than he could assimilate quickly, still, after the child was adequately oriented, he could often respond spontaneously. Or, like Chester, he could, after retreating, recover control quickly and return to active dealing with the situation.

Some of the children moved flexibly from a narrow focus at the beginning of their orientation to a new situation to a gradually widened perceptual approach; they did not need to cling to a narrow, safe island beyond the time it took to become clear about the situation as a whole. Or a child could make trial and error efforts up to a reasonable point, then give up, ask for help, or shift his interest when these failed. Barbie could hesitate when a structure was unclear until she was able to discover what it was about, then move into action rapidly once she had clarified things for herself. She could not only distinguish between social givens, such as green and red lights, but perceive many nuances of what might be safe or risky, socially acceptable or unacceptable behavior, and direct her own activity accordingly. Even Martin who appeared at the party to be one of the most constrained children was apparently comfortable and free within the assumed limits of the rug in the Miniature Life Toy situation. He never explored or used anything out of bounds, but his movements were not constricted and he was able to develop his own ideas in his own way.

Ingenuity and spontaneity in putting things together, considering more than one percept for the same area, shifting their mode of integration from inductive building up from small units to larger ones to more integrative inclusion of part processes; flexibility in response to changing stimuli, color and forms, or from foreground figures to background figures; even Susan's ability to combine fine perception with distorted, vague, even confabulatory forms, or the magical ability to make anything into anything else were among the different expressions of perceptual flexibility we saw in these children.

Affective flexibility expressed in variations in mood were sometimes elicited in response to external stimulation such as music: Roddy's moods shifted from brash noisiness to absorbed stillness when he heard the music box. Ronnie's variations of roles, positions, and feelings appeared in response to changes in his sense of relatedness to people and the situation. Friendly and intimate with Dr. Moriarty after his early slow warming-up period and spontaneous in the Miniature Life Toy play session, he had been anxious to the point of tears in contacts with other examiners and in the pediatric examination, and the Sheldon body-photograph situation.

We are accustomed to expect mood changes in children between two and five, but actually extreme changeability was characteristic of fewer children in this group than in more highly stimulated metropolitan groups. We saw how some of the children did vary strikingly from a sober, poker-face initial approach to warm, glowing resonance when they had become at ease in a situation, and free to respond fully. Patsy appeared sober and even a little sad at times, where at other times she could be even ecstatic. The speed with which her mood shifted suggested a quick response to changes in situations and atmospheres and lack of carryover, perseveration, or pervasive effects of emotional reaction when she felt she could not manage the adult. Other children with a wide emotional range like Susan could be solemn and thoughtful at one time, angry and spiteful at another, or radiantly loving at still another time. Flexibility in emotional quality, intensity, and openness was characteristic of many children in this group.

This emotional and cognitive flexibility appeared important in the capacity for recovery, restoration of perceptual clarity, realism, and emotional well-being in children like Susan and Roddy. The latter showed a conscious awareness of the process of recovery from confusion, suggesting that already at this early age there was an element of conscious control involved in his flexibility. At a deeper level Chester showed a capacity for flexible shifting from an attitude of armored defense to a relaxed and spontaneous approach, for instance, in the Rorschach situation.

In situations such as the blocking game, social flexibility appeared in children like Janice who could play on a win-and-let-win, crash-and-let-crash-basis, now proving her ability to dominate and now giving the grownup a break.

Flexibility in the quality of goal-directedness or purposefulness of activity appeared in Donald.

He could be thorough and persistent at times, or fluid, as he explored new possibilities at other times; and efficiently flexible when a substitute had to be accepted.

The children also differed greatly in their range of styles. Susan could be a little lady or quite a rowdy, tomboyish character with many nuances between. Similarly Patsy, typically gentle, soft, often dreamy in situations such as the Miniature Life Toy play session, could occasionally be rough or impetuous at home, especially when blocked by her mother.

Flexibility was closely linked with autonomy; the attitude of ability to choose, to make a decision between alternates, involved both an autonomous stance and freedom to consider the range of possibilities and to make a decision one way one time and another way another time, depending upon the personal implications of the situation to which one was exposed. It is also not surprising to find flexibility linked with creativity in these comments on the children's behavior since the exploration of new possibilities and new combinations involved in creativity would itself imply freedom to move beyond accepted patterns.

Flexibility in fantasy

Children like Ray and Steven also showed marked flexibility in their ways of dealing with play and fantasy. Steven's play was highly realistic at times and imaginative at other times, within an over-all tendency to initiate and sustain fantasy with a degree of coherence and organization beyond that of some of the other children. Ray was able to maintain clarity about reality in the midst of an elaborate fantasy, moving flexibly between realistic play and primary process level of play, and maintaining the ability to pull himself back consciously from a regressed level of play. Donald also showed a tendency to vary from realistic to symbolic or extremely primary-process type of play (at the same time all of it consisted of compact, clear units) and he always seemed definite and clearcut in carrying out his action. By contrast, we can note children previously reported in other studies[1] who remained either very literal and reality-bound in play or were typically fantastic in their themes—in neither case showing the flexibility just described.

It is obvious that these various forms of flexibility involved not only the capacity for easy shifting of bodily stance and posture, the ability to shift attention, interest or cathexis on objects, ideas, and goals, and the capacity for flexibility in expression of affect, but also flexibility in highly complex integrations of ideas and feelings.

Variability

Flexibility or the capacity to respond appropriately in varying ways to different situations and demands can be seen as a function of, if not a wholly conscious use of variability of many different kinds.

We saw shifts from tension to relaxation, from restless, rapid, loose-jointed activity to smooth functioning, from insecurity to vigorous ambitious effort in certain children. Variability often suggested that the changing level of tension or anxiety in the child under different circumstances was quickly reflected in changes of behavior. Other types of change in the quality of motor behavior in this normal group included shifts from quiet to quick, impulsive movements, from slow tempo to fast. Such alternations are under less conscious control than are variations in focus of motor activity. Variability in the pace and quantity of speech in other children reflected variations in tension, both positive in tone and negative or anxious in quality. Grace Heider has discussed the relation of shifts involving decreases in the level of integration, in her monograph on vulnerability in these children during the infancy and preschool stages.

While the capacity to shift attention, emotional response, goals, body postures, motor style, defenses, roles, quality of give and take with the grownup, types of gratification expected, were all important in the child's positive ways of coping with the situations in which we saw these children, the capacity to shift in a constructive way which sustained a gratifying response to the environment and supported the inner integration of the child, must be distinguished from the tendency to shift attention in a distractible, uncontrolled compulsive or impulsive way. The latter was apt to be an expression of tension, restlessness, inability to sustain effort toward goals, inability to control the flexible pattern of shifting as we have been describing it.

Flexible changing of goals or of attention was also distinguishable from a tendency toward compulsive self-interruption or abortive action shown, for instance, by Roddy in Miniature Life Toy sessions; he acted as if he could not count on the grownup to let him carry through ideas on which he had started to work.

Dealing with limits

He can use delay as a way of implementing resistance to conforming, or as a way of gaining time during which he may assert his own autonomy so that while he ends up doing what was asked, he does it of his own choice; in his own good time, as it were. He turns a demand from adult into an autonomous act.

We saw the capacity of many of the children to follow their own initiative when the situation permitted, yet at the same time to accept help or even ask for it when they come to the end of their rope. This parallel autonomy and realistic acceptance of their own limitations seemed to be basic factors in their security in relation to the world.

This gave the impression of alternations between being helpless little children, perhaps a little infantile at moments, or being businesslike, mature, and grown-up when they were dealing with situations they could handle alone. Being able to be realistic at times or imaginative at other times was characteristic of most of them; they did not need to stay obsessively within an area of forced creativity and imagination or cling to an utterly safe realism.

Realistic flexibility was also expressed in the capacity to delay, to postpone gratification, to wait; Donna especially recognized that she would have to bide her time, or wait for her turn.

The use of flexibility in managing frustration, difficulty, failure

Most striking were the evidences of ability to deal flexibly with failures, difficulties, and frustrations. Comments such as the following illustrate this:

She did not seem deterred or disturbed by failure. Sometimes she gave up, sometimes she tried substitutes, sometimes she made one trial after another—she could be persistent or ignore the frustration. She handled it in flexible ways that varied from one time to another.

If confronted by an obstacle she does not care too much about, she ignores it.

She copes with external reality with a variety of trial and error attempts; when confronted with difficulty she substitutes, combining materials from different sources, adjusting, manipulating, or restructuring reality—all maneuvers which could be well used to maximize her strengths and compensate for or minimize her weaknesses.

While not many children were observed to have the ability to "make anything serve in the place of something else" as did Ray, numerous children were described as being able to accept substitutes easily in situations of frustration. This ability was facilitated in certain children by such capabilities as the following:

She distinguishes between the issues that are worth coming to grips with and those that aren't for her, with a capacity to bypass the latter in an energy-conserving way. She used protective selection, automatically and deftly.

Susan was one of numerous children who utilized gratifications of various sorts to balance frustrations and to stave off threats. The ability of Susan and other children to turn away from potentially overwhelming stimuli and toward satisfying, safe, loving, or humorous stimuli; to shift attention to the less ambitious projects in which skill had already been established ("Do you want me to do something I *can* do?") was made possible partly by the range of resources for gratification which we discussed in the previous chapter. Adaptably and realistically discarding an unsuitable tool and substituting another can be seen as a highly integrative use of ideas and skill available to the child.

Changing the subject, or offering confidences about daily experiences instead of responding to the question asked were among the children's ways of offering substitutes to deal with difficult intelligence test demands which they could not quite handle.

We saw children for whom failures were left behind casually instead of being experienced as frustrations; there was always something else to turn to, if not objects, then one's own interesting fantasy. For instance, a child who is unable to draw was able to cut out a smaller piece of paper; one who could not build a bridge built a tower instead; one who could not draw a square drew a circle; one who could not repeat the digits accurately, counted instead. Here apparently the child was able to shift his aspiration level to another level, or another area of functioning; he was able to give up an inaccessible goal to invest his interest quickly in a new goal. These characteristics were also involved when children who had asked for a given toy as a prize in a competitive game were quite happy with a second choice even if it were quite a different sort of toy.

Daryl showed considerable patience in replacing a block when a structure she had made tipped over. Teddy was able to deal with frustration by including a frustrating object in a larger context: picking up a soldier and finding that it was broken, he said, "Look, you've lost your head . . . well, anyway we can use him."

In certain instances a child would circumvent a difficulty by finding another way of communicating his idea. For instance when Roddy's speech defect caused difficulty in communicating to the examiner about an object involved in an answer, he pointed to an actual example of the object. Sometimes a child was able to put aside a difficulty and come back to it later with renewed energy. Teddy was able to take the initiative in looking around for alternatives when he could not find exactly what he wanted in the MLT play session, and when he came to the end of the resources there, he was ready to change to other games.

Sometimes this flexibility went to extremes where it appeared almost fluid. For instance, in the Miniature Life Toys play session Cynthia "seemed to be a fluid coper in the Dodge floating drive fashion. She could easily disengage her grip on something that might be taxing, float or shift lightly to another gear, putting considerable force into her determination to move ahead when she decided to come to grips with the challenge." Typically she seemed soft and appeared to be using minimal effort, but at times could become pivoted, quiet, perseverative, even stubborn or forceful.

While most of the children were able with one device or another to bypass frustrations and difficulties, occasionally there was an instance of real expression of frustration. For example, Terry threw the pieces on the floor in an MLT session with an explosive gesture when he could not accomplish what he was trying to do. But, on the whole, when alternative solutions were available regression did not occur in this bold form.

For the most part these children were not perfectionistic; perhaps we should say they were not perfectionistic as yet, since they had not been exposed to school pressures or concepts of perfection dominated by a marking system. We saw that it was often possible for them to pass over tests presenting difficulties by recognizing failures and tolerating imperfection (Chapter 4). In the Miniature Life Toy session Martin's attitude was that broken things were there to be fixed, or if you couldn't fix them, use them as they were or let them be. One didn't stop to worry about them. The attitude, one might say, was that the show goes on; it was more important to go on to the next thing and to carry on the over-all activity. It was rare to see anyone compulsively clinging to completing a given goal. As we have implied, ignoring failure was often simply part of a process of acceptance of minor imperfections, forging ahead without bothering to be critical.

Sometimes the child would find new solutions not apparent at first. For instance, Jo Anne, who was one of the most resourceful copers in general, after difficulty in opening one of the barn doors of the Bonhop Play House reached it from the inside through another door after a process of vicarious trial and error, looking for alternative methods to solve the problems. With this new approach she quickly found possible ways to deal with the problem.

Sometimes a child would forcefully or arbitrarily shove objects into place or manipulate material in a way to get past the difficulty. Even Karen, whose perceptiveness was so subtle, and who was often so ingenious, resorted to sheer force to push a Bonhop Play House block into its appropriate roof hole when it didn't go in easily. At other times she struggled her way through by trial and error, somewhat compromising the level of reality testing usually characteristic of her, in the process of throwing extra effort into her attempt to solve the problem. Sheila used her teeth ingeniously to handle the string of beads when fingers alone could not manage it. Barbie coped more subtly with a problem in the play session by narrowing the field with which she was trying to deal.

Asking for time, "Wait till I get this in" or "I'm not ready yet, I gotta tie it. Pretty soon I'll be ready," was a way of keeping the adult at bay while the child continued his effort to master difficulty.

Certain children, like Trudy, could learn from experience even to the point of doing better on a harder test than they did on the original test which was new to them.

Shifting aspiration level

In a few instances, as we have seen, children tried to set the aspiration level lower in order to prevent the disappointment of failure. "I don't know if I know," said Ronnie, thus protecting himself from initial failure by not definitely expecting success or permitting the examiner to expect it. Simply anticipating the difficulty had some of this value. With some children this pattern of lowering the aspiration level went beyond simply admitting the difficulty, or the limitation of one's own ability, or the doubt of success, to actually shifting to an easier or different task.

The tendency to relinquish the usual standards of perceptual clarity was not characteristic of many of the group, although the capacity to tolerate defects, which was characteristic of many children, might seem to be sufficiently related to this to lead to lax standards. Diane had an unusually firm and secure self-image. Comparable to this willingness to settle for poorer form, might be the tendency of another child to make less effort when failure was imminent, as if the realistic appraisal of the likelihood of failure made it obviously not worthwhile to make a strong investment.

Underlying all these aspects of flexibility appeared to be the child's sense of ability to control what he would react to, how much he would accept and express, how much he would respond to or invest in a situation, how close he would let the grownup come, what demands he would allow the grownup to impose. The capacity to forestall frustration by such controlling efforts probably contributed to the security which made possible quick recovery after moments of shaky integration. Susan could use her flexible affective and cognitive responses, and ability to vary her relation to people and situations in order to give herself a chance to recover from overstimulation or threatening moments.

Perhaps this same inner flexibility contributed to the fact that many of the children were able to tolerate ambiguity, to include both sides of the picture, to deal both with foreground and background, and to shift their orientation to handling a situation.

The flexibility of different children in relation to difficulty was described in brief summaries such as the following:

(Teddy could) assert, select, direct, organize, ask for help when necessary though rarely, and accept difficulties philosophically. He adapts, invents, finds compromise or creative solutions and in conflict situations modulates his drive to maintain harmonious relationships and avoid any real clash. He can win or let the other person win. He can destroy innocuously or be creative. He is well able to do boys' things and channel aggression into culturally accepted directions without apparent anxiety about getting hurt.

Or, in the case of a girl:

She did not seem deterred or disturbed by failure; sometimes she gave up, sometimes she tried substitutes, sometimes she made one trial after another. She could be persistent or ignore the frustration.

Of another girl:

She copes with external reality with a variety of trial and error attempts; she substitutes, combining materials from different sources, adjusting, manipulating, restructuring reality; these are all maneuvers which could be well used to maximize her strength and compensate for or minimize her weaknesses.

And of still another, Jo Anne, other examples of whose flexibility we have already seen:

The speed with which her mood shifted when blocked suggested a quick response to changes in situations and atmospheres and lack of carryover, perseveration or pervasive effects of emotional reaction when she feels she cannot manage the adult.

Ideational range and flexibility are brought out here as elsewhere in her Rorschach. This capacity to shift from one aspect of the blot to another, to derive percepts, to entertain more than one possible percept for the same area, to reality test for the preferred percept, to document the secondary one as well was outstanding.

Variability ranged from rejecting to accepting, from tension to relaxation, from restless, rapid, loose-jointed activity to quietness, from insecurity to ambitious efforts.

In these instances the variability appeared to be an expression of an effort to deal with the changing stress or threat of frustration in different kinds of situations.

Flexibility in the use of defense mechanisms

Along with these ways of coping with difficulty we find certain characteristic defense mechanisms: a tendency in one child toward self-punitive critical reactions; in another, a tendency to retreat psychically from the situation. Occasionally we found children denying the failure, or seeming not to hear, or defending a wrong answer. Others would compensate by citing superiority in other areas, for instance, to a sibling or mentioning previous successes, or anticipating success in the future; a child who could not tell time said "No, but I will some day." Here the aspiration level is maintained and referred to another time period. Clinging to a known success and asking for more tasks of the sort already successfully handled or fending off demands that were too difficult would be an example of maintaining self-esteem by holding onto known achievements.

Another defensive reaction occurred occasionally; for instance, Barbie used a narcissistic orientation to fill the gap when she was at a loss. Mature as she was, she also fell back on a childish cliché game response, playing peek-a-boo, thus substituting an easy game for an effort to deal with a realistic difficulty—a standard child-adult maneuver of regressing to a specific act belonging to an earlier stage in which one knows oneself to have been competent.

Bluffing and implying that success is a matter of choice, referring inadequacies to the external world in a critical way; depressive musing about one's handicap, perhaps to get comfort or preclude criticism from the outside or to come to terms with one's superego by accepting one's failure—these are other defensive ways of dealing with difficulty.

Darlene's range of coping devices and defense mechanisms was striking in a Miniature Life Toy situation. At the end of a play session which had begun stiffly we summarized as follows:

> She uses a range of coping approaches, from rigid and exaggerated conformity and assumption of a demure little girl role, to casually bypassing frustrations or difficulties which might be frustrating to others; regressing to a dependent or narcissistically self-interested position at times of insecurity while at other times she is able to let out energetic, decisive, aggressive, competitive efforts with a gay spirit and with an undoubted capacity for strong determination. At other times, she can become a demure martinet. She can look at the world through her own eyes and though apparently devoid of the sparkling or imaginative characteristics of some of the other children she can even, though awkwardly, go after what she wants with astonishing directness. While one misses the colorful nuances of expression shown by other children, Darlene may develop some shrewdness out of her forceful determination to master reality.

We have often observed the tendency for the happiest children as well as those who were more threatened to show comparable ranges of and variability in the use of defense mechanisms; the difference between these groups seemed to lie in their success in using defense mechanisms in such a way as to keep large areas of freedom for satisfying response to many situations. This flexibility in the use of defenses contributed to the resilience of even such vulnerable children as Rachel as well as to the triumph of a child exposed to such severe stress as Susan experienced.

We are not so surprised to find the resourceful, sensitive, and flexible Karen showing a highly complex orchestration of coping and defense patterns. The same child may, as Brennie did, combine denial or evasion at one time with initiative and direct coping efforts at another time.

It is easy to be misled by superficial impressions. While Rachel seemed to make great use of avoidance techniques particularly in party and play situations which were unstructured and which did not involve explicit, formal adult direction or support, the appearance of withdrawal could be most misleading. At one time we commented that even if she is admittedly a shy spirit, she is not a broken one; she still has an eye out for what life can hold for her and what she can get out of it. Once back at home, as we noted, she gave her mother a vivid and detailed account of everything that was going on around her. At the end of the Miniature Life Toy play session which had begun with her characteristic immobilization in strange new experiences, we summarized her positive coping assets as follows:

A remarkable flexibility and resilience enable her to respond with quiet freedom once she is out of the immobilizing, awesome or frightening new experience; a capacity for deep sensuous delight and gratification and for sensitive, nonverbal interpersonal communication through smiles and eyes contributes to a genuine relationship; the music is there if not the words. A capacity for resourceful manipulation and problem-solving leads to constructive use of the play opportunity; a capacity for representation and symbolization of disturbing experiences and fantasies helps her to tolerate frustrations and stress.

In other words, while this initially silent little girl was unable to take first steps into new opportunities without support and guidance, so that externally she seemed to be coping less well with the environment than most of the other children, she was all the time stowing away observations which she could use under circumstances more favorable for an active response on her part. Her defensive surface immobilization was not paralleled by a real inner rigidity or apathy, blank as she sometimes appeared even to the careful observer.

We have already seen in more detailed reports on Patsy and Susan the extremes of success and difficulty that characterized their coping efforts. In certain situations Patsy's very strong conscious alertness seemed to serve a defensive function, watching and controlling all the time, curbing her spontaneity at threatened moments. By contrast, in situations free from threat and the need for watchfulness that provided safe stimuli to Patsy's interests, she could be ecstatic and joyful beyond most of the other children. Watchfulness for her involved guilty feelings. We see, then, areas of extreme defensive restriction under the surveillance of her very strong conscience and also great spontaneity in areas where conscience was not invoked to protect her from dangerous impulses. In the same way, Barbie could swing between impulsiveness and inhibitions, with a characteristic pattern of control in many situations which presumably evoked suppression of her—at other times—strong impulses.

The occasional use of defense operations in an over-all pattern of direct coping efforts can be illustrated by Jo Anne. She was spontaneous and often original in her behavior and ways of dealing with many situations. "If I eats lots of soup, I'll grow up," was one of her various formulations of means to ends, indicating that at this early age she had grasped the possibility of exercising control to reach her goals. She was a child who was able to say on her way to one of the first testing situations "If you give me trouble I'll go home," with apparent confidence in her ability to leave if she wanted to and let the adult know that she was by no means helpless vis-à-vis big people.

At the same time she was capable of avoidance reactions, saying defensively "I don't know," in a situation where she might have and subsequently did contribute more. On the Rorschach her ordinarily good form perception broke down on Card IX and further pressure led to less well-discriminated responses with a tendency toward perseveration. Dr. Kass suggested that when pressed beyond her immediate interests and needs, Jo Anne would continue to try to meet demands, but would do so in a stereotyped and much less adequate way than was customary for her. He also noted that her avoidance reaction was not deeply ingrained, but tended to be only a temporary order of response and was easily given up as she experienced mastery, success, and recognition. Her control was apparent also on projective tests where Dr. Kass commented further:

This is a very competent little girl. The number and strength of her coping patterns seems to make her quite a formidable coper and even though she has a few problem areas it seems that she is doing a very nice job handling them. We see perhaps a little overcontrol but certainly if we want to develop a great many coping devices demanding more energy and strength perhaps than she has, one would have to be a little restricted. She seems to use her restriction in a healthy way.

She has been able to deal with sibling rivalry problems and to repress her vivid oedipal struggle. By the time of her second CAT she seemed to have become so efficient in her favorite coping devices as not to need such a wide range as she used in the original situation. Initially on the CAT she had needed to interrupt a dynamic sequence, breaking with the reality of the picture stimulus and negating aggression which had apparently been perceived and partially developed. As it approached culmination she shut it out or scotomatized it. She had then resorted to massive denial as she took off on a new tangent, allowing the monkey to escape from the tiger and concluded that there was really no aggression at all because the animals were stuffed! This was an interesting sequence of perception with partial admission into conscious awareness and then obliteration of aggression through denial, reflecting the ingenuity she was capable of at an early stage before her confidence in her capacity for mastery made such extreme defense unnecessary.

Flexibility as a general trait

If what we have said about the flexibility of these children in many different aspects of their motor and emotional behavior—their communication and relationships, their handling of their bodies, their use of objects, and their dealings with fantasy and play—seems to imply that flexibility was a general trait which permeated all aspects of the child's functioning (to the degree that he possessed it) we need to scrutinize this point. Actually we find many children flexible in some areas and much less so in others. Perhaps one of the most striking examples would be that of Vernon whose cognitive flexibility is implied in his I.Q. of approximately 140, one of the highest in the group, while we have already illustrated more than once the relatively narrow range within which he moved emotionally and socially. Similarly we have already noted Rachel's inner flexibility and integration and its contrast to her tendency to be physically immobilized and to restrict the range of her activity and involvement with people in all the situations away from home in which we saw her. Martin showed the same kind of motor flexibility in handling his body in the Miniature Life Toy play session which was typical for most of the boys in this group but he often appeared emotionally and socially rigid and inhibited. The actual patterning of flexibility varied for different children; in some cases it was maintained in one or two areas but not in others, while certain children like Ray and Susan were flexible in virtually every aspect of their functioning.

Summary

We often noted how these children would watchfully feel their way to see how far they could go, test out the limits, then accept and yield. Along with this adaptability was the capacity of such children as Darlene to recognize realistically that she would have to bide her time before carrying through an action which was not possible at the moment. Accepting substitutes easily, offering them, making something serve in place of something else; the ability to change plans, shift to other games, easily make a transition from one activity to another, respond to changing moods in the environment; to alternate winning and letting the adult win in the crashing game; shifting from armored defense to relaxation; using their own resourceful ideas to make a resilient recovery after failure or frustration; taking another look for alternative solutions; flexibly using a variety of defense mechanisms; or swinging between impulsiveness and control as the situation allowed for or needed one or the other, were among the examples of flexibility reviewed above.

Such emotional and cognitive flexibility appeared important in the capacity for recovery, restoration of perceptual clarity, realism, and emotional well-being in children like Susan and Ronnie. The latter showed a conscious awareness of the process of recovery from confusion, suggesting that already at this early age there was an element of conscious control involved in his flexibility. At a deeper level Chester showed the capacity for flexible shifting from an attitude of armored defense to a relaxed and spontaneous approach, for instance, in the Rorschach situation and also others.

We have belabored this point to an extreme degree, because—perhaps due to our reliance, for psychological thinking, on mechanical models or others from physical science—our concepts of development and of learning have tended to overemphasize static structures: perceptual, cognitive, verbal, motor. The range of variability which each child possesses merely sets the limits within which the constant new integrations of response can be creatively formed.

NOTES AND REFERENCES

1. Murphy, L.B. *Personality in Young Children,* Vol. 1, pp. 35-52. New York: Basic Books, 1956.

COPING STRATEGIES

When we discuss the coping devices and qualities of functioning involved in mastery, we have only described the a, b, c's, elements, as it were, which are utilized in a complex process. The coping process is a matter of strategy, of flexible management of different devices for dealing with the challenges from the environment. This process is shaped by the child's experience of the challenge and the resources currently available to him. Even specific learned patterns like Brennie's manners (Chapter 2) are utilized in strategic ways and have a place in a sequence which involves far more than acquiescence to the prescriptions of the adults. Whatever the adult expectations, pressures, or responses, the child has his own view of the situation and copes with it according to his own lights. We saw this most sharply in the children's spontaneous dealings with the—to them—often unreasonable or irrelevant demands in the intelligence test.

By strategy we also mean that the child often (if not generally) makes an effort to reach his own goals while at the same time keeping within the limits of adult acceptance or tolerance. Despite all of the criticisms and protests at the intelligence tests, for instance, these children did nothing that called for direct discipline from adults. Even Molly's vigorous action seldom if ever risked any real break in rapport with her understanding mother, and whenever she saw that her mother was angry at what she had done, she herself initiated loving reparation to restore harmony.

As we saw in accounts of beginnings at parties, the child often goes through a series of steps in the process of orientation, selection, and the use of stimuli offered. This in turn often involves maintaining an alert appraising attitude while participating at a minimum safe level, following which the child is able to become more involved in newly presented activities.

Coping strategies, then, are the child's individual patternings and timings of his resources for dealing with specific problems or needs or challenges. Both methods of managing of the environment, and devices and mechanisms for managing tension aroused by the stimulus, or likely to result from a given response to it, are often involved.

From the various illustrations of sequences through time, we can also see that the deployment of various devices at different phases of the child's orientation, his cognitive mastery, available resources, and perception of himself, cannot be conceptualized as the resultants of a simple process of learning to meet specific situations in a standard way. Learning of many kinds is involved. A major example is the learning which accompanies reality-testing—the child's own efforts to answer questions about the nature of an object, what is it for, how does it work, what can I do with it? Such reality-testing includes, above all, clarifying the answers to the questions; "How dangerous is this actually?" "How much freedom am I allowed to experiment with it in my own way?" "What are the consequences of such experiments?" Reality-testing is both cognitive and manipulative, and also proceeds by creative restructuring in order to test potentialities, along with asking questions.

When we say that coping is a synthesizing or integrative concept, and that it deals not only with techniques but with *strategy,* we are emphasizing the role of a function, the way in which a child uses a tendency (to focus on details versus ignoring details, etc.). While coping methods use such resources as alert perception, a reservoir of memories, and so forth, as well as defense mechanisms such as denial and repression, we are also concerned with the nuances, or modulation, or flexibility and adroitness with which these resources are organized and used. We look at the sequelae of specific coping operations and the new coping devices to which they lead.

As Dr. Karl Menninger pointed out in a discussion of this material the child may cope directly with problems presented by the environment with a sense of confidence and ability to handle these problems; or the problems arising in the first efforts to cope with them may give rise to anxiety as a by-product of the results of some of the coping devices used, or the failure of these coping devices to solve the problems as the child considers adequate. Thus, while the child may be confronted initially with a primarily external threat, if his efforts to cope do not reduce the strain, tensions aroused by internal upheavals and by reactions to the external threat rapidly become mingled and reinforce each other.

When the first coping step fails, subsequent coping devices or efforts may then be regarded as "secondary coping"; along with the results of the first efforts it is important to watch the differences between the initial coping orientation and the secondary coping efforts. Some children, for instance, leap first and then only settle down to reflection and make efforts at cognitive mastery after the initial active approach fails, whereas other children reflect first and look before they leap. We could see examples of this in the intelligence test responses especially, and also in the sequences of efforts to deal with motor challenges at the party.

A major hazard then exists for the child in the development of coping strategies. If his first efforts fail, and secondary coping devices are developed, do these restore the balance? If they do, they leave the child free for continued spontaneity. But if not, they may lead to defensive rigidity, such as we saw in Martin's building efforts (p. 104 f.), which prevents further exploration of potential gratification. This may result in continued frustration, leading to further anxiety which in turn leads to further defensive attitudes.

The coping process thus involves, as we saw (Chapter 8), sequences which will be different for different individuals, in addition to the different use of specific devices by different children. To say that such sequences have a purposive direction is to say that they have become individual strategies. The process includes control of the direction of attention, interest, and feeling; control of anxiety and efforts to manage this stress, whether inner or outer, in such a way as to reduce the tension or anxiety; and along with efforts to reduce this tension or anxiety, in some cases at least, efforts to balance the anxiety or negative feelings with positive gratification.

Ordinarily we think of maturation of a function grounded in

structures at a given stage of development, but here we have to think not only of its maturation in genetic terms but also of its evolution in the context of the goals and the values which the function has served, and the results of its use.

What are the purposes for which, for instance, children (like Brennie) develop a strong tendency to observe the environment around them both in terms of a wide range and in rather minute detail? What are the conditions for the development of delaying, retreating, avoidance tactics, or of fantasy, or of control, and what do they do for each child? When the strategies in which ego functions and defense mechanisms are used, and their sequelae are explored, we get a better understanding of how a given function, or organized group of functions, manifests its own evolution in the service of phase-specific needs of the child; how it develops and is integrated within the child's character as this changes with his over-all growth.

Situations which call for coping strategies

We can now differentiate coping functions from other response patterns of the child. Coping involves encountering something new or not yet mastered: a novel situation, an obstacle, or a conflict. It also involves some means-end element in the process of the activity. Anger as such is not coping; reducing or controlling this anger (as by reflecting on the question whether the consequences are worth the satisfaction of expressing it) is one way of coping with it. When a two-year-old snuggles into his mother's arms, it may not be coping; when he effectively pins his mother's arms down in a show of apparent affection which prevents the mother from reaching for the crawling baby, it is a method of coping with his rival.

The situations confronting the children we saw included one or more of several potentialities; they could be (1) gratifying, (2) challenging, (3) threatening, or (4) frustrating. Gratification and frustration were generally mutually exclusive, with frustration as the response to failure to receive a potential or expected gratification. The two intervening terms, challenging and threatening, relate to anticipated gratifications or anticipated frustrations or injuries to self-esteem or to the physical self. Some situations, of course, combined more than one of these features; for example, the psychiatric examination was sometimes both challenging and threatening.

A child may approach a situation involving new opportunities, challenges, or potentialities of gratification with a simple, direct act to obtain the gratification, as in sucking a piece of candy. If there are no obstacles or problems in this process at all—that is, if gratification is right there—we can hardly refer to coping. We must remind ourselves that primitive reflex and instinctive activities which can take place without plan or strategy—blinking, swallowing, defecating, laughing, crying, hating—are not "coping" activities. Neither are habits which have become automatic, an irreversible part of the person, almost like reflexes. Adaptation is thus a wider concept than coping; it includes habitual and routine, unchanged, automatic, and reflex responses.

When a situation involves some threat, the child's action in relation to the threat may move in any one of several different directions: he may attempt to reduce the threat, postpone, bypass it, create distance between himself and the threat, divide his attention, and the like. He may attempt to control it by setting limits, or by changing or transforming the situation. He might even try to eliminate or destroy the threat. Or he may balance the threat with the security measures, changing the relation of himself to the threat or to the environment which contains it, but which also includes sources of reassurance. Instead of dealing with the actual threat itself, he may deal primarily with the tension aroused by the threat: discharging tension by action, or by affect release displacement of affect into fantasy, dramatizing activities or creative work. Or he may attempt to contain the tension via insight, conscious formulation of the nature of the threat, defense maneuvers such as being brave, reassuring himself that he would be able to deal with it; or by fantasy which contained a counterthreat through elaboration without necessarily releasing affect.

In all of these kinds of coping operations we can see the role of specific coping acts in the sequence of steps involved in dealing with a threat or achieving gratification: preparatory steps toward coping, coping acts, and secondary coping efforts required to deal with the consequences of the first two; for example, using more drastic methods or retreating further.

Whether we consider the coping strategies in relation to results which obtain or maintain gratification, or in relation to managing threats or stress, we can see that the child's aim in terms of tension control may be to decrease tension, to maintain it, or to increase it. The choice depends on whether the tension level is part of the context of gratification, or of stress, and the level of tension needed for the gratification or for relief of stress. Subsidiary aims to avoid, or discharge, or contain the tension will also be involved here. This already implies that under certain circumstances the child may be trying to maintain a status quo under gratifying conditions or conditions when a threat might be increased, or to move toward a change under conditions when a change would reduce a threat or increase gratification. It is also obvious that at times the child may be occupied with temporarily decreasing or increasing tension as a means toward a further end in a series of steps.

In his initial contacts with a complex situation, a child may attempt to decrease tension during a period of familiarizing himself, achieving cognitive mastery, making his own appraisal or a cognitive map of the situation. Following this, he may mobilize a large amount of energy for very active efforts, having once selected the goals which are important to him in this situation. This dramatic contrast between decreasing or limiting factors arousing tension during the initial orientation, and the ensuing dramatic increase of energy and use of it in active participation, was seen in the behavior sequences of Donald at the party (pp. 100 ff.).

We saw that the coping efforts made in trying to achieve mastery involved different kinds of sequences for different childen, and also different devices, for controlling trial solutions and building next steps upon them. These processes included control of attention, interest, and feelings; control of tension and efforts to manage the stress aroused in the situation in such a way as to keep it at desired levels. In some cases this meant efforts to balance tension and negative feelings at any point with increments of gratification.

Especially when obstacles are present, but not only then, we can speak of the child's coping strategy and its purpose, namely, to obtain gratification after the obstacles are overcome. If obstacles are not easily surmounted, supplementary coping efforts may be involved when it is necessary to take steps to maintain the continuity of energy needed to reach a goal in the face of these obstacles or difficulties. Thus, at the party there were wide differences in the tendency of different children to persist in the search for hidden caches of candy and peanuts which could be found only by exploring through the bushes and shrubs, some of them prickly, over a wide area, part of it far enough away to take the child down a slight hill and out of sight of the group.

Here, we can distinguish between the ultimate gratification of an instinctual need—for instance, oral satisfaction—and the accompanying value of surmounting the obstacle for its own sake. For some children, once they had discovered what was involved, mastering the situation and its challenges became at least as exciting in itself as finding and consuming the candy and peanuts. While surmounting obstacles could be initially motivated only by the prospect of gratification of a basic need, the success in surmounting the obstacles en route then developed its own autonomous drives.

When a child fails in his effort to reach one goal, he may cope with this situation either by developing new ways of trying to reach the goal or by setting lower goals which are more certainly within his grasp, as we frequently saw the children doing in the intelligence test. In other words, flexibility in the setting of goals may be as much a part of coping as flexibility in methods or means of attempting to reach goals. Coping may operate by taking things one at a time; as in fencing, one uses all sorts of positive techniques which may often include what look like symptoms. Screaming to scare the four-year-old bully as Arthur* did may be as effective as hitting him; wetting the bed when mother is paying too much attention to problem brothers may win her attention as Joyce* did. Getting aggressively rebellious, as Molly did, may alert the mother sufficiently to bring changes in the situation.

As we have seen, especially in Molly's records where long-time sequences in her efforts to deal with certain problems were available, these strategies are constantly being developed, revised, relinquished and supplanted by new ones. Methods of dealing with her little brother which were typical at the age of four are rare at six or seven when solicitude had taken the place of overt jealousy.

These complex, yet flexible and changing patterns of managing difficulties vary greatly from child to child; in each case, they depend partly on inborn factors we may assume, partly on long-past and recent experience, with the conscious and unconscious insights, skills and defense mechanisms resulting from this. They also vary with the meanings of immediate situations, as we saw when we found children dealing with a male examiner very differently from the way they behaved with a female examiner; or when we saw them handling a free undirected situation very differently from the way they behaved in a structured situation dominated by specific adult demands.

Coping capacity or resources, then, draw upon the child's native equipment, integrative capacities, and ability to make flexible use of these, along with the environmental supports he needs in any situation, when they are available. We shall discuss later detailed aspects of factors in coping capacity and still later we shall discuss the development of coping methods and the contribution of coping to the development of the child.

While we think of coping problems as arising from the environment, and its demands, pressures, deprivations, and frustrations, we see how relative these are to the needs of the individual child, especially his own capacity to use the environment in a way that satisfies him, which provides gratification and at the same time protection from overstimulation. The coping problems which arise from strains

* Children in earlier records.

within the child—due to developmental imbalances, differential sensitivities, autonomic reactivity, tenuousness of integration following illness—all add burdens to his efforts to deal with the environment.

Structures contingent upon a given stage of development may be temporary and dependent on the individual-social configurations of available and acceptable resources at a given time, thus changing with age. We saw that as the child matures and gains new equipment and meets new social demands, former coping resources may be relinquished and new equivalents are employed. Crying is an important resource for communication until language develops; for many children and some adults, it may remain an important channel for release of severe tension even after language has matured, the number depending on the severity and consistency of restrictions on crying imposed by the culture.

Developmentally contingent structures grow out of successive emergents in equipment and their responses to demands from the environment, and appreciation by the environment. In the infant, perceptual maturation, teeth, grasping, locomotion, sphincter control, language, understanding of time, and ability to grasp larger social units, each lead to new interpersonal transactions, awareness, conflicts, and coping structures. Increasing capacity for repression and other defense mechanisms, for fantasy, and for symbolization contributes to new coping levels, modulations of methods, and a possibility for intrapsychic equivalents of action or overt affective discharge. Alloplastic coping is more modulated, refined, flexible, and creative as intrapsychic coping resources (fantasy, constructive defense mechanisms) are developed.

At any given time variations in coping methods in a given child use developmentally contingent structures dynamically dependent on the motivation elicited by the individual-social experience at that time and the residual (unresolved or only partially repressed) conflicts rearoused by interactions between the current external and internal situation. For example, dominating the female examiner versus cooperation with the male examiner, or ignoring mother versus giving in to grandma, are greatly influenced by the status of the child's feelings about his relation to father and to mother, his competition with one for the other, etc.

Affective pressure may disorganize previously established coping structures. Severe traumata, or threats, illnesses, excessive demands, overstimulation, or intrapsychic imbalance of developmental origin (as at puberty but also earlier) may lower thresholds for tension or lead to shifts in the balance of transactions between inner and outer forces. The child may, in the effort to handle excessive tension, become hyperactive, withdrawn, or immobile, or may show distortions of perception, etc. Disorganization of previous coping patterns may lead to new ones, either more or less effective for the child. These new reorganizations may be assisted by guidance (suggestions, coaching, interpretations from persons in the environment) or may emerge spontaneously as intrapsychic restructuring operations comparable to alloplastic restructuring of the environment.

While the specific coping strategies vary from one time to another, and the coping problems vary with environmental changes and changes in the condition of the child along the lines just reviewed, many of the children in this group, especially the balanced and stable ones, or those with extreme characteristics which persisted through the period of our observation, showed a persistent coping style. By this we mean the over-all orientation of a given child with its tendency to elaborate and consolidate certain kinds of coping strategies rather than others. This is the resultant of many factors that contributed to the child's use of his equipment in dealing with the environment.

Levels of awareness, and levels of integration of coping strategies

The level of consciousness—the extent to which a child is fully aware and accepting of his own behavior, including the degree to which his coping efforts are implicit (preconscious) or even to a large degree deeply repressed (unconscious)—is seen when we are considering large segments of behavior such as the child's total use of a play session, but cannot or should not be evaluated in terms of individual items of behavior out of the context of the child's over-all response to a situation.

The degree of integration—whether the child's coping efforts proceed by a series of single units of behavior, or by combinations of parallel activities, or by complex symphonic integrations—can be evaluated only on the basis of samples of large units of behavior in a variety of situations. Related to this would be the appraisal of the child's pattern of strategy, his tendency to reach for immediately accessible gratifications, or to separate himself quickly from threats, as compared with a tendency to move through an extended sequence of coping efforts toward postponed and perhaps more elaborate gratifications.

Strategy in terms of expectable effects

Coping strategies can also be evaluated in terms of the expectable effects as seen from the viewpoint of effects on tension-level as well as gratification of specific needs: whether the effect on tension is the one intended or not. Attempting an interesting but highly dangerous feat, such as jumping from a high wall (as Roddy did, for instance), would be an example of a process likely to increase the tension for almost any child; in other instances, certain activities might increase the tension for some children when this is contrary to their aim.

The expectable effect on feelings, the tendency for a given strategy to produce pleasure, anxiety, or guilt could be foreseen by the adults for most of the children, although we have already seen that the need systems of the children, and the punishment experiences vary enough even within a relatively homeogeneous group to create great individual differences here. Darlene, Martin, and Gordon were especially prone to feeling guilty, and their coping strategies were motivated in part by their need to avoid guilt.

Similarly, the expectable social effect—whether a child's behavior will be greeted with acceptance or rejection by adults or by other children—can be judged or foreseen only if we know the value patterns of the group in which the child is being observed. Even in one limited geographical area there are differences in what parents accept or reject sufficiently great to lead to mistakes unless we know the standards of each parent. From this point of view, "adaptiveness" is a relative matter; what is adaptive in one family is not in another.

Likewise, the expectable effect of a coping effort on the child's self-image and evaluation of himself, whether this will be improved, remain the same, or be depreciated, requires a knowledge of the values, needs, and goals of each child. The same thing is true of the effect of his efforts on the tolerance or resilience of the child. "Adjustment" is also relative to the capacities, needs, and tolerance-level of the child.

It is thus important to look at and evaluate the results of the coping strategies not only in terms of the immediate effect on the environment or relation to the specific gratification at which the child is aiming, or the alleviation of the frustration, but also the relation of the coping effort to the child's level of integration. This cannot always be evaluated immediately since, as we have seen, temporary regressions may appear in the service of new integration at different stages in the child's development.

Coping as an integrative function

Coping thus includes not only the more elementary situation-oriented devices but also all of the complex ways in which the child deals with reality as he sees it; defense mechanisms which temporarily deny reality, evade it, distort it, or set barriers against it are involved in coping when direct efforts to handle reality are not possible, or fail.

These defense mechanisms—projection, rationalization, denial, etc.—are subjective manipulations of reality to take the sting out of it, to make it bearable. Emphasis on the normal, flexible use of defense mechanisms must not limit our conception of the ego, and of the total range of coping resources which it uses. The child's direct and indirect efforts to handle reality in such a way as to reach his goal, to change the state of affairs to suit his needs, are included; the concept of coping focuses attention on the purpose, function, and result of the behavior for the child.

The "ego" is not only a fort protecting the self from instincts, i.e., a center of defense mechanisms; it is, as Schilder and others have suggested, a center of impulses to mastery, to respond to and use the environment constructively, a process which can involve defense mechanisms as well. Coping is the term we use to describe the manner in which this is done, the strategy by which the child attempts to achieve mastery, gain satisfaction, gratify himself, and prevent tension levels or disorganization which would disable him or interfere with this process of mastery. It includes therefore the strategy of maintaining frustration tolerance, of deactivating frustration-responses which would interfere with further attempts at gratification.

Coping can be literally "adaptive" with the emphasis on fitting in. Or it can be creative, producing actual transformations in situations in the environment at large or in the attitudes of people. From this point of view it is a broad category with room to include different ways of dealing with life.

PART IV

COPING AND DEVELOPMENT

❧❧❧ 14

THE BEGINNING
OF COPING*

THE TRANSFORMATION of an apparently dimly seeing, chaotically moving, avidly sucking, yet sleepy neonate into a smoothly coordinated, alert, and constructive adult involves many processes, not all of which we understand. "Maturation" and "learning" go on. The organism "interacts with" or "engages in transactions with" the environment.[1] These are very broad abstractions which serve a purpose, yet leave many questions unanswered, questions concerned with exactly what happens in these interactions and transactions. Moreover, when we are concerned with the universal hows of development we are apt to neglect the problems related to individuality—the variations and even the laws which can be seen only when we consider the widely different designs of growth and interaction with the environment in differ-

* This chapter utilizes material previously published in L. B. Murphy, Coping devices and defense mechanisms in relation to autonomous ego functions, *Bulletin of the Menninger Clinic,* Vol. 24, 1960.

ent individual children. First, let us review some of the general laws underlying the development of individual ways of coping.

In our study we take for granted and build upon general laws of development characteristic of all children (and many other species) such as the mutual patterning or programming of structures and functions: the more or less genetically determined and therefore unique equipment of each infant provides a foundation; but action instigated by the need to cope with obstacles to gratification or tension-release modifies the pattern. Thus effort and exercise improve even such a simple pattern as the sucking reflex; through the first days after birth it is incorporated into more complex response patterns.

Something like imprinting, although it might better be called "programming," may underlie the child's attachment to familiar places and people, an attachment which has been observed in a few very young babies (eight weeks) although usually it is not observed until later. Among observations of infants there is no evidence for the instant formation of an attachment at a given hour after birth, comparable to the imprinting process in geese described by ethologists.[2] Since conditioning has been experimentally demonstrated in the neonate, with wide individual differences in the number of exposures to the unconditioned stimulus required to establish the conditioned response, and since attachments demonstrated in infants appear after dozens or hundreds of opportunities for such conditioning, we must assume that learning is involved in the development of attachments in human infants. The capacity of the infant to use and to evoke the help of the mother in coping with discomfort grows out of such conditioning processes through the early weeks and months.

The infant evidently develops feelings of familiarity supported by the many experiences of satisfactory tension-release in relation to his mother and other personal and impersonal aspects of the environment. We have seen that some of the infants in the group were observed or reported to show restlessness or anxiety in strange situations or in reaction to strange people as early as eight to twelve weeks.

However, sudden, definite, or new visual, auditory, and other stimuli evoke orienting reflexes from birth[3] which become integrated into larger orienting patterns including either immobilization or heightened exploratory activity to facilitate the orientation process. These orientation processes increasingly involve greater differentiation and integration as stimuli become more meaningful cognitively and affectively, and more usable by the motor apparatus of the child. We have to assume, as we have mentioned earlier, that orientation and familiarization processes are aroused directly by the occurrence of stimuli of a certain intensity or degree of difference from the usual.

These orienting processes may be seen as precursors of the differentiating and integrating functions of the ego which continue through life and are prerequisites for all mastery or coping efforts. In Hartmann's terms,[4] these are among the most primary autonomous functions of the ego; phylogenetically, these can be understood as evolving from the organisms's need to be acquainted with the environment before it can use any part of the environment for need gratification or tension release. Piaget's thinking carries us a step further here.[5]

Registration of impressions of external stimuli as denoted by Piaget's "assimilation" and modification of internal schemata which he refers to as "accommodation" lead to a tentative equilibrium. This however has to be constantly recreated as new stimuli, inner needs, and other demands produce a succession of not unwelcome disequilibria.

Motivation is generally understood to be aroused by both internal stimuli (drives, needs of the organism leading to restlessness and search) and external stimuli which arouse impulses for exploration and manipulation. The young human as well as the young of another species also has needs for what Hebb has termed "perceptual nourishment."[6] In the clinical field the absence of adequate perceptual stimulation has been seen by Spitz[7] and others to contribute to developmental disturbances. In addition, sheer maturation of structures also brings along the urge to use the new equipment (e.g., motility urge [Mittelmann][8]) and also brings new possibilities of integration emerging from their use, which are differently exploited in different cultures.

So far we have been talking about various basic processes without reference to their coordination; this goes on under the organizing tendency which we refer to the ego. Without these organizing processes development does not go on. There are individual differences at every point, however, which qualify the pace, interaction, balance, and resultants of these processes. Great differences have been noted in the number of exposures required to effect conditioning in the young infant. There are also wide differences in the strength of such basic motivations as hunger and other facets of the oral drive such as the need to suck or to mouth small objects. There are wide differences in the pace of maturation and gratification potential of different functions, such as eye-hand coordination, locomotor skills, language, and social responses. These and other differences all mean that at the most basic level development in each child follows a somewhat unique design with individual problems of dealing with the environment and individual styles of managing tensions, obtaining gratification, and coming to terms with the demands of society.

Individual and changing balances of equilibrium and disequilibrium

Some other concepts tend to focus again on broad common-human tendencies. When our thinking is guided by the connotations of "adaptation" we tend to emphasize, as we mentioned above, the aim of reaching an "equilibrium" as a goal of activity. This is supported by our observations of infants in a hungry phase, whose restlessness recedes when they are satisfied, yielding to quiescence.

If, however, we watch children, even young infants of two to six months, after feeding, when hunger drives are satisfied, we find great variations in evidence of concern with maintaining an equilibrium. Many an infant, and even more, a young child, acts as if he wanted to obtain stimulation, to make something happen, to stir things up, to initiate changes, to create excitement, and by implication to enjoy the delights of pleasurable disequilibrium. Undoubtedly anthropologists will say that the interest in disequilibrium-creating activity also varies greatly from culture to culture. It certainly varies from child to child—in terms of differences in the capacity to arouse, sustain, and to tolerate tension, excitement, and new stimuli.

Longitudinal studies have documented very well changes in the equilibrium, whether growing out of internal events, external changes, or interactions between these of a given child, at different points in his growth, and his varying levels of coping capacity at different times. Variations in the structuring and management of his pattern of intake demand, and response to the environment, are to be expected as well. When we find the children in Macfarlane's study[9] showing peaks of problems at the age of five and of ten, or when we look at the cycles of equilibrium and disequilibrium or irritability observed by Gesell and his workers, it amounts at the most general level to the same thing: There are phases when the child can cope with more and times when he has to limit himself to less. There are times when he needs to reach a more stable equilibrium and times when he not only tolerates more disequilibrium, challenge and change but actively seeks it. These times come at different ages for different children, depending on the maturational pattern, external pressures, and capacity to deal with problems as they arise.

These phases of disequilibrium involve changing distributions of both physical and psychic energies related to a changing pace of physiological growth at different periods and changes in the level of physiological integration at different times, as well as changes in the internal pressures of conflicts with which he must cope, and the many differences in environmental pressures at different points in development. At one time skeletal growth is creating new problems of body and muscle adjustment. At another time hormone growth introduces both new energies and disequilibria at the level of autonomic nervous system and affective responses. Along with these alternations of equilibrium and disequilibrium within the child's own body, he is faced with changing opportunities and demands from the outside world.* These lead to conflicts between old interests and new emerging capacities. Thus he is involved in a complex shifting pattern of give and take which results from the interaction between these very complex changes within himself and sometimes equally complex changes in the outside world and its demands upon him.

If this statement about sequences, cycles, and changes in relation to the changing balance of equilibrium and disequilibrium seems to be placing the emphasis on the problems to be met, we also want to emphasize the gradually increased, if fluctuating, capacity for testing of reality, grasp of situations, understanding the environment, and understanding oneself which comes with growth. This is facilitated and integrated at times when the child is not too overwhelmed by the overstimulations intrinsic in the cumulative effect of inner and outer changes and their interrelationships, especially when new insights are stimulated by problems of mastery of inner or outer change or both. We find differing emphases on these two factors for different children. Some children show spurts of new integration under the stimulus of new challenges, others achieve new integration at times of quiet, or relief from a period of excessive pressure.

Maturation, to be sure, means increased capacity for delay, planning, mastering problems in fantasy, and manipulating the environment. These rich improvements are optimally supported by and strengthened by the learning experiences of the child in school, but sometimes they have to go independent of or even in antithesis to the school experience—depending on the extent to which teachers and the school administration appreciate the complexity of the total process of maturing, and depending also on the extent to which the needs of the individual child at each phase can be met by the program of the school at that time. Wise teachers around the world in many different kinds of schools are able to say, "He needs time to find himself; right now he has been growing so fast," or "There is much that is new to him this year and he'll need to take it in for a while before we expect too much of him."

Let us now consider the relation of this gradually increasing

---

* Entering school at the age of five or six is one such environmental change; shifting to junior high school is another; moving to a new city is another.

"capacity to cope with the internal and external problems" to concepts of adjustment and adaptation.

Adaptation and the capacity to change the environment

The concept of adaptation includes such basic physiological reactions as shift in blood pressure, the child's ability to tolerate changes in temperature, as well as the total range of reflex responses which the infant brings into the world, many of which become part of his basic resources for defense and maintaining himself in the environment as an organism. Some initial reflexes become incorporated through use and by conditioning into more complicated adaptive structures; only when activity of the ego is involved, as in selection of response patterns, do we speak of coping.

Adjustment is often used with the implication that the child is accepting, satisfactorily conforming to the demands of society around him; these demands may relate to his physical management, for instance, his acceptance of the basic routines of schedules of eating or sleeping, the diet, etc., his acceptance of the social rules and regulations common in his society, his acceptance of an ability to adequately meet the demands for learning, the skills and tools which he will need as an adult in his society. In practice, though not necessarily in theory, this has often led to a one-sided view of healthy dealings with the environment, overlooking the struggles and effort to change the environment itself which are seen in coping efforts.

Both adaptation and adjustment tend to be used with the connotation of fitting in, as if the environment were something static out there and the child were a pliable thing to be somehow squeezed into it. If the child does not meet the expectations of the adult he is not adjusting. Recently such phases as "mutual regulation" have been coming into the literature, implying that the mother and child do not consist of a couple, one of whom fits into the patterns of the other, as the programmatic philosophy of infant care during the 1930's seemed to expect, nor that the mother is capable of an infinite adaptability and extension of herself as the extreme self-demand approach of the 40's seemed to imply; but rather, that mother and baby together find a way of living which meets the baby's need and tempo and approach to life to a sufficient degree, while at the same time expecting him to utilize and to some extent fit into the patterns of his mother.

However, even this phrase hardly does justice to the active self-initiated responses to the environment made by the young infant. Even at birth the baby is not only as an organism which strives for an equilibrium, or which fits into the environment; he is an active, self-propelling, creative being, able to stimulate others to initiate changes in the environment from the time he arrives in the world. This activity, capacity for effort, capacity to initiate change, including the creative aspects of his dealings with the environment, we have for convenience referred to as coping.

The mother who makes her decisions about the baby in terms of "what he likes," what "satisfied" him and so forth, who permits free movement from the beginning even while she holds him supportingly, who lets him decide when to take and leave the nipple, when he wants to rest, and when he wants to work hard at a new motor skill, when he wants more exchange of stimulation, recognizes this intrinsic active capacity which the baby brings with him.

How does this approach view the tasks of infancy and early childhood?

The tasks of infancy

In infancy and the early years the following major tasks face the child:

1. Managing the various basic bodily functions, breathing, feedings, eliminating, sleeping, etc., and the drives which evolve from them.

2. Persistent day-by-day dealing with the stimulation from the environment, especially that associated with newness, pain, and overstimulation; as part of this, strong stimuli; developing ways of using the environment, dealing with the opportunities and frustrations it offers, and developing a capacity for deriving and contributing pleasure.

3. Coping with periodic challenges arising from "developmental crises" or "critical phases" at times of maturation of new functions, or major shifts in the relation of the child to the environment (such as weaning) as he gets older.

4. Mastering special impacts, traumata, or threats to integration from illness, accidents, and the like.

5. Learning to use all of his resources to move, both autonomously and with help, toward his goals and toward mutually gratifying exchanges with the environment.

6. Becoming a member of his culture who can deal with the deepest feelings and conflicts involved in relationships with the parent of each sex and with siblings and peers and can communicate and participate in play and work.

The first task of managing basic bodily functions including breathing, circulation, sleep, sensory and motor exercise, as well as feeding and elimination, involves gratifying the drives and needs which are represented in consciousness and others which usually remain unconscious. Special attention has been given to sucking which is an intense instrumental drive during the early period where rapid growth is required; but although intense it does not entirely displace the perceptual and motor drives. The latter come into play as fast as hunger and sucking needs are satisfied and are often parallel with this activity.

The second task, of managing stimulation from the environment, involves dealing with drive aspects as well as stimuli imposed by the outside. The need for body contact and, more generally, the need to maintain optimal interaction and tension—neither too little nor too much—are involved along with the need to utilize the functions of the organism as mentioned above.

Developmental crises and critical phases are essentially variants of these first two tasks; weaning may involve too sudden a loss of an accustomed drive gratification. Periods of new levels of sensory awareness, whether at the eight-weeks' level of auditory-visual maturation, or the so-called "eight-months'-anxiety" phase of new differentiations between people (which may occur at any time between five and ten months in different infants), involve risks of being overwhelmed by too much newness. As Freud [10] made clear, an essential aspect of a trauma, whether from pain, illness, fright, or other causes, is precisely the problem of being overwhelmed by a degree of stimulation that cannot be mastered.

Essentially then, we come down to two central tasks—managing the drive processes, including the needs and goals to which these gradually give rise, and managing the impacts from and relations with the environment, including the conflicts arising between drives and the limits or demands of the environment. The residues of each of these major areas of management at each period of development contribute to the child's resources for dealing with the demands and opportunities of the next stage, but also to the burden of conflicts carried into each new phase.

A dynamic conception of development must include not only the role of drives including libidinal and aggressive drives, but also the interacting roles of cognitive and of motor development as these are utilized, channeled and in part motivated by the former drives and also by the need to avoid pain, whether from overstimulation of customarily gratifying stimuli, or from directly distasteful and painful stimuli.

Phases in cognitive and in motor development are easily observed and have been described in detail at the level of operation of specific functions. The interactions of these with libidinal drives have been less fully studied, although Spitz[11] and others have emphasized the fact that weaning and its partial relinquishment of libidinal gratification in nursing can best take place at the six to eight months period when the infant's interest is increasingly drawn to sensory and motor interchanges with the outside world.

Interactions between libidinal drives and autonomous ego functions

Interactions between libidinal drives and autonomous ego functions include the following, all of which can be documented from our records:

Ego functions take over in early infancy after the libidinal drives are gratified: when he is neither sleeping nor eating, the baby a few weeks old looks, listens, explores, and contacts. If there are difficulties in achieving gratification, or gross distress in the gastrointestinal area, emerging perceptual functions may have difficulty in maintaining autonomy.

Drives intensify ego functions: the baby may discriminate the bottle from other objects before he differentiates his mother from other women.

Ego functions help to control, temper, or modulate drives: hearing or seeing mother's activity makes it possible to wait for feeding.

One function may substitute for another: a child insufficiently gratified in the area of oral or contact needs may develop intensified visual and auditory interests.

The style of functioning developed in one zone may be transferred or generalized to other zones as when oral aggression contributes the style to social contacts.

Ego functions are increasingly used to implement drive-gratification, as motility makes it possible for the child to reach his own drive objects.

Regression to primitive libidinal gratification may be used to refresh the child for further concentration on intensive ego efforts.

Attitudes developed in a libidinal context may be transferred or generalized to the use of ego functions.

Management of pain

Phases in the response to and management of pain and its interaction with both developing drives and ego functions have been barely studied at all. Freud's concept[12] of the stimulus-barrier which protects the organism from overwhelming stimulation has been utilized by

Bergman and Escalona[13] for their discussions of sensitivity, and by Ramzy and Wallerstein[14] for their consideration of pain in relation to fear and anxiety. There is also a need for study of sequences or phases in the development of pain-management, its relations with other aspects of the infant and young child's development, and its sequelae for the ego or for personality as a whole. Experimental and observational data have dealt chiefly with a narrow range of pain stimuli such as pinpricks, the inoculation needle, or tight restriction.[15] An infant that tolerates a circumcision during the neonatal period, with little or no evidence of pain provided it has a sugar lump to suck, is still likely to respond with a startle to a sudden noise, and to an unpleasant taste by spitting out. It looks as if the organism has been prepared to be sensitive to and to avoid initially certain kinds of threats and sources of overstimulation more than others.

We can offer the following tentative conclusions and hypotheses on the basis of the observations on our limited sample. Management of sources of stimulation including those which bring discomfort or pain develops with the maturation and experience of the child. While the young infant is able to turn away from, spit out, or visually shut out momentary or mildly unpleasant stimuli, he is extremely vulnerable to severe or prolonged discomfort. Extreme disintegrative reactions involving massive autonomic upheaval, disruption of motor coordination, as well as marked respiratory and circulatory changes along with screaming are characteristic, and for the infant with prolonged colic or other gastrointestinal distress, occur frequently. The extent to which this can interfere with integration of perceptual-motor processes and other aspects of cognitive functioning is implied in our statistically significant correlation between oral gratification and perceptual clarity, and related correlations.[16] We also saw more hostility and ambivalence in children who had experienced prolonged distress. Daryl's persisting suspiciousness was one example of this. Since this degree of weakening of the integration of the child can be seen even within a selected normal group, it is easy to see the difficulties which might result from prolonged overwhelming distress in early infancy to children already threatened by developmental imbalances, sensory defects, or by any degree of brain damage. These conditions evidently interfere with the autonomy of emerging ego functions, differentiating and integrative capacities, and present special problems in the management of anxiety, the maintenance of healthy narcissism, and the development of trusting relationships with the environment.

Factors influencing mastery at successive phases

Each of the tasks of mastery of each successive phase initiated by the ripening of new drives or of new ego functions can be handled optimally well only if the child's development up to that point has been relatively free from distortion or disturbances due to illnesses, oversensitizations, overstimulation, deprivation, erotization, aggression from the environment, and the infant's anxious or angry or disappointed, or affect-hungry reactions to these. Some sort of difficulty with the environment due to one or another or a combination of these factors was visible in a majority of the children we observed despite the capacity for mastery which they generally showed. That is, few children, with the possible exception of Barbie, Teddy, and Diane, were without some scars which interfered with some aspect of dealing with the environment. A concept of the fully and serenely developed child, able to use all of his functions optimally well, able to handle all of the age-appropriate demands that are placed upon him and to respond to all of the opportunities offered to him, is an abstract ideal, which is very rarely approximated.

The interaction of coping capacities

In clinical work we constantly see children whose inability to deal with certain aspects of their relations to the environment interferes with other aspects of their development. We also see the reverse, and make use of it in education. In nursery schools, we have seen children who could not manage the complexities of a spontaneous music hour remain on the sidelines, or refuse to "go to music" and thus miss not only the music but the group activity, the shared fantasy, and other aspects of the experience as a whole. By contrast, we have seen children who could not cope with free play in a large group of children, but did respond eagerly to the opportunity for directed activity in an organized music hour.* Motor blocking, and speech difficulties commonly interfere with social participation in young children. These are obvious. Less obvious integrative difficulties are evidently involved where a child cannot cope with a situation involving a larger group of children, but is able to participate freely in a small group of three or four. Sam, the highly verbal child we saw in Chapter 2, was able to say that he felt "confused" by the nursery school group in his first days at school, at the age of three and a half. We saw much evidence of the

* Observations in the Sarah Lawrence Nursery School music hour with Marian Gay.

detail with which he observed different aspects of the environment, as well as his awareness of people, his strong feelings, and his fantasy. Where a child responds at so many levels, with such intensity, "confusion" is, we can assume, a likely result at first of entrance into a large group in a new environment which would flood him with a wide variety of new stimuli. A less perceptive child could assimilate new aspects of the situation more gradually, and with less danger of confusion. It is important here that Sam, like Molly and Donald in the present group, had shown evidence of uneasiness or something like anxiety at the age of three months.

From the first sucking experience to the first entrance into school, through all the activities rooted in the maturation of libidinal, aggressive, motor, and cognitive drives, there is always a question: Will the child be able to carry through the activity satisfyingly? If he does, if he is able to master the opportunity presented by the concomitance of his emergent ability and relevant environmental stimulation, we say that he was able to cope with it; if he fumbles to the point where he gets discouraged, gives up, settles for incomplete mastery of the new function, or retreats to a preceding level of functioning, we say that he could not cope with it. Mastery and coping, then, are resultants of the functioning of drives including those which activate ego functions. A child does not simply have a drive toward mastery in general, he is selective. He is interested in mastering specific challenges—others are ignored. He has a drive to master a motor skill, as Darlene did (p. 168 f.) or a fear, as Molly did.* We could say that drives and functions to some degree carry with them their own drive to completion, to adequacy, which are necessary for full gratification. When mastery of the use of a developmental capacity is interfered with by other limitations, we can expect to see a frustrated, restless, or troubled child. The child wants to use what he has got, and use it well, effectively.

Children differ in the degree of their persistence in trying to achieve the full potentialities of each developmental capacity and to surmount the difficulties presented by developmental transitions, conflicts, frustrations; to this extent they have differences in the drive to mastery. No other infant was observed to struggle with the same persistence to master an emerging incomplete motor function as Ronnie struggled to master the coordinations involved in getting up on all fours. These differences also vary in different modalities. Few other infants showed the avidity in exploring multiple oral pleasures as did Karen.

No infant showed maximum pleasure in mastering all of the potentialities in all modalities—there was always an order of preference

* See Chapter 3.

as to the stimuli and activities to which the child would give his most intent concentration. Since adults differ in their awareness of what a baby likes, wants, and strives for, there were of course differences in the extent to which the infant was able to exercise or to obtain gratification in the preferred areas, related to the awareness and the cooperation of the environment in providing adequate stimuli and opportunities.

In view of the enormous importance of reality-testing efforts, the attempt to achieve cognitive clarity in new situations, and the role of motor exploration, on the one hand, and of communication and the ability to ask questions, on the other hand, we can see that disturbances which affected the pace of development and of the integration and stability of motor coordination and speech would hamper the child's capacity to deal with new situations. In this group, despite their great motor freedom in many situations, sixteen children showed some sort of motor retardation or tendency to lose coordination under stress. Thirteen showed some sort of speech difficulty at the pre-school period including tendencies to stutter under stress. (These numbers do not include children who simply tended to be inhibited in action at the beginning of new situations, like Donald, or children who tended to be silent, like Vernon.) Seven children showed difficulties in both areas.

In four instances, Lennie, Patsy, Sally, and Brennie, no infantile precursors of motor difficulties had been observed. In the case of Lennie and Brennie, severe illnesses and their sequelae may have contributed to part of the difficulties in this area, while with the girls motor difficulties may have been related to environmental deprivation, or deep conflicts, and ambivalence not anticipated in infancy but rather severe by the age of four to five.

We can see that expectations of or doubt about the ability to deal with new opportunities and demands from the environment are successively reinforced or modified as the child is or is not able to manage the new challenges of successive developmental levels as he experiences them, from birth on.

Beyond this, changes for the better in coping capacity (reflected in a few children less well predicted by Escalona), were in several instances the apparent result of intense efforts by the child (Karen, Janice, Ronnie) to master difficulties which could not be dealt with adequately at earlier periods, whether because of weaknesses resulting from illness, or developmental difficulties, or lack of support from the environment at the earlier phase. In these instances, as the child succeeded in mastering one crucial area, other capacities for mastery improved.

The full meaning of each phase of development can only be seen in relation to what came before and what comes afterward.* The preschool period for many children is a period of experimenting with sex and age roles, with different identities, with different feelings about parents, siblings, peers; with different ways of dealing with the opportunities and obstacles life offers. It is not the only experimenting phase; at three to six months the baby did a great deal of experimenting with ways of handling his body—rolling over, arching, stretching, tumbling. At the beginning of adolescence the boy and girl in our culture typically experiment with their appearance; later comes sexual experimentation. Some young adults experiment with work opportunities. Against the background of this view of development we can now look at the first efforts toward mastery.

The earliest coping efforts: control of stimulation

Along with orientation processes, one of the first steps toward mastery is the infant's attempt to develop a pattern of control of stimulation, self-dosing, and overt demand for stimulation congruent with his own intake needs and capacity for assimilation. In addition to his capacity to respond to potential need-gratifiers, this will include his ability to limit stimuli from the outside, to give himself time out when he needs it, to have his protest accepted when demands are too much. It also includes obtaining respect for his own need to increase the quantity of stimulation or change the quality, make it more varied, richer, or more related to his own interests. His early coping devices include such elementary and basic items of behavior as selective looking, looking at, looking for, looking away from; shifting attention from

* Erikson says, "Finally, I must emphasize again, that all these stages are intrinsically related to the psychoanalytic theory of the basic drives and of the ego. . . . The first stage was related to what, in psychoanalytic psychosexual terms, is called orality and sensory-tactile erotism. The stage of autonomy versus the stage of shame and doubt is related to anality and to muscular development. For 'libido-development' as well as 'child development' and social accentuation have in common certain modalities, such as holding on and letting go, retaining and releasing. The sphincters, as part of the muscle system, can become the dramatic place where holding on and letting go is particularly emphasized to a degree dependent on how much the culture wants to emphasize it, and how much emphasis the individual can tolerate. From intense experiences of being held on to, of holding in, of holding in, of holding on, of being freed, of letting go in relation to persons, objects, and feelings, can come a sense of autonomy; that is a sense that the child can master himself and his environment more than he needs to be mastered and to have things done for him. This basic ratio can later influence many modalities, characterizing, in turn, basic social attitudes such as a hostile ejecting, letting loose, or repudiating, or a tolerant letting pass, letting live, letting go." 22 Excerpt from Discussion on Child Development, edited by J. M. Tanner and B. Inhelder, Vol. 3, New York: International Universities Press, 1958, pp. 170-172.

a threatening object to a safer one, alternating attention by shifting to a safe stimulus for a time in order to consolidate a feeling of adequacy, then shifting back to the threatening stimulus in order to master it further perceptually, or as preparation for doing something to it or with it. The latter illustration comes close to the level of coping which we have called coping strategy, in which sequences of different kinds are to be seen. The infant may withdraw momentarily as preparation for a more active response later on; or he may go through tests or experiments on a basis of which he draws inferences leading to a change in his way of dealing with a situation. Initially these are not consciously purposeful, but as the child becomes increasingly aware of the sequelae of his behavior become so.

This capacity of the child to control the impact of the environment through the ability to evoke, select, and limit the amount and kinds of stimulation, on the one hand, and to increase them both quantitatively and qualitatively, on the other, includes the capacity to change the patterning of limitation and augmenting, the narrowing of interest or the broadening of interest, the getting involved in activity, or keeping a distance—at different periods of development. Some infants need much more help with this than others do.

Coping attitudes

We can now consider steps by which basic coping attitudes develop. While the birth cry may have the primary biological function of guaranteeing breathing, subsequent cries bring the experiences of relief, food, contact, warmth, drying, and other comfort satisfactions and also new stimulations required to relieve boredom. It has been experimentally demonstrated both in this country and in the U.S.S.R. that classical or Pavlovian conditioning can take place under controlled experimental conditions in the neonate.[17] Following, moreover, the principle of operant conditioning,[18] we may assume that a varying number of experiences of positive responses of the mothering person to an infant's cry succeeded by the relief of discomfort provide a rather complex foundation for the following: the infant experiences that crying as such makes something happen; crying then very shortly becomes a communication to the environment and a signal, although first it may be merely a built-in reflex. The repeated experience of positive responses from the environment to crying—which is the baby's only resource for communication for a considerable period of time—may be assumed to lead secondarily to the orientation toward communicating, ultimately including talking in order to express needs, desires, feelings. But another secondary aspect of successful experiences of achieving a response to crying may be assumed to be some vague experience of mastery or sense of resources for manipulation, control, and making something happen.

The effort to suck, whether nipple or fingers, coupled with alleviation of hunger tensions or merely the gratifying sensory experience of sucking per se also involves, we may assume, not only the pure operation of reflex followed by alleviation of hunger but the secondary or "deutero-learning," as Gregory Bateson* calls it, that making the effort produces results.

Each successive type of effort made by the baby, including the effort to hold up his head momentarily in order to see, in the vague way that we assume that he sees a bright light when sometime between the age of a week and a month he is able to hold up his head in order to focus better—each such positive effort followed by a positive gratification may be assumed to have its own secondary learning effects constantly reinforcing the value of effort. Other primitive vaguely goal-directed activities such as shoving away oppressive blankets, pushing with his feet and thus varying his position in the crib, whatever the particular gratification involved, can also be seen in relation to this secondary learning which supports making an effort, or struggling, or trying to make something happen, or to manipulate something, or to control the environment or one's own body. In other words, coping efforts begin practically at birth and insofar as active efforts succeed, an active or positive coping orientation is becoming established. All such experiences of relief from discomfort or achievement of positive satisfaction which follow upon expressions or motor actions of the child then contribute to the formula effort-brings-satisfaction.

Conversely, when a baby cries in distress and no relief comes, as with institutionalized babies, or when the efforts of the adult to give relief persistently fail to do so, we can assume that some difficulty or lack of confidence in the potential positive results of expressions and of making an effort will be the consequence, along with loss of cathexis of or interest in the potentially gratifying environment, and possibly even withdrawal to the point of apathy, sleep, or a persistent tendency to give up.

The basic coping orientation becomes enriched as the various aspects of equipment of the baby mature sufficiently to make possible increasing perceptual clarity in visual, auditory, tactual, and kinaesthetic areas. A considerable part of a very young infant's waking time, at least for many infants, is used in explorations and focusing in one or

* Refers to deutero-learning as the attitude of learning or "learning to learn" which comes along in the process of learning a specific skill. Bateson, G. *Naven*, 2nd ed. Stanford: Stanford University Press, 1958.

another sensory area in ways which can only be described as making an effort to achieve perceptual clarity in contact with the environment. The drives to see, to hear, to touch, and to move are as spontaneous from the beginning of life as the hunger drive. We noted earlier that experiments in the U.S.S.R. have demonstrated that a neonate will even stop sucking when a loud sound is heard.[19]

The relative dominance of the hunger drive during the first six months or the first year yields during the second year to a shift in the priority of sources of gratification. Many babies of this age are less interested in food, have less appetite, and are far more interested in gratifications in the motor area than they are in food. During the first year the baby has been rewarded for his preoccupation with feeding by tripling his weight; once this steep climb has been achieved the need for constant interest in food has begun to taper off.

But long before this loss of appetite sets in, the sensory and motor spheres have been claiming a larger and larger share of the baby's time, interests, and effort. This varies enormously with different babies but preoccupations with pushing up the head, pushing up the shoulders, learning to roll over, pulling up to a sitting position, to a standing position, and then walking can be very absorbing for many babies who make astonishingly persistent efforts to practice and improve these skills, as was true of Ronnie.

Defensive uses of different systems in infancy

In between the active efforts to manage its relation with the environment, and the intrapsychic mechanisms which serve defensive purposes, we can see defensive reactions of the body; individual infants tend to use one or another body zone for such defense purposes. We can group these operations according to the zone and the act.

DEFENSIVE USES OF MOTILITY

We saw these infants showing markedly different patterns of reaction to unwanted stimulation. In the motor area:

Stiffening—Freezing. Some babies of three to four months and over stiffen their backs and legs when they are being put through procedures which they do not like. Not all the babies did this. Vernon was one of the stiffeners and from his total record it looks as if stiffening in early infancy was a precursor of "freezing," or immobilization at later stages. This is a motor defense pattern that prevents the adult from putting the child through operations which the child does not propose to cooperate with. The child takes a stand, as it were, even before he is actually able to stand vertically. The attitude seems to be "I'm not going to put up with this," "I'm not going to go along," "I won't have anything to do with it," or something of this sort.

Relaxing—Going Limp. This is about as effective as stiffening. The baby turns into a limp bag of meal and offers no cooperation. However, the adult can accomplish more with a limp baby than with a stiffened one. The attitude here seems to be "Well, do what you like but I won't help."

Moving away, against, or toward something. Babies who have achieved any control over locomotion may scramble, crawl, creep, stretch, pull and in other ways try to get away from, for instance, a diapering situation. Terry was an example of this. Others push away the mother's hands, kick, or in other ways try to protest against and fight against the unwanted activity. Still others reach *for* goals of their own, objects to play with, etc. Mittelmann[20] notes the "loosely organized slashing of the extremities in rage of the infant after six months, with increase in tempo, amount, angularity and amplitude of movement in less intense rage reactions."

He also reports the toddlers' pattern when anxious, to "scurry back to the mother or surrogate and clutch her." He adds that the anxious child organizes space so that the loved adult is the center of it. In this reaction, "motility, i.e. flight and search for safety, becomes livelier" and he notes a contrasting pattern of the anxious infant, when in the safety zone of the mother, "to stare at the stranger without moving."

Since the infancy records provide intensive data at one stage only for each baby we do not have material to show to what extent these patterns of stiffening, going limp, and moving away, against, or to are mutually exclusive. The same babies may use one or the other at different stages of infantile development, but Mittelmann observes consistent tendencies in different infants to use one or the other, among the small group of infants he studied intensively. Nor do we have data on the period of the second year of life.

DEFENSIVE USES OF SENSORY APPARATUS

It is harder to be sure of our ground here. At the age of four weeks, Stevie seemed to withdraw from stimulation into an unresponsive passivity. At twenty-eight weeks Patsy was seen to shut her eyes and go to sleep at the moment when three observers converged on her crib for a simultaneous time-sample recording—as if she found the concentrated attention too much or found it hard to distribute her own attention among three people giving her such close attention. In nursery schools we have seen children who "don't hear" or who "don't see" either specific things or very much in general; in other words they limit the range of vision or of hearing. We also see those who are hyperalert, who have very low thresholds in the visual and auditory areas, and we see those who move away from disturbing visual or auditory stimuli to substitute ones which are safer or more gratifying.

Dr. Heider[21] has also pointed to important instances of variations in sensory functioning: children who do not show reactions to strong stimuli such as loud noises but do startle at slight stimuli; it is as if they were caught off guard and react to the slight stimuli while with the sudden, loud, more violent or unexpected ones they are able to institute defense operations which inhibit the startle reaction.

VOCALIZING

Here we see the following:

Silence or complete inhibition of vocalizing, including crying and experimental vocalizing.

Hypervocalizing or agitated, birdlike, rapid, noisy chatter.

Expressive vocalizing: protesting in anger; whimpering for attention or consolation; vocalizing as if to comfort oneself, etc.

Notice the wide variations in different babies including those who (in some cases quite early) have an extraordinary range of differentiated vocalizations.

ORALITY

Here we see:

Ejecting, spitting out or spitting up, dribbling, vomiting, drooling.

Loss of appetite or not eating, not swallowing, "playing with the food in his mouth," not receiving or accepting food, with an inhibition of oral gratification and response.

An increase of appetite or a compulsive repetitious oral demand in over-eating or uninterrupted eating.

The use of any of varied kinds of substitute oral comfort, pacifier, thumb or fingers, sucking on bottle, toys, or on blanket, etc.

It is not clear to what extent blowing bubbles and other kinds of lip and tongue activity are also used by the babies for defensive purposes in addition to being developed just for the fun of it. By and large they seem to go on in an atmosphere of enjoyment and spontaneous playful exploration of the kinds of things that one can do with one's mouth.

Precursors of defense mechanisms

Even in the records of infants observed during the first three months many of these activities might be regarded as precursors of both later coping devices and defense mechanisms. In common with very simple organisms such as worms and ants, a baby soon after birth will turn its face or body away from a threatening stimulus, shut its eyes to avoid such a threat, or curl into itself. Some neonates will also push away or in some other way crudely attack a stimulus which is a source of discomfort, such as an uncomfortable blanket pressing on its face. A baby's cry, at first a primitive discharge mechanism of the organism, soon becomes a technique or device for obtaining help. It is used as communication and demand as well as an expression of anger, fear, discomfort, or pain and anxiety.

As soon as the development of motor skills and locomotion makes it possible for the baby to turn over, creep, or pull or push himself away from the stimulus, his primitive turning away or shutting his eyes is extended to removing his body. As fine motor control develops, his initial amorphous hitting out yields to more coordinated methods of hitting or throwing away. These are all active ways of defending one's self against discomfort or external stress—that is, they are forms of defensive behavior. Thus we can see a series of steps between the earliest and later methods of defending one's self, some of which become patterned into defense mechanisms. For example: The baby turns away from a threatening stimulus. This makes it possible for him to forget; or parallel with forgetting, to deny the existence of the threat. When forgetting is maintained consistently, we might call it repression. It is hardly reasonable to assume that all forgetting is repression under emotional conflict, since when the infant is very young such a multitude of stimuli are pressing upon him in succession that memory must be regarded as a positive development and an achievement in itself, and forgetting as a normal consequence of the shifting of attention from a previous stimulus to a new and more absorbing one.

When the baby reaches an age where the threat comes from the reaction of the environment to something he has done, whether it is a matter of biting the nipple of his mother while nursing or throwing something frustrating or annoying to him out of his play pen or high chair, we find the beginning of anger at the external person who punishes or reproves for the painful or socially destructive action.

It is not uncommon to see forceful spirited babies look angrily and defiantly at the grownup who has slapped the baby's hand or protested some action. It is as if the baby said, "It is you who are bad, not I." This quick exchange seems to serve the purpose of forestalling recognition or acceptance of guilty feelings by the baby, especially in those cases where the baby maintains a proud autonomy after such accusing looks at the grownup. In some instances a baby may follow such an angry accusation with a shy, withdrawing, retreating appeal as if for forgiveness or for reinstatement of love, a look expressive of reparation. This is a distinct next step, however. In a setting of exchanges of anger before a baby has clearly differentiated concepts of self and of mother, such responses may involve precursors of later projection.

Among the children in our study, Stevie and Patsy, who turned away from strong stimulation in infancy, used withdrawal as a major defense operation throughout childhood. Children like Sheila, who protested vigorously in their early weeks, tended to continue this but with modulation through the latency years.

Critical phases in the early years

We have been discussing the infant's ways of dealing with some of the earliest problems of managing unwanted, excessive, or unpleasant stimulation. But the ongoing daily challenges faced by the baby are not the whole story; at critical phases in the emergence of new functions there are special hazards, tasks, and problems to deal with.

Each of the peak phases of unfolding of instinctual and of ego functions can contribute permanent parts of the child's makeup under certain conditions. The phase of emergence of a function may lead to different outcomes, however, depending on the state of the organism, previous development, readiness for the new capacity, the stimuli from the environment at the time and their relation to the emerging functions. Our understanding of the problems appearing in connection with successive "critical phases" as these are often called, has been growing slowly over a long time.

In 1890 William James[22] stated the law of transitoriness: many instincts ripen and then fade away. "If during the time of an instinct's vivacity, the objects adequate to arouse it are met with, a habit of acting on them is formed, which remains when the original instinct has passed away; but if no such objects are met with, then no habit will be formed; and later on in life, when the animal meets the objects, he will altogether fail to react, as at the earlier epoch he would instinctively have done." Embryology has documented this at a physiological and neurological level.

Today we are familiar with the concept of the "critical phase" as it is used by the ethologists: if the proper or necessary environmental stimulus does not appear at the time of emergence of a new function, the function will develop and will never develop thereafter. The term has been used by Freud,[23] Erikson,[24] Benjamin,[25] and Spitz[26] with modified meanings. Each of these uses, in one way or another, is concerned with the capacity of the individual to deal with the pressures created by newly experienced stimulation from the environment at a time of emergence of new functions. A special hazard has been generally associated with the period of adolescence, but to different degrees it exists at all turning points in development. The critical phase aspects of each psychosexual stage have been discussed chiefly in psychoanalytic literature; critical phase aspects of development of ego functions has had less attention.

If we now sketch in series the major critical phases of the first six years we see something like the following:

1. While many writers in psychoanalysis have dealt with the potential or actual trauma of any birth experience, pediatrics, neurology, and psychology have limited their concern to the effects of abnormal birth (and pregnancy) conditions—those involving some degree of anoxia, tissue damage, etc. The fact that birth itself, for any infant, is a critical phase which involves hazards intrinsic to the shift from one environment to a grossly different one is not so widely recognized. Ribble[27] and Greenacre[28] have discussed these in terms of the tasks of achieving adequate *integration of physiological functioning.*

At birth, the very first challenges and risks involve the problems of breathing and establishing circulatory functioning in the new environment. Soon after, the necessity of sucking presents difficulties to certain infants who may confront nipples hard to suck from, or who may have little energy to suck persistently, etc. Sucking is the first effort to earn a living, or to work, and for some involves considerable struggle or requires considerable encouragement; this was true of Greg in the present group. This fact has been overshadowed by the adult fascination with "greedy" infants who suck passionately and effortlessly.

2. Parallel with the early problems of integration, the neonate, even with its limited sensory capacities, is nevertheless often confronted with problems of *managing stimulation from the environment.* We believe that some of these earliest coping efforts are seen in the use of sleep, turning away, spitting out, etc., to avoid or get rid of unpleasant stimuli. These were seen in this group at the age of four weeks.

3. As Benjamin has recently pointed out,[29] at about the age of eight weeks, visual and auditory perception become dramatically more available to the infant, who is observed to "actually see" and not merely look or stare. Parallel with this development of perception, at least in some of the infants in this group, is the emergence of the "human" smile coordinated with the visual glance of the infant, and responding to the visual attention, voice tactual stimulation, or movement by the adult. This responsiveness tends to evoke activity from adults which elicits more responses; this involves a danger of overstimulation.

More broadly, we can see this stage—whatever the age at which it occurs—as critical for the integration of autonomous ego functions, especially perception and the earliest reaching. There is some evidence that either over- or understimulation at this time may disturb the development of these ego functions; ethology has emphasized the need for stimuli adequate to the needs of each new emerging function. The infant, with some limited control of his body by that time, in terms of raising his head, turning it more freely, wiggling his body into different positions, restlessly evoking adult attention to posture needs which will increase the visual range or provide protection, is himself coping with the problems presented by the need for an optimal relation with the environment at this phase.

In this early stage of patterning of perceptual functions, colic or other gastrointestinal difficulties, frustration, or deprivation in the alimentary system may also threaten the autonomy of these emerging functions.

An important issue in these instances is whether the infant can use soothing tactual or vocal stimulation from the mother to assuage distress and reduce difficulties and discomforts arising from inadequacies in his interchanges with the environment in other modalities. The infant who is hard to comfort, who is unable to make use of balancing gratifications from the environment runs the risk of establishing a more shaky foundation for his relations with the environment than the infant who, though disturbed by colic or shifts in temperature, is successfully soothed by the mother's voice or by rocking or stroking.

This critical phase may be considered to last until, at about the age of three to four months, the infant achieves markedly greater control of hands and trunk and is able *to manage his own body* in such ways as to diminish, increase, or modulate stimulation for himself. It is interesting to note that "three months colic" seems often to terminate, parallel with this increase in the coping capacity of the infant, as if his capacity for management of his body contributed to a spontaneous decrease in tensions, and less need for external help in getting rid of excess air through burping. Further, he can reduce muscle tensions from uncomfortable postures by spontaneous movements of his own. It is also important to note that this three-to-four month phase is marked by a conspicuous development of affect, expressed often vividly by infants of four months or more, and used by them to evoke further responses from the environment. With Teddy, Escalona's[30] "best predicted" child, this capacity to evoke responses from others was outstanding at the age of twenty weeks. It was dramatic in Donald at sixteen weeks. This greater capacity for expressiveness probably also contributes to resources for tension-discharge, and thus to the "happiness" of the baby at this stage.

4. The three-to-four month phase then can be regarded as a critical phase for development of reciprocal exchanges with the environment and *early differentiation of self from the environment*. This does not imply that the infant can yet distinguish different individuals clearly, although some infants do. It means that in healthy mother-child couples, some expectancies have been established, some sense of being-able-to-count-on a response to certain evocative efforts. The use of crying is involved here, and by this age, many mothers report their ability to distinguish between tired cries, hungry cries, cries of pain, and other cries. The process of differentiation goes on in the mother as well as in the baby.

Differentiation of other affects[31] proceeds rapidly at this stage also; the provocative laughter and crowing of a four-month-old baby was notably contagious for Escalona's staff. The baby begins "cooing" somewhat earlier, but now begins to use syllables and expressive vocalization, to which the mother may respond in kind. It is possible that the frequency of speech disturbances in this country may be related to the failures of the environment to respond adequately to these early differentiations of vocalized sounds, so that smooth and steady progress in connecting one's own sounds to those of the adults is not promoted.

Since at this phase, infants are reported to "like" and "not like" and to accept or reject many different foods, toys, other stimuli from the environment, we assume that this is a period of rapid differentiation in stimuli in many modalities, as well as differentiation within both positive and negative feelings about such stimuli in the normal infant.

It is important to note that this is the phase of the "paranoid position" as Melanie Klein[32] termed it on the basis of experience in analyzing disturbed children and adults. If we think of this in relation to the description of observed aspects of the differentiating process just discussed, we can see that the phenomena she describes are probably due to the failure of: adequate differentiation of the external environment, the development of appropriate affective responses to it, and capacity to master it to some degree by abilities to evoke desired stimuli and responses from the environment. In other words, the so-called "paranoid position" can be seen as a resultant of failures in coping with the tasks of this phase, failures which obviously jeopardize the subsequent development of the infant who has to continue his struggles with the environment without adequate basic differentiating of objects and affects related to them. The confusions resulting from chaotic projections of bad feelings onto the imperfectly perceived environment leave residues which threaten to undermine later reality-testing.

5. In the six-to-ten month phase the infant goes through several kinds of development more or less simultaneously, and with different interactions, depending on the frustration, pain, struggle, or gratification and success accompanying each. He gets teeth and the possibility of chewing, and in our culture, an increased range of foods, with the task of adapting to new textures. He becomes able to sit up, and perhaps to crawl, and to stand up. These greatly expand his range of vision and tactual contact with the environment, as well as the range of satisfactions in movement, body contacts, kinaesthetic experiences, and other body experiences. Primitive games of exchanging objects, peek-a-boo and the like contribute to the capacity to manipulate the environment, and to know what to expect from it. At the same time vocalization is also increasing rapidly and with it, vocal interplay with adults.

The continued development of differentiating capacity generally results in a new ability to differentiate his mother from other women who now become stranger by contrast, just at the time that he is exposed to many other new sensations from the environment and from his body. The expanded world, combined with his increased capacity for differentiation, greatly increases the hazard of overstimulation; he exposes himself to more than he can integrate, or respond to in an integrated way. He may become fretful, not just because he is teething but because he is somewhat frustrated by his inability to cope with all of the newness his expanded awareness and capacities put before him.

Quiet, equable infants, of moderate drive, well-balanced development, free from special sensitivities, may go through this phase serenely. But sensitive infants, like Susan, Terry, Ronnie, in this group, appear excited, restless, fussy, or irritable, quite apart from the specific threat of anxiety at intrusion of a stranger, or at loss of the mother at this time.

This phase, often critical for "separation anxiety" or loss of mother, is a complex stage, where the threat is probably not due simply to the emergence of the new capacity for differentiation of mother from stranger, but where this occurs against a background of complex challenges which may be difficult for the infant to cope with, quite apart from the new discriminatory capacity. In fact, our records, along with those of K. Wolf,[33] Leon Yarrow,[34] and others, show that the discrimination between mother and other persons often occurs much earlier. It may be threatening only when the total context of the baby's world as he experiences it from new angles of vision and new sensory contacts is shifting, and places new demands for perceptual differentiation upon him at a pace he cannot completely master, and which therefore lead him to need the support of his mother with special urgency.

6. In the next phase, the latter part of the first year and early part of the second, locomotion in terms of walking introduces a period of wobbly uncertainty, often culminating in vivid expressions of triumph and delight as the struggling infant succeeds in walking by himself. This eager pleasure in mastery, first glimpsed in the infant's response to adult recognition of his evocative efforts at the four-month phase, is repeated as language develops and as he discovers the magic power of a word to bring what he wants from a comprehending adult. Both locomotion and language bring many hazards in their varying impact on infants with different zones of sensitivity, levels of stability and resilience. Some infants refuse to walk again for some time after an accident due to failure to maintain balance.[35] Speech may be interrupted if a trauma occurs during its emergence.

At the time that the infant is exposed to new vistas for exploration, and new possibilities for communication and cognitive mastery of objects through attaching names to them, his sense of autonomy may be intensely augmented. He may, with delighted abandon, run from adults who complain they "cannot keep up with him," but have to chase him all day long. This goes on at the same time that the child is developing a new kind of control of his body, with the maturation of conscious sphincter control, and its accompanying exploitation by the adults for the development of cleanliness habits. Motor, verbal, and toileting modalities of assertion, rebellion, defiance, and withholding may appear all at the same time, in sequence, or in alternation. This phase brings common hazards of rigidity when the child stubbornly defends himself against adult pressures at a time when he is savoring a new capacity to "do it myself."

Coping efforts in the second year of life

The children in this research group were not studied in the second year of life, but in order to illustrate some of the everyday problems of dealing with the environment faced by a child who is in the highly transitional phase between infancy and the independence made available by mastery of speech and locomotion, we can draw on the record of another child observed periodically from birth to ten years.*

* This summary based on LBM's records on this child.

Greta, at fourteen months, had many wishes, needs and interests; she did not talk much and had few words. But she communicated a great deal, with considerable expressiveness and motor agility. Waking up in the morning she pointed at the window shade, looked toward her mother and motioning upward, indicated that she wanted the shade to be pulled up, then she stood up in her crib, leaned far over the edge, and pointed down to indicate that she wanted to get down. If she was picked up without being offered anything to eat she became restless and when asked, "Do you want a cracker?" nodded her head vigorously, with wide approving smiles.

She used many different methods of getting around. She liked to walk and to dance but crept upstairs on her hands and knees. In the yard outside if she felt insecure on a piece of rough ground she used the sit-creep locomotion that she used before she could walk. Sometimes she played kitty and doggie and crawled on all fours, more in fun than as a real method of locomotion.

When she heard rhythmic music, either sitting or standing, she kept time with her back, swaying or jumping or waving her arms, or dancing in a circle of her own. Being danced was a source of delight.

She loved "Ride a cock horse," and somersault games and would initiate them by climbing onto an adult leg and jiggling up and down, leaning backward or making other appropriate movements.

She liked to feed herself, and like any other fourteen-month-old baby, smeared food on her face and bib and tray as she did so. When her mother brought out the washcloth Greta happily swished it around in the tray to "help" in the cleaning up.

One day she was in the car with her grandparents; Greta was next to her mother who held her tiny baby brother in the back seat. She started fussing and poking at her grandmother who asked, "Do you want me to come back there and hold you?" She nodded her head excitedly and smiled; when her grandmother moved back and took her on her lap, Greta leaned back and went to sleep.

When an adult was sitting in the living room reading, Greta came in, turned the knobs on the radio until she found some music, trotted over to the adult, began to dance, then raised her arms, asking to be picked up and danced. She seemed thrilled when this was understood and the adult responded.

She liked to give. Whenever she had a cookie or a cracker she took a bite, then offered the adult a bite, then took another herself. She accepted substitutes easily when something was taken away from her.

She was very eager to maintain contact; it came naturally to her, and in moments when she felt doubtful about a relationship, when an adult was preoccupied or expected something from her which she did not understand, or was on the verge of disapproval, Greta would smile in a rather forced, squeezed-up grin and squint as if to say, "Let's keep everything cheerful, shall we?" Very different from her spontaneous smiles, this forced smile was used in a definitely manipulative and controlled way: it was Greta's device for trying to keep the world in a good mood, and avoiding strained relationships.

As a younger infant she had shown evidences of skin sensitivity and at this age, she did not like to have her face washed and her hair combed. But she accepted the fact that it would be done (protesting while it was going on, shoving the washcloth away from her face), in the sense that she forgave the adult after it was over and did not hold a grudge. She put up with it with minimal protest when a soft washcloth was used in small quick dabs that did not cover her whole face at one time. Evidently she did not like the feeling of not being able to see, when her face was covered with the washcloth all at once.

Once when a piece of dirt was removed from the tip of her nose she fussed, but when it was shown to her she made brushing motions on her hair as if perhaps to say, "Yes, I know it is one of those things that has to be done to make me look nice."

She wanted to do as much as she could by herself, and in general was independent. In new situations when her mother was near she ran around and around like a little dog, exploring and touching everything until she made herself at home. She took things out of boxes, shelves, or drawers, or off of tables, as long as she could find anything new. But when limits were set she respected them: When an adult said, "No, no," as she started to pull out the encyclopedia she refrained from completing the act, and when another adult later said "No, no," about other books lying on the coffee table, she ran to the encyclopedias and smiled, pointing to them without touching them, looking up with a knowing smile as if to say, "I'm not supposed to touch these either, am I?"

Left without her mother in a situation where strangers were present, she would hunt for a familiar person, reaching to be picked up, hiding in a shoulder and peeking around while she observed the new person.

She handled her jealousy of her baby brother in various ways. When she saw him in bed with her mother she rushed to her mother's side with hugs and kisses, jumped up and down and pulled at the bed until her mother took her into bed too. Observing his penis, she took a small stenographer's rubber finger-guard and neatly covered the penis; another time she tried a thimble. Then she ran around pointing to her umbilicus and those of other children as if to say, "This is something we all have."

Playing with a favorite kitten, she patted, hugged, and fed it, pulled its tail and lugged it around by neck or stomach; the kitten usually came back for more.

She enjoyed other children and liked to explore them, patting, poking, rubbing them all over, putting her finger into their eyes or mouth.

When she was given painful ear treatment by a doctor, she reproduced the procedure on grownups, even to the extent of selecting the comparable ear. This pattern of turning a passive experience into an active one was typical of her.

Mild bumps she could take in her stride with a perhaps proud grin. When upset after a more severe hurt she was responsive to being comforted;

after a brief dance or song or moment of play her cheerfulness was restored. She was very empathic to the distress of others, and quick to sense their moods. Once when an adult made a comment to Greta's mother about a difficult experience, the child caught the tone of voice and ran to the adult, throwing her arms around the adult's neck, kissing her as if to offer comfort.

This was a direct and expressive child as well as an active one. Another little girl, with equal motor skill, was both more and less direct in coping with her feelings about a new baby. At first she climbed on the bed and hit the baby. After her mother had several times restrained her, substituting gentle patting motions for the attack, Sandra focused her attention on her own baby doll, repeating in elaborate detail what she saw her mother do with the baby, although at seventeen months she could verbalize nothing more than "night-night" as she tucked the baby doll into its crib following a long sequence of caretaking activities.

These illustrations are enough to demonstrate the roles of many devices we have described in older children which develop rapidly as motility becomes available, although we do not mean to imply that all children would show all of these patterns at the same stage.

Residues of early struggles

By the age of two and a half to three years, at the time when we first saw the children whom we then studied to the age of twelve years, the residual attitudes, coping styles, and devices, developed during these successive phases, presented us with the highly individualized patterns we have glimpsed. Only a minority of children in this normal group had come through this sequence of critical phases with all of their coping resources intact. We can see that in human infants development is so complex, and the precise variations of parallels among emerging functions so different from one child to another, that we have to be careful to avoid oversimplifying of the sort which we tend to do when we follow models developed from lower species. The crucial aspect of a critical phase may be the interaction of emergent functions within the child, not just the relation of stimulus offered by the environment to the demands of the emerging function. It is this internal interaction which may determine the infant's capacity to cope with the new impacts of the environment.

Throughout the growth period and to some degree throughout life, especially for those most affected by the pace of change in today's culture, new challenges occur, with their new difficulties and threats of failure, along with their new potential gratifications. Even within the limited span of the first ten or twelve years, we have seen marked changes in the capacity of some of the children in the group we have been studying to deal with the new opportunities and risks they confronted at different points in the developmental span. Others, but a minority in this group, have been remarkably consistent in their approach to each successive stage; these are chiefly the children of smooth, well-balanced development, moderate drive, and affective response, who are also free from developmental stresses caused by illness or by severe disturbances in their families. For such children the impact of new demands, we may infer, is less severe and energy for new integrations is maximally available. At any rate, their flexibility within the range of the continuity of their style of development is maintained, and their coping methods and defense mechanisms do not freeze their capacity to develop new solutions to the new problems they confront.

From this point of view, it is important for those concerned with a child to be alert to specific periods which constitute a critical phase for a given child—periods characterized by indications of loss of the accustomed capacity to cope with environmental opportunities and pressures typical of the phase. It is, similarly, important to be aware of the specific focus of sensitivity or coping difficulty for the given child; in the anal phase, the motor relations to the environment may be threatened in one child; another child may be affected in the development of language and concept-formation connected with it; in another child, smooth gastrointestinal functioning may be threatened. Each child has his own table of problems emerging from the exchange between his specific nature and his particular environment.

Emergence of defensive processes

With some children, whose parents were teasing, punitive, or in other ways aggressive, rigid defensive patterns developed in the first years. By the age of two or three years, defensive processes have gone far enough so that some children (for example, Martin in our group) develop a pattern of anticipating blame, protest, accusation, or punishment from the adult and forestalling it by (1) projecting threats to the adults, and (2) acting in a way which takes into account the possibility of their threatening behavior. Even when there is no objective evidence that a specific new adult is hostile, the child retreats to a safe area where dangerous activity will be avoided, in this way taking no risk. In other words, early experiences of exchange of hostilities leads to a pattern of anticipation of threat from the grownup. This can become an intrapsychic device which operates automatically and autonomously, finally emerging as a "defense mechanism."

In the early stages of turning away, denial, repression, and projection, we can see the steps in the baby's actual behavior. After an end product such as projection has been repeated to the point where it becomes crystallized into a mechanism, the child does not go through these steps and the pattern can seldom be broken. In exactly the same way, other higher units are established which then become autonomous and capable of incorporation into still more complicated configurations of response; the defense mechanism has become an autonomous response pattern.

By the age of two to four years, all of the children in our study group had already developed a repertoire of such patterns—defense mechanisms which played their part in the total resources of coping used by each child. This was true regardless of the over-all level of happiness or adjustment or prognosis of future comfortable development as seen by the psychiatrist. Furthermore, the most normal and happy of our group of children drew upon defense mechanisms as part of their total strategy for coping, with considerable flexibility and with changing emphases over the period during which we observed them. We saw the sequences in coping with fear of thunder which showed Molly's way of progressing by a series of steps in which defenses and overt efforts were combined (pp. 178-179). We noted that the cognitive mastery and the denial were both important in the total process of coping with fear of thunder. As we reviewed through the sequences, one defense mechanism yielded to another and her projection of fear onto her little brother was essentially another form of denial, or was used in the service of denial as part of the total process of outgrowing her fear.

As we follow the development of such efforts to master fears and other stresses on the part of our children, we are struck by the flexibility with which they used defense mechanisms along with overt defensive maneuvers as part of the total coping strategy. This flexibility includes the capacity to use one mechanism at one time and another later, as well as the capacity to use different ones together, when they are needed. An important point in relation to Molly is that she was not an inhibited, withdrawn child who was unable to deal directly with the environment. She was very direct in her ability to seek comfort from her sister, to go to her parents' room, or to actively snuggle into bed herself. The intrapsychic defense mechanisms did not appear as substitutes for these active efforts or as a result of failure to make active efforts but rather went hand in hand with her active efforts as part of her total progress in coping.

Up to this point we have dealt with the development of defense mechanisms in relation to defensive operations. We saw a continuity between the baby's first efforts to turn away even through such a limited act as shutting his eyes or turning his head, and his later efforts to turn away bodily, efforts to deny and repress, and then his subsequent patterns of denial and projection. We can speak of the emergence of defense mechanisms as autonomous response patterns which have developed by a series of steps from primitive overt defense operations, but which, once reaching a state of effective operation at an intrapsychic level, function automatically without going through the preliminary steps.

We cannot see the whole process adequately, however, unless we also look at the defensive use of ego functions which are a natural part of the child's total cognitive, motor, and affective development. Normal babies who are not hungry, sleepy, or in pain respond with varying degrees of vivid interest in visual, auditory, tactual stimuli as fast as their neurological development provides the equipment for responsiveness to the stimuli of the outside world. Babies differ widely in their use of such stimuli. The analysis of records of our children as infants shows wide differences between the tendencies of certain babies to pay more attention to faces and to people than to things, or to pay more attention to colorful, shiny, and in other ways interesting objects in contrast to faces. Our knowledge is not at a point where it is possible to stand on firm ground in any theory regarding the basis for such differences in eager excitement about and response to things as compared with faces. Preference for things may develop like other preferences from very specific patterns of stimulus-gratification by people or discomfort in contact with them; or from deprivation of contact with people. Controlled studies of differences between babies whose first oral gratifications come through being nursed, or being fed while held cuddled and smiled at by the mother, as compared with babies who are played with very little, or are fed by bottles held on mechanical bottle holders, might contribute something to the understanding of this difference.

Whatever the factors are which contribute to spontaneous preferences for things (in the manner of engineers at the adult level) there is also evidence for defensive *turning to* objects which can be selected, managed, and controlled more easily than people can be managed. The child's management of his relations with the environment involves the selection and orchestration of both impersonal and personal stimuli with a view to keeping over-all stimulation at an optimal level for him, and finding the materials he requires for use of his own equipment and satisfying his own needs. The first five years are the time when his basic pattern of managing stimulation from the environment is established, during the emergence of fundamental ego functions, affects, and drives.

NOTES AND REFERENCES

1. Lorenz, K. The nature of instinct. In Schiller, C.H. *Instinctive Behavior.* New York: International Universities Press, 1957.
2. Hilgard, E.R. *Theories of Learning* (rev. ed.). New York: Appleton-Century-Croft, 1958. This is an important review of major principles of learning including conditioning.
3. Sokolov, E.N. *Perception and the Conditioned Reflex.* Moscow: Moscow University, 1958 (expected English translation).
4. Hartmann, H. *Ego Psychology and the Problem of Adaptation* (Tr. by D. Rapaport). New York: International Universities Press, 1958.
5. Piaget, J. *The Origins of Intelligence in Children.* New York: International Universities Press, 1952.
6. Hebb, D.O. *The Organization of Behavior.* New York: John Wiley, 1949.
7. Spitz, R., Hospitalism: An inquiry into the genesis of psychiatric conditions in early childhood. *Psychoanalytic Study of the Child,* Vol. 1. New York: International Universities Press, 1945.
8. Mittelmann, B. Motility in infants, children, and adults: patterning and psychodynamics. *Psychoanalytic Study of the Child,* Vol. 9. New York: International Universities Press, 1954.
9. Macfarlane, J., Allen, L., and Honzik, M. *A Developmental Study of the Behavior Problems of Normal Children Between Twenty-one Months and Fourteen Years.* Berkeley: University of California Press, 1954.
10. Freud, S., Inhibitions, symptoms and anxiety. *Standard Edition of the Complete Works of Sigmund Freud,* Vol. 20. London: Hogarth Press, 1959.
11. Spitz, R. *No and Yes.* p. 125. New York: International Universities Press, 1957.
12. Freud, S. *Beyond the Pleasure Principle. Standard Edition of the Complete Works of Sigmund Freud,* Vol. 18. London: Hogarth Press, 1955.
13. Bergman, P., and Escalona, S. Unusual sensitivities in very young children. *Psychoanalytic Study of the Child,* Vol. 3/4. New York: International Universities Press, 1949.
14. Ramzy, I. and Wallerstein, R. Pain, fear and anxiety: a study in their interrelationships. *Psychoanalytic Study of the Child,* Vol. 13. New York: International Universities Press, 1958.
15. Levy, D. The infant's earliest memory of inoculation: a contribution to public health procedures. *J. Genet. Psychol. 96:* 3-46, 1960.
16. See my Preventive implications of development in the preschool years. Chapter 10 in Caplan, G. (ed.) *Prevention of Mental Disorders in Children.* New York: Basic Books, 1961.
17. Marquis, D. Can conditioned responses be established in the newborn infant? *J. Genet. Psychol. 39:* 479-492, 1931.
18. Skinner, B.F. *Science and Human Behavior.* New York: Macmillan, 1953.

19. Sokolov, E.N. *Perception and the Conditioned Reflex*. Moscow: Moscow University, 1958 (expected English translation).

20. Mittelmann, B. Motility in infants, children, and adults. *Psychoanalytic Study of the Child*, Vol. 9. New York: International Universities Press, 1954.

21. Heider, G. *Vulnerability in Infants and Young Children* (to be published).

22. James, W. *Principles of Psychology*, Vol. 2, p. 398. New York: Henry Holt, 1890.

23. Freud, S. Three essays on sexuality. *Standard Edition of the Complete Works of Sigmund Freud*, Vol. 7. London: Hogarth Press, 1953.

24. Erikson, E.H. Problems of infancy and early childhood. In *Encyclopedia of Medicine*, Vol. 12. Philadelphia: F.A. Davis, 1945.

25. Benjamin, J. Lecture to Topeka Psychoanalytic Society, January 26, 1961.

26. Spitz, R. *A Genetic Field Theory of Ego Formation*. New York: International Universities Press, 1959.

27. Ribble, M. *Rights of Infants*. New York: Columbia University Press, 1943.

28. Greenacre, P. *Trauma, Growth and Personality*. New York: Norton, 1952.

29. Benjamin, J. Made this statement in the course of a discussion of a lecture on "The Innate and the Experiential Indevelopment" given at the Topeka Psychoanalytic Society on January 26, 1961.

30. Escalona, S., and Heider, G. *Prediction and Outcome*, pp. 154-164. New York: Basic Books, 1959.

31. Bridges, K.M.B. Emotional development in early infancy. *Child Development, 3:* 324-341, 1932.

32. Klein, M. A contribution to the psychogenesis of manic depressive states. In Klein, M. *Contributions to Psychoanalysis*, pp. 282-310. London: Hogarth Press, 1948.

33. Wolf, K. Observations on individual tendencies in the first year of life. In Senn. M. (ed.) *Problems of Infancy and Childhood*. New York: Josiah Macy Jr. Foundation, 1952.

34. Yarrow, L. Maternal deprivation: toward an empirical and conceptual re-evaluation. *Psychol. Bull. 58:* 459-490, 1961.

35. Shirley, M. *The First Two Years*. Minneapolis: University of Minnesota Press, 1933.

☙☙☙ 15

COPING STYLES

WE THINK OF COPING STRATEGY as a specific behavior sequence—however simple or complex—used to deal with a specific challenge or type of problem. Individual differences in drives and equipment, and discrepancies between developmental levels in different areas have been visible at every stage of observation of our normal group. These differences interact within the child and with the environment; the result is coping style expressed in different sequences of steps toward mastery, the development of different strategies and uses of them. A given child may develop a large range of coping devices and strategies or he may limit himself to very few. The total range determines his coping *style*.

Most of these children came from families of several children; in five families there were two children in the study, and in many others we were acquainted with one or more of the children closest to the one we studied. Rarely did the siblings have similar coping styles.

While Steve was from early infancy one who turned away, Sheila was a protester. Chester at four and a half years was stoical while Ray tended to regress under stress. Trudy absorbed herself in activity with puzzles and other nonpersonal objects, but Molly refused to come without her mother. Vernon was constricted and reserved while his brother Mervin was outgoing and spontaneous. Donald was initially a detached observer, his older brother a friendly participant. In all of these instances each child's coping style can be seen as the outcome of predispositions in the child interacting both with the early and contemporary handling by the mother and relationships with other members of the family; experiences personal to each individual child had also helped to evoke individual ways of feeling and responding. In this book we cannot present a full account of all the factors contributing to a child's style of dealing with the situations in which we observed them. We are focusing here on the task of presenting the role of certain basic constitutional tendencies interacting with certain basic patterns of environmental impact.

Individuality of style can be seen best when we look at the development of a few children from infancy. Three kinds of development of coping styles can be illustrated: First, styles which appear throughout childhood to be shaped by configurations of drive, activity level, sensitivity, and tolerance levels visible in the first six months of life, and dominated by the child's own constitutional tendencies which either never met, or which won out over, severe pressure from the environment. Second, we have seen styles which emerge from the confluence of constitutional tendencies and environmental influences going in the same direction. Third, we see more complex patterning of style when the child's own natural inclinations are deprived, blocked, repressed, or in some other way defeated, so that coping methods are developed in layers, which include complex defensive patterns. These in turn make it increasingly difficult for the child's natural tendencies to find expression. We shall illustrate these several kinds of development of coping style in the following pages.

We can begin with two children in the same family: the robust and forthright Sheila with whom we became acquainted earlier (pp. 81 ff.), and her softer brother Steve (two years older), as quiet and easy-going as Sheila was direct and forceful. Despite their differences the infants shared a tendency to be disturbed by loss of autonomy, as when an adult interfered with activity instigated by the child and at a later age, blind analyses of Rorschach tests commented that these children "could not be forced into a mold." Their mother was very permissive with all four of her children.

The children were two years apart in age; Steven was the elder.

Each one had been seen at the age of four weeks in infancy, at which time precursors of their later styles were clearly defined: Sheila protested what she did not want; she terminated feeding decisively when she was finished; she demanded—and, as her mother later reported, "always" succeeded in getting what she wanted. Steve was by contrast a quiet, passive infant who, though he sucked efficiently, did not even withdraw his lips from the nipple when he had had enough, but let the milk dribble down his chin and chest. In both the positive and negative sense he was a child who tended to "take what comes" and this mode of response was expressed in the oral zone par excellence. He was never a go-getter. Sheila was sturdy, Steve was easily fatigued. Sheila's thresholds were high, Steve's very low. Throughout the ten to twelve years we have watched the two children, the decisiveness of Sheila, her firm stance, and her capacity to protest have continued to be characteristic while Steve has continued to avoid conflict or direct encounter with opposition. He has seldom been known to fight, because, as he said at the age of twelve, "I wouldn't win."

Of course, no two children in the same family are born into exactly the same constellation, or in exactly the same maternal situation; we observed certain differences in the infants' environments or relations to their mother which might explain part, though hardly all, of such clearcut differences in their behavior at four weeks. At the time of Steve's birth his mother was worried about the possible loss of her own hospitalized mother. When Sheila was a tiny baby, her mother was worried merely about finances and her physical condition. The father worked on a night shift; his work had changed by the time Sheila was born so that he was no longer working at night. We saw some important similarities first. With both pregnancies the mother had severe nausea during the first three months. Both deliveries involved long labor but were otherwise uneventful. Both were large babies weighing over nine pounds. Both times she described herself as loving babies, and both times her breasts literally overflowed with milk which sustained nursing until the child was a year old or more.

Both babies were rocked by the parents, and the maternal grandfather played with them so much the father was jealous. According to the mother, both she and the father were easy-going, but some other members of the family were different: the father's father was energetic and a "wonderful money maker." Mrs. R's younger brother was energetic; he planned to be an athletic director. He assumed some authority over the children and spanked them if they did not do what they were told to do. In other words, while there were specific differences, there was little evidence of gross difference in the family atmosphere at the times the two children were born. There was evidence, on the other hand, of widely varying stocks in the family line, contributing to differences in equipment and personality.

Here are summaries of each when seen a little under the age of one month:

Sheila seemed a "monstrously large baby." Her birth weight (nine pounds six and one half ounces) was, however, only a few ounces above that of Stevie. At four weeks she weighed more than twelve pounds. Dr. Leitch said that she could not remember ever having seen a four-week-old whose arms and legs were so rounded and firm. Her movements were forceful, jerky, and moderately extensive, and much of her behavior showed what seemed to be a characteristic vigor and definiteness. There was, however, little of that force in her sucking, perhaps because her mother offered the breast so frequently that she was rarely in a state of hunger.

She seemed to relate actively to the world, apparently focusing readily on people and showing greater than average interest in objects for an infant of four weeks. She seemed to have distinct preferences, responding especially to shiny and to red objects; she was more responsive to her siblings than to adults.

She showed only mild fatigue after the psychological test and within perhaps fifteen minutes seemed alert and rested again. She did not seem to mind strong stimuli, for instance, the ringing of a bell or fairly rough handling with which her sister tried to soothe her when she cried, and the mother did not report early sensitivity to loud sounds such as she had described in the case of Stevie. It was noted that in the face of strong illumination she closed her eyes and went to sleep instead of showing discomfort as some babies did.

Her capacity to respond to and evidently to experience the world in an active and fairly differentiated fashion did not seem to involve enjoyment. Her face wore a frowning, distinctly unpleasant expression most of the time. While she accepted the tests of tissue resistance she did not seem to enjoy this contact and frowned more when her skin was touched. She protested, crying vehemently, when she was laid down after being held. The impression was that she was "an infant who was not willing to put up with much and who was easily offended."

Stevie was in appearance a sturdy baby, weighing at birth nine pounds one ounce, and almost eleven pounds at the age of three weeks when he was first seen at the Well Baby Clinic. Except for an occasional tremor, his movements were unusually smooth and strong for an infant of his age, moderate in range and tempo. When undisturbed his facial expression usually seemed to indicate contentment.

He seemed so sensitive that Dr. Escalona described him as a baby who often seemed to experience fairly intensive stimulation as a kind of insult. His mother said that he minded wet diapers and had shown marked reactions to loud sounds and that he would jump if he was moved into the sunlight even when he was asleep. It was difficult to gain his attention either to objects or to social stimulation; but when he once responded he showed alert attention. In contrast to Sheila such attentiveness was soon followed by apparent fatigue, and such evidences of stress as an increase of jerkiness in his movements, heightened irritability, and whimpering. Changes of color came and went slowly.

Although he seemed to enjoy some moderate sensory stimulation, Steve seemed to avoid or to withdraw from strong stimulation even at this very early age, but it was not at first clear how much of his passivity was in fact a resultant of soft musculature and low tonus (which though not interfering with good coordination constituted a zone in which stress was shown) and how much was an acquired method of reducing environmental stimulation to his tolerance level. His infancy ratings on "adaptive" measures were lower than ratings on other aspects of his development. The presence of sensitivity in the auditory area from early weeks is suggested by the later development of musical interests which led to considerable competence with a clarinet by the age of eleven and a tentative plan to continue with music professionally to earn his living. (Perceptual clarity and differentiation were implied in his later very precise organization of Miniature Life Toys, beyond the level typical of most of this group, and within the confines of a limited area his play was unquestionably creative.)

If then we see Steve as a constitutionally sensitive boy, quiet, lacking in vigor and motor drive, with very little inclination to deal with frustrating situations aggressively, and comparably limited tendency, if not capacity, to discharge tension through motor channels, his coping style appears to be largely shaped by this equipment. He always avoided overt conflict, stepped aside when a fight was brewing as a school boy, and "kept out of trouble" consistently. Naturally, there was less basis for the development of guilty feelings about destruction as these are seen in some aggressive children who did get into trouble, received more punishment, and realistically had more basis for feeling threatened by their impulses. And, naturally also, he did have other fears, but they did not disturb the integrity of his thought processes. Steve kept the peace, and along with this managed to have some boyish pleasures—although he missed many colorful experiences he would have encountered through more active coping methods.

Steve illustrates a style of coping with environmental stimulation which is dominated by the child's tendency to maintain comfort at the expense of not striving to get as much as he otherwise might have gained from life. At the opposite extreme we find highly responsive children, like Susan and Jo Anne, whose orientation is toward getting as much as possible; their liveliness, zest, and initiative contribute to a high gratification level which may compensate for the discomfort or strain involved in reaching it. At any rate, when we evaluate the over-all capacity to cope with the opportunities and challenges of the environment in the sense of making maximal use of them, Susan and Jo Anne were rated high, while Steve and Vernon (who was also very selective and even aloof) were rated lower at the preschool level.

Many other illustrations could be offered of children whose coping styles seemed to be rooted directly in basic constitutional factors. These contributed to certain kinds of responses to "an average expectable environment" and certain ways of dealing with the tensions, conflicts, and needs to which these responses gave rise. The reader who is familiar with Escalona and Heider's *Prediction and Outcome* may remember Teddy, the stable, consistent boy whose behavior as a preschool child was (as we noted earlier) so well predicted by Escalona.

But if so, the reader will also remember Janice who was least well predicted, partly because her reactivity to environmental changes produced new behavior and partly because of subtle resources which had not been recognized in her infancy. We have to say that the extent to which constitutional factors, as seen in the early months, continue to dominate a child's coping style, depends partly on the stability of these factors or their resistance to change; it also depends partly on the range and strength of environmental influences, especially in relation to whether they work with or against the child. Pressures against the child can defeat his natural coping tendencies and force the elaboration of complex strategies which mask the original patterns.

Coping styles of two children with similar equipment and family influences

The interplay of constitutional equipment and drives with family patterns and cultural setting can be illustrated with children showing certain marked similarities.* Vernon and Sally had comparable I.Q.'s of 136 and 137 on the first series of preschool tests. Both children showed a down-to-earth practical judgment, superior vocabulary, and ability to express themselves in explicit, concise, if not laconic terms. Both were quick to understand and both made careful, sharp observations which contributed to their high test scores.

* Based upon a comparison by Alice Moriarty.

Both are middle children, each having both older and younger boy siblings and seeing themselves as part of a family of children; rivalry appears to be considerably repressed. Both come from similar socioeconomic backgrounds where life was moderately comfortable at what might be classified as the lower middle-class level; yet the families had to be practical and self-sufficient and work had to be continuous if they were to survive. Both fathers do skilled work with their hands. Intellectual ability was not valued highly in either of these families but each child had observed the father using his skills to improve the home: for example, Sally's father made the children a swing set, and Vernon's father built kitchen cabinets for their own home.

Both children usually exhibited excellent motor control in gross and fine movements; yet there was a wide range of degrees of smoothness of coordination. Some rigid movements and awkwardness in posture appeared when strain or pressure was felt. In both children strong locomotor and manipulation drives were noted in infancy; these were evidently reinforced by observations of their fathers' skilled manual work. Vernon showed especially good differentiation in movements involving fine muscles.

Parallel with their tendency to rely upon motor ways of coping, in line with their excellent motor control and locomotor and manipulation drives, both children learned to talk earlier than their siblings, although Sally's speech appeared to be infantile in enunciation. While Vernon was quite capable of expressing himself when he felt like it, he tended to be laconic. The fact that grammatical construction was rather poor in both appeared to be a reflection of the language usage in the two families; verbal expression was inferior to observation and conceptualization. Further, both children invested more interest in motor activity than in speech and relied upon it more readily despite their excellent vocabulary and high intelligence quotients.

Both children were in general emotionally undemonstrative at the preschool stage, with poker-face countenances and only rare expressions of delight or displeasure. When he was an infant Vernon's smiles were very rare, but then and later, when they appeared they seemed especially "meaningful" to observers. With both children, some autonomic signs of strain appeared in labored breathing and facial pallor under stress. Strong aggressive drives were not fully expressed, communication of pleasure was delayed, and considerable anxiety in each child seemed to inhibit more open expressions of emotion. This was true of Vernon as early as the age of twenty-eight weeks. Both children fatigued easily; and both showed inertia in shifting their attention while also persisting, even to the point of exhaustion, in completing anything undertaken.

Both children were unusually self-sufficient and autonomous in many respects, as their competence might lead one to expect, but even so they displayed a certain tinge of basic insecurity about the world around them. Vernon was from infancy anxious about strange situations. At the preschool stage both children seemed slightly distrustful. Sally at times had considerable ability to share pleasure and Vernon communicated a subtle warmth at times, yet with both one felt an unobtrusive way of maintaining distance from the adult. This was more marked with both children when they were in situations directed by adults of the opposite sex, Sally in Dr. Toussieng's session, and Vernon in his sessions with Dr. Moriarty and Dr. Murphy. With both children a relationship with a new person seemed to progress through definite phases characterized by careful watching, then accepting an activity while excluding the examiner, then including the examiner, then quietly sharing pleasure in the activity with the examiner.

Both of these potentially very able children have experienced strong feelings of being small and less able than their fathers. Perhaps as a method of compensating for this imagined inadequacy both of the children showed off mildly at times, Sally talking about her capacities while Vernon demonstrated them.

In a new situation both children tended to cling to an initial activity (such as a pegboard in Toussieng's session, or repeating similar drawings in the Moriarty session), perhaps as a way of establishing and staying within an area of security. Both children tended to explore, try out and vary activities only within a limited scope. Their play remained unintegrated in both the Toussieng and Murphy sessions. Responses to pictures as in the CAT and the Binet were maintained at an enumerative, descriptive level which, in such bright children, seemed constricted. They did not develop an ego-involved, affectively toned continuous story with logical consequences following a series of related events. Fantasy was thus not highly developed, or perhaps not easily communicated by either child.

Aside from these similarities the children differed in certain respects; Sally was more free to use the wide variety of toys in the Miniature Life Toy session, and in this way appeared to get more out of such experiences than did Vernon. This freedom in Sally was in such striking contrast to the consistent inhibition of girls like Rachel, Daryl, and Vivian that her rating on capacity to cope with the opportunities of the environment was higher among the girls than Vernon's was among the boys. No boy was more reserved or showed less gratification from his encounters with the environment than Vernon, despite his great competence, fine motor coordination, and capacity to manipulate objects.

We cannot say that socioeconomic level in and of itself, or being a child of a father who worked with his hands, was responsible for these similar constricted patterns, since other more emotionally expressive children, like Chester and Ray, came from equally low economic status. An important factor may lie in the mother's emotional relationship to each child: in both instances there were hints of dissatisfaction. Vernon was a third boy—his mother might have preferred a girl. Moreover, his sensitivity and reserve as a baby was in contrast to his mother's forthright vigor, efficiency, and somewhat teasing attitude. Sally's mother was glad to have a girl but wanted a more feminine doll-like girl to dress up. That is, there was a certain incompatibility or disappointment in the relationship, in contrast, for instance, with the unalloyed contentment of Chester and Ray's mother with her boys, in a considerably more economically deprived family.

In Sally and Vernon we have children whose initial tendencies (alert observation, motor skill, low affective expressiveness) were reinforced by the family life, and by the children's relation to each parent. Both children developed a guarded, selective, constrained approach to new situations and especially to the world of adults. With peers at the latency period they were well-liked and more spontaneous. Their motor skills were an asset and they were respected in their school groups. These were children whose coping style developed along a rather straight line, initiated by their early individual tendencies, but with an element of caution exaggerated by the subtle strains of the mother-child relation.

Deprivation and overstimulation as contributors to styles of coping

We mentioned above that a child's coping may be greatly influenced by handling which deprives or goes against the early needs or inclinations of the child. To see this, we can briefly describe Patsy's style which illustrates a more complex development. She was a baby of average activity and drive level, consistent in sleep and waking. Her development as measured in tests was well balanced. But at twenty weeks there were many evidences of a strong need for contact and tactual stimulation, along with strong oral drives. Her most delighted laughter followed upon Escalona's vigorous pull on the Taylor-tot in which she was sitting and her mother reported that Patsy enjoyed most of all roughhousing with her father. By contrast, we saw a four-year-old who seemed sensitive and tended to keep her distance so that she seemed at times isolated and shy, while showing highly differentiated visual perceptiveness on projective methods and an ecstatic response to aesthetic stimuli such as a musical toy.

What accounted for this shift? Without going into the rich in-tricacies of her development we can note here the role of her mother's fatigue when Patsy was a baby and inability to hold or cuddle her much, with the relative deprivation or contact-hunger which must have resulted. Patsy's mother was responsible and attentive insofar as she would smile at the baby or speak to her from a distance; this, we infer, stimulated the infant's investment in visual and auditory zones as areas of attention substituting for the tactual contact she naturally craved. Not only did she develop these intense responses in visual and auditory areas, but she herself withdrew, perhaps identifying with her somewhat distant mother, or relating to her by adopting some of her mother's ways, in direct contrast to her natural inclination toward physical closeness. It will not be surprising that this solution was only partially satisfactory, and Patsy remained one of the children who "liked to hang around mommy" into her school years beyond the time when most children were roaming autonomously over a wide territory. In other words, her unsatisfying solution of a basic and deep need led to a hierarchy of coping patterns, defensive in character, thus keeping her from the flexibility in development shown by other chil-dren whose coping styles reflected their natural inclinations.

Daryl's coping style had an even more complex background.* She was a premature baby and had a long history of illnesses; her dainty constitutional pattern contributed to the impression of frailty. Her mother combined solicitous protectiveness with exploitation of Daryl's prettiness; an emphasis on appearance made the infant an extension of her mother's highly narcissistic self-image. While the mother gave much attention to grooming her pretty, fragile baby, and hovered over her, she provided little social stimulation. Two younger siblings, the youngest a boy—close to her in age—threatened the symbiotic dependence of Daryl on her mother, and aroused strong hostility. Daryl developed in a self-centered way, accepting the emphasis on clothes and propriety; she continued to cling to her mother. She handled the separations enforced by the arrival of five younger siblings one after another by recreating this neurotically symbiotic relation with her younger sister—dominating, controlling, and defend-ing her. Daryl was dependent on her for a context in which it was pos-sible to be spontaneous. Outside the protective and releasing symbi-otic situation she appeared immobilized, mute, shutting out the adults; or she was passive, or expressed the wish to avoid impending de-mands; this may have contributed to a retardation of verbal and social development in comparison with her motor level. Her verbal responses were immature; social interpretations were limited. Another early

* Based on a summary by Dr. Heider.

factor must also be considered here: that everyone but her mother wore a facial mask as protection against infection when approaching her during her first two months of extrauterine life.

She could be extremely hostile and expiated the hostility by self-punishment—mouth-washing—after chewing the baby in MLT. Daryl at four showed various oral preoccupations, along with persistent anxiety and hostility and shutting-out patterns, and evasive, amorphous generalizing; but the group doubted that she would run into acute difficulty unless she encontered severe stress. Rather, they felt that she would continue to deal with the environment through re-creating symbiotic relationships with a mother figure and a younger sister figure, in the context of which she could achieve some security and spontaneity; being attractive and well-dressed would help her to do this easily. She apparently did this at kindergarten where the teacher reported that she was "the most popular child."

Brief flashes of spontaneity in certain situations suggested that she had potentialities for a more colorful, enthusiastic, or creative use of the environment. Her anxiety (accumulated from the infantile difficulties, repeated illnesses and the extended protection accompanying them, limited social contact, dethronement by and competition from younger siblings) seemed to be handled by narcissistic satisfaction in her own prettiness, and her abilities to either shut out, control, or to elicit positive responses from others. We may say that she has used dependence as a major coping device, in which she could be relatively secure and free. It is likely also that her hostility has saved her from a more extreme passivity which might have resulted from all of the protection she received.

The structure of a parochial school appeared to be satisfying and Daryl's beauty continued to attract the support she required. Gradually she became able to go to school without her sister by her side. But even at the age of eleven, when confronted alone again with the unstructured Miniature Life Toys setting, she was smilingly mute until a younger sister, Katrina, only four years old, was brought in. Now Daryl became the protective one, supporting, aiding, and abetting the younger child's ideas with an alacrity of which no hint had appeared before her little sister came into the room. At the end of the session she "generously" gave Katrina the small flashlight which had been provided for each older child. The infancy pattern was now reversed and Daryl had become the protective, symbiosis-inviting mother, making a place for herself in the environment by protecting and hovering as she had been hovered over.

Relation of coping styles to predicted variables

In Escalona and Heider's *Prediction and Outcome*,[1] the following basic group of capacities and tendencies were predicted correctly, as judged by themselves, in from sixty-five to ninety-five per cent of these children: (1) motor coordination and development, activity pattern and range, activity level, freedom and use of space, motor habits; (2) attention, concentration, involvement, decisiveness, and goal striving; (3) complexity and intensity of affects, and expressive behavior; (4) perceptual sensitivity and intake, intelligence level and pattern; (5) interest patterns and play patterns; (6) fantasy and imagination; (7) appearance, demeanor, and reaction of staff to the children; (8) sex role acceptance, sex conflicts, oedipal conflict, relationship with siblings.

Of these, the first six groupings rely heavily on the assumption of probable continuity of characteristics of functioning observed in the first six months. But Escalona's predictions also took into account the mother's handling of the infant, the family constellation at the time the infants were seen, and the characteristics of the physical environment and ecology of Topeka. We can say that precise observations of qualities of perceptual, cognitive, motor, and affective functioning, and of the infant's responses to impersonal objects and to people permit a psychologist experienced with infants and children and familiar with the environment and the parent-child relation to predict accurately some aspects of the child's later style of functioning and probable coping approaches.

In addition, certain other inferences were based on such assumptions as these: infants who were immature or awkward in their motions and who showed relatively greater interest in inspection and exploration of the environment by looking than in physical activity were expected not to excel in the latter. The later development of fine coordination necessary for skillful manipulation of objects requires the capacity to delay responses to stimulation, and to modulate direct motoric expressions of impulse. Where this capacity for delay was not seen it would also not be expected that a child would later develop a high degree of fineness of manual coordination.

Similarly, thinking, concept formation, and the development of solutions to problems depend on a capacity to delay; these would not be expected to become a major basis for a child's coping style if the infant was highly impulsive from the beginning. In addition, babies whose behavior was explosive and who responded with acute distress and tension to restraint of movement would not be expected to grow into children who easily learned to stand delay, or were able very early to give up immediate gratification of needs. Such factors have a major role in shaping the child's coping style.

All predictions were made with knowledge of the cultural norms in this area, so that a tendency would exist to predict behavior congruent with the cultural norm except where factors had been observed which would tend to produce contrary or deviant behavior.

A major factor in the failure of less successful predictions was the failure to foresee adequately the extent to which a child might later be able to outgrow early vulnerabilities—through improved health, his own drive, and persistent effort toward mastery, or insightful and resourceful compensations for limitations. Karen and Roddy were conspicuous—among the children who appeared most vulnerable in infancy—for their ability to gain strength during the childhood years. Karen as a baby seemed unable to protect herself from external stimulation and pressures; impersonal objects were not satisfying, and she could not get enough social, tactual, or oral satisfaction. Roddy's high drive and low sensory thresholds, with low capacity to select and exclude stimuli, created an intrinsic coping problem in infancy; this was augmented by his autonomic reactivity and loss of motor integration under the stress of overstimulation. Yet, by the time of the preschool parties, both of these children had developed an impressive capacity to enjoy the opportunities that were offered. In both instances, the child's own high drive—supported by a basically stable family life, whatever its specific frustrations to the child—found a way to take hold of life and get satisfaction from it. We can see a somewhat similar development in Jo Anne and Ronnie, who also had strong drives. And even Janice, with her many handicaps as an infant—and, in various ways, unfavorable environment—was able to use the environment much better than expected as a preschool child, and still better at a later level.

The lowest level of confirmation for Escalona's predictions occurred for basic attitudes to self and to the world; responses to unfamiliar situations; shyness; achievement needs and competitiveness; thematic content of free play; internal psychic mechanisms in response to frustration; and relationship with mother at the preschool stage.

This does not imply a lack of continuity with tendencies in infancy—it could result from failure to observe precursors of some of these factors as well as the earlier well-predicted ones were observed; or failure to judge accurately the probable resultants of interacting factors; or failure to anticipate shifts in the mother's attitude as the child developed; and especially to the impossibility of guessing the impact of unforeseeable experiences (favorable or unfavorable) in the next few years of the child's growth, as well as the effects of decrease of deleterious health factors, and improvement resulting from the child's own efforts as we illustrated above.

The role of perceptual sensitivity in coping style

Because perceptual sensitivity determines to a considerable degree both the scope of the stimulus pressures upon the young child and his awareness of resources he can draw upon in meeting his needs and implementing his interests, we shall pause for special consideration of its role. Twelve children in our group were rated by Dr. Heider as sensitive infants. Interestingly enough, nine of these were also rated high in drive and two were average. Only Steve was rated as highly sensitive and low in drive. It looks as if the typical pattern is one of generalized vividness of response of the organism to the environment. This intensity is expressed both in a lowering of perceptual thresholds and a heightening of drive and also activity level. From this point of view we do not expect passive or "quiet" children to be as involved perceptually with the environment as more intense, vivid, active children. If we now consider the different groups of children, according to drive and sensitivity level, we see that among those with balanced development which provides the child with maturationally comparable equipment in the major areas (as defined by Gesell) we find certain similarities. Greg, Roddy, Jo Anne, and Susan (all children of high sensitivity, high drive, and good developmental balance) tended to initiate activities, to evoke responses from others, to control situations, or to make them different. They left their own stamp on any situation they entered, even as infants.

Children with high sensitivity and drive but low balance—who, therefore, had complex patterns of strength and weakness—were highly individual in their coping styles. In Part I (pp. 104-105) we saw Martin's need to find a safe area, Donald's need for more time than most children required. Terry used both verbal and motor techniques to concentrate on solitary activities of his own choosing. Brennie sometimes seemed to throw out a smoke screen of manners and of fantasy to keep relationships where he wanted them.

Children with markedly low sensory thresholds (or high sensitivity, since sensitivity is high where threshold is low) were evenly divided between those whose mothers were anxious, tense, unstable or in other ways might have contributed in obvious ways to the sensitizing of the baby, and those whose mothers were unusually relaxed, permissive, and giving (Chester, Steve, and Donald), or who were actively aware of the baby's needs and responsive to them as well as apparently well-adjusted (Ronnie, Martin, and Susan). Children who reach clinics are often both sensitive themselves and have anxious, tense mothers; this has tended to lead to the assumption that the mothers cause the child's sensitivity. But there is a flat contradiction here to the hypothesis that low thresholds in the baby are necessarily a resultant of anxious interaction with the mother. It might be suggested, however, that unusually gentle mothers give the baby minimal occasion for the development of defenses against stimulation, and this may tend to stabilize thresholds at a low level when the infants are initially sensitive.

The reader will remember Donald's extremely slow, cautious orientation pattern (pp. 100 ff.). This becomes intelligible when we also see that from infancy he was a child of low thresholds; a certain amount of stimulation was pleasurable, while too much became distinctly unpleasant; the child had a narrower range within which a tactual stimulus was pleasant than did many other children. Thus he had a tendency to find tactual stimulation, at least, both pleasurable and a source of discomfort. This "pleasure-pain ambivalence," as we shall call it, was also observed in quiet Steve and seclusive Martin. But cautious reserve or distancing, both of which could protect such children from the danger of overstimulation were not used by all such children. Jo Anne, Chester, Roddy, Susan, and Brennie were all as infants observed to show this pleasure-pain ambivalence—in contrast to Molly, Ray, Patsy, and Ronnie for whom tactile stimulation appeared to be generally pleasurable. Jo Anne and those mentioned with her used masterful selective or manipulative techniques to keep stimulation from the environment at a level they wanted. They could seek more, or move out of the field, evoke or reject stimulation.

We got hints as to reasons for the different choices of ways to deal with the threat of overstimulation, or unpleasant stimulation, when we saw that Donald and Martin, at least, had very low levels of balance, with adaptive functions as rated on the Gesell scale lagging behind language and personal-social functions. We can infer that this vocal and personal-social responsiveness would tend to evoke responses from people which might easily become overstimulating. And since their adaptive resources were less adequate for their age, they were unable to do much effectively to avoid overstimulation except to develop the cautious reserve we have seen, used by Donald chiefly at the beginnings of unfamiliar situations. By comparison, Chester, Roddy, and Susan were all exceptionally well-balanced in their general development, with all resources at a superior level. They were, then, much better equipped to deal with the potential threat of their sensitivity and of their ambivalent pleasure-pain responses to tactual stimulation. Steve and Jo Anne, who are exceptions to this last generalization, were both seen at the age of four weeks, when we have less basis for evaluating adaptive-motor development. This was the area considered to be lagging in both children. (It is important to note that at the preschool level Steve though quiet was considered very smoothly coordinated though still a quiet child, and Jo Anne's motor achievements were outstanding.) Brennie, the other exception, was advanced motorically, which probably contributed to the development of masterful manipulative orientations. But it is interesting to see that while his language was considered less advanced at that time, he developed into a very talkative child.

Another factor of great importance in the child's interaction with the environment and way of managing it is the range of modalities in which sensitivity occurs. Roddy, of all the infants, showed the widest range—sensitivity in auditory, visual, and taste areas being observed in addition to tactile sensitivity. Moreover, this was complicated by digestive difficulties, susceptibility to infection, and fatigability, thus placing him among the children with difficult vegetative functioning. These experiences could be expected to add to the pain and discomfort from external stimulation, further discomfort from within his own body, and to reduce the usual infantile narcissism or sense of well-being expressed by the robust child. Frequent illnesses might also be expected to increase autonomic variability. All of this together could be expected to make him dependent on help from the mother to balance his discomforts with positive feelings. Since infections come and go he might have experienced alternations of comfortable and uncomfortable times, which could contribute to the variability related to instability in autonomic functioning.

In such a child we can see several sources of difficulty which would add to the problem of managing the environment. If, as we find in actuality, he was also a child of high drive as well as well-balanced equipment, we would expect to find tendencies toward active control of the environment; at the same time these illnesses and sensitivities would tend to make him dependent on his mother for her help and comfort. Thus the pleasure-pain ambivalence noted in the area of tactile sensitivity might well be just one point of ambivalence among several, including strong love-anger feelings toward the mother who would be associated both with pleasurable and with painful experiences.

We can see, then, a broad foundation for, or multiple precursors of, later ambivalence in personal relations as well as toward the environment generally, aside from the tendency toward ambivalence rooted in the double pleasure-pain sensitivity we noted at first. Such a pattern would almost inevitably call for a variety of ways of managing the environment and would put a heavy burden on the task of integration and acceptance of different feelings about himself and about the environment.* With less strong drive or lower activity level we could have expected him to have to handle stimulation by some forms of distancing device.

We cannot exaggerate the great difference between the tasks of management of stimulation encountered by such a child in contrast to children like Sheila, Barbie, Sally, and Diane, who had a robust start, with easy vegetative functioning, high sensory thresholds and thus relatively few sources of discomfort from within themselves or from their own contributions to interactions with the environment.

Rigidity, as contrasted with the free use of distance devices in the process of selection of stimuli, was part of Daryl's pattern, and of Darlene's and Martin's; here, with different antecedent experiences, was great hostility, and it was only where considerable hostility was kept under tight rein that we found such rigidity in our own admittedly small sample of children. Daryl and Darlene had the most hovering restrictive mothers of the group. With Daryl this was associated with the early frailty and illness of the child. With Darlene intense religious commitments required strict limits. Martin's hostility was directed to a more active, physically strong brother a year older with whom he was locked in the grip of bitter rivalry, intensified by the factors contributing to ambivalence and hostility which we discussed above (p. 335).

Children with high drive as infants but early low sensitivity included Sheila, Lennie, Karen, Gordon, Diane, Sally, and Tommy. We cannot describe the later behavior of these children as a group because some of them had a large proportion of disturbing experiences of different origins. Lennie and Tommy suffered illnesses which lowered their vitality and auditory acuity, but both were responsive to help and resilient. Gordon suffered the most severe environmental threat but was able to maintain his ability to respond to adults who were interested in him. Karen was relatively deprived of gratification for her strong contact and affection needs partly because her mother had become pregnant again when she was only two months old. Sally's mother had an emotional disturbance which led to her absence from the home for some time. All of these children with high drive and low sensitivity compared to others were able to make continued efforts to maintain rapport with people; Lennie, Karen, and Gordon were

---

* Some aspects of Roddy's development are discussed in S. Escalona and G. Heider, *Prediction and Outcome*, pp. 221 and elsewhere. The infancy ratings quoted here are from G. Heider, *Vulnerability in Infants and Children*, to be published. An extended discussion of Roddy will be included in L.B. Murphy, and collaborators, *Vulnerability, Stress and Resilience*, in preparation.

conspicuous for their ability to use relationships with adults in coping with their difficulties.

Most children of low drive in infancy (Steve, Vivian, Ralph, Ray, Barbie, and Vernon) did not reach out for or actively seek stimulation as did the previous group. They did not tend to restructure the environment. They "adapted" in the passive sense of the word, chiefly going with the tide, not initiating activities, nor controlling the adult, nor actively trying to make things different from the way they were. They enjoyed certain aspects of each situation in their own way but did not aim at increasing the level or range of gratification.

All of them but Steve were considered by Dr. Heider to be relatively low in perceptual sensitivity as well as drive; since Steve was seen at four weeks it was not clear whether his tendencies to ignore stimuli were an expression of low sensitivity or of defenses already developed against stimuli to which high sensitivity exposed him. Assuming that it was the latter, Steve and Teddy were the only infants with high sensitivity who also showed a marked tendency to delay response in infancy. Steve had low drive, and Teddy moderate drive, and it may be important to note that both boys, though at very different levels in their capacity to respond to a wide range of opportunities of the environment and in their alacrity and forcefulness as people, were contained, and well-organized, and both came through the first twelve years of childhood with a high degree of consistency. Both showed a capacity to cope with the environment in ways that contributed to their tolerance for the stimuli it offered and avoided pressures which might threaten their integration.

Children of average drive and marked sensitivity included Molly and Chester as well as Teddy. All of these we have seen to be active, flexible, and resourceful in dealing with many of the new situations in which we saw them. Like the high-drive, high-sensitivity children, they left their mark on each situation in which they appeared. Each one was a definite, strong personality. But this group of average drive and marked sensitivity also included Patsy, Daryl, Cynthia, and perhaps Rachel—children whose capacity to make use of the opportunities we provided were limited in different ways. Each of these had special environmental deprivations or pressures to which they responded by different kinds of resentful withdrawal. They did not show the capacity to struggle actively with deprivations as did the children, like Karen, observed to have higher drive as infants. Without high drive, high sensitivity tended to produce withdrawing tendencies, and little effort to develop active, direct methods of dealing with the environment.

Without further examples we can see here something of the early backgrounds for devices of managing stimulation: shutting out stimuli that come at an unwanted time, by turning away so as not to see, covering up ears, protesting; rejecting habitually stimuli that cannot be handled successfully; diminishing or terminating stimulation that is too much for pleasure, or after satiation; or in greater extremity, destroying or attacking painful stimuli. On the positive side of stimulus management we see the beginnings not only of choice and selection, approach and seeking, but of techniques for evoking response, getting more of interpersonal stimulation as well as impersonal stimuli; restructuring or merely organizing stimuli to enhance the satisfaction from exchanges with the environment.

We see, then, that styles of dealing with the environment are formed in the process of these dealings and take shape from the intake equipment, the output capacity, and the integrative pace and level of the child at a given time, and interacting with each other and with the environment.

We referred earlier (p. 295) to Freud's concept of "stimulus barrier" as a feature of the ego which limits the amount of stimulation; research in the 1950's, following earlier demonstrations by Spitz and others of effects of inadequate environments, has pursued the problem of too little stimulation or stimulus deprivation. Most of these experiments have sought generally applicable conclusions about effects of stimulus deprivation.

In the records of these children we look from another angle at the individual differences in stimulus need, and its relation to styles of dealing with the environment, drive for contact with new stimuli in relation to capacity for gratification; tolerance of stimuli; and capacity to manage, structure, and integrate stimulation from the environment. From this point of view we can see that the average expectable amount of stimulation is more than some infants and young children can handle while it is insufficient for others. Thus the area of management of stimulation, whether eliciting more of it or selecting and reducing it, is not only a basic coping task, related to sensory thresholds, sensory need, demand, or drive, and integrative capacity, but is central for shaping the coping style.

We see then that the interaction of the organism-environment level of mutual influence (due to drives and sensitivities on both sides) and the child's economic situation (needs, capacity to discharge tension, thresholds for and tolerance of tension) and the total dynamic setting, especially the mother-child relation, tend to determine both the coping problem and the pattern of the response.

Basic determinants of coping style

We have given special attention to drive and activity level, sensitivity, and developmental balance as rated from infancy data in children whose later style of dealing with the environment we have been observing. Other groupings determined by differences in autonomic reactivity, or in abilities could be followed in the same way. We can now suggest a series of patterns or models of styles dealing with the environment.

1. Children of low sensory sensitivity, low autonomic reactivity, low drive, and good developmental balance will function smoothly and naturally with moderate encounters with the environment, ease of control, mild gratification, and little compulsion to obtain more intense or a wider range of satisfaction. Their ease both of gratification and of control will help them to avoid guilt and hostility-arousing conflict with the environment.

2. By contrast, children of high sensitivity, high drive, autonomic reactivity, and good developmental balance will make active, vivid, quick contact with opportunities, maximize their use of them with a wider range of coping techniques, and show evidence of a high level of gratification. But their high drive will lead to more conflictual encounters with the environment. Other things being equal, the flexibility and adaptive resources implied in their good balance will help them to solve the problems resulting from these conflicts, with a resulting frustration-gratification balance on the positive side. But the greater tendency to get into conflict with the environment is apt to lead to a more complex emotional life, more fantasy.

3. When high sensitivity and high drive are accompanied by developmental imbalance, the danger of unpleasant sequelae of encounters with the environment will be greater. If the high drive precludes a capacity for delay, a child may deal with these possibilities by cautious or slow entrance into new situations, a tendency to be selective and to maintain safety within a narrow range. But gratification will be pursued energetically within this range and can be intense when difficulties are mastered.

4. When high sensitivity is combined with high autonomic reactivity (especially with slow recovery), and with high drive but marked developmental imbalance involving deficiency especially in the adaptive areas, the child will have great coping difficulties; he may have difficulty in the use of delay, selection, and other ways of controlling the impact of the environment, and be prone to disappoint-

ment except when he finds exactly the right scope for his areas of good equipment.

These hypotheses could be extended, and should be, on larger groups. For the present they are important as illustrating the interaction of different factors in a cluster, to produce an individual style of coping with the environment.

NOTES AND REFERENCES

1. Escalona, S., and Heider, G. *Prediction and Outcome.* New York: Basic Books, 1959.

16

ASPECTS OF ACTIVITY
AND PASSIVITY

IN THIS NORMAL GROUP that we studied, marked limitations in the child's capacity to make active efforts occurred chiefly among children who were from infancy very quiet or passive, who had low drive, or were easily inhibited. In addition, a child who had been a premature baby who was much hovered over, and a child whose infantile eczema had seriously limited activity during the period of development of motility, lacked initiative during the entire growing period, especially in new situations or when faced with new opportunities. Some of the children we observed to be quiet in infancy—such as Vernon and Sam—had active siblings; we have no evidence that the quiet behavior was induced by the mother's handling. Sam's mother was relaxed and permissive and her ways gave freedom for Sam's sister Sheila to be as vigorous as Sam was permissive. In other words, constitutional tendencies in the child himself, as well as major developmental impacts connected with the handling of health problems by the environment, were of chief importance in the activity-passivity patterns. Most of the children who had been infants of average or more drive and activity level (and were free from severe illnesses) continued to deal with the environment in active ways, although from latency on we found continued modulation of early impetuousness in Susan, Karen, Molly, and Roddy. When we studied relationships between infancy patterns and preschool behavior we found statistically significant correlations between such specific infantile expressions of an active attitude as the "capacity to protest unwanted foods," "terminate after satiation," etc., and the later preschool tendencies to "fend off pressures from the environment" and to make other active coping efforts.[1]

Thus, while many differences in constitutional tendencies such as autonomic stability, affective intensity and range, subtlety of perceptual differentiation, and others contribute their share to the coping style of a child, among the most basic is the difference in activity pattern. We shall discuss this here because our data may help to clarify some of the confusions which sometimes appear in discussions of activity and passivity.

In the infants in our research group we find impressive differences in activity level in terms of the over-all amount of motor activity during the four hours of observation; and in zones of motor discharge, some babies are more active with legs or arms or both while others do more rolling and turning with their bodies; in area of activity, some infants move through very much wider arcs than others; in tempo and rhythm—some babies move quickly while others move in a slow and gentle way, and some move in smooth, regular rhythms while others move in more staccato rhythms; in the vigor or force of activity, some infants are mild although they move through as wide an area and with about the same tempo, while others seem to be discharging much more energy, moving in a very forceful way; in persistence of activity as contrasted with alternating periods of activity and passivity—of course, all infants have to alternate activity and passivity to some degree but these alternations are more frequent and more dramatic in some infants than in others. All of these different aspects of vigor, tempo, smoothness, area, zone, and so forth go together to color each infant's own style of activity, and thus of coping with the environment, as well as level of activity. Many different qualities and degrees of activity seen in these babies suggest that the following distinctions need to be made. We may see babies as generally active in contrast to being quiet, as Margaret Fries[2] described many years ago. Quiet babies like Steve do not move a great deal and are also not apt to be highly demanding. When they do move their activity does not have the forceful, energetic, or staccato quality typical of some other babies.

We do not find an opposition between activity and an oral orientation. Activity is often contrasted with the passive-receptive orientation assumed to be involved in oral functioning, but it is interesting to note that when we are observing young babies it is not always easy to abstract qualities of oral functioning as distinct from other response tendencies of the organism. Demand level, persistence of goal-orientation, capacity to protest or terminate, and degree of gratification appear in the oral area parallel with the same kinds of response in other areas to a considerable extent. Of course there are infants like Patsy with moderate activity level and high oral drive and also children with low oral drive and high drives in other directions, but by and large the enthusiastic feeder is also an enthusiastic baby. Babies with high oral drive are typically active feeders—they "go for it," "work at it," "stick to business."

Those infants who feed with gusto generally respond in other modalities with similar vigor. Similarly a baby who is passive in the oral area is apt to be passive when seen in other contexts. For instance, Steve as a quiet baby protested little, never terminated feeding decisively and seemed passively receptive in his feeding in contrast to Sheila, who made clear demands when she was hungry, terminated feedings when she had had enough, and in general was decisive in the oral area, although not greedy, engulfing, or aggressive. Steve continued to be a "quiet" if very well coordinated and in many ways smooth-functioning boy. Sheila continued to be decisive.

We mentioned above our statistically significant correlations between infantile capacity to protest (as when offered disliked foods), as well as capacity to terminate feedings, and later capacity to fend off the environment; we found comparably significant correlations between autonomy in the feeding situation permitted by the mother, and later autonomy in coping with the environment. Here the oral or feeding situation can be regarded as a situation with major reinforcing potentialities; whatever style of activity has been experienced as part of a gratifying feeding situation tends to become established as at least a tentative pattern for coping style generally. In Erikson's terms,[3] the mode of behavior in a given zone tends to become a mode of response to the environment.

This is quite different from looking at "activity" in contrast to an "oral orientation" as if there were actually a contrast. In our group the most active babies included some of the babies with highest oral drive who used one or another sort of activity for direct food gratification, for body satisfaction, for comfort under stress, or as a means of facilitating recovery and resilience at times of extreme fatigue. At the adult level we can see this in the vivid people who accomplish a great deal, are very interested in the world around them, enjoy people very much. They also enjoy their food, drink, and smokes with equal enthusiasm, and readily use these for direct satisfaction, for relaxation, for facilitation of social intercourse and for comfort and tension release, as some of our active children like Susan used oral pleasures.

Passivity has many aspects and roles—it is universally a resting orientation necessary for all the babies and children at certain times. When resting and sleep are associated with preliminary and concomitant gratification of sensory needs or welcome release from overstimulation this like other experiences may be reinforced. Passivity may be seen as a receptive orientation, an attitude of waiting to see what is going to be done, waiting until things are brought to one. In this sense, Rachel is passive since she does not initiate activity but responds to overtures from the environment. A controlled orientation in a quiet child like Vernon may be confused with passivity although his psychic orientation or attitude is highly selective—he is by no means indiscriminate in the way in which a passive orientation would imply. Very refined cognitive operations are going on all the time even when he is not active in a motor way. Such a child might be considered to have a highly economical pattern. Everything he does is precise and functional; he never wastes energy. His preliminary explorations are typically visual rather than motor, and he does not engage in potentially wasteful trial and error activity. When he goes into action each move counts.

So far, then, we have observed that what may roughly be regarded as "passivity" may actually have the functional value either of rest, of waiting until the structure of the situation has been made clear and opportunities are explicitly offered, or of economical use of energy. These are different from the receptive drinking-in orientation of the child who may stand quietly absorbing, with much satisfaction, sensory, perceptual, and emotional cues from the environment. That this is not necessarily a psychically passive process, however, is clear from such cases as Joyce[4] whose creative productions were much more rich and complex when she came to the point of externalizing what had been in the process of getting integrated during weeks of sitting in the sandbox in nursery school. The very highly receptive child may need long periods of quiet in order to permit maximal openness of the senses to the surrounding world, and also the necessary time for the absorbing, and for the integrating which precedes the often unusually original products of such a child.

Neither in activity level nor drive level, as rated by Heider, were girls noticeably more passive than boys as infants in this group, although by the preschool age only Jo Anne was as much interested in running, jumping, and climbing as were the most active boys. Here we are talking about the pleasurable use of motility rather than actively directed coping efforts which were, as we have seen, typical of many girls.

We have not yet referred to "feminine" passivity at all, and when one is dealing with infants it is not easy to recognize such a quality as typical of girl rather than boy babies in general. Certain delicately built, dainty, mild little girls like Vivian who seem typically feminine may fit into the group of gently moving, mild-activity children we mentioned above. Actually, in our group, there was no girl baby who was more "quiet" or passive than the quietest boy baby, Steve.

However, a startling difference between girl babies and boy babies is hinted at in our study of the nursing patterns. Certainly with many of the boys the mothers treat the nursing situation with a high degree of respect for the boy baby's autonomy; her attitude of "come and get it" and of following his rhythms of starting and stopping tend to build into the infant boy in the very first six months of life an expectation that he can be autonomous, which provides a foundation for later freedom to be active in a masculine way.

The girl babies are more hovered over, more fiddled with; their clothes are arranged more; and with them the mother is more apt to take a "mother knows best" attitude, imposing a pattern on the girl baby which leads her to learn that she is expected to conform, to follow, to fit in. The most outstanding example of this was Daryl. There are conspicuous exceptions, as with Sheila, whose mother took the attitude from the first that this baby girl knew exactly what she wanted; the mother seemed to enjoy this quality and respected her protests. Molly and Susan were others who were given a considerable amount of autonomy. By contrast with the girls who accepted the dependence imposed by their mothers, Sally, whose mother wanted to treat her baby daughter in a feminine way, demanded and obtained independence.

If we relate the observations above to other research data such as those from the Strong Vocational Interest Test, the Terman-Miles Masculinity-Femininity Test, etc., we could see that our data are by no means inconsistent with the latter; that is, it looks as if there is an enormous overlapping in what popularly is called "masculinity" and "femininity," with few girls who are outside of the range of the quiet boys generally and only a small number of boys who are more active than the most active girls. The question arises then whether the feminine-passive attitude is not, as Margaret Mead suggests in her volume *Sex and Temperament*, [5] to a considerable degree a culturally inculcated orientation rather than a biological given, manifested through differences in drives and expressed in part by differences in activity level.

We also tend to think of tactile sensitivity and related sensory drives as part of an oral, or a passive, orientation. Our data do show explicitly that tactile sensitivity emerges as a more important variable for girls than for boys in our sample. If we put this alongside of the point just made, that mothers, according to our cultural orientation, tend to let even very young infant boys have their rope, as it were, while baby girls are handled much more, we can see that from birth more tactual stimulation is given to girl babies. This tactile responsiveness also appears in our data to be related to the affect depth, if not affect range, characteristic of the little girls as compared with boys.

Looking at this in a slightly different way, we can say that if girl babies are handled more, dressed more, and confined more, etc., they are also being exposed more to a kind of stimulation from the environment which evokes sensory experience and affect. If, at the same time, they are limited, not given the opportunities for motor discharge, exploration, and tasting of the environment (as well as in a few cases not having the capacity for motor discharge which the boys have), we can see the basis for low thresholds of affective reactions and for expressive discharges as well as internalization or somatization of these. In other words, we might hypothesize that the foundations of the so-called "passive" feminine pattern of coping are laid in the combination in early infancy of greater tactual stimulation and evocation of affect, combined with limitation of vigorous motor discharges. Our data repeatedly show the greater use of affect in the girls' coping.

While the infants with a high activity level such as Lennie, Brennie, and Terry were also very active preschool children, we also saw children like Karen and Janice who were not so active as infants, but who became very active during the following years. By contrast, certain moderately active infants became less active as children of three and four years. These increases and decreases in activity level expressed differences in ways of dealing with frustration or other stress: certain children became more active, in response to frustration, while others seemed to lose energy and become less active.

The way in which the active children spontaneously leaped over terrace walls at the party, climbed the huge lion and bear statues at the zoo, and raced up the diving tower in the park showed a degree of coordination achieved through years of wide roaming range and other opportunities for free movement available in their neighborhoods. Ecology, then, along with constitutional factors, contributed to the level of activity in these children.

So far we have not said much about the relation of aggression to activity, although it might have been implied in the vigorous protests described in some infants—both girls and boys. It is worth enlarging on this for a moment. Vigorously protesting infants will protest a taste they do not like, will protest when they are satiated, etc. In other words, they exercise active controls of the kind and quantity of stimulation which they are willing to accept.

Beyond this, some of the infants even as young as four and eight weeks were very decisive and clear about postures which they would tolerate and those which they would not accept. For instance, Lennie simply would not stay in a prone or supine position even at the age of four weeks, but insisted upon being held more or less vertically. Years ago, when first observing this in some babies, we thought it was associated especially with the desire of babies to be able to see more and more interesting things, since obviously when held in a vertical position they can see the objects and people in the room much more adequately than they can when lying on their backs or on their stomachs. However, in the Escalona-Leitch records this occurs in some babies who do not have a strong visual interest; other aspects of the baby's freedom for movement and interaction with the environment are probably involved here as well. For instance, when held in a sitting position, the baby can move his arms around, can explore the mother's body; he has more interesting parts of the environment to get into contact with than he has when he is lying down, either prone or supine. It might even be that babies can also hear better when held up in a sitting position than they can when they are lying down, often with one ear buried in the mattress.

We have seen that the degree of selectivity, vigor of choice, decisiveness, and general capacity to insist on having the opportunity to relate to the environment in the way in which the baby wants to relate to it are expressions of very young babies (as young as at least four weeks if not earlier), expressions which imply an active orientation to the environment. Occasionally one can see a baby during the neonatal period vigorously bat away covers encroaching on his face. Such acts have not been recorded much in the literature, probably because of the fact that people who do experiments on infants are watching them under certain limited conditions which preclude the opportunity to see this kind of thing. Or if the observers did happen to see it they were still impressed by the relatively uncoordinated fashion in which the baby moves, and relegated the event to the general category of "mass activity," rather than observing the situation in which the baby found himself and what he did with it. By the age of three, four, or five months, we often see some babies reaching for the bottle or the breast with a kind of avid vigor or force which could be called aggressive. Here activity, aggression, and oral vigor are part of the same response.

It is also interesting to see that when we scrutinize the behavior of the babies it is very hard to differentiate anything that we could ascribe to a high aggressive drive as such, apart from such qualities of alacrity, vigor, activity and energy in feeding situations, response to toys, turning to and seeking the attention and care of the mother. The active interest in the surrounding world, pleasurable response to it, and capacity to make use of stimuli and experiences which are offered, are not considered by the environment to be "aggressive" except when a very insistent, demanding, screaming baby "gets the upper hand," and is regarded as a "little tyrant."

Most of the babies who showed steady, positive, stable interest, responsiveness, and capacity to be gratified emerge as children who, like Chester, do become able later to defend themselves in aggressive ways. Typically, these Kansas girls and boys, active as they were, were not aggressive at the preschool stage in the sense of "looking for a fight." Only two, Brennie and Donald, worked up a wrestling bout at the parties. As we have seen the children, they were typically cooperative, adaptable, capable of utilizing, finding, or offering substitutes, and they consciously controlled destructive impulses. Most of them did have some aggressive fantasy when we scrutinized the play records and CAT's and Rorschachs, that is, concepts of aggressive defense against the threats of the world. It was quite common for the children to show evidence of very strong feelings of being threatened by forces much greater than themselves, whether tornadoes, bulls, or snakes (all of which are part of the Kansas landscape) and they were often concerned about their limited power as compared with the power of the big, strong father who metes out the spankings or "lickings" when they overstep the limits.

It is, therefore, extremely difficult to talk in a simple way about differences in "the aggressive drive" as distinct from vigor and activity level and the experiences to which they had contributed in infancy. Since all infants do have experiences of frustration, or failures on the part of the environment to meet the needs of the baby, and since those with any spirit do protest or in one way or another defend themselves against intrusions or deprivations or failures or other rough treatment of the environment, we see how the aggressive reaction develops typically as part of the active exchanges between the baby and the environment. Whether there would be any aggressive reaction in the sense of destructive behavior in children who literally had not experienced frustration, we cannot say. Every baby may have greater or less potential for aggressive reactions, a potential which is "released" by one or another kind of violation of the organism or threat to the organism—such as excessive, painful, or uncomfortable stimulation, angry or hostile responses from the environment, etc. The best "copers" in our preschool group had already modulated their defensively aggressive responses sufficiently so that they were usually flexible and could be handled in such a way as not to jeopardize the next step in gratification or the next interchange with the environment.

Now we saw a small group of children, containing both boys and girls, whose aggressive fantasies and whose behavior in one way or another, whether active or passive, expressed a degree of hostility or negative rejecting feeling beyond that typical of the group in general. In every single instance of this sort there was some obvious, persistent and, for the child, insuperable frustration in the picture: for instance, the imbalance between Martin's nearly total gratification in his early infancy and his later frustrations, experienced as he moved into the world of his older brother and got into competition with him, was complicated by the intrinsic conflict due to the disparity between his verbal and intellectual interests and his relatively limited ability. Janice, the fifth and "menopausal child" of a mother in an unstable phase of her life, was never able to depend on consistent care, and developed skillful capacities to push other people around and get what she wanted in a demanding and aggressive way. Karen, "the odd one" whose mother "didn't quite know where she came from," in contrast to the other half-dozen children who seemed to fit into the family, chronically lacked the basic warmth, contact, and attention she craved; she was a child who showed extreme affect hunger and stimulus hunger, consistently doing things with objects and with people to stir up interaction, a kind of behavior which seemed aggressive to some, not all, of the observers.

We are making these distinctions because it seems very important to discriminate between the kind of overt activity which produces benign and welcome changes in the environment, appreciated by others whether child or adult, and the kind of activity which interrupts or bothers or hurts others. For instance, the active, stimulating quality of Greg, who could always start things going, attract others with his interesting, original ideas, keep things lively and in other ways function as a dynamic force in any social situation, can be compared at the other extreme with the annoying and even destructive activities carried on by Colin[6] at a period when he had to prove himself in terms of power after an illness which gave him a terrifying experience of helplessness. If we use the term "aggression" to describe both the capacity to move into the environment in an active, discovering, creating, and stimulating way which produces welcome results for other people, small or large, and activity aimed to destroy, depreciate, demote or which in other ways bring discomfort for others, small or large, we create enormous difficulties for our thinking. It seems much clearer to use the term "activity" as a general category referring to acts within which there may be constructive acts and destructive acts from the point of view of the object or the person who is affected by them. Hostility refers to the inimical orientation toward the object and may be expressed in aggressive activity. "Aggression" can mean almost anything from hostility to the vigor with which either constructive or destructive acts are carried out.

Greg was extremely active in the sense that he had a vivid, self-initiating, self-directing, and stimulating orientation toward the environment and capacity to participate in exchanges with it, but with little evidence of hostility or of aggression insofar as the latter implies destructive effect or intent, or even marked force.

In a more heterogeneous group of children, or a group which includes disturbed children, we see tension discharged through hyperactivity, disorganized activity, destructive activity, or poorly integrated motor expressions such as grimaces, etc. This type of activity was almost totally absent in the present group and probably distinguishes them from a disturbed or clinic group more than any other differentiation we could offer. At the same time we also see that control is used at times of stress in ways which can give the appearance of, or actually have the effect of, passivity.

We are apt to call "passive" those children who are easily inhibited by apprehensiveness and new situations, new people, demands for performance which go beyond their capacity, and the like. As we saw (Chapter 2), it was quite typical and normal for many of the children in new situations to seek physical contact with the mother, keep her near, hold her hand, play with parts of her dress or body. Here ordinarily we would refer to the necessary dependence of the young child on the mother in the sense that he needs her support when he is under stress and feels threatened. At the same time he is quite active in obtaining it and in making his own use of her in his own way insofar as she will let him. At this point then we have to distinguish between different expressions of autonomy: meeting the situation in a self-reliant, independent way as compared with actively seeking the support, help, and comfort of the mother in order to proceed with the approach to the new situation, an approach which may actually be quite active in its own way.

When the mother is not present, inhibition, and the passivity which it seems to produce, may continue for a very long time, as was true with Donald when he came to the party without his mother (pp. 100 ff.), and earlier when he came to the play sessions with me. Initially in these situations he could not make immediate use of physical support or assistance from a new female adult, but seemed to need a long time to "size up the situation" before he could move from his inhibited-passive orienting position to an active encounter with the situation and participate in the games and activities which were going on. Yet, when he became active, he was extremely active in the party—not only participating in the run-jump games on the steps and high walk apparatus but also tumbling, rolling over on the ground, and inventing his own forms of acrobatics. Despite the very, very long periods of "passivity," then, that were typical of Donald in new encounters or at times when he felt threatened, it would not be accurate to call him a passive child in the sense in which we described Steve as a passive child from earliest infancy in terms of his low energy and his very quiet way of handling himself and the environment. Donald's temporary passivity was in the service of goal-directed activity and represented a stage of orientation and effort toward cognitive mastery which he had to pass through before he came to grips with the situation overtly. This stage was shorter or longer depending upon how strange it seemed to him, how complex it was, and the degree of anxiety which it aroused.

Martin, by contrast with Donald, could be described as passive perhaps in the sense that he retreated to a quiet part of the garage when he came to the party, playing very quietly by himself, and not engaging in vigorous interchanges with the rest of the children. However, the likelihood that the inner picture was not consistent with an interpretation of a passive character was suggested by the fact that what he did in the garage was to build the tallest possible structure with the blocks available, with evident pride in his ambitious undertaking, which had the value of establishing himself in terms of competence and mastery within an area which he marked out for himself. In other words, looking at Martin, we think in terms of zones of activity and zones of passivity, and the need of certain children to differentiate the zone within which they will be active, ignoring the other areas where they may be called passive because of nonparticipation.

Ronnie, one of the boys who showed a great deal of apprehension in approaching new situations, was also inhibited initially and to that extent passive during the early phases of his entering a new situation, but moved into very vigorous activity including participation in the give and take among the boys. From infancy on he had his own style of retreating to passivity in a constructively regressive way to recover his energy before getting back into the struggle. His fatigability, like that of some others (Martin), seemed to be associated with a high degree of tension and some accompanying hostility and controlled aggressive feeling which he apparently carried around chronically.

We can then talk about the activity-passivity axis in terms of a number of variables: (1) energy level and constitutional activity level, style, scope, rhythm, tempo; (2) activity level in relation to the management of energy distribution in terms of needs for rest and alternating periods of motor discharge and restful quiet; (3) receptivity to the sensory, affective, and other cues from the environment; (4) passivity in the service of cognitive mastery; (5) passivity imposed by the culture patterns of the environment, as mediated especially by the mother in infancy; (6) passivity as a result of constraint imposed by medical problems or inhibition—this is the child's way of dealing with tension or anxiety-hostility problems which add to the threat he senses in strange situations. In dealing with the relation between activity and aggression, we pointed out the many different variants of activity and passivity which have nothing much to do with aggression, and the necessity for distinguishing between forceful expression of energy in creative or constructive ways and, on the other hand, those activities which involve threat to other people, whether of a mildly competitive or grossly destructive sort. We could also distinguish between aggressiveness and the sex drives of individuals who can be quite adequate sexually while showing very little of energetic or competitive drive to master other people in the environment.

Thus, active and passive tendencies do not seem to be mutually exclusive but seem to exist in different patterns whose configurations help to shape the child's coping style. Some of the strongest, most autonomous, vigorous, constructive, and independent males are those who most long for some loving appreciation and warmth. The term "passive wishes" does not seem to do justice to what is involved. It is passive in the sense that these boys or men want to be loved as well as to give love. Other types of boys or men defend their masculinity in terms of aggression at the expense of a total renunciation of tenderness. Nor does activity preclude tenderness in the children we studied. Lennie cuddled a big white teddy bear in his left arm while he was vigorously shooting a noisy gun with his right arm, in his play session. The cuddling was as important as the shooting, and the loving and shooting were two aspects of "activity."

Differences in activity-receptivity patterns

Very conspicuous in this group is the fact that activity is not polar-ized in relation to receptivity; rather, receptivity is a separate variable which may be high both in active and in quiet children. For instance, Greg and Terry, different as they are, are extremely sensitive, receptive boys with low thresholds for sensory responsiveness and impact of stimulation from the environment. In fact, it is easy to surmise that their high degree of receptivity exposes them to an amount of stimula-tion which heightens their activity level because of an increased need for discharge of tension. In other words, if they were less sensitive to the impact of the environment and less receptive, they might not have such a strong need for activity in order to discharge tension, on the one hand, and to manipulate the environment so as to keep its impact within manageable limits, on the other. Chester and Ray are interesting examples of boys both of whom are quite sensitive and receptive, while Chester is a high activity boy and Ray a more quiet child. Similarly among girls, Jo Anne and Susan are both very active girls and have been so from infancy, parallel with a high degree of sensitivity to nuances of social and sensory stimulation; the same is true of Karen. By contrast, Patsy is more moderate in activity, although in receptivity and sensitivity she is comparable to the others mentioned above. All of these girls would contrast with Diane, who is very balanced at a moderate level in respect to sensory thresholds or intake and motor reactions or discharge resources. Diane was one of the most balanced girls in the group at the infancy and preschool stages.

Relationships between activity and capacity to cope with the environment

Now, while we have seen that activity is not opposed to drive to gain oral pleasure, nor is a high activity level required for creativity or for a consistent masculine-role orientation, in our group there are certain differences in the development of the coping style of active and passive children which we have not yet discussed. Active childen come into contact with more aspects of the environment, have more opportunities to develop varied cathexes, relationships or interest, more choices, more possibilities of substitutes as ways of handling frustration, more experiences to use in trial and error solutions, more practice in skills, and thus more motor and affective resources for coping. Evidently it was for such reasons as these that we found positive correlations between activity and capacity to cope with the environment.

But the highly active child also encounters more obstacles and frustrations, risks more failures, and, like Susan, Jo Anne, and Greg, is more apt to keep going to the brink of fatigue and to run into the danger of loss of integration or control secondary to the lack of a margin of energy. Thus, when we consider emotional stability, we find an important interplay between the management of reserves of physical energy and the maintenance of psychic integration.

NOTES AND REFERENCES

1. Our statistical analyses are being presented at length in Murphy, L. B., and Raine, W., *Methods in the Longitudinal Study of Children,* to be published in 1963.
2. Fries, M., and Woolf, P. Some hypotheses on the role of the congenital activity type in personality development. *Psychoanalytic Study of the Child,* Vol. 8. New York: International Universities Press, 1953.
3. Erikson, E.H. *Childhood and Society.* New York: Norton, 1950.
4. Heider, G. *Vulnerability in Infants and Young Children* (to be published).
5. Mead, M. *Sex and Temperament in Three Primitive Societies.* New York: Mentor, 1935.
6. Murphy, L. Colin: a normal child. *Personality in Young Children,* Vol. 2. New York: Basic Books, 1956.

17

HEALTHY NARCISSISM
AND IDENTITY

WE HAVE SEEN HOW the baby and young child go through amazing sequences of learnings and relinquishments in the process of finding out how to get along in new situations constantly being presented by the environment. Babyish ways have to be given up almost as fast as they are formed, and a relatively limited proportion are incorporated into more enduring complex configurations. The mouthing of the six-month-old baby as a way of reality-testing is a thing of the past some months later, not included in more complex tactual and verbal reality-testing methods. What is left may be the residual trying-out effort, which expresses itself in manual activities—tapping, poking, rubbing, putting together—in the two-year-old, or still later in chiefly visual methods of reality-testing. That is, the coping efforts at any one stage contribute to the development of both skills and the drive toward further mastery in subsequent stages. These early experiences also contribute to attitudes toward or feelings about both the environment and the self.

Through his mouthing the baby discovers the many-ness of the world out there to be explored, the varieties of interest it can arouse, the range of satisfaction it offers; and he discovers himself as an active agent in exploring. In other words, what remains is the out-there-ness of many things, and the potentiality of putting himself in relation to that out-there-ness, and doing something to know it better—if not mouthing, handling—or just looking. This drive to go ahead and do something about discovering the infinite muchness of what is out there is still being expressed fifty or sixty years later in the avidity with which people now fly almost as fast as the speed of sound to reach within a few hours far corners of the earth and look, feel, and—to be sure—even taste the variety which it offers. The baby's way of coping with the outsideness and varying degrees of accessibility of the environment contributes to the development of his interest in it, his invest-ment in it, his lifelong concern with making it part of himself, and also his sense of himself as finding satisfaction in it.

Thus in this process he also discovers himself—he finds that it is he who can, with Terry, "know" many things exciting to know; with Susan, pick up more than one thing in one hand; with Diane, meet the demands of adults "very, very well"; with Molly, be brave "like the big kids." His satisfaction in being himself, his self-image, and his identity are constantly being shaped by his awareness of his encounters with and interactions with the environment, and his assessments of his own potentialities for dealing with it and the potentialities for satisfaction which it offers him. This is an individual process, as we saw in the preceding chapter.

Erikson[1] has discussed the ways in which the modes of dealing with drives originating in different libidinal zones become generalized as modes of ego-functioning. The baby learns not only how to get food —he learns to get whatever he wants. He learns in other words, about "getting" things. Similarly, his early experiences in making something happen, or making himself comfortable, or stimulating a response from the environment leave residues of modes of dealing with the environment which may be generalized beyond the immediate situation.

We saw that the process of orientation begins at least as early as birth and is a step in the process of devising ways of dealing with the stimuli offered by the environment. The baby pays attention to noises, lights, and voices in the first few days. What he dislikes he objects to; or he recoils. A tentative style of responding to and managing stimulation develops in the first weeks so that his mother says, "he likes" the sunlight through the leaves; he likes his orange juice but not his vegetables; he likes to sleep in the dark; he likes to be tightly covered; he likes faces, or lights, as the case may be. Already he has communicated preferences, he has succeeded in conveying the fact that certain things are satisfying and pleasurable and he would welcome more of them; he does not want to put up with certain other things. He is thus selective, insofar as the environment will "cater" to his preferences.

Each infant tends to have his own rhythm and tempo of doing the things that babies do. One infant pauses over his milk, to look around or to rest, or to smile at his mother; another keeps at it, not stopping at all until the bottle is finished. If his rhythm is interrupted, he has to deal with the interruption, and he may learn something about interruptions. He may come to expect them, to hate them, or to endure them. Just because he has been interrupted we cannot predict what his residual feelings will be, Roddy was typically interrupted by a loving, attentive, but not very flexible or perceptive mother. Is this connected with the fact that at twelve he was a gracious host, as if he had learned from his own experience how not to interrupt, but how to go along with people? Apparently he learned to give what he had not received. What remains then is a subtle and complex resultant of the multitude of aspects of the experience of interaction at any given time.

The role of coping in human maturation

Certain questions about maturation, learning, and mastery and their relation to motivation in the growing child may be answerable if we consider the relation of the coping efforts to these. During the entire process of development we are constantly confronted with the fact that children give up or abandon activities, ways of behaving, attitudes, etc., from one period to another. It is at least as much of a mystery why children outgrow and abandon response patterns as it is a mystery how they come to learn and develop them in the first place. Why do not children simply go on sucking their thumbs, crawling, or screaming? We may say that our rewards and punishments take care of the problem. Crying gets punished and being brave or not crying is rewarded. But where external rewards and punishments are not involved, economy of energy may be invoked. A child discovers by observation of other children or adults or by trial and error that another pattern is quicker or more efficient or more acceptable as a means of reaching a goal than the former pattern, which is then consciously or unconsciously rejected. Walking and runnning are faster than creeping.

In still other cases, the basic motivating need which supported a behavior pattern is reduced in strength as maturation brings new needs into stronger places in the hierarchy. Thus sucking, including thumbsucking, is not as satisfying or interesting after new motor and play gratifications are available.

But if we carry our observations down to the first six months of infancy, where external reward and punishment is not actually used very much by the environment, where the picture of economy is not so relevant since most of the needs of the child are met through the agency of the mother or some other person, and where the needs themselves are not changing much as yet—that is, during the period of eight to twenty-four weeks—we have to look for another factor which may also be relevant at the older stages once we have identified it. This is the element of effort or struggle. Struggling to hold up one's head continues to be satisfying until holding up one's head is not only mastered but integrated into other responses. After this time the baby holds up its head when this is necessary as part of a larger effort directed toward some other goal. The process of holding up the head in and of itself is no longer a stimulus. More obviously the process of turning over or rolling over is fascinating as long as it is a struggle to do so. The child works at it, keeps on rolling over and turning over, sometimes for a long period of time. After he has come to the point where turning over and rolling over may be done when necessary as part of a larger pattern aimed toward an external goal, it is no longer of interest in and of itself. We are all too familiar with the same general tendency in relation to, for instance, the period when the baby is learning to grasp and hold on to and let go, or the period when he has discovered throwing, or the period when crawling begins. With each of these new possibilities, the baby is preoccupied with the motor pattern itself as long as it involves effort or coping with an incomplete body function —that is, as long as the pattern is incompletely mastered. After the behavior becomes easy it loses interest in and for itself and is again utilized only as a means to end part of a larger coping pattern, or goal-directed motor sequence.

What we are saying here then amounts to the proposition that the struggle toward mastery has a motivating force of its own. The question may be raised: does this not belong under the general heading of aggression; but aggression must always have some object even when it is being used in a constructive as well as destructive sense. Coping in the sense of struggle toward mastery of skills is not necessarily a matter of doing something to anything outside oneself or to oneself, which is implied in aggression, but rather doing something *with* oneself. Observational records of infants contain many illustrations of the delight, or exhilaration and sense of exuberant well-being expressed by the infant with each of these steps in mastery. Each one adds to his reservoir of narcissism or pleasure in being and doing.

If coping or making an effort or investing some energy in the process of mastery is satisfying in and of itself, one corollary would be that objects which had involved such effort or investment of energy would have greater value than objects which did not involve such efforts. This hypothesis has been tested by Lila Weissenberg,[2] who demonstrated experimentally that children when offered a choice of two identical objects, one of which has been made by their own efforts as compared with one which might be slightly more perfect but involved no effort of their own, chose the object that had been produced by their own efforts.

It is not hard to see the place of this factor of effort in coping once we have identified it. Nature provides the equipment for many skills, for instance, but in the human being the skills are not actually polished up or fully available except through practice, often long practice. In the human young, not even such a basic and elementary skill as walking is automatic or well integrated when the structures are first mature enough to make it possible. Practice, effort, and willingness to tolerate failures are all involved before walking is mastered; all of this might be quite loathsome to the child unless the process of coping with incomplete functioning were satisfying in itself.

Another corollary would be that when complete mastery has been attained an activity will lose its motivating value in favor of another activity for which the maturational level of the child is sufficiently ready to make progress through effort possible but which is yet incomplete. Thus one would expect a child to prefer new, recently acquired skills to old and well-polished ones. This can easily be verified through relatively short-term longitudinal observations of any group of children and is in fact a major reason for the outgrowing of certain phases of intense absorption and interest. Such a phase of intense absorption typically accompanies the coping phase of the effort to master new activity.

The role of expression and discharge in the preschool years

In the preceding pages we discussed the role of making an effort, the capacity to keep on trying, to use the resources available in one's self combined with sustenance and support from the environment and the consequences of mastery and triumph resulting from these efforts. We found here that the retroflex effect of coping on development is more complex than is implied in the formula that function modifies structure, insofar as in this statement we tend to think primarily of motor skills alone.

What we have said so far fits with the everyday assumptions in our culture expressed in such maxims as "If at first you don't succeed try, try again." Such maxims were a heritage of the pioneer era in our culture when enormous value was placed upon individual effort. At an extreme this was expressed in the "let him sink or swim" policy.

A different contribution to an understanding of the relation of coping to development comes from a scrutiny of the role of expression and discharge of angry and fearful feelings in the preschool period: failure to express and discharge affect is related to vulnerability. The children who become more vulnerable, with the exception of those like Lennie who had severe illnesses, were conspicuous for their tendency to repress negative, hostile, and anxious feelings. By contrast only a small proportion of the children whose vulnerability decreased, or who held their own, were inhibited in this way. Susan and Karen among the children of decreasing vulnerability were quite open in expression of aggressive tendencies; Chester, Molly, Jo Anne, and others in the group who held their own were even more so.

We infer in the light of the total developmental picture of these children that in the preschool years as well as in infancy the child has too few verbal, motor, and social skills to permit modulated and socialized management of angry feelings in reaction to the frustrations and conflicts of this period. Successful discharge of anger, as we saw it with Molly in the preschool years, permits the child to liquidate resentments and the guilty feelings associated with them and thus to be capable of continued spontaneity and response to the emergence of new solutions both to conflicts and to external problems. In contrast, repression of hostile, angry, resentful, and guilty feelings as in Vernon, Gordon, Martin, and some others binds these feelings, ties up energy required to maintain the repression, and thus reduces the energy available for continued spontaneous problem solving. Along with this, he may be afraid to try his own methods further. Instead of achieving new and better coping techniques the child is burdened with a package of repressed hostile feelings.

Concretely, Molly's overt struggle and ready discharge of angry feelings toward her little brother left her free enough to begin to enjoy him when he became a companion who might be a source of fun, and then to use a mild form of repression through displacement, on the one hand, and the development of protectiveness, on the other. Karen's constant overt search for response, aggressive as it seemed to members of the study group, satisfied enough of her affect hunger so that gradually she was less driven by it, and was able to develop increasingly modulated and differentiated channels for her aggression while accepting the forms and manners expected by society around her. Similarly Janice's effort to make a niche for herself produced some odd and sometimes unpleasant results as a small child, yet left her free enough to use the new opportunities for participation in a social group at the prepuberty stage when her family moved into a better organized social situation.

What we see empirically, then, in the children who go through the preschool years in a setting of family life which persistently represents the demands of society—yet leaves the child free for internal awareness, feeling, and successful discharge of anger, and of other negative feelings and aggressive impulses—is that this process is accompanied by continued coping efforts characterized by increasing modulation and differentiated expressions of aggression.

We have been speaking here of motor and affective aspects of coping and their contribution to progress and development. We can add certain aspects of cognitive functioning which we have seen in the children who maintain or improve their coping capacity. We have already noted that the intelligence quotient as such is in this group less highly correlated with coping capacity than are warmth, resources for gratification, and flexibility. Of course if a wider range of I.Q.'s had been studied, the correlation would be expected to be higher; this group included only children of average intelligence or better.

To discover the resources which the individual may find useful in coping takes active exploration of the environment, either in motor or visual terms or both, since motor exploration is usually in the service of visual exploration. We noted the role of these steps toward orientation and familiarization in our early discussion of the children's response to new situations. We can add here that the constant effort at cognitive mastery of the environment, and the discovery of new possibilities, contributes both to the increase in the latter, and to a cathexis for the process of cognitive mastery itself. It proves worthwhile to know the score, to have ideas which could be put to use, and the "good copers" have a store of such concepts for coping. Children like Rachel who were confined to a narrow environment had fewer ideas of what one might do in problem situations outside of routine home events, as tested by the Engel Children's Insight Test.

It is obvious from what we have been saying that our division into motor, affective, and cognitive factors in the contribution of coping to development is highly arbitrary; at every point we have found all of these moving along together inextricably and contributing to each other. The motor explorations, surveys, and efforts contribute to attitudes of hope and confidence, on the one hand, and to knowledge of coping resources and insights into ways of problem solving, on the other. The motor efforts implicitly increase the skill of the child as repeated actions become more efficient and successful simply through their repetition (cf. Darlene), but could not take place without affective and cognitive support which are enhanced as the efforts themselves reach the expected goals. The effort to cope always involves an integration of what we, from our outside point of view, differentiate out into motor, affective, and cognitive aspects and contributes simultaneously to development as a whole which is not experienced in a piecemeal way by the child.

Effects of coping   *to tolerate stress*

Positive effects of coping are implied in the results of our statistical analysis of resistance to or freedom from a tendency to disintegration under stress. Here we find "competence," "courage," "capacity for free-wheeling attention," and the "capacity to use substitute gratification" as intimately related to freedom from a tendency toward disintegrative reactions. Also significantly related to freedom from disintegrative reactions are the "capacity to mobilize resources" and "accuracy of reality-testing" together with freedom from difficulties in relating to others, depth of relatedness, and social insight. "Positive self-feeling" is also found here.

We can infer that something like the following goes on: the child with stable positive self-feeling is apt to be able to maintain and to develop good relationships with others, and to sustain a flexible relation to the environment; this is expressed in perceptual freedom and courage, which together contribute to the capacity to mobilize resources including substitute gratifications. That is, the child with unassailable positive self-feeling is able to meet threats resourcefully, find solutions, and thus reduce the stimuli to disintegrative reactions.

The effectiveness of coping methods varied from a few children who repeatedly collapsed into tears, seemed heartbroken, became hyperactive, or immobilized, or in some other way lost ego control to the point of being unable to function without help from the adult, to instances where certain children were able to keep going under all of the conditions in which we saw them and who seemed very resistant to tendencies toward disintegrative reactions. A middle group of children were able to manage well under most stresses but had not yet developed adequate defense mechanisms to cope with acute anxiety or disappointment or conflict.

Being able to select or to control the part of a situation to which they could attend was important for certain children, and those who collapsed in the pediatric examination and in the body-photograph situation were faced with requirements which made any selection impossible—thus evoking a maximum sense of helplessness vis-à-vis the controlling adult.

Control of stress was implemented not only by selectivity in the situation, but by modifying the child's own behavior. Of our children, seven had at some time little or no capacity to control stress by delay, keeping their distance, and selecting the areas or objects to which they would respond; these were children who were either passively incapable of taking any stance at all and were therefore vulnerable to all stimuli, or they were impulsively active like Lennie and indiscriminately exposed themselves to difficulty by plunging headlong into situations.

By contrast, twelve others were frequently very definite in their efforts to control stress, by protest or refusal, or by manipulative efforts or by keeping their distance until they had mastered the potentialities of the situation sufficiently to move into it. We also saw children who varied from one extreme to the other, at times appearing to be stymied or overwhelmed while at other times they were clearly selective although never able to manipulate the adults or the situation as the above group did.

Very important here is the degree of control over motility—either low inhibitory capacity (as with Lennie), or low capacity to release motor responses under stress (as with Darlene), or lack of flexibility in shifting from activity to passivity and vice versa created difficulties in the child's management of himself and of the environment at times when a need arose to decrease the stress. The average level of activity seemed less important than the degree of ego control and flexibility in making use of whatever tempo and drive the child naturally had. For example, Greg was very active, Teddy moderately active, and Steve was quiet, but all three were able to handle themselves flexibly in contrast to highly active Terry, Lennie or Jo Anne, moderately active Roddy or Darlene, or quiet Rachel or Daryl. Thus "control" in our children involved both releasing and inhibiting capacities, and flexibility in management of both. The too easily inhibited and the uncontrollable have equal if opposite difficulties in selectivity, delay, distancing—approach and fending-off operations, and were thus less able to deal with the environment under stress.

Cognitive factors work hand in hand with motor factors and contribute to the degree of flexibility with which the latter can be handled. Certain children with high sensitivity to detail in the environment, like Patsy or Donald, required longer orientation times and periods of observation and survey before selecting parts of a situation to deal with; but Greg, Brennie, and Karen, also richly observant of detail and sensory qualities, had sufficient speed to orient themselves, make choices, and move into action fast, not only in contrast to the slow orientation time of Patsy and Donald but in contrast to the initial time-out for appraisal typical of most of the children. Our data do not justify speculation on factors involved in speed of visual orientation, since both the slow and fast orientors were children who were affectively sensitive and responsive and able to invest much interest in their exchanges with the environment. Further studies are needed to differentiate the steps between recognition of aspects of the environment, selection of portions to engage, formation of goals or intentions in the activity undertaken, and movement toward the goal—steps involving increasing integrative effort and allowing possibilities of delay or inhibition at any step.

That is, anxiety may intervene at the point of initial survey, if features of the same involve a threat; or at the point of selection, especially if prohibitions against touching or exploring have been strongly imposed at home; or at the point of goal formation if, for instance, possibilities of aggressive or other prohibited action are inviting and arouse conflict.

Delay in movement toward the goal may be related to discrepancies between goals and abilities as with Darlene and Diane, who on different occasions attempted motor achievements beyond their mastery at the time.

The effectiveness of such cognitive-motor integration depends on the integrative tempo of each system. Donald was slow in initial orientation but could be fast in action once he was oriented; Sheila was quick to grasp possibilities of a situation but had limited range of large motor capacities. Most boys in this group had high or moderate motor skill—only Lennie, Tommy, and, in relation to certain athletic feats, Teddy, were hampered in coping by motor limitations; by contrast, several girls—through severe external interference due to medical problems in the case of Rachel and Susan and restricted opportunities with Darlene, Diane, Daryl, and Vivian—were blocked in motor implementing of coping efforts. In all of these instances except that of Susan, energy and vigor were moderate or low.

These limitations in larger motor activities in the party and the psychiatric sessions did not apply to demands for motor dealing with small toys and other objects; Rachel, Susan, and Daryl had considerable skill and could express their ideas well here, in contrast to Sheila, who was less interested in the toy world.

In the group we studied, motor resources were not sufficiently varied among the boys to provide statistically significant correlations with coping adequacy; since infants with evidence of motor or any other defect were excluded, the lower end of a random sample was missing. In further studies we hope to include the children who were excluded from this original infancy group selected for normality.

Since statistical analysis of the motor variables was hampered by this limitation of the sample, it is especially important to recognize the extent and importance of the quality of motor dealings with the environment characteristic of most of the boys through the many experiences in which we saw them.

The role of triumph

We saw earlier many instances of the role of triumph or mastery in the development of a sense of capacity to cope with a challenge and threat. We saw Ronnie exclaiming that he could master the cognitive challenge, Darlene's "I jumped!", Susan's repeated assertions of what she could do, Molly's triumph in mastering fear. We also gave special attention to Ronnie's struggle for mastery of the all-fours position in infancy.

Susan, Ronnie, and Karen are three of the children who were judged by Dr. Heider to be less vulnerable at the preschool age than they seemed to be in infancy, and in view of the capacity for gallant struggle shown by these children especially we should pause to reflect on the contribution of success in coping, and the effort that goes into it, to development.

At an earlier point we noted the different ways in which investigators such as Piaget (observing infants and young children) and Sherrington have emphasized the principle that sheer functioning modifies structure. In everyday parlance, we say that success breeds success. This is more than a matter of the modification of structure by function which constantly contributes to the improvement of skill. What we have seen is a combination of this improvement in skill resulting from the active coping effort; an emergence of belief in or confidence in the worthwhileness of this coping effort which has produced success; a reduction of anxiety as a result of this success; the development of a self-image as the child who can master a challenge by his own efforts. That is, triumph or successful results of coping efforts produce motor, affective and cognitive changes which predispose and equip the child for more efforts.

In all the instances mentioned above the child's drive to use the resources available to him at the time led to changes in perception and feelings about the originally threatening situation, and about himself.

We could summarize this by saying that each experience of mastery and triumph sets the stage for better efforts in the next experience. Confidence, hope, and a sense of self-worth are increased along with the increase of cognitive and motor skills, which can contribute to better use of the resources. In this way the foundation is laid for spontaneous use of new potentialities made available by maturation as the child moves from one developmental stage to another.

The contribution of mastery to healthy narcissism and identity*

Throughout the Coping Study we were impressed by the fact that many of the children who coped most readily with the environment, and also those who seemed most resilient and integrated, were children who expressed a spontaneous, naive pride in themselves and often in their families. This pride seemed to flow naturally into a positive feeling about the environment generally, and included responsiveness to people and capacity for love. In the happy child, spontaneity was expressed both in warmth toward the environment and delight in himself.

No conflict existed, apparently, between strong enjoyment of self and strong response. There seemed to be a mutually energizing or contagious effect here. With Greg, Susan, Chester, and many other children, the child's capacity to enjoy himself aroused a response from others which was invigorating to both; the response from others reinforced the child's investment in the environment which provided gratifications supporting his enjoyment of himself and appreciation of his mastery and specific skills in dealing with the environment. This mutually energy-releasing effect attracted our attention and suggested the value of considering the relationship between narcissism and related aspects of self-feeling and the child's capacity to deal with the environment.

This observation came first as an intuitive impression of a number of children and led us to reconsider the role and some sources of pride. The productive and invigorating pride of these Kansas children had evidently not been inhibited by that aspect of Western tradition from Biblical proverbs and Sophocles which thinks of pride in terms of the aphorism "pride goeth before destruction and a haughty spirit before a fall." Antisocial and self-destructive aspects of excessive pride or haughtiness which contribute to detachment from or rejec-

---

* Based on L. B. Murphy, Pride and its relation to narcissism, autonomy and identity, *Bulletin of the Menninger Clinic*, Vol. 24, 1960.

tion of others are discussed in literature and philosophy, in the Old Testament and New Testament, Sophocles, Spinoza, and Shakespeare.

But Schopenhauer[3] makes the following statement: "Pride is an established conviction of one's own paramount worth in some particular respect; while vanity is the desire of arousing such conviction in others. Pride works from within; it is the direct appreciation of oneself. Vanity is the desire to arrive at the appreciation indirectly, from without."

Van der Waals' discussion of narcissism[4] showing, as it does, the growing aspects of Freud's concepts of narcissism[5] and in particular the room that is allowed for what he terms "healthy narcissism" as an aspect of every personality, thus emphasizes the importance of positive self-regard. The implied healthy self which does not have to be aggressively defensive is expressed in Woodrow Wilson's "too proud to fight." Pride in this sense is related to a secure sense of self-worth which does not have to be defended except when it is genuinely in danger. Realistic discriminations regarding the conditions and times when it is necessary to be aggressive (granted that successful aggression is well within the possibility of the individual) and confidence in one's capacity for self-defense contribute to the strength of this type of pride.

Helen Lynd[6] points out the relationship between pride and shame, on the one hand, and the sense of identity: the undermining of the sense of identity which occurs when the child is shamed, humiliated, made to feel helpless, and the importance of supporting the kind of pride we have just been discussing. Alice Moriarty has described the role of positive self-feeling in some children's capacity to cope with failure or difficulty in tests. Other children illustrate the contribution made by a vivid sense of an appreciated self to the ability to balance and control, if not master, inner as well as outer problems.

What are the sources of this pride and its more fundamental aspects of self-feeling and narcissism? Erik Erikson[7] speaks of the early subjective experience of recognition, and being recognized, as dating probably from the beginning of the baby's smiling response to the mother's smiling face. Among our research group this baby smile was very apt to occur during or after feeding or immediately after some other gratifying care involving sensory pleasure—including the baby's experience of being cleaned and dried and having his diapers changed, and after the bath, being cozily wrapped up and tucked into blankets. The experimental approach used by investigators who have shown that the baby will smile even to a mask showing eyes and mouth on a blank drawn face, or even parts of such a mask face, lures us away from the usual experience-setting of mutual gratification and stimulation in which the smiles of the baby in his home setting normally take place. These mutual smiling recognitions are of the deepest importance for the development both of object relationships and of healthy narcissism.

Erikson's comment leads us to reconsider the relation of the earliest narcissism to the contribution of all sensory, kinaesthetic, visceral, and action experiences to the development of the self-image, as discussed by Gardner Murphy.[8]

We meet a certain paradox when we talk of the helplessness of the young baby and also of his sense of omnipotence without adequately dealing with the realistic relation of these two. The fact is that the baby experiences both, often in relatively quick succession, and that growth consists of a modulation of each, not the elimination of either. That is, again on the basis of records of infants, the baby moves from the omnipotence assumed to be the inner quality of sensation accompanying objectless satiation, or the moments after feeding or being cared for which have led to a temporary freedom from need for a feeding or caring person, to periods of the opposite.

The omnipotent feelings in a tension-free or blissful state alternate with the helplessness of the tiny baby when he cannot satisfy urgent needs. However, this helplessness does not describe his total experience, for as soon as the mother is in contact with the baby, he is apt (although it differs from one child to another) to start an active rooting for the nipple, as instinctive as the rooting done by a kitten or puppy or any other young mammal; instinctive as it is, it still involves persistent, active, goal-directed effort which is rewarded with gratification by the food. Schachtel,[9] Bernfeld,[10] and others have developed this point at length. Consequently, the baby, almost from birth, participates in the process of gratifying his needs and to this extent his helplessness is already reduced or modified.

There are some other needs as well which at least some infants make an attempt to handle even from neonatal days. We noted earlier that some neonatal babies can push away covers encroaching uncomfortably on the face, and it is a common source of amusement to nurses that some babies when they are still in the hospital can wiggle themselves down into a cozy corner of the crib (as did our four-week-old Vivian). A baby who repeatedly achieves this maneuver can be assumed to be learning something about what he is able to accomplish for himself, and to be acquiring a positive feeling about effort, and about his capacity to deal with the environment.

We also see some neonatal babies struggling to hold up their heads when held, and to stare at a bright light or some other conspicuous visual stimulus. The repeated efforts which such babies make (and this kind of thing is most apt to happen when other needs have been gratified) point to the importance of satisfaction in autonomous ego-functioning for its own sake—that is, looking for the sake of looking, and listening for the sake of listening. Thus, even during the very first weeks of life—for some babies the first two weeks of life—we infer primitive if vague experiences of mastery associated with the baby's various efforts, not only in basic libidinal gratification and feeding, but also with more diffuse need satisfaction in achieving bodily comfort, and with autonomous ego-functioning which begins to operate especially at times when other needs or libidinal cravings are not present as far as we can judge. These primitive beginnings of experiences of mastery and autonomy are parallel with the primitive beginnings of self-esteem and well-being rooted in primary narcissism.

The concept of early objectless satiation which has been associated chiefly with oral gratification should probably be extended to experiences of comfort and satisfaction when any needs are met, and also to experiences of satisfaction in using all functions available at a given level to the extent of their potentialities at that stage. This satisfaction or pleasure, experienced probably as undifferentiatedly internal and external, is in the self as well as in the contacts with stimuli from the environment.

Rudimentary awareness of differences in these contacts must contribute to the foundation for a gradual but multidimensional differentiation of self from objects. We can accept the idea that the first differentiation is stimulated by such experiences as the loss of the nipple when acutely hungry, from which the infant finds in some dim way that the source of satisfaction is not himself but is something outside. This experience begins very early, and is probably reinforced by his efforts to regain the nipple. The capacity of the baby to integrate some sense of me-ness versus object out of such an experience will doubtless vary in relation to other aspects of integrative capacity, about which we know very little. Certainly in the first week or so of life many babies react by screaming at such interruptions in such a way that it could be expected to reinforce the perception of difference.

As the baby becomes able not only to succeed in retrieving the nipple but to wait, to look at, to keep an eye on the mother during such an interruption, or to listen to her voice, we assume that integration is taking place and that the baby has, at some level, command of the idea that "mother is there and will come back." By this time, if not before, pleasure from renewed contact with the gratifying object begins to come into the picture as an experience different from the experience of undifferentiated self-contained bliss or primary narcissism.

In the next stage, usually between three to six months, this capacity to regain the source of satisfaction becomes well-established in many babies. Pleasure in being a cause, getting action from the mother, getting results, and arousing activity by the object to gratify one's needs becomes clear and controllable. In the records of infants in this group we see spontaneous expressive babies "crowing," as we say, with eager delight at the age of three and a half to five months to attract the attention of a loved adult. The pleasure associated with gratification from the mothering person is actually used as a stimulus for further attention from her for its own sake, whether or not any basic libidinal needs are directly involved. (We say then that the baby wraps his mother around his little finger, he rules the roost.) What Fenichel[11] calls the infant's passive receptive mastery often involves considerable initiative in order to bring the stimuli within the range where he can be receptive. From this stage, where enough differentiation is present to permit waiting and delay, responding to signals, and giving signals —and all of this is very clearcut by the age of six months—we find very rapid development along three lines simultaneously.

From the time the baby's autonomy has expanded through being able to handle his body enough to cooperate in dressing, diapering, and bath, to make things happen by batting at toys in his cradle gym, reaching, banging, manipulating, demanding, commanding, and stimulating—all of which are well underway between three to six months in many babies—through the period where the baby is able to sit up with help, then pull himself up, to crawl, to pull himself to standing, finally to walk, we find the development of exuberant delight, triumph, and other expressions of pleasure in mastery. The narcissistic pleasure in being able to do, to manage one's own body, to get satisfaction by what one can make it accomplish, parallels the development of autonomy through these dramatic stages of the expanding motility during the rest of the first year of life.

In our culture, the delight and appreciation of the adults and siblings as the baby almost miraculously achieves these new accomplishments provide a pleasure for the baby reflected back from the object. The combination of his own zest in autonomous achievement and the secondary narcissism or feeling of well-being arising from the pleasure reflected back from the object contributes to the pride of the newly walking child whom we now consider "autonomous" because he can go from one place to another and is no longer dependent upon being carried.

Autonomy in the management of sphincter control normally comes after the child has already developed a considerable sense of control through his overt motor achievements. It seems, then, to be only one aspect of a deeply rooted feeling of accomplishment and independence which has been growing ever since the very first primitive active efforts he made within a few weeks after birth. Also it seems to be only one aspect of an autonomy which is expanded and enriched by the sense of being able to do things to objects, to put things inside other things, to bang things together, to make sounds (with some children, even to put records on their own phonographs), and to accomplish primitive restructuring and creating.

I have reviewed these sequences on the parallel development of narcissism and autonomy without describing the concomitant development of the sense of identity. I referred earlier to Erikson's comment on the first dim sense of recognition and being recognized as perhaps the beginning of identity, and along with this (perhaps in some cases stimulated by it), the beginning of baby's differentiation of self from others.

As soon as the baby begins to get an experience of "I stimulate myself," through patting his hands together, touching and exploring his body (these things can begin around four months) or looking at his own hands (which usually begins before three months), we can assume an experience of pleasure from the self as a stimulus or an object which is assimilated into the enriching process of narcissism.

The repertoire of devices for managing stimulation increases rapidly as grasping and other manual coordination patterns increase and as he gains more and more control of his body. All efforts to put distance between himself and stimulation by so much can be assumed to increase his awareness of himself versus the environment, distinct from it, more or less comfortable, depending on the kind of impact from it, and more or less able to do something to it. When the things he does to it increase his comfort or gratification, we assume that a rudimentary sense of satisfaction in what he did, that is, in his achievement, ensues. Expressions that can only be called triumphant are seen as early as the infant experiences success over obstacles after persistent effort. Struggling to grasp something almost out of reach, especially after he has begun to crawl, is a familiar example among infants in the second half of the first year, but a crow of triumph when he succeeds in evoking by his actions or sounds a response, such as being picked up, from a delaying adult, can be seen in some infants in the latter part of the first six months. This is the basic "I *can* do it" feeling, which along with pleasure in bodily activities supports the natural healthy narcissism of infancy.

This is a different expression from the "bliss," seen and often envied by adults, after a satisfying feeding, and also when the baby is peacefully relaxed in the mother's lap in a phase of quietness, letting the world go by. The blissful baby does not at that moment care about the world. At a moment of triumph, however, the baby experiences delight in what he has begun to do with it. Both feelings must contribute to a sense of well-being. Something like the feeling of triumph or sense of mastery in coping with the opportunities and the pressures of the environment can be seen through the successive stages of expanding capacities, from the eight-month-old infant's gleeful excitement as he discovers that he can pull himself to a standing position, holding to the railing of his crib, to Darlene's triumphant "I can jump!" at the party.

A great many of these "I can do" feelings get consolidated before the child turns to "I am" expressions, as in Susan's "I am five!" The urgency underlying "I can do" feelings can only be realized as we see more clearly some of the underlying anxieties commonly reflected in the children's responses to projective tests; here a typical concern deals with the problem of being small in a world of big people who can and are free to do more. Each experience of mastery is not only a momentary conquest but a promise of more to come, a reassurance of the capacity to grow up. The sense of mastery is also closely related to a sense of worth, importance, and ability to gain respect from others and maintain one's own self-respect.

Erikson[12] has focused attention on the deposits for healthy ego development provided by the satisfactory experience of each stage of development seen primarily in terms of the libidinal phases. Here we can add and extend the contribution of Mittelmann,[13] whose presentations of the motility urge and the stages in the development and vicissitudes of motility have provided an important anchor for the understanding of some of the relationships between autonomous functions of the ego, as seen by Hartmann,[14] and libidinal development as seen at earlier periods of psychoanalysis.

All ego functions arise from genetic dispositions which carry their own energy; at the same time their development takes place in an interpersonal context which has much to do both with the support and patterning of narcissism, and with the investment in the environment that augments and nourishes or deprives the so-called autonomous ego functions. The latter are also constantly interacting with the environment in the service of libidinal gratification, and are reinforced by basic pleasures when autonomous efforts implemented by motility and sensory apparatus produce gratification of primitive needs. In addition to residues for the affective orientation of the ego which are carried over from experiences at successive libidinal phases, we also have to include residues from a complex interaction between these modes of experience connected with different libidinal zones and the modes of experience emerging autonomously in connection with sensory and motor functions. Thus pride, self-esteem, and the feeling of well-being are the resultants of autonomous efforts, healthy narcissism, and the sense of identity which they produce, and also the interaction between these and libidinal phase experiences.

We can now speculate on some of the consequences for development of the behavior we have reported. Taking a cue from the preschool child's frequent use of "I can" or "I cannot" we may infer that mastery and coping ability are closely involved with the sense of identity. If this is sound, we must conclude that this aspect of identity has precursors or roots in all of the infant's contacts vis-á-vis the environment—acts upon, against, or at the environment, in contrast to the acts with the environment which contribute to relatedness, identification, and empathy.

Over and over again we saw how the impact of a new challenge intensified the child's awareness of himself; his capacity to meet such a challenge enhances his pleasure, his sense of adequacy, and his pride. Through the successive experiences of spontaneous mastery of new demands and utilizing new opportunities for gratification the child extends and verifies his identity as one who can manage certain aspects of the environment. Through his coping experiences the child discovers and measures himself, and develops his own perception of who and what he is and in time may become. We can say that the child creates his identity through his efforts in coming to terms with the environment in his own personal way.[15]

NOTES AND REFERENCES

1. Erikson, E.H. *Childhood and Society*. New York: Norton, 1950.
2. Weissenberg, L. Relation between previous effort and attractiveness of goal object. On file at Kansas University Library.
3. Schopenhauer, A. Essay on pride, pp. 63-64. *Complete Essays of Schopenhauer* (translated by T.B. Saunders). New York: Wiley, 1942.
4. van der Waals, H. Lectures on Narcissism. Topeka Psychoanalytic Institute, 1962.
5. Freud, S. On Narcissism: An Introduction. *Standard Edition of the Complete Psychological Works of Sigmund Freud*, Vol. 14, 1957.
6. Lynd, H. *On Shame and the Search for Identity*. New York: Harcourt Brace, 1958.
7. Erikson, E.H. *Young Man Luther*. New York: Norton, 1958.
8. Murphy, G. *Personality*. New York: Harper, 1947.
9. Schachtel, E. *Metamorphosis*. New York: Basic Books, 1959.
10. Bernfeld, S. *Psychology of the Infant*. New York: Brentano, 1929.

11. Fenichel, O. *The Psychoanalytic Theory of Neurosis*. New York: Norton, 1945.
12. Erikson, E.H. *Childhood and Society*. New York: Norton, 1950.
13. Mittelmann, B. Motility in infants, children, and adults: patterning and dynamics. In *Psychoanalytic Study of the Child*, Vol. 9. New York: International Universities Press, 1954. See also Mittelmann's articles in Vols. 12 and 15.
14. Hartmann, H. The mutual influences in the development of the ego and the id. In *Psychoanalytic Study of the Child*, Vol. 7. New York: International Universities Press, 1952.
15. Dr. Cotter Hirschberg suggested this way of putting it after reviewing the book.

POSTSCRIPT

AT THE PRESENT TIME all of these children are approaching or entering adolescence and we have been watching them meet the changing demands of school, church, and neighborhood during the intervening years. Ronnie, Donald, and Terry are expert Boy Scouts, athletic and proud of their skills, while still sensitive to new situations. Lennie showed unusual responsiveness to the help of his mother and teachers in mastering school difficulties related in part to his early speech problem. Teddy has maintained a high level of consistency and maturity through some major family crises. Brennie had difficulties after a very severe illness but is resiliently recovering his integration. Steve has continued to be the boy "who waits for life to happen."

Daryl, Vivian, and Rachel have continued to be shy in the face of the unpredictability of newness in research sessions but have been more at ease in the formal atmosphere of parochial school. Molly has done well in every area of school and home life but is still reluctant to venture very far from home on her own. Susan mastered the threats involved in two additional hospitalizations for a body cast and for fusion of vertebrae; now she swims, rides horseback, dances, plays the piano, and has many other skills. But it has been difficult for her to catch up on the years lost in experiences with peers; with them she is diffident.

Marked changes in their ways of meeting life have come with some of the other children who have been exposed to severe stress or frustration of different kinds. We are now studying the deeper aspects of struggle which can be seen as the children cope with loss, intense conflicts, recurrent disappointments, and the inner and outer stresses of early adolescence.

APPENDIXES

A. BIOGRAPHICAL DATA ON CHILDREN

Name (Pseudonyms)	Age (Sept. '54)	Religion	Father's Employment (Business includes salesmen)	Siblings (y: younger o: older)	Grandparents (gg: great)
Vivian	2:6	Catholic	Business	1-o, 1-y	4
Molly	2:7	Protestant	Professional	2-o, 1-y	3
Sheila	2:8	Protestant	Business	3-o	3
Raymond	2:8	Protestant	Unskilled	3-o, 2-y	4
Brennie	2:10	Protestant	Business	1-y	3-1 gg
Darlene	2:10	Protestant	Unskilled	1-y	4
Donald	2:10	Protestant	Unskilled	2-o	3
Vernon	3:2	Catholic	Skilled	2-o, 1-y	3
Ronald	3:5	Catholic	Business	2-y	1
Diane	3:5	Protestant	Skilled	3-o	3
Sally	3:5	Protestant	Skilled	1-o, 2-y	3
Lennie	3:5	Protestant	Semiskilled	1-o	4
Charlotte	3:7	Catholic	Unskilled	1-y	2
Rachel	3:8	Catholic	Unskilled	2-o, 2-y	1
Daryl	3:10	Catholic	Business	2-y	4
Ralph	4:0	Protestant	Skilled	3-o	2
Tommy	4:1	Mixed	Skilled	1-o, 1-y	6-2 step
Barbie	4:3	Protestant	Business	1-o	2
Chester	4:5	Protestant	Unskilled	2-o, 3-y	4
Gordon	4:7	None	Business	None	3
Susan	4:9	Protestant	Professional	1-y	4
Patsy	4:9	Catholic	Business	2-o, 1-y	4
Janice	4:10	Protestant	Business	4-o	3
Martin	4:11	Catholic	Skilled	3-o	3
Roddy	4:11	Protestant	Skilled	1-y	4
Teddy	4:11	Protestant	Army	1-y	4
Greg	4:11	Protestant	Professional	None	2
Steven	5:0	Protestant	Business	2-o, 1-y	3
Trudy	5:2	Protestant	Professional	1-o, 2-y	3
Terry	5:3	Catholic	Semiskilled	1-y	4
Karen	5:4	Protestant	Semiskilled	2-o, 3-y	4
Cynthia	5:7	Protestant	Skilled	2-o, 1-y	2

Introduction

Modern ways of obtaining correlations in mass numbers by IBM techniques made it possible for us to intercorrelate over 640 variables of several different kinds. These variables with their raw scores or ratings are contained in a volume popularly referred to as "the Bible." In the following paragraphs I shall review the major sources of the scores and ratings included in "the Bible."

The first 85 variables describe the neighborhood, the house and its equipment, the child's living space, parents' room and occupancy, child's possessions and clothes as rated by the parent interviewer who saw the mothers in their own homes; and also her ratings on aspects of the functioning of the child as an infant based on the records made in infancy together with ratings on the Gesell test given in infancy, and the interaction between the mother and baby in infancy.

The next group of variables include the scores and measurements obtained by the pediatrician in her examination of the child together with ratings of her observations and report of certain other factors such as pregnancy and delivery conditions. Ratings on the amount of illness, ratings on the rank orders and variability in blood pressure, pulse reactivity, etc., as well as bodily measurements are included in this group.

The next 10 variables refer to intelligence test scores and the variability of Sheldon ratings at the preschool period.

Following these are 134 variables describing the child's equipment under the headings of motility, sensory responsiveness, cognitive functioning, affect, response to the environment, social responses, sexual responses, language, and symptoms. For the purposes of the "prediction study" these were rated by a group of noncontaminated outside raters, all clinical psychologists who were, however, not well grounded in the study of the preschool children. The ratings were made on the basis of detailed but concise summaries of the functioning of the children at the preschool period written by Dr. Heider; the ratings involved transferring verbal statements regarding qualitative and quantitative aspects of the child's functioning into rating form and in some cases transferring inferences based on these summaries into rating form.

Next there is a series of variables based on the detailed records and summaries by the psychiatrist, as rated by Dr. Moriarty following a process of abstracting and excerpting these psychiatric records. The basic evaluations of the psychiatric records were charted in detail before the ratings were made. These variables refer to drives, impulse control, specific aspects of ego functioning, integrative functions, and level of adequacy of self-image.

Next a series of variables rated by the examiner and observers during the Witkin experiments, followed by variables rated on the MLT session, included such items as active orientation, feeling one's way along, capacity for free-wheeling attention, resistances, knowing the score, grasping sequences; pleasure in tactile experiences, ability to accept substitutes and the like.

Another group included ratings on 55 variables dealing with autonomy expression, tension or anxiety, cooperation with authority demands, accepting own limits, readiness to ask for help, level of self-feeling, orientation speed, and the like rated by Dr. Moriarty and Marie Smith independently on the basis of the child's behavior in the intelligence test situation.

About 150 variables dealing with such aspects of integrative functioning as ability to postpone, wait for gratification, ability to synthesize thinking, affect, action, keeping one's distance temporarily, creative potential, ability to restructure the environment, were rated either by Moriarty and Murphy or by Moriarty, Murphy, and Heider, who met as a group to give a concensus rating based on their combined knowledge of the child. Finally, global ratings of capacity to cope with the opportunities, challenges, difficulties, and frustrations of the environment and the capacity to maintain internal integration were rated separately by Murphy and Moriarty and also by averaging Murphy and Moriarty's ratings. These global ratings together with Moriarty's ratings of cognitive, affective, and motor coping capacity were made by pairing each child with every other child in the group to arrive at a finely differentiated rank order of coping capacity as designated.

Ratings on these aspects of ego functioning were made on one varible at a time, each child in the whole group being rated on each variable before another variable was presented. This same process was used for Moriarty's ratings with the difference that each variable was rated for every child in each of four phases of the testing situation before the rater turned to work on another variable.

The actual list of 640 variables was arrived at empirically—that is, derived from the observation records themselves; thus many variables, such as simple qualities of pride and courage, capacity for free-wheeling attention, strategic withdrawal, ability to control the impact of the environment, sense of importance, being taken seriously, had not been thought of and not listed in any of the preliminary outlines which had been developed to sensitize the observers to the different levels of functioning to be observed.

The degree of agreement between raters differs depending upon such matters as the nature of the variable, the nature of the situation in which the child was observed, the closeness of the rater to the observations of the child, etc. The correlations between independent ratings by Moriarty and Smith on observations in the delimited intelligence test situation were extremely high (88 to 96) while the agreement between raters who did not know the children and in fact were not well acquainted with preschool children generally and who based their ratings on data in and inferences from summaries varied widely among different pairs from about .3 to .6. For purposes of the statistical study of these ratings variables correlating at an .05 level of significance with the global rating of Coping I or Coping II were studied most extensively. This does not mean that other variables were not important since low correlations were in many cases obviously due not only to limitations of the raters but to limitations of the evidence in the setting of this research study, and to limitations of this homogeneous sample.

A larger group of children including a wider range of personalities, level of ability, and so forth would probably have made it possible to translate into quantitative form certain relationships which we can document only by individual outstanding cases.

Since the study was planned from the start as an exploratory and pilot study to produce hypotheses, all the findings are primarily directed toward the formulation of these hypotheses and to the conceptualization of this area of study rather than definitive demonstration of any individual hypothesis.

On pages 226 and 344 we commented on relationships between ratings on infancy behavior in feeding situations and various preschool variables. The following are examples of these:

Among the substantial correlations between infancy oral gratification and preschool variables for boys are the following:

.607	clarity of perception
—.701	critical of people, depreciates others
—.753	loss of perceptual clarity under stress
.610	sense of self-worth
.643	strength of interests
.532	ability to control the impact of the environment
—.522	tendency to get fatigued
.457	reality level

.457   autonomy
.463   positive self-appraisal
.463   degree of differentiation of affect
.455   flexibility of emotional management and control (AM & LBM)
—.434   tension level
.416   capacity to maintain internal integration

Among the significant correlations between infancy ratings on protest, termination and resistance in the feeding situation, and preschool variables for boys are the following:

.789   can forestall danger—knows when to stop
.668   impulse control
.618   reality testing
.624   ability to control the impact of the environment
.605   over-all ability
.566   clarity regarding own identity
—.548   tendency to give up easily at failure
.555   ability to restructure the environment
.552   development level of speech
.575   orientation: speed with which the child was aware
.455   determination
.536   mastery (drive for, struggle capacity)
.596   sense of importance, being taken seriously
.594   problem-solving attitude toward life

Among the significant correlations between infancy ratings on "autonomy permitted by mother" and preschool variables for boys are the following:

.614   capacity to maintain internal integration (Coping II—LBM)
.571   ability to limit or fend off excessive stimulation
.511   resistance to discouragement
.610   ability to mobilize energy to meet challenge or stress
.784   sense of self-worth
.646   clarity in sex role
.700   separation (differentiation of self and others)
.513   discharge efficiency for the child who has discharge resources

On pages 226-227 I comment on correlations between autonomy and other aspects of ego-functioning.

Significant correlations between preschool ratings of autonomy and other variables, for girls, include the following:

.559   energy level
.881   ability to organize and provide own structure
.919   tendency to use environmental areas selectively
.874   speed of orientation (in new situation, AM)
.586   appropriateness of affective responses
.670   ability to solve problems directly
.715   determination

.821   "knowing the score," grasping sequences
.718   satisfaction in mastery
.771   range of areas of gratification

Significant correlations (.50 and up) with combined Coping I (capacity to cope with the opportunities, demands, frustrations of the environment) include:

Boys and Girls:

freedom to translate ideas into action
faces world with open anticipation
autonomy
uses environmental areas selectively
is stimulating to others
competence
active orientation—acting on, doing to
range of areas of enjoyment, gratification
ability to ask for or get help when needed
motor and visual motor control
ability to restructure the environment
intensity of interest, enthusiasm
has emotional sending power, reaches others
ability to take different roles

Girls:

motor coordination
purposefulness of movements
speed or tempo
energy level
eagerly explores environment in new situation
interest in mastering space

Boys:

over-all ability
depth of affect
clarity of distinction between reality and fantasy
breadth of perceptual field
pleasure in tactile experience
tact
ability to balance gratification and frustration

The higher correlations for girls in motor areas reflect the wider range in ratings on motor variables among girls; similarly the correlations with affective and sensory variables for boys reflect the wider range for boys on this group of variables.

C. PUBLISHED REPORTS AND DISCUSSIONS OF FINDINGS FROM THE STUDIES OF THESE CHILDREN

Infancy Data:

Escalona, S., and Leitch, M. *Early Phases of Personality Development: A Non-Normative Study of Infancy Behavior.* Evanston, Ill.: Child Development Publications, 1953.

Brody, S. *Patterns of Mothering.* New York: International Universities Press, 1956.

Heider, G. Vulnerability in infants. *Bulletin of the Menninger Clinic 24,* 104-114, 1960.

Preschool Data:

Escalona, S., and Heider, G. *Prediction and Outcome.* New York: Basic Books, 1959. (Predictions based on the infancy data studied in relation to the pre-school data.)

Heider, G. What makes a good parent? *Children 7,* No. 6, 1960.

Moriarty, A. E. Coping patterns of preschool children in response to intelligence test demands. *Genetic Psychology Monographs 64,* 3-127, 1961.

Moriarty, A. E. Children's ways of coping with the intelligence test. *Bulletin of the Menninger Clinic 24,* 115-127, 1960.

Escalona, S., and Moriarty, A. E. Prediction of schoolage intelligence from infant tests. *Child Development 32,* 597-605, 1961.

Murphy, L. B. Psychoanalysis and child development. *Bulletin of the Menninger Clinic 21,* Nos. 5, 6, 1957.

Murphy, L. B. Effects of child-rearing patterns on mental health. *Children 3,* No. 6, 1956.

Murphy, L. B. Learning how children cope with their problems. *Children 4,* No. 4, 1957.

Murphy, L. B. The child's way of coping: a longitudinal study of normal children. *Bulletin of the Menninger Clinic 24,* 97-103, 1960.

Murphy, L. B. Pride and its relation to narcissism, autonomy and identity. *Bulletin of the Menninger Clinic 24,* 136-143, 1960.

Murphy, L. B. Preventive implications of development in the preschool years. Chapter 10 in *Prevention of Mental Disorders in Children,* Gerald Caplan, ed. New York: Basic Books, 1961.

To be published

Murphy, L. B., and Raine, W. *Methods in the Longitudinal Study of Children.* To be published in 1963.

Heider, G. *Vulnerability in Infants and Young Children.* Monograph to be published in *Psychological Issues,* International Universities Press, New York.

Moriarty, A. E. *Variability in Cognitive Functioning* (monograph).

Murphy, L. B., and Gupta, V. *Vulnerability, Stress, and Resilience* (monograph).

Murphy, L. B. Character development in normal children: sources of flexibility. To be published in the *Journal of Projective Techniques.*

INDEX

abandonment, feelings of, 42

Abraham, K., 247

accidents, aftermaths of, 139; coping in, 115-144; defense mechanisms in, 136; doctor relations in, 132-133; friends' curiosity following, 129-130; hostility and anxiety feelings following, 143; mastery and control in, 137-138; mother's role in, 134; questioning in, 143; role reversal and play in, 134-135; triumph and pride following, 138-139

accommodation, assimilation and, 194

accomplishment, pride in, 88, 159, 167, 368

achievement, self-esteem and, 97

achievement drive, 4

Achromycin, 122, 132

acting out, 149

activity, aggression and, 348; coping capacity and, 354-355; vs. delay, 175-176; passivity and, 342-355; reduced level of, 83-84

activity-receptivity patterns, 354

adaptation, concept of, 292-293; coping efforts and, 6

adequacy, language of, 2

adjustment, adaptation and, 292-293; see also coping

adolescence, 308

adults, at "party," 97; pressure from in test situations, 80-86; threatening behavior of, 316

affect, development of, 309; goals and, 241-243; gratification and, 232

affect hunger, 241

1976

Holidays, Holy Days and Commemorative Days

Jan. 1 New Year's Day

Feb. 12 Lincoln's Birthday
14 St. Valentine's Day
16 Washington's Birthday

Mar. 3 Ash Wednesday
17 St. Patrick's Day

Apr. 11 Palm Sunday
15 Jewish Passover
16 Good Friday
18 Easter Sunday

May 9 Mother's Day
15 Armed Forces Day
31 Memorial Day

Jun. 13 Trinity Sunday
13 Children's Day
14 Flag Day
20 Father's Day

Jul. 4 Independence Day *

Sep. 6 Labor Day
17 Citizenship Day
25 Jewish New Year

Oct. 4 Jewish Yom Kippur
11 Columbus Day
24 United Nations Day
25 Veterans Day
31 Halloween

Nov. 2 Election Day
25 Thanksgiving Day
28 First Sunday of Advent

Dec. 25 Christmas Day

JANUARY

S	M	T	W	T	F	S
				1	2	3
4	5	6	7	8	9	10
11	12	13	14	15	16	17
18	19	20	21	22	23	24
25	26	27	28	29	30	31

FEBRUARY

S	M	T	W	T	F	S
1	2	3	4	5	6	7
8	9	10	11	12	13	14
15	16	17	18	19	20	21
22	23	24	25	26	27	28
29						

MARCH

S	M	T	W	T	F	S
	1	2	3	4	5	6
7	8	9	10	11	12	13
14	15	16	17	18	19	20
21	22	23	24	25	26	27
28	29	30	31			

APRIL

S	M	T	W	T	F	S
				1	2	3
4	5	6	7	8	9	10
11	12	13	14	15	16	17
18	19	20	21	22	23	24
25	26	27	28	29	30	

MAY

S	M	T	W	T	F	S
						1
2	3	4	5	6	7	8
9	10	11	12	13	14	15
16	17	18	19	20	21	22
23	24	25	26	27	28	29
30	31					

JUNE

S	M	T	W	T	F	S
		1	2	3	4	5
6	7	8	9	10	11	12
13	14	15	16	17	18	19
20	21	22	23	24	25	26
27	28	29	30			

JULY

S	M	T	W	T	F	S
				1	2	3
4	5	6	7	8	9	10
11	12	13	14	15	16	17
18	19	20	21	22	23	24
25	26	27	28	29	30	31

AUGUST

S	M	T	W	T	F	S
1	2	3	4	5	6	7
8	9	10	11	12	13	14
15	16	17	18	19	20	21
22	23	24	25	26	27	28
29	30	31				

SEPTEMBER

S	M	T	W	T	F	S
			1	2	3	4
5	6	7	8	9	10	11
12	13	14	15	16	17	18
19	20	21	22	23	24	25
26	27	28	29	30		

OCTOBER

S	M	T	W	T	F	S
					1	2
3	4	5	6	7	8	9
10	11	12	13	14	15	16
17	18	19	20	21	22	23
24	25	26	27	28	29	30
31						

NOVEMBER

S	M	T	W	T	F	S
	1	2	3	4	5	6
7	8	9	10	11	12	13
14	15	16	17	18	19	20
21	22	23	24	25	26	27
28	29	30				

DECEMBER

S	M	T	W	T	F	S
			1	2	3	4
5	6	7	8	9	10	11
12	13	14	15	16	17	18
19	20	21	22	23	24	25
26	27	28	29	30	31	

1977

JANUARY
S	M	T	W	T	F	S
						1
2	3	4	5	6	7	8
9	10	11	12	13	14	15
16	17	18	19	20	21	22
23	24	25	26	27	28	29
30	31					

FEBRUARY
S	M	T	W	T	F	S
		1	2	3	4	5
6	7	8	9	10	11	12
13	14	15	16	17	18	19
20	21	22	23	24	25	26
27	28					

MARCH
S	M	T	W	T	F	S
		1	2	3	4	5
6	7	8	9	10	11	12
13	14	15	16	17	18	19
20	21	22	23	24	25	26
27	28	29	30	31		

APRIL
S	M	T	W	T	F	S
					1	2
3	4	5	6	7	8	9
10	11	12	13	14	15	16
17	18	19	20	21	22	23
24	25	26	27	28	29	30

MAY
S	M	T	W	T	F	S
1	2	3	4	5	6	7
8	9	10	11	12	13	14
15	16	17	18	19	20	21
22	23	24	25	26	27	28
29	30	31				

JUNE
S	M	T	W	T	F	S
			1	2	3	4
5	6	7	8	9	10	11
12	13	14	15	16	17	18
19	20	21	22	23	24	25
26	27	28	29	30		

JULY
S	M	T	W	T	F	S
					1	2
3	4	5	6	7	8	9
10	11	12	13	14	15	16
17	18	19	20	21	22	23
24	25	26	27	28	29	30
31						

AUGUST
S	M	T	W	T	F	S
	1	2	3	4	5	6
7	8	9	10	11	12	13
14	15	16	17	18	19	20
21	22	23	24	25	26	27
28	29	30	31			

SEPTEMBER
S	M	T	W	T	F	S
				1	2	3
4	5	6	7	8	9	10
11	12	13	14	15	16	17
18	19	20	21	22	23	24
25	26	27	28	29	30	

OCTOBER
S	M	T	W	T	F	S
						1
2	3	4	5	6	7	8
9	10	11	12	13	14	15
16	17	18	19	20	21	22
23	24	25	26	27	28	29
30	31					

NOVEMBER
S	M	T	W	T	F	S
		1	2	3	4	5
6	7	8	9	10	11	12
13	14	15	16	17	18	19
20	21	22	23	24	25	26
27	28	29	30			

DECEMBER
S	M	T	W	T	F	S
				1	2	3
4	5	6	7	8	9	10
11	12	13	14	15	16	17
18	19	20	21	22	23	24
25	26	27	28	29	30	31

Holidays, Holy Days and Commemorative Days

Jan.	1	New Year's Day
Feb.	12	Lincoln's Birthday
	14	St. Valentine's Day
	21	Washington's Birthday
	23	Ash Wednesday
Mar.	17	St. Patrick's Day
Apr.	3	Jewish Passover
	3	Palm Sunday
	8	Good Friday
	10	Easter Sunday
May	8	Mother's Day
	21	Armed Forces Day
	30	Memorial Day
Jun.	5	Trinity Sunday
	12	Children's Day
	14	Flag Day
	19	Father's Day
Jul.	4	Independence Day
Sep.	5	Labor Day
	13	Jewish New Year
	17	Citizenship Day
	22	Jewish Yom Kippur
Oct.	10	Columbus Day
	24	Veterans Day
	24	United Nations Day
	31	Halloween
Nov.	8	Election Day
	24	Thanksgiving Day
	27	First Sunday of Advent
Dec.	25	Christmas Day*